JOURNEY TO HOPEFUL FUTURES

"*Local communities around the world are caught in the dangerous riptides of ecological crises producing social and economic ruptures that are unprecedented and not of their making. What to do in practical terms? Working together at the local level, with care, compassion, and co-creativity providing the guiderails, as Helena advocates, has to be an essential part of the solution. With a richness of resources and practical exercises to hold hands, hold each other, and hold together along personal and collective journeys of hopeful futures, this book facilitates learners and co-workers from right across our wonderfully rich and diverse communities to work together to fashion alternative futures and take collective action. It is a beautifully optimistic book, and just what we need right now*".*

**Sally Randles, Professor in Sustainability and Innovation,
Manchester Metropolitan University**

"*Kettleborough offers us a toolkit for life journeys in incredibly difficult times, helping us see ourselves as an integral part of the unfolding cosmic drama; anyone can walk the path, feel the magnificence, share in the joy. This book is an inquiry that can be transformative. It begins with the simple and the small and carries the capacity to take us all the way to celebrate the sacred in all that we can see, feel, touch and immerse ourselves in.*"

Jagdish Rattanani, Journalist, Foundation of The Billion Press; teacher in communications and ethics, SPJIMR, Mumbai, India; Director, ASP, UK

"*I have huge admiration for the way Helena Kettleborough has pursued her quest for a different, participatory way of being in the world ethically, intellectually, practically, and spiritually over many years. She is right to claim that she continues to 'walk her talk'. This is a truly attractive book, profound but clearly written, which will be a valuable resource to readers in many different walks of life.*"

Peter Reason, Writer, Emeritus Professor University of Bath

"*The multiple crisis we face are rooted in separation from the Earth, the denial that the earth is living, and an anthropocentric arrogance that we are superior to other species who are our relatives. This world view creates hopelessness and despair. Dr. Helena Mary Kettleborough 'Journey of Hopeful Futures' is a guide to once again find humanity's place in a living earth, to rediscover our relations as members of the earth community, reclaim the sacred, and through participation in living processes, regenerate Gaia.*"

Vandana Shiva, Ecologist, Philosopher, Physicist & Ecofeminist; Founder of the Research Foundation for Science Technology and Ecology and of Navdanya, the seed saving movement

Journey to Hopeful Futures

A Handbook

Helena
Kettleborough

Centre for
Connected Practice

COMMUNITY CREATIVITY COSMOS

Published in 2023 by Centre for Connected Practice
Manchester, UK
Web: https://c4cp.net

ISBN 978-1-9163008-1-1

The information contained within this book is strictly for educational purposes.
If you wish to apply ideas contained in this book, you are taking
full responsibility for your actions.

Pages designed and typeset according to the author's creative direction

Dedication

To Phil, for consistently believing in me and travelling with me
on this journey

To my family, human and more-than-human for giving me hope

To my children, and all of the children, of this beautiful
and ancient universe

Contents

○ Author's Note to her Hopeful Companions

This book contains numerous signposts to help the reader on their own Hopeful Journeys.

Many of them are now, of course, online and the links are included in the text. In order to make this easier, you can also access them all on the Centre for Creative Practice Website where there is also more information about my work.

You will find all the weblinks in this book and a statement on publishing and sustainability on the Centre for Connected Practice website: https://c4cp.net/blog/project/journey-to-hopeful-futures-a-handbook/

In Chapter 5, page 167, I suggest ways to find resources not obviously publicly available.

Many of the excercises in the book call for self-reflection. If you feel at any time in need of information and support for your own mental health you will find reliable and free information at: https://www.nhs.uk/mental-health

I wish you well on your lifetime journey and send you my love and support.

Helena Kettleborough
Manchester UK
January 2023

Introduction

"A journey of a thousand miles starts with the first step"
Tao Te Ching (Kwok et al, 1993, chapter 64)

Gaia's Graveyards

In 1999, my family was debating how to celebrate the Millennium. Our two younger children wanted to make something. Their elder sister had made cuttings of her favourite band and they decided to follow suit and create a scrapbook. There were Millennium celebrations all around the world and the children pasted in pictures of fireworks from California to Sydney. They each decided on a topic – the younger chose animals, and her sister, marine life. The cuttings came from newspapers and magazines lying around the house. Their grandmothers helped too and sent stories out from newspapers they read. The children wrote their own stories, drew pictures and pasted everything into a rapidly expanding scrapbook: 'New mammal discovered in South America', 'Ocean warriors', '300,000 sea birds dead – now Europe counts the cost of an ocean of filth', 'The end of the Arctic'. We began to realise that something was terribly wrong. The animals were losing their homes, they were being hunted or poached, or they were being fished to extinction. At the end of 2000 the children completed their scrapbooks, but I carried on collecting. Soon, the cuttings filled an old desk, boxes under the desk and multiple cupboards. Five years later, one evening over a pint, my partner Phil mused that the reason I collected the cuttings was because they were my graveyards. Another four years passed and my youngest daughter, now 17, told me not to be so depressing and to

News

Last chance to save great apes from extinction

Conservationists launch desperate effort to stop humanity killing closest relatives

Tim Radford Science editor

An international push to save the great apes – the gorilla, orang-utan and chimpanzee – from extinction is being launched today by UN chiefs and environmental campaigners.

All three species are in serious danger. The great apes survival project – known as Grasp – will target 23 countries in Africa and south-east Asia where apes survive. Habitats are being disturbed by farmers and miners, and destroyed by loggers, and the apes are being killed for food.

"The clock is standing at one minute to midnight for the great apes," said Klaus Toepfer of the United Nations environmental programme (Unep). "Some experts estimate that in as little as five to 10 years they will be extinct across most of their range.

"Local extinctions are happening rapidly and each one is a loss to humanity, a loss to the local community and a hole torn in the ecology of our planet. We can no longer stand by and watch these wondrous creatures, some of whom share over 98% of the DNA found in humans, die out."

Botanists reckon that up to a third of the flowering plants on the planet could

Figure 0.1: Last chance to save the great apes from extinction
(Source: Tim Radford, 2001,The Guardian, 21 May, Photographer: Mark Lennihan/AP).

collect stories of solutions too. They became not my graveyards, but Gaia's graveyards, graveyards for a dying planet. Twenty years on from the Millennium and I am still collecting. I now have thousands of cuttings. This book grew out of those cuttings and is rooted in them, in the voices of millions of mammals, birds, insects, fish, plants and people all crying out for our support, love and action.

Stepping out

The scale of the challenges facing our planet and our species has never been greater. These challenges are everywhere but they are not always immediately visible. Over the years, as I collected the Gaia's Graveyards cuttings, sad and disturbing news kept accumulating, often the same stories repeated but the facts getting worse. I presented some of these stories in an installation called *An Ark for Gaia*. It included the melting ice caps and glaciers (Vidal, 2011a; Sufi, 2019), carbon dioxide levels in the atmosphere that last existed on Earth three million years ago (Carrington, 2013), plumes of methane further contributing to rising temperatures (Watts, 2020) and the threat of sea level rise to low-lying countries and coastal cities around the world (Harvey, 2021). The last decade has been the hottest on record, bringing with it extreme weather, heatwaves and floods (Harvey, 2019).[1] These changes, combined with the continued destruction of habitat by humans, monoculture farming practices and the overuse of antibiotics and chemicals, seriously threaten biodiversity (Jowit, 2010). All megafauna face extinction this century (Lydall, 2012). Malaysia's last Sumatran rhino died on Saturday 23rd November 2019. Insects and birds are slipping away, noticeable by their silence (Connor, 2014). Entire systems face irreversible tipping points. The world's rain forests are threatened with destruction. In the early 2010s, it was feared that the Amazon could become a carbon emitter with mass tree deaths. This became reality a decade later (Carrington, 2011, 2021). The oceans are being overfished, sharks are diminishing in number, the blue tuna is threatened, and acidification of the oceans, caused by their warming, not only threatens coral reefs but the plankton on which the entire marine food web relies (Independent 2010; Gray, 2010; IPPC 2021).

The International Panel on Climate Change warns that beyond 1.5°C of warming, life on Earth will be seriously threatened. Our rapidly warming oceans demonstrate the extent of the crisis as they absorb more than 90% of the heat trapped by greenhouse gases (Abraham, 2019). In 2021, the international annual Climate Action Tracker demonstrated that national Greenhouse Gas Reduction Plans, one outcome of the Paris Climate Agreement, are still not enough to meet the targets established in 2015. The planet is a living system, yet we do not understand how these forces interact. Therefore, we continue to create new and unexpected challenges that we lack the knowledge to deal with. A primary one for the third decade of this century was the COVID-19 pandemic, highlighting how human penetration of nature allows diseases to jump from animals to humans (Carrington, 2020). As governments and civil society struggled with the pandemic, scientists have unanimously given humanity 10-20 years to make the difference needed to save biodiversity and until 2030 to make serious and unprecedented cuts in carbon emissions (IPPC, 2018; Harvey and Carrington, 2019; UNEP, 2022).

These ecological challenges sit underneath the progress of human societies. The United Nations Human Development Reports, first published in 1989, chronicle major improvements for human life across the planet.[2] Substantial progress has been made in human health and in keeping people healthier and alive for longer. Maternity care and services have improved, as has the early life expectancy of children. There have been great improvements in education, with more children all over the world attending school, university and participating in lifelong learning. The UN reports that more students are enrolled in PhD programmes globally than ever before. Hunger has been reduced in many countries and millions of people lifted out of extreme poverty. Countries such as China and India have seen a substantial expansion in the middle classes. The provision of local services for health, education, care for the vulnerable, libraries, community development, and youth services have been pioneered and developed during the twentieth century. Far-reaching improvements can be seen in human rights and equalities and in access to rights to vote and participate in society. Social movements for gender equality, civil rights, anti-racism, LGBTQ+ and disability rights have grown and are established as key forces around the world.

At the same time, there have been advances in technology. More humans than ever live in heated homes and in greater comfort. The technological revolution of the twenty-first century has networked the entire world in ways not before imagined and has provided most people with more power in their phones than that which took the Apollo astronauts to the moon (Kendell, 2019). The industrial processes of the nineteenth and twentieth centuries are translating into a renewable energy revolution and we are now at the dawn of a new era of fossil-free fuel production. The technological revolution over the past four hundred years has occurred in tandem with a vast expansion in scientific knowledge. In the twentieth century, for the first time in the planet's 4.5-billion-year history, humans and robots explored beyond our planet, sending back awe-inspiring photographs of other planets and moons. The intrepid spacecraft, Voyagers 1 and 2, are now journeying in interstellar space, another cosmological first for our planet.

O   **Hopeful Companions**

To begin to understand what is happening to our planet Earth.

Books
Ghosh, A. 2021. *The Nutmeg's Curse: Parables for a Planet in Crisis*. London: John Murray.

Films
11th Hour. 2008. Warner Independent Pictures.

Resources for Action
Actions that individuals can follow: advice from Vanessa Nakate, Ugandan Climate Activist 2021: https://www.thebookseller.com/author-interviews/newsvanessa-nakate-climate-change-pushing-millions-people-extreme-poverty-and-leaving-them-nothing

United Nations Development Programme, *Human Development Report*. 2020. The Next Frontier: Human Development and the Anthropocene: http://hdr.undp.org/sites/default/files/hdr2020.pdf

United Nations Environment Programme. *Emissions Gap Report 2022: The Closing Window:* Calls for 'urgent system wide transformation to achieve the enormous cuts in greenhouse gas emissions needed to keep to 1.5 degrees of warming': https://www.unep.org/resources/emissions-gap-report-2022

An introduction to the Hopeful Companions boxes is given later in this chapter.

However, we live in a time of tension between the progress we have made and threats to the functioning of the planet. These two are interconnected. Despite, or perhaps because of, the progress we have made, our sheer numbers and the reach of our technologies threaten to overwhelm all the systems of the Earth. In addition, enmeshed in a complex economy dominated by powerful forces increasingly beyond the control of national governments, let alone individuals, maintaining a sense of hope, optimism or agency has become increasingly difficult. Tensions have been exacerbated by the economic politics of austerity, introduced by governments at the start of the twenty-first century (Toynbee & Walker, 2020), which has reversed trends in reducing wealth inequalities, with many countries in the developed world experiencing growing inequality. Half of the world's pay goes to 10% of the world's workers (Kollwewe, 2019). COVID-19 has exposed the deep inequalities in society, with, according to

Pidd et al. (2020), "people in poorer areas dying at twice the rate of those in richest areas"; trends seen all over the world, according to Berkhout et al's report for Oxfam International (2021). Public Health England found that Black, Asian and other minority ethnic groups suffered disproportionately from COVID-19, both in being more exposed to the disease and more likely to die than those from a white ethnicity (LGA, 2021).

Choosing hope

This book cannot offer solutions to such meta-problems. But it does offer a new perspective and practical positive approaches to help individuals and communities to find the energy and commitment to tackle the challenges ahead and focus on solutions and techniques, maps, tools, exercises and practices to enable everyone to chart a course through the mountainous challenges ahead.

Beyond academic and public policy circles, reports on what is happening to the planet are generally delivered through social and broadcast media. Although many of us are concerned, we do not always know how to respond, as we feel the crisis is too big and individual actions too small. Meanwhile, elected governments shy away from disruptive (and potentially electorally disastrous) policy changes and businesses remain committed to externalising environmental damage, with many companies actively backing so-called 'climate change deniers' and spreading paralysis-inducing confusion.[3]

In response to what is happening, individuals often feel despair, despondency and the sense that what they do will make no difference, so why even try? A common reaction is to make one or two small changes and hope that someone else will take action. Another common reaction is to simply ignore the situation. Many of us do not make a serious attempt to fully understand carbon dioxide emission figures or the human politics dominating our thoughts and actions. Apocalyptic fiction and non-fiction tell us that it is all going to end badly. In the UK, progress at the community level to reduce carbon dioxide emissions has largely been destroyed by government austerity measures. It is easy to see why we have a looming sense of going backwards.

However, over the past 50 years, there have been many sparks of hope and this book seeks to build on the good work that has gone before.

The 1970s saw the first Earth Day and Greenpeace volunteers placing their small boats between whales and whaling vessels. The decades that followed have seen great changes at the international level. The Brundtland Commission's report on sustainable development was published in 1987. The UN Conference on Environment and Development was held in Rio de Janeiro in 1992, leading to, among other things, Agenda 21 for local authorities and communities. Thus far, this century has seen the creation of the Earth Charter in 2000, the Millennium Development Goals 2000-2015, the UN Sustainable Development Goals 2016-2030, and the International Conference on Climate Change in Paris in 2015. Civil action has grown too, with the school climate strike movement and Extinction Rebellion calling loudly for change and Black Lives Matter inspiring action globally. Despite all this activity, emissions continue to rise.

The past teaches us that this will be a long journey and a hard struggle because so many of those who have grown wealthy have so much invested in the present system and, as individuals, we largely welcome the increased comfort and ease that the technological boom has brought to our lives.

This book is about choosing hope as a way forward, rather than choosing despondency and despair, cynicism or inaction. It is about choosing long term optimism, and choosing action over our entire lifetimes. It is about not seeing 'work' as separate from 'home', or friends as separate from family. It is seeing that every aspect of our lives can be hopeful and part of ongoing change. It is about optimism, love, and spirit. It reflects Michael McCarthy's call to fiercely love nature in the knowledge that nature may not be here next year (2015). It is about seeing our lives as part of an embedded cosmological whole.

This book is also about seeing humanity as part of a meaningful universe and gaining spiritual and physical energy from that understanding. The book proposes a powerful form of learning known as first-person action research. This is an ongoing process of action and reflection in our daily lives to help us to undertake a journey that will give us a new perspective on everyday life. First-person action research is a reflective journey between our interior and exterior lives and offers a sustained inquiry into our daily lives that is curious and constantly questioning. This approach helps us to take action while reflecting on our internal motives, values and ethics. First person action research is part of the broad action research family. Action research has a number of key characteristics which can help in our journey of inquiry. A notable one is learning through cycles of action and reflection, which can range from small to mega cycles over years.

The book draws on my own personal journey over the past twenty years as I became aware of the scale of the challenges facing our living planet, Gaia.

Reflecting on my own life, I can see that my first-person inquiry has been going on for nearly thirty years, from well before I had a name for it, or was aware of the academic literature on the subject. Over time, I have developed effective action research practices in a variety of settings: in my inner-city Manchester community, at regional learning and training centres for neighbourhood management and community empowerment across North West England and in local authorities where I worked for social inclusion and women's equality. First-person inquiry has informed my participation in GreenSpirit, a UK NGO based on green spirituality, and at management and business schools at Lancaster and Manchester Metropolitan Universities.[4] I have also brought this practice to my work at the Centre for Connected Practice, where I am a community development activist, researcher and facilitator.[5]

Throughout this book, I recount my own ongoing relationship with first person inquiry, so that others may learn about these practices and adapt them to the particular situations of their own lives. During the course of my journey, which is ongoing, I have discovered methods and models, developed tools and techniques, drawn on academic evidence and my own interventions in the world, and discovered new ways of knowing and thinking. I want to set that journey within the context of a living planet experiencing unprecedented human-induced stress, and I want us to learn to place both our progress and our struggles within the wider cosmic context.

Embedded cosmological perspective

In the 1970s, James Lovelock published the first of his seminal books about the Earth as a self-regulating living planet (1979) and, over the past thirty years, Thomas Berry and his collaborators have described humanity as integral to the 13,800,000,000-year history of the universe (1988, 1999), while Leonardo Boff (1997) has described the Milky Way as "our cosmic homeland".

These paradigm shifts give us a sense of our planet as an interconnected whole. We had our first glimpse of our place in the Cosmos in 1968, when William Anders, an astronaut aboard Apollo 8, captured an image of planet Earth as a sphere floating in endless space. Lovelock and Margulis's Gaia hypothesis of a self-regulating system that has evolved over billions of years, has contributed to the development of earth systems science and our understanding that everything is integrated. This paradigm shift arises from an emerging history of our planet over hundreds of years, and growing scientific understanding that Earth is part of a universe of transformations stretching back 13,800,000,000 years. This understanding enables us to locate ourselves within the neighbourhood of the Solar System, in the Cosmic homeland of our Milky Way Galaxy.

However, the scientists are not alone. This paradigm shift also builds on notions of spirit and mind. As we begin to understand that humans are innately spiritual, we see that the cosmos that gave birth to humanity and, therefore, to spirit and consciousness, is part of us and part of all matter. We are led back to the wisdom of faith communities and indigenous worldviews, to an Earth that is alive and full of spirit.

This way of perceiving the world involves a deep understanding of our planet within the broader history of the universe, embracing the knowledge that it has taken 13.8 billion years to make each strand of complex life that now exists on Earth. It is about seeing both the Earth and the universe as sacred and understanding that we live in a meaningful Cosmos in which each one of us is responsible and accountable to something greater than ourselves. We may well be the only planet in the Cosmos to have evolved complex life, which means that we are part of something very special and unique.

This embedded cosmological paradigm enables us to see ourselves as part of the history of this living planet, but not the summation or the whole. By looking through the lens of geology, past events can teach us about what we are currently doing. Two hundred and fifty million years ago and, again, 55 million years ago, the Earth experienced a huge increase in carbon emissions, causing temperatures across the planet to rise by around 5-6°C (Ward, 2007; Stager, 2011). Biodiversity was severely disrupted, but many species survived by moving to higher latitudes or altitudes. However, in the twenty-first century, species are unable to do this because humanity and what we have created literally stands in their way. Fifty-five million years ago, it took around 170,000 years for the planet to recover, a timescale far beyond that of our present human civilization (Stager, 2011). Geologists have pinpointed five major crises that have threatened life on Earth over the planet's 4.5-billion-year history. Humanity has created the sixth crisis simply by pouring our waste products into the land, the sky and the oceans (Lenton and Watson, 2011). An embedded cosmological perspective begins with the understanding that we have outgrown the childish norms of liberal economics, mechanistic science, consumerism and of perceiving the Earth as the inanimate servant of humanity. Structural racism, gender based violence, vast global economic inequalities, discrimination based on prejudice towards the LGBTQ+ and disabled communities have no place on our only home in a vast cosmos.

An embedded cosmological perspective offers a unique approach to living in the world. First, it is grounded within our daily lives, in the way we work, raise our children, go on holiday, care for each other, care for the dying and the new-born. Second, it grows out of and embraces many centuries of social, political and community change, and suggests that we need to learn from those struggles to achieve improvements in human health, education, poverty reduction, human rights and equalities, and the role of community development and community learning in building more just societies.

Third, this perspective is premised on the belief that everyone is part of the work for an ecologically and socially just world. As Abraham Maslow (1962) reflected, whatever our skills, we are all part of the work for this ideal. We are like the cathedral builders of old who did not live to see their dream completed, but built anyway. Therefore, this perspective is for all human members of the planet Earth community, respecting and honouring our differences,-and requires that individuals work within their work, home, faith or interest group communities for collective learning, action and spirituality.

Instead of feeling overwhelmed by the challenges facing our planet, an embedded cosmological perspective helps us to see these challenges within the context of the long history of our Cosmos.

This perspective adds to our human dreams of a better future, the science of our place in the universe and our understanding and appreciation of love. Martin Luther King inspired generations by sharing his dream of racial and social justice[6]. This book grows from these dreams and seeks to inspire you to create dreams embedded in the Cosmos, of thriving individuals and communities, of a flourishing planet and of hopeful futures.

A cyclical journey

This book is both a journey and a toolkit for action that draws on these embedded cosmological perspectives. Through a series of six cycles, I break down this cosmological perspective into manageable chunks from the scale of the self to community, our planet, the cosmos and back again. These cycles offer hopeful perspectives based on extended ways of knowing and understanding, using a practice called first-person action research, through which we can explore lived personal practices related to the self, home, family, work and organisations, and engage in more meaningful personal action, individual participation and a renewed ability to influence the world around us. Throughout the book, I use my own personal experience to illustrate how change can take place in each of us. The book also contains a series of practical exercises to provide you with the tools to develop and live this new paradigm. The exercises will help you to counter the sadness and grief of what we are doing to the Earth and the feelings of powerlessness that many of us experience in the face of the mechanistic, consumerist paradigm that has long dominated the West. These exercises will help you to replace those feelings with more useful and hopeful strategies for life.

My own first person action research journey is ongoing. For instance, the Black Lives Matter Movement led me to undertake a deep cycle of research exploring my own privilege and the gaps in my knowledge, academic practice and understanding and recognition of racism caused by that privilege.[7] As a result, I am engaging with a broader body of literature beyond the white US/UK canon and addressing why we need to pay deep attention to the effects of racism, slavery and colonialism in order to build anti-racist societies. I have been guided by the work of the Runneymeade Trust in collaboration with the Fawcett Society, which notes that:

'In the UK there are a number of terms used to describe a person's race and ethnicity...There is no agreed consensus on the appropriate language to use and we respect that people have different preferences when it comes to racial terminology.' (Day et al, 2021, pp 5,6) [8] [9]

◯ Hopeful Companions

Some initial resources on Black Lives Matter and anti-racism.

Books
Holding, M. 2021. *Why We Kneel, How We Rise.* London: Simon and Schuster. International cricketer and sports commentator, Michael Holding uses story and sport to explore racism and ongoing practical action to bring about equality and anti-racist societies

Films
Channel Four News: *Black Lives Matter: A History.* 16 June 2020: https://www.youtube.com/watch?v=YG8GjILbbvs

Resources for action
The Ahmed Iqbal Ullah Race Relations Resource Centre and Education Trust, online and in person: https://www.racearchive.org.uk/

Black Lives Matter: a global social civil rights solidarity movement. We kneel together for peace and unity, asserting that Black Lives Matter and that Black People are treated as humanely and fairly as white people: https://www.blacklivesmatter.uk/

I also recognise that this work and my own development are ongoing.

My hope is that through an ongoing examination of those areas that need development and the continuing of my journey of exploration, learning and action in these fields, I can advocate with anti-racism and social justice at the heart, for Earth as Community and for our Planet and Cosmos as sacred. Whilst recognising that a long road lies ahead, this is for me, a hopeful journey where racial and all forms of human justice are intertwined with ecological justice and become part of one shared journey towards better futures within our ancient and beautiful Cosmos.

The book as a toolkit

This book contains tools, maps and approaches to help you create hope and positive energy for the major and seemingly insurmountable challenges facing our planet. The approaches enable each one of us to contribute to changing the world for the better through being part of a wider universe. They give us renewed hope, enthusiasm and energy for the arduous journey ahead.

Each one of us must make a journey of discovery and learning within ourselves, our communities, our planet and our cosmos to develop a loving understanding of what is happening to our planet and to own the pain in our hearts. This love for the planet is the same love we feel for those dear to us. It extends Matthew the Evangelist's commandment to "love your neighbour as yourself" to include love for the more-than-human and the other elements of planet Earth. From such an understanding and practice of love we can start to take action individually and in the company of others. Through love, we can contribute to transforming the predominant exploitative paradigm that is damaging the Earth and its human and more-than-human inhabitants into a paradigm that respects the natural systems on which life depends, and work to restore the Earth and transform society. The cultural historian Thomas Berry hopes for a new era, the Ecozoic, "when humans will be present to the Earth in a mutually enhancing manner" (1999:55). This is the 'hopeful future' at the heart of this book.[10]

The love required to transform our world can be nurtured through a reflective process that combines academic and spiritual concepts with practical community action. Action research can be used as a framework to help us develop spiritual and practical personal responses to global challenges and to create a vision of a transformed world. I illustrate the use of action research by reflecting on my own thirty-year practice of neighbourhood and community regeneration in the northwest of England. In so doing, I provide a 'how to' guide to enable others to explore and create their own journeys towards hopeful futures.

Sometimes, it can feel as though our actions for social or environmental change are merely rearranging the deck chairs on the Titanic. The book's six cycles offer constructive techniques to help you to overcome the paralysis you may experience in the face of such monumental challenges, enabling you to find your own path and to understand the important role you have to play in creating hopeful futures for all of us.

The most important of these techniques is developing the practice of first-person inquiry. This practice offers a means of individual empowerment by linking evidence, practice, spiritual need, personal development and learning through cycles of practice and reflection. It is particularly valuable for the meta-challenges we face – ecological survival, social justice, diversity and inclusion – and for the development of a new paradigm and stories that empower individuals, organisations and groups to challenge conventional wisdom and to take action.

At the heart of this first-person inquiry is using writing as inquiry. This includes reflective writing, storytelling and autoethnography to understand your own place in the Cosmos. I use different metaphors to visualise the journey ahead, and I create maps, tools and practices for that journey, using different creative approaches.

Whether you are an activist, a professional, an academic or a caring citizen concerned with the problems facing humanity in the twenty-first century, the ideas and approaches set out in these cycles will help you to more effectively rise to the challenge in family, community, work, faith or academic contexts. These approaches engage with the interior as well as the exterior journey we all must make, and they offer techniques to keep on going when things get tough. I write for every conservationist and social activist who knows that things are wrong but is struggling to be heard or to make headway. These practices will give you the confidence to move forward. Everyone can, and must, play their part to make space for biodiversity, halt the speeding train of climate change, tackle social inequality and build a hopeful future for all of Earth's inhabitants.

The scholar Lester Milbrath (1989) describes how he wanted to write a book about imagining a sustainable society and instead wrote about values, ethics and social learning. My experience has been similar. I wanted to write a book about sustainable management. Instead, I found myself writing about inquiry, learning and reflection. As my awareness grew that individual journeys of discovery are central to our route to a sustainable future, I realised that we lack practical maps or guidebooks to help us on our way. The tools, maps and underlying theories included in this book are relevant to teachers of responsible business and sustainable development at high school, undergraduate or postgraduate levels, to managers and professionals in public, private and NGO sectors working towards sustainable economics and communities, to community educationalists and activists, to trade unionists, to concerned members of faith communities and to individuals wrestling with the dilemmas of modern living.

The tools that guide our journey contribute to an emerging intellectual tradition of Gaia and Cosmos to counter the current hegemonic myths of consumerism and a mechanistic worldview. The twenty-first century zeitgeist, with its prevailing narratives of doom and gloom, demands new tools to support new worldviews that will lead to the creation of hopeful futures for all of the inhabitants of planet Earth.

Those already committed to the journey will find sustenance in these pages. Those debating and wrestling with the research, professional, faith, management or other challenges of practice, will find meaningful expression for their profound concern about the meta-challenges facing humanity and hurdles to mounting effective challenges to 'business as usual' paradigms. Students from many different disciplines will find a way of looking at their subject in a new and participative light.

Using material from my own first-person research to illustrate the nature of inquiry will, I hope, help you to imagine travelling on your own journey and will encourage you to embark on that journey. I explore how the voices of the planet and the more-than-human world can be heard through media as disparate as newspaper cuttings, scientific reports, and the insights of cosmonauts, astronauts and taikonauts who have had the privilege of journeying into space. By adopting meditative and reflective learning practices, these voices can emerge into and become part of our daily lives. I hope to speed you on your journey, while avoiding some of the dead ends and detours that I have experienced, for time is of the essence, and the next 50 years will prove critical.

Each of the book's six research cycles of action, inquiry and reflection begins with a brief overview to give you the opportunity to think about the application of what you are learning in the context of your own life. The book does not need to be read in sequence. Each of us will start our journey from a different point and follow a different route. You can start at whichever cycle is most appropriate to your stage of the journey.

Dancing Lightly: Reflections on the holding of ideas

My teacher, Professor Judi Marshall, often reminded her students of the need to dance lightly with ideas. This is reminiscent of St Benedict's teaching that "in the vast reaches and endless memory of the universe...our greatest triumphs and our meanest actions are as lasting as a mark in sand" (McQuiston II, 1996). The Gospel of Matthew, Chapter 10, verse 29, tells us that every sparrow is counted.[11] The ideas investigated in this book are held and offered with simultaneous lightness and seriousness. The purpose of first-person inquiry is not to find the 'truth', but to be constantly inquiring into our actions, values and resources studied. I encourage you to ask questions of yourself, this book, and the wider world around you.

In the same spirit, the action research presented in this book is not an *'ism'*. Instead, it is a creative space, enabling us to work together as human beings with all our imperfections and in ways that enable us to address the mighty and systemic challenges we face. In the face of immense environmental damage, biodiversity loss and climate change, and our actions to date, pedagogue Steven Stirling (2010) suggests that we must face the music and dance into the night, acknowledging the enormity of what we are facing, but never giving up the dance. I hope the ideas in this book will enable us to dance together towards the dawn.

Starting your journey

Scattered throughout each chapter are the items in the tool kit. The tool kit consists of three tools – Hopeful Companions, Creative Learning Exercises and Invitations to Reflect (see Figure 0.2). *Hopeful Companions* suggest resources for further exploration. *Creative Learning Exercises* are designed to draw you into experiential learning both individually and in groups or organisational settings. *Invitations to Reflect* present reflective writing or other inquiry exercises to help you to create your own map to a hopeful future, guiding your practice as an individual, as a member of a community, as a citizen of planet Earth and as an inseparable part of the Cosmos. To prepare for such experiential learning and reflection, I invite you to gather the resources you'll need.

Creative learning materials

What learning materials will help you on your journey? These can be very simple, such as a notebook and pen. The physical act of writing and drawing on paper is an important part of the process of engaging with these ideas. Find a notebook tucked away in a drawer, or buy, preferably, a recycled one. You will need a good pen – perhaps you might choose a reusable ink pen, so that you do not have to keep throwing away. Have fun – use coloured pens, coloured pencils – make sure you have a pencil sharpener and a rubber so that you can experiment, change if needed, be creative. For the drawing exercises, try using paper of different colours and sizes. You may

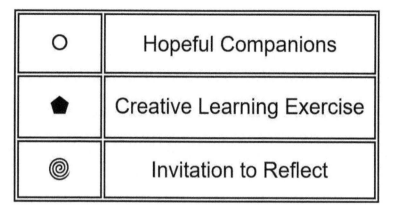

O	Hopeful Companions
⬠	Creative Learning Exercise
◎	Invitation to Reflect

Figure 0.2: Three tools in your Hopeful Futures Tool Kit.
You will find boxes with these symbols at intervals throughout the book.
You are invited to follow them up as you go along or later.

want to take notes and you could use multiple colours for different sections and themes. You may prefer working electronically. If you are writing on a laptop, create a dedicated word document or a series of folders for different subjects. You may want to gather inspiring material that you come across, such as poems, music and art and you could have a separate folder for each. On your laptop you could colour block your notes, experimenting with all the different colours available. Either way, you could create a supply of craft materials to work with, gathering odds and ends and asking friends and family to contribute. Materials might include discarded packaging, string, paper, wool, used envelopes, greaseproof paper from the kitchen, ink and paint, or natural materials such as wood, water, leaves and seeds. All these items can be stored in a box or basket dedicated to your journey, or in a craft drawer. All these resources can be used with the different exercises in the tool kit.

O   Hopeful Companions

These boxes offer signposts and introduce you to motivational resources within a variety of media and offer broad horizons to explore.

The Hopeful Companions allow you to engage with the thoughts of others and, over time, enter into debate and discussion and join in a global conversation. Many of these resources can be accessed online. Others can be accessed through your local library or interlibrary lending scheme including, in the UK, the British Library. In some cases, as a local resident, you can join the library of your local university. Your community may have a local resource centre. Think about ways to gather and share resources on your street, including a mini street library. Why not take as many opportunities as you can to engage in the discussion?

Remember to engage reflectively with these resources. Take note of who the author/creator is and where their perspective might have come from. As you proceed with your journey, be open to all voices, allowing them to be heard and included in the developing conversation.

You might want to record your responses to these resources. The creative learning materials will help you do this.

Creative Learning Exercises

Throughout this book, there are invitations to write, draw, or in some other creative way, explore what you have read.

These Creative Learning Exercises allow you to creatively respond to what you are learning about. Sometimes you will be invited to undertake these exercises in nature. The exercises aim to release your creative energies, so that the challenges of the planet become not overwhelming problems but creative challenges to be addressed with all your creativity, hope and energy. Each exercise invites you to explore and record your responses so that you can reflect on them in the future. There are many ways to record your responses, through journal writing, photography, art, sewing, embroidery, music, singing, poetry, sculpture, gardening, cooking and baking. You might take your responses further, through performance, Instagram and other social media. These Creative Learning Exercises offer a bridge between the Hopeful Companions and Invitations to Reflect. [12]

Invitations to Reflect

These learning exercises invite you to reflect and meditate on what you have encountered, both in this book and in the Hopeful Companions boxes. I encourage you to find a space where you feel comfortable and enjoy reflecting, perhaps outside in nature, in a library or café, on a park bench, or in a quiet corner of your home.

A key element of the Invitation to Reflect is reflecting over time on what you are learning and the actions you are taking in your life. In this way, you can enter into the practice of cycles of reflection and action which, I hope, will continue long after you have reached the end of the book. In essence, the Invitations to Reflect allow you to catch your breath, to stop, to carve out time for reflection, so that you do not feel rushed. Over time, these cycles of action and reflection might mirror the seasons of our planet.

For some, this journey of reflection may become a spiritual journey. For others, it may not. It may be a journey of individual reflection or reflection in the company of others.

 Invitation to Reflect

Gather your Creative Learning materials. Start as simply as you like – a pen, paper, a pencil and an eraser. Find somewhere quiet and set aside 15 minutes or half an hour to think about the following questions. Come back to these questions in a day or two or a week and consider any further responses you might have.

Consider your current practice of inquiry. Do you usually take time out of your day to reflect? Do you write or draw or daydream? Do you pray? Are these processes valuable to you? Do you have a favourite spot for reflection?

If you don't currently take time out to reflect, did you do so in the past? Do you know anyone else who does? Do you have any concerns or fears about reflective practice? If so, what are they?

Think about your day. When can you set aside time for reflection? What time or times of days are best for you?

Where can you engage in reflective practice? Do you have a quiet space at home? Do you have an outside space where you would like to reflect? Do you have a space in your workplace? Or on your commute to work? Or in a café? Or in a faith-based building?

Consider the types of learning you like to engage in. Do you like reading? What types of reading material do you prefer? Do you find it easier to listen? Do you prefer watching television or internet programmes? Identify the ways you most enjoy learning and reflect on how you can maximise those opportunities to learn?

Think of your own journey ahead, identify who you can work with and support you on the journey. This could be from friends and family, to members of your local community group, faith community, NGO or trade union, to colleagues at work.

Developing your own tools for your journey

As you work with these tools, you may start to develop your own signposts, creative exercises or reflections. You might start to seek out your own Hopeful Companions resources and develop your own Creative Learning Exercises in a medium most suited to you, and develop your own reflective questions and practices.

You are now ready to begin your journey to more hopeful futures.

Notes

[1] Heatwaves affect wildlife adversely in many different ways, including fires killing species and young, to dehydration and heat stress killing marine shore life: 'Too hot. As fires rage and birds faint, the heat is taking its toll on wildlife'. Phoebe Weston, The Guardian, 25th July 2022.

[2] For a complete list of the Human Development Reports from 1990 by year and key theme, see: http://hdr.undp.org/en/global-reports

[3] For example, the action of oil companies in misleading the public on the science of climate change: https://www.theguardian.com/environment/2022/mar/10/oil-companies-corporate-free-speech-laws-climate-litigation. Also the profits made by the oil companies: https://www.theguardian.com/environment/2022/jul/21/revealed-oil-sectors-staggering-profits-last-50-years

[4] For an exploration of academics in service of communities, see Remi-Joseph Salisbury and Laura Connelly's exploration of struggles around anti-racism (2021).

[5] The Centre for Connected Practice was co-founded in 2015, with my civil partner Phil Barton: https://c4cp.net/. We are inspired to create connections and share ideas, resources and creativity across community, academic and professional boundaries to improve the quality of life for all the residents of Gaia, within the context of humanity's awe inspiring 13.8 billion year history.

[6] King, M.L. Jr. 28 August, 1963. I Have A Dream, March on Washington for Jobs and Freedom. Video: https://www.youtube.com/watch?v=vP4iY1TtS3s

Text of the speech: http://freedomsring.stanford.edu/?view=Speech

[7] In working towards an anti-racist paradigm, my personal reflective cycles of action, learning and reflection are explored further within chapter 5.

[8] Dey, M., White, W., and Kaur, S. 2021. *The Pay and Progression of Women of Colour. A Literature Review.* London: Fawcett Society and the Runneymede Trust: https://www.fawcettsociety.org.uk/the-pay-and-progression-of-women-of-colour-literature-review A Note on Language: Pages 5 and 6.

[9] Gyimah, M., Azad, Z., Begum, S., Kapoor, A. Ville L., Henderson A., Dey, M. 2022. *Broken Ladders: The Myth of Meritocracy for Women of Colour in the Workplace.* London: Fawcett Society and the Runnymede Trust: https://www.runnymedetrust.org/partnership-projects/broken-ladders A Note on Language: Page 5

[10] See the short video: Thomas Berry – cultural historian and geologian: *A Human vision for the Earth Community*: https://www.youtube.com/watch?v=-5vVJ1y2PMs

[11] Matthew 10: 29 -31. King James Bible (ND). Containing the Old and New Testaments, King James version. Oxford: Oxford University Press.

[12] For work on creativity in learning, see Chrissi Nerantzi, who developed the Creativity in Learning Unit as part of Continuous Professional Development at Manchester Metropolitan University: https://chrissinerantzi.wordpress.com/

First cycle: Beginning our Journey

"Within the lifespan of someone born today, our species is currently predicted to take our planet through a series of one-way doors that bring irreversible change…. In such a future, we will bring about nothing less that the collapse of the living world, the very thing that our civilisation relies upon."
David Attenborough (2019: 120)

In this cycle, we will establish 'Base Camp' from the perspective of Earthrise – a view of planet Earth from the Moon: where we are now in relation to our planet home. We will explore our human achievements and search for the contours of the mountains on the journey ahead.

This cycle will enable you to see that the challenges our planet faces are interconnected and can be solved. I encourage you to engage actively with what is happening to the planet, so that you can understand your own view of the mountains ahead. As a species, we have reached rock bottom and the only way forward is through love and participation.

Through cosmic worldviews or paradigms, we can learn to experience and participate in the world in different ways. In this cycle, I present a family of interconnected cosmological, Gaian and participatory paradigms that offer different ways to approach the sacred, including the 'awe and wonder' of the Cosmos.

These new paradigms will enable humanity to escape our present 'stuck' thinking, allowing us to dance lightly with new ways of knowing and engaging.

Chapter 1: Exploring base camp

"We have [predicted] a ghastly future of mass extinction, declining health, and climate disruption upheavals...and resource conflicts this century. Yet our goal is not to present a fatalistic perspective, because there are many examples of successful interventions...instead we contend that only a realistic appreciation of the colossal challenges facing the international community might allow it to chart a less-ravaged future."
Corey Bradshaw et al (2021: 6)

"My advice is to spend your time on those who are reachable, teachable and movable. They need assistance.... Too many have fallen into climate despair, having been led astray by unscientific, doomist messaging, some of it promoted by the inactivists, in a cynical effort to dispirit and divide climate activists."
Michael Mann (2021: 262)

Gaia's Graveyards – sharing

As I collected the cuttings of biodiversity loss over the years, I amassed a heart-rending list of species threatened or in severe decline. How could I share this with others? I got into the habit of taking the cuttings to workshops and spreading them on the floor or giving them to workshop participants to look at. My aim was to share the sadness of seeing so many animals threatened with extinction as a spur to urgent action. With my partner, I created *Pilgrimage for Gaia* workshops for faith communities to explore what is happening to nature and to encourage participants to use arts and crafts materials to create ideas for solutions. My partner, who is an artist,

Figure 1.1: Gaia's Graveyards: Timeline, Barborough Kettleton (2015).
Exhibition view at The Tower Gallery, University of Chester.
(Photograph: Mike Pumford).

created a number of installations over several years. *Timeline* consisted of one cutting from each year pasted onto small pieces of wood and suspended as a downward line, illustrating, over fifteen years, the increasing gravity of the threats facing biodiversity.

The Washing Line was created by workshop participants who cut out newspaper stories related to biodiversity loss and hung them alongside the newspapers from which they had been cut. This visually and physically demonstrated the lack of serious attention given to biodiversity loss.[13] Meanwhile, *The Cabinet* illustrated how few newspaper stories related to biodiversity, with hundreds of newspapers cascading out of an old lacquer cabinet, and those relating to species under threat suspended from a birdfeeder. A final installation, *An Ark for Gaia*, contained thirty cuttings of biodiversity loss, with a headline, a photograph and text, mounted on board. During *Pilgrimage for Gaia* workshops, participants studied the cuttings in the Ark and each chose one that called to them.

Throughout this journey, the work of artists and creatives will be integral to our understanding of what we are doing to planet Earth.

Figure 1.2: Gaia's Graveyards. Washing line, Phil Barton (2015).
Exhibition view at St Agnes' Church, North Reddish. (Photograph: Phil Barton).

Threats to biodiversity are reflected in the scientific literature. In 1979, conservationist Robert Lamb highlighted the threats to trees as they are immobile in the face of danger.[14] Trees in the UK are currently threatened by six pathogens (Vidal, 2011b). In the 1990s, Harvard ecologist E.O. Wilson studied the effects of humanity on the natural world, and concluded that we have been a planetary killer for thousands of years, attributing the deaths of megafauna to human expansion and development (Anderson, 2001; Wilson, 2002).

Stephan Harding (2006) uses the phrase 'desperate earth' to describe the decimation of elephant and rhino populations. But it is not only megafauna that are threatened with extinction. Insects, often unloved, but key species in our ecosystems as pollinators, decomposers and food are also gravely threatened (Oates, 2015; McCarthy, 2015). Our seas face depletion and the WWF (2018) estimates that half of all shallow water corals have been lost in the last 30 years, with many species of fish classified as endangered or threatened. Some species, having faced pressure over many years, can disappear, as if overnight, as happened with North Atlantic cod in Newfoundland in the 1990s, leading to the decimation of local fishing communities.[15] In 2020, the WWF global Living Planet Index reported "an average 68% (range: -73% to -62%) fall in monitored populations of mammals, birds, amphibians, reptiles and fish between 1970 and 2016" (WWF, 2020).

Meanwhile, the International Union for the Conservation of Nature (IUCN) Red List of Threatened Species lists 35,000+ of its 128,918 species as 'threatened' with extinction.[16] Nature writer Michael McCarthy (2015: 16) reflects:

> "It is extraordinary: we are wrecking the earth, as burglars will sometimes wantonly wreck a house. It is a strange and terrible moment in history. We who depend upon it utterly are laying waste to the biosphere, the thin planet-encircling envelope of life, rushing to degrade the atmosphere above and the ocean below and the soil at the centre and everything it supports: grabbing it, ripping it, scattering it, tearing at it, torching it, slashing at it, shitting on it."

 Invitation to Reflect

Find news, magazine or online reports of animals threatened with declining numbers or extinction.

Over time, collect some of these stories. Perhaps there is a species or group of animals in which you are particularly interested.

Consider species that are not cute or cuddly, not mammals, not charismatic megafauna. How do you feel about threats to these animals?

Record the stories you find and write down the headlines.

Identify the challenges faced by different species.

Continue to collect these stories while reading this book.

Reflect on how these stories make you feel.

Starting out – Earthrise

Space exploration has been a passion of mine since I watched the Apollo Moon landings as an excited child. One of my favourite images from space is the famous *Earthrise*.

On Christmas Eve 1968, Commander Frank Borman, navigator Jim Lovell and astronaut William Anders were on the far side of the moon

Figure 1.3: Earthrise - Basecamp: exploring what is happening to planet Earth. (Source: NASA, 1968. Earthrise, https://www.nasa.gov/image-feature/apollo-8-earthrise)

aboard Apollo 8. The surface of the moon was pitted and grey. Borman began to roll the spacecraft in its orbit when suddenly, out of one of the capsule windows, they glimpsed a blue and white disc and realised, with a shock of recognition, that they were seeing the Earth rising above the moon. "Here's the Earth coming up. Wow, is that pretty," Anders exclaimed. Lovell and Anders scrambled for the camera and the film, while Borman told them they couldn't photograph Earth because it was not in their schedule! Then, devastatingly, they lost sight of Earth. However, as their spacecraft rotated, their home planet came back into view and Anders captured the first pictures of Earth from another celestial body, 250,000 miles away from home. Earthrise has become one of the most well-known photographs of all time.

The photograph inspired scientists studying Earth and space. It is a photograph that emphasises how fragile and exceptional our planet is. For the first time, we saw ourselves as one, the animate and the inanimate on our home planet. We saw ourselves as a watery and rocky sphere spinning in the cosmos, held together by gravity. As we noticed the contrast between the lifeless moon beneath the astronauts and the living Earth, our consciousness grew of how special the Earth is. In extending the view of ourselves, we began to see the Earth as much our home as our more immediate houses and streets. The photograph is credited with helping to stimulate the creation of the first Earth Day in 1972 and the rise of the environmental movement.

Scientist James Lovelock was influenced by NASA programmes he worked on to find life on Mars and Venus. This culminated in his work to understand the Earth as a living organism, which he called "the Gaia hypothesis" (1979). The photograph encourages each of us to see ourselves living in multiple homes: in our houses, on our streets and regions and countries and continents, and on our home planet, Earth. Seeing Earth from the moon helped us to understand how exceptional our planet is to have her moon, how exceptional is our place in the solar system, and to understand our neighbouring planets not as lumps of dead matter but as participating beings in the history of Earth. In short, this photograph caused a paradigm shift in how we see the world and how we see our place in it.

 Creative Learning Exercises

Visit the NASA Image Library, which holds an amazing collection of photographs and images of our solar system, the Milky Way, and further afield https://www.nasa.gov/multimedia/imagegallery/index.html

Why not download or print your favourites, add them to your journal or display them at home or work?

Visit NASA's wonderful collection of footage from the Apollo era and enjoy the first moments when humanity saw Earth from space: https://www.nasa.gov/mission_pages/apollo/index.html

A narrated reconstructed video version for the 45th anniversary of the taking of the Earthrise photograph can be seen at: https://earthobservatory.nasa.gov/images/82693/earthrise

Draw or paint your own version of the Earthrise photograph and hang it in your work place or home.

Earthrise – inviting a creative and spiritual response

For much of our history and for many indigenous communities in the twenty-first century, we are part of a living planet. Yet, with the rise of consumerism, much of this knowledge has been lost. Towards the middle of the twentieth century, our species began to overwhelm the planet's ecosystems.[17] How might we understand what we are doing to planet Earth? Earthrise shows us that we cannot solve our planet's problems by focusing on single issues or on our own streets or in our own countries. It presents a radically different view of the Earth as a living, interconnected whole, suspended in the velvet blackness of space. How might we respond to such a vision of the Earth in order to make our own journeys to hopeful futures? I have found the spiritual tradition of Al-Anon, a programme to help the families and friends of alcoholics, based on the Alcoholics Anonymous (AA) 12-step recovery programme, very helpful.[18] Step 4, in both programmes, 'Make a searching and fearless moral inventory of ourselves' allows for a complete and honest review of all our qualities, both good and bad. Step 4 is followed by a journey of renewal that includes Step 9, 'Making amends to those you have harmed.'

We will not complete the journey unless we start with an understanding of what humanity is doing to our planet. This is the work of thousands of scientists all over the world and a situation that changes all the time. I cannot cover every aspect of harm in one chapter of one book. However, I have been bearing witness and using first-person action research for over two decades to deepen my awareness of what we are doing to the planet. This is a method that will help you to find out what is happening to the world and to create your own responses.

You may feel that you already 'know' the content of this chapter and that it is too depressing to read about these things again. But, from the perspective of the AA and Al-Anon spiritual programmes, if we cannot honestly face the actions of our lives and express those actions aloud to supportive others, we cannot move forward. We must first face up to our behaviour and any harm caused. Before moving forward, we must also be able to say sorry. Earthrise helps us to recognise the fragility of our planet and encourages us to apologise for what we are doing. Seeing planet Earth as a whole helps us to recognise the needs of all communities and not just the powerful and rich and to make social justice and human rights integral to this journey.

Creative Learning Exercises

Create your own record of what is happening to our planet. There are many creative approaches you could take to doing this:

Create a collage of pictures of the many ways humanity is challenging the planet.

Use coloured inks or water colours to paint what is happening to the planet. You could take a roll of wallpaper and paint over many days.

Create your own art installation – for example, your own timeline since Earthrise was taken in 1968, pinpointing important dates related to threats to wildlife, increased carbon dioxide in the atmosphere, dates around social justice issues.

Choose and gather together pieces of music that evoke for you what is happening to our planet.

Keep track of this evidence through written notes of stories, articles, books or research. Keep the list in a notebook or on your laptop. Add each new reference to that list.

Earthrise – A wasteful challenge on a planetary timescale

How can we examine the challenges facing humanity in ways that are helpful to our journey? Earthrise helps us to see our planet in the context of her 4,500,000,000-million-year history. Within this timescale, scientists Tim Lenton and Andrew Watson (2011) believe that our waste is at the root of many of the problems our planet faces.

A 2006 study found that the average human in the US "uses his or her weight in materials, fuel and food every day" with a corresponding high amount of waste (see Primack & Abrams, 2006: 241). In December 2018, BBC's Blue Planet II drove home, with great poignancy, the fact that, each year, mountains of plastic find their way into our oceans, having been produced by industry, used by consumers and then discarded. Images of dying turtles gave a sense of urgency to the need to end single and short-term plastic use. The Great Pacific Garbage Patch, estimated to be anywhere from the size of Texas to the size of Russia, highlights the need for immediate action.[19] All plastic eventually breaks down into micro-plastic. Such is the size and number of micro plastics that they literally rain down upon us (Wetherbee et al., 2019). A global research study by Lau et al. (2020) concluded that US and UK citizens are the "biggest sources of plastic in the world" and urged concerted global action to achieve zero plastic waste. A study by Elhacham et al. (2020) reported that, for the first time in human history, "global human-made mass exceeds all living biomass." One particular waste product of our over consumption is the emission of greenhouse gas.

Rising temperatures, caused by these greenhouse gases, are having a disastrous effect on ecosystems. In pre-industrial times, the atmosphere contained 280ppm of carbon dioxide. Since the start of the Industrial Revolution, the quantity of carbon dioxide in the atmosphere has increased and is now increasing at an exponential rate. The atmospheric monitoring station at Mauna Loa Observatory in Hawaii has been monitoring carbon dioxide levels since 1956. In 2013, it recorded 400 ppm for the first time and, at the time of writing this chapter in 2021, concentrations are 416.09 ppm with an upward underlying trend.[20] Some countries have both an historic and a current carbon footprint. Therefore, when determining how countries should cut emissions, historic footprints must be taken into account to achieve climate justice.

 Creative Learning Exercises

Check out today's carbon dioxide reading – and keep following – at https://www.co2.earth/

Watch the World Meteorological Association video: Climate Change, the Relentless March: https://www.youtube.com/watch?v=hIcJCwvTFfg

Read the World Meteorological Association Report on global warming and 2020: https://public.wmo.int/en/media/press-release/2020-track-be-one-of-three-warmest-years-record

What is the CO_2 level today? What was it last month? What about last year? Five years ago? Twenty years ago? Illustrate your findings through painting, collage or drawing.

In your journal, create a timeline of increasing CO_2 in the atmosphere. How does this make you feel?

Trace the relationship between carbon dioxide emissions and the Industrial Revolution in countries such as the UK, the USA and Germany.

Earthrise – Our warming planet

Carbon dioxide traps the sun's heat in the atmosphere, causing it to warm up. In recent years, temperature records have been repeatedly broken, with 2020 the hottest year on record, 2016 second and 2019 third (NASA, 2023) and the decade 2011 to 2020 is the hottest decade on record. Some places on Earth now experience temperatures that are too hot for species to survive; in parts of Australia for bats (Cockburn, 2019) and Seville, in Spain, for baby swifts (Bourne, 2022). Some formerly habitable places are now nearing the upper limits for human survival. In spring 2022, for example, temperatures of 49°C were recorded in New Delhi, 44°C in Phoenix, Arizona and 40°C in Madrid (Harvey et al., 2022). Rising temperatures increase atmospheric moisture, leading to more rain and flooding over land and increased storm intensity. Some excess carbon dioxide is absorbed by the oceans, reducing the pH level, making the water more acidic. Widespread acidification threatens coral reefs and the plankton which forms the base of the food web. Higher temperatures at high latitudes are causing permafrost to melt, resulting in the release of methane, a far more potent greenhouse gas than carbon dioxide. Methane is also trapped in sediments around the edges of the continents and, as our oceans warm, this too is released into the atmosphere, threatening to cause runaway climate change that may already be beyond human control.

Our planet is faced with an unprecedented great burning. With the warming of the planet, extensive and long-lasting fires are burning around the globe. The 2019-2020 fires in Australia, exacerbated by years of severe drought followed by very hot temperatures, demonstrate how a situation can suddenly escalate. California now faces annual extreme bush fires which rage out of control. Nor are the rainforests spared. Indonesia faces huge threats from fires, with over 2,000 burning at one time in 2019, turning the sky 'blood red' over Sumatra,[21] and the 2019 fires in the Amazon raised fears that we have reached a tipping point beyond which the Amazon rainforest – Gaia's lungs – cannot recover (Amigo, 2020). The 2021 fires in Australia were accompanied by pictures of darkened skies and humans and animals trapped or forced to flee to beaches to find safety. On first reflection, these fires appear to be far from our own doorsteps and their immediate impact seems distant. Yet, the view of planet Earth from the moon teaches us that we are all one. If we destroy the Amazon rainforest, we destroy our own life support system. Forest fires across the world add more methane and carbon dioxide to the atmosphere, increasing the temperature of the planet from which none of us can escape, as it is our only home.

At the same time, glaciers and ice sheets are melting. Both the Arctic and the Antarctic recorded unprecedently high temperatures in March 2022 (Harvey et al., 2022). Cold fresh meltwater pouring off Greenland as its icecap melts may slow the Gulf Stream current that regulates temperatures in Europe. The diminishment or collapse of the Gulf Stream would have drastic consequences for life in Europe. Meanwhile, in Antarctica, the great Western ice sheet is on the verge of collapse. This destabilisation is beyond humanity's control and its eventual collapse is predicted to result in at least one metre of sea rise globally by the end of this century (Goldenberg, 2014; Goodell, 2018).

Rising temperatures also threaten the planet's fresh water resources. The retreat of Asian glaciers that are a source of fresh water for millions of people signals the start of a major water crisis (Immerzeel et al., 2020). In Africa, rising temperatures are leading to prolonged drought. In 2019, the Victoria Falls in Zimbabwe slowed to a trickle as a result of multiyear drought (McKenzie & Swalis, 2019) while, in the US, the southern states face increasing drought, with human development causing the overuse and non-replenishment of aquafer water. In India, it is estimated that, by 2030, millions will be without fresh water (Banerji, 2018) while rising sea levels in Bangladesh threaten to salinate underground freshwater reserves (Vimela et al., 2011).

○ Hopeful Companions

What we are doing to our planet:

Films
She is alive, she's beautiful and she's hurting (4 minutes):
https://www.youtube.com/watch?v=nGeXdv-uPaw

Climate change: The facts.
https://www.youtube.com/watch?v=EOctIuyVfnA

An Inconvenient Truth (trailer):
https://www.youtube.com/watch?v=Bu6SE5TYrCM

Resources for action
The North-South Divide:
https://prezi.com/dwhvbzpvuzax/the-global-northsouth-divide/

Fighting Racism and Discrimination: The Durban Declaration and Programme of Action at 20:
https://www.ohchr.org/sites/default/files/Documents/Issues/Racism/
OHCHR_DDPA_Booklet_EN.pdf

Earthrise – Interconnected scientific assessments

If many of these challenges were studied as single issues in the twentieth century, scientists increasingly describe them as systemic and interconnected. Several international scientific assessments have sought to understand these challenges. In 2005, the Millennium Eco-Assessment (MEA) drew together the work of 1,360 ecosystem scientists and found that all seven of Earth's ecosystems are in crisis and, in the long term, human well-being is threatened. The MEA analysed the impact of environmental degradation on humanity, highlighting how dependent humanity is on healthy ecosystems. Although the lives of billions have been improved in the short-term, these improvements have been dependent on the exploitation of the Earth's ecosystems to meet food, fresh water, materials and energy demands. Such demands have weakened all seven ecosystems and threaten sustained improvements to human life (MEA, 2005).

In 2012, the Blue Planet Laureates, scientists who have won the prestigious Ashanti prize for their contributions to the environment over a twenty-year period, came together to issue a report on the dangers facing the planet. The report unequivocally linked the health of the planet with human health (Ashanti Glass Foundation, 2012). In 2013, the International

Programme on the State of the Ocean (IPSO) with the International Union for the Conservation of Nature (IUCN) published an analysis of the threats facing the world's oceans. These threats include overfishing and dead spots and revealed the increasingly interconnected nature of the threats facing the oceans (IPSO, 2013). The Assessment Reports of the Intergovernmental Panel on Climate Change report each year on climate change and its effects on different aspects of the planet, providing detailed scientific evidence. In 2017, a meta-analysis of research concluded that the planet faces "biological annihilation" (Cebellos et al., 2017). In 2019, building on the work of the MEA, the report from the Intergovernmental Science-Policy Platform on Biodiversity and Ecosystem Services found that over a million species are threatened with extinction. In all, the planet faces the sixth great extinction in geological history (Kolbert, 2014). The only difference is that, this time, the extinction is caused by human action.

◯ Hopeful Companions

Books
Goodell, J. 2017. *The Water Will Come: Rising Seas, Sinking Cities, and the Remaking of the Civilised World*. Carlton VIC, Australia: Black Inc.

Resources for Action
Carbon Brief (2022) *In depth Q and A: What is Climate Justice?* 4 October: https://www.carbonbrief.org/in-depth-qa-what-is-climate-justice/

Climate Action Tracker, independent scientific analysis tracking progress against the 2015 Paris Agreement, for 36 countries and the EU: https://climateactiontracker.org/

International Panel on Climate Change: 2014 IPPC *Report on mitigation and adaption to the climate emergency*: https://www.ipcc.ch/report/ar5/wg2/ an accompanying short film: https://www.youtube.com/watch?v=jMIFBJYpSgM

IPPC 2018 *Special Report on the importance of not exceeding 1.5°C of warming above pre-industrial levels*: https://www.ipcc.ch/sr15/

Earthrise – Listening to planet Earth

In 1972, *The Limits to Growth* (Meadows et al., 1972) was published. The authors argued that humanity was outstripping the planet's capacity without regard for its limits. In the fifty years since, humans have failed to listen to what the planet is telling us about the impact of our actions.

In 2009, Rockström et al. (2009) presented a new way of conceptualising these limits to growth, involving nine planetary boundaries, all of which humanity must remain inside. According to their analysis, humanity was already outstripping the carrying capacity of three of these nine boundaries: the nitrogen boundary, the climate change boundary and the biodiversity boundary. Nitrogen, used in the production of artificial fertiliser, runs off the land into rivers and gets carried to the sea, where it causes ocean dead spots. The use of potassium and phosphates has also reached dangerous levels. All three chemicals are used in the production of artificial fertiliser. By 2015, a fourth boundary had been crossed: land-system change due to the appropriation of so much of the planet for food production (Steffen et al., 2015). The human desire to consume meat is causing the destruction of ecosystems such as the Amazon rain forest, while the demand for palm oil is destroying the rainforests of Indonesia. The total number of livestock for human consumption crowds out all other animals on the planet (Elhacham et al., 2020). Computer scientist Stephen Emmott, author of *Ten Billion* (2013) has found that population growth, energy use, food consumption and resource use trends are all growing exponentially, a phenomenon that he refers to as an "unprecedented planetary emergency." A study in 2019 identified the systemic ways the Amazon rainforest is threatened, including the political withdrawal of environmental protection, the farming of maize and soya on the forest edges causing changes to weather patterns and the cessation of the rains that sweep over the rainforest, attacks on indigenous peoples who protect the forest and a reduction in biodiversity (Xavantina & Santarén, 2019). Each of these factors further weakens the rainforest's resilience.

So great is humanity's impact that many believe we have initiated a new geological era, the Anthropocene. So great is our impact on the planet that it will be visible in the fossil record even though we have lived on the planet for only a blink of the Cosmic eye. Our geological legacy will include plastics, chicken bones and a great disconnect signifying the extinction of so much life.

Creative Learning Exercises

Identify a part of the planet that interests you and research the changes which have taken place in the past fifty years. Record your feelings about the changes.

Research the terms 'Anthropocene' and the 'Great Turning' and draw your responses to what you find. You can start your research using the following resources:

'Ten things you should know about the Anthropocene' a talk by Erle C. Elis based on his 2018 book: *The Anthropocene, A Very Short Introduction.* Oxford: University Press: https://www.youtube.com/watch?v=1RlVnaxTUv4

Understanding the Anthropocene is essential to how humanity can change direction. Watch Johan Rockström 'Beyond the Anthropocene' at the World Economic Forum, 24 February 2017: https://www.youtube.com/watch?v=V9ETiSaxyfk

Kathryn Yusoff's 2018. *A Billion Black Anthropocenes or None – Forerunners.* Minneapolis: University of Minnesota: 'a transdisciplinary conversation between feminist black theory, geography and earth sciences to address the politics of the Anthropocene'.

Understanding the Anthropocene with an anti-racist perspective: UCL News: Professors Maslin and Lewis: 'Why the Anthropocene began with European colonisation and mass slavery', 25 June 2020: https://www.ucl.ac.uk/news/2020/jun/opinion-why-anthropocene-began-european-colonisation-and-mass-slavery

---

⭘ Hopeful Companions

Books
Mann, M. 2021. *The New Climate War.* London: Scribe.

Films
Planetary boundaries explained:
https://www.stockholmresilience.org/research/research-news/2015-01-15-planetary-boundaries---an-update.html

Veteran climate scientist and activist James Hansen illustrates what is happening to the climate: http://www.columbia.edu/~jeh1/

Resources for Action
Covey et al. 2021. 'Underestimating the challenges in avoiding a Ghastly Future'. Papers, ideas and debates on how to avoid a ghastly future: https://www.avoidingghastlyfuture.org/explore-resources/

Global Forest Watch. 2022. Forest Monitoring Designed for Action: https://www.globalforestwatch.org/

Meet 13 Young Indigenous Rights Activists, Office of the UN Secretary General Envoy on Youth: https://www.un.org/youthenvoy/2021/08/meet-13-indigenous-young-indigenous-rights-activists/

Earthrise – Human development and rights

Given the human dimension to the environmental crisis, it is also critical that, as a society, we address the challenges of eliminating poverty, hunger and inequality. The 2000-2015 United Nations Millennium Goals have been replaced by 17 Sustainable Development Goals for the period 2016 to 2030, with 189 nations ratifying these targets. These too need to be added to the map of our journey (see Figure 5.1, p. 164).

The Human Development Reports demonstrate that, in the twentieth century, millions of people have been lifted out of extreme poverty. Education levels have risen to previously unheard-of levels, and more children than ever now attend school. This has had an especially positive impact on the lives of girls and women. Health care is improving around the world. The number of women giving birth without medical care and attention continues to fall. However, the COVID-19 pandemic threatened to reverse decades of improved health care (UN/DESA, 2020). War and conflict remain issues for humanity. In 2019 over one hundred civilians were killed each day in armed conflict and the number of people fleeing war, persecution and conflict exceeded 79.5 million, the highest number ever recorded (UN SDG, 2020).

A key aspect of recent human development has been the creation of the concept of human rights. My own hometown, Manchester, and the Greater Manchester Region, are illustrative of our advances in human rights. The city was the site of the 1819 Peterloo Massacre, a peaceful demonstration for suffrage that was violently suppressed by sabre-wielding cavalry. It was also the site of the 1844 founding of the Co-operative Movement in Rochdale. In 1863, the working people of Manchester supported the abolition of slavery in the US. The first meeting of the Trades Union Congress took place in 1868 at the Mechanic's Institute. At the start of the twentieth century, Emily Pankhurst worked for female suffrage and, in 1945, the Fifth Pan-African Congress took place at the former Chorlton-on-Medlock Town Hall, attended by, among others, Kwame Nkrumah and Jomo Kenyatta. In the 1970s and 1980s, it was the site of the radical Asian Youth Movement which fought against racism and discrimination and, in 1964, it was the site of an early meeting of the movement for LGBTQ+ equality in the offices of the Diocese of Manchester, as well as the site of the pioneering Gay Village and the *Queer Up North* International Festival, established in the 1990s. Well before the national Disability Discrimination Act, Manchester had become a site of the disability rights movement, campaigning across all parts of society.[22]

Such movements for human rights highlight the need to include power in our journey to hopeful futures. The needs and rights of poorer communities, local communities and Indigenous communities must be specifically considered as we proceed on this journey.

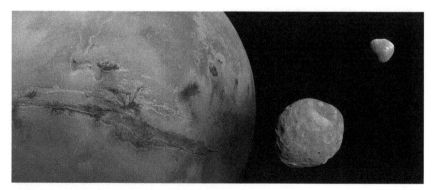

Figure 1.4: Mars and her moons: a metaphor for re-examining our lives. (Source: NASA, 2019. Mars and Her Moons, https://solarsystem.nasa.gov/moons/mars-moons/in-depth/)

⭕ **Hopeful Companions**

Human development and history.

<u>Books</u>
Ramamurthy, A. 2013. *Black Star: Britain's Asian Youth Movements*. London: Pluto Press.

<u>Organisations</u>
United Nations Declaration of the Rights of Indigenous Peoples: https://www.un.org/development/desa/indigenouspeoples/ declaration-on-the-rights-of-indigenous-peoples.html

United Nations Human Rights website: https://www.ohchr.org/EN/pages/home.aspx

United Nations Refugee Agency: https://www.unhcr.org/uk/

<u>Museums and libraries</u>
The International Slavery Museum virtual tour: https://www.liverpoolmuseums.org.uk/international-slavery-museum/virtual-tour

The People's History Museum: https://phm.org.uk/

Reflections – Mars and her moons as a metaphor for humanity

One way to think about the present situation is to reflect on how we see the world in our daily lives. Earthrise is one obvious image that comes to mind. However, if we think about the reality, often we are far more aware of our own immediate human concerns, while we ignore those of the planet and wider cosmos. One way to conceptualise our present situation, is to turn our attention to our neighbour, Mars, with her two small satellite moons, Phobos and Deimos. Deimos, the smaller of the two moons, represents our human focus: our individual lives, our communities, our families, our organisations and businesses, our art, culture and sport. Phobos, the larger moon, represents how we increasingly see the environment, as something that has some growing significance in our daily lives. But what we fail to notice is the huge planet of Mars which represents the vast and ancient Cosmos of which we an integral part (Figure 1.4). This way of seeing the world has devastating consequences, illustrated so poignantly by the *Timeline* at the start of this chapter. We need to change our perspective, so that we see that our daily, human-focused concerns are, in fact, part of something much much bigger. We must stop ignoring the fact that without a healthy ecosystem, humanity and the civilisations it has created cannot function. Our progress as humans throughout the twentieth century is not ecologically sustainable. The social justice effects of the climate emergency will fall disproportionately, and the lowest-emitting poorest countries will suffer the most.[23] Indeed, theologian Anne Primavesi (2013) argues that the treatment of poorer communities is akin to how the planet herself has been treated.

There is no doubt that we need to change our way of living and restore a sustainable balance between human activity and the natural systems that sustain us. Yet, amidst the rush of modern life, the multitude of messages bombarding us and the dominant consumerist paradigm of our time, it can seem impossible to change or to do things differently. Hundreds of books have already been devoted to analysing what is wrong, scientific consensus is overwhelming and the evidence continues to mount. Positive action can seem inconsequential in the face of such overwhelming destruction and degradation. Many of us, much of the time, find we are unable to cope with the scale of the problems and "just go along with the status quo", booking out deckchairs on the Titanic.

Earth rise – Arising from rock bottom

Our final viewpoint brings us back to the view of the Earth from the Moon. Wang Yaping, the first Chinese teacher and second Chinese woman in space, wrote, "When I looked out of the window for the first time, I realised the true meaning of the power of life…. That kind of beauty was just beyond comprehension." (in Jackson, 2017: 116)

Wang's words echo those of all who have travelled to space, giving those of us who remain Earthbound the opportunity to see our planet as unique, special and worthy of our care and love.

In the AA spiritual tradition, rock bottom is when the alcoholic can go no further. It is often only at this point that she or he turns to AA for help. As a species, we have reached rock bottom. In order to climb up from rock bottom, the alcoholic must acknowledge all the harm they have done. In this chapter, I have tried to confront some of what we have done to the planet, in order to start the journey of recovery to hopeful futures. In his

2015 Encyclical, *Laudato Si'*, Pope Francis put it perhaps most succinctly: "We need only take a frank look at the facts to see that our common home is falling into serious disrepair."

A further challenge facing humanity and our planet is the complexity of twenty-first century human society. This makes the challenge of appropriate action even more difficult. The challenges we face are psychological as well as structural. The New Scientist, for example, has listed thirty-three reasons why we cannot cope with climate change. These range from the fact that if we do not like something we can decide to disagree with it and not give it further attention, the fact that we spend time with people who reinforce our own viewpoints and are never forced to face up to facts that challenge us. Social media has reinforced this tendency (Gifford, 2015).

Climate change writer Michael Hulme suggests that our differing standpoints and worldviews make it hard for us to talk about climate change. He argues that we have stripped out the mythology and spiritual meaning from discussions about climate change, making it difficult to talk to each other across our different meanings and experiences (2009). Some of us, for example, see the planet from a scientific perspective while others see it from a more metaphysical perspective, and we have difficulty understanding each other across this divide. Hulme suggests bringing the spiritual and the mythological into this conversation.

Another way to understand our differences is through George Lakoff's (2010, 2011) concept of "unconscious structures". These are the "frames" or "schema" through which each individual processes knowledge. To understand complex knowledge, a system of frames must exist to hold such knowledge. Lakoff argues that each individual must use the frames appropriate to them. We need time to construct appropriate frames, such as around the climate emergency, and repetition of such framing is needed. In the next chapter, I will explore how we might create a family of interconnected frames or paradigms across different cultures and people.

In the early 1980s, James Hansen was one of the first scientists to report the phenomenon of climate change and urged humanity to take urgent action to curb carbon emissions. At first, US politicians paid attention to what he had to say. However, oil companies soon started to sow doubt about the science and a number of climate deniers gained prominent access in the media.[24] Such is the complexity of the problem and the lack of time to make meaningful change, that some scientists are pessimistic. In his account of the exponential nature of the challenges facing the planet, Stephen Emmott concludes with his younger colleague's solution "to teach [his] son how to use a gun", an apocalyptic response mirrored in popular culture (2013: 198). Other scientists use the state of the planet to argue that geoengineering is the only solution. Such responses are not helpful and make for paralysis and inaction. In her book, *Under a White Sky*, Elizabeth Kolbert (2021) movingly explores the dangers of using geoengineering even though we are up against the limits in halting global warming and biodiversity loss. While climate scientist Michael Mann (2021) argues against doom and gloom and the need for geoengineering, he stresses that we urgently and systemically need to decarbonise society, a task that is within our technical capabilities. In an interview with the Dublin Community Project, climate scientist Kevin Anderson from the Tyndall Centre in Manchester, reflected,

> "We are choosing to fail, we make all the right noises but we are choosing to fail...we are all in a collective delusion together...at the moment we are running scared of changing the direction in which are heading" (in Gibbons, 2016).

The complexity of human culture and thought adds to the challenge. We feel unable to stop what we have set in motion. Elizabeth Kolbert (2006:187) reflects,

> "It may seem impossible to imagine that a technologically advanced society could choose, in essence, to destroy itself, but that is what we are now in the process of doing".

Earthrise – Choosing Hope

This book is concerned with the very practical need to overcome paralysis and powerlessness and to support humanity in travelling towards futures that are more hopeful. Is such a journey even possible? Kevin Anderson argues that, "We have the opportunity to choose to succeed."

This book is about how we might choose to succeed by creating and following our own path to creative futures within our home planet, our home galaxy and our home Cosmos. It is a journey of hundreds of years of scientific discovery and the many achievements we have made as and for human beings. It is the journey of our emerging understanding over the past fifty years since we first saw Earthrise and our dawning understanding of how we are destroying our beautiful, ancient and infinitely precious home. It is a spiritual journey of hitting rock bottom in our consumerist culture, seeking forgiveness and recognising the spiritual nature of the journey ahead. It is a journey of working in harmony with the planet and with our Cosmos, in the full knowledge of our inability as humans to know the consequences of intervening in complex ecosystems that have evolved over millions of years.

 Creative Learning Exercises

Read the UN Sustainable Development Goals and identify at least one that calls to you. Learn all that you can about your chosen goal. https://www.undp.org/content/undp/en/home/sustainable-development-goals.html

Reflect on personal agency, consider various perspectives, reflect on your own response:

Greta Thunburg's address to the 2019 UN Climate Action Summit: https://www.youtube.com/watch?v=TMrtLsQbaok

Malala Yousafzi's Nobel Peace Prize Lecture 2014: https://www.youtube.com/watch?v=c2DHzlkUI6s

Mia Motley, address to the Opening of the COP 27 World Leaders Summit: https://www.youtube.com/watch?v=5J0egwAfO0w

---

We have no time to lose and the journey ahead will be perilous and full of challenge. Starting the journey equipped with the knowledge of what we are doing to the planet is essential. So too is feeling such knowledge in our hearts. We must continue to face this knowledge, not with despair, but with hope.

Reflections: Learning to listen

It is a challenge to fully appreciate what is happening to our home planet. More than half of humanity now lives in cities or urban areas. Often, the temptation to put our heads down and look at our shiny mobile phones and iPad screens is overwhelming. Much of the information in this chapter may seem remote and unreal when, despite the challenges and difficulties, our own immediate lives are actually good. Yet, we know from seeing our planet from the Moon that everything on Earth is connected.

We need to don our waterproofs!

How then do we need to journey? Business as usual is clearly not a sensible option. From the challenges identified, it is clear that we need a fundamental change in our thinking and actions if we are to successfully travel to hopeful futures. During my own twenty-year journey, I have explored widely and I propose that we each embark on a journey of discovery and learning, that we travel with social and ecological justice, with ethics and values and that we travel both individually and together. I believe that we need to change the way we see the world. Such a task is not easy. But it is to this question of seeing the world differently that I turn in Chapter 2.

Invitation to Reflect

Explore what is happening to planet Earth through your five senses. This will help to make the ecology of the planet more real and immediate. It is through our senses that we experience the Earth and can develop a systematic understanding of what is happening to her.

Listening
Listen for the singing of the birds. Notice where you hear birdsong. In spring, listen for the sound of frogs croaking. In summer, listen for the insects. Listen out for flies buzzing, bees flying through the air, crickets. If there are no sounds but traffic, listen to the silence of nature. Experience sadness at the silence that has fallen. Listen to the sound of the rain. Is it as you remember from years ago? Is it soft? Or fierce? Find your local water courses. Can you listen to the water in the brooks and the rivers?

Seeing
Look up from your mobile phone through the branches of the trees. Notice what is around you. Are there bees or butterflies, daddy longlegs, birds? What do you see on the ground – small animals, a hedgehog, road kill? Notice the domestic animals around you? Are they communicating with you? What are they saying? When you pass walls, notice the moss and the lichen. Observe the habitats where birds, insects and mammals live. Look at the surfaces of ponds moving with frogspawn in the spring.

Touching
Hug a tree. Feel the great smoothness of the bark of a silver birch. Feel the barks of different trees. Touch a leaf; feel its softness and turn it over and observe how the leaf converts sunlight into energy. Connect to the soil and turn it over in your hands. Touch wet leaves lying on the ground and appreciate they are creating the soil of tomorrow. Appreciate the years needed to turn leaf mould into soil. Notice where there are no trees or where trees have been cut down.

Smelling
In the city, smell the freshness of the early morning air. Smell the freshness of the air in the countryside. Smell the pollution from traffic. If you are near a fire, smell the burning. Try to imagine the smell of the Earth's burning forests.

Tasting
Taste and saviour the foods you eat. Explore the taste of different foods. Remember the taste of being thirsty. How does wanting water make you feel? Imagine not being able to get the water you need.

Put all of your senses together to start to feel what is happening to our planet. Begin to pay attention to what Gaia is feeding back to you.

Notes

[13] The Installation was made in the run up to COP 21 at which the international Paris Agreement to limit CO_2 rises to 1.5°C or well below 2.0°C increase on preindustrial levels was agreed: https://unfccc.int/process-and-meetings/the-paris-agreement/the-paris-agreement

[14] For an account of Lamb's life's work to protect trees, see his obituary by John May in the Guardian, https://www.theguardian.com/environment/2005/oct/14/guardianobituaries.conservationandendangeredspecies

[15] For an account of the moratorium on fishing and its effects on the community: https://www.cbc.ca/news/canada/newfoundland-labrador/furlong-the-tides-still-ebb-long-after-the-moratorium-1.1236995

[16] http://www.iucn.org/about/work/programmes/species/our_work/the_iucn_red_list/

[17] The first Earth Overshoot day was recorded in 1970: https://www.overshootday.org/newsroom/past-earth-overshoot-days/

[18] The Al-Anon programme has Twelve Steps to guide the spiritual growth of families and friends of alcoholics: https://al-anon.org/for-members/the-legacies/the-twelve-steps/. These Steps are very closely modelled on the Twelve Steps of Alcoholics Anonymous: https://www.alcoholics-anonymous.org.uk/About-AA/The-12-Steps-of-AA

[19] For further information on the garbage patch, which consists of several huge concentrations of marine waste, see: https://oceanservice.noaa.gov/facts/garbagepatch.html

[20] See https://www.co2.earth/ for daily CO_2 levels

[21] See a vivid report in the New York Times: https://www.nytimes.com/2019/09/25/world/asia/indonesia-red-sky-fires.html

[22] See Gradwell, L. 2017. Manchester Firsts: https://tonybaldwinson.com/manchester-firsts/

[23] At COP 27, the Prime Minister of Barbados, Mia Motley argued that "poor nations are 'paying twice' for climate breakdown." Quoted in Greenfield et al 2022.

[24] James Hansen is interviewed in Sir David Attenborough's 2019 film: *Climate Change, the Facts*, directed by Serena Davies: https://www.bbc.co.uk/programmes/m00049b1

Chapter 2: Emerging paradigms for Earth & Cosmos

"A new type of thinking is essential if [humanity] is to survive and move to higher levels."
Albert Einstein (1954)

"The best we can do is offer our children good direction, positive direction, direction that comes from experience and observation—that's what indigenous people have."
Chief Oren Lyons (2004)

"The pressures on ecosystems will increase globally in coming decades unless human attitudes and actions change."
Millennium Ecosystem Assessment (2005)

The universe is enormous and ancient. Just how ancient is hard to imagine, but I try. It is summer and I am on holiday with my family in Co. Kerry, Ireland. We go for a walk, starting at an old Mass path on the Iveragh Peninsula.

From the mountainside, we look across Dingle Bay to the hump-backed silhouette of the Great Blasket Island. As we climb higher, two lakes appear below, in a U-shaped valley formed ten thousand years ago by glaciers. Where ice once lay thick and heavy, there are now the still grey waters of the lake and boulders scattered down the mountainside. At the peak, we are rewarded with a breath-taking view down the Ferta Valley to Cahersiveen. The valley is covered in green and brown fields, crisscrossed with stone walls. We sit for lunch, with moss, bog flowers and insects at our feet. I notice a small rock and pick it up. To my delight, the ripples of an ancient beach are clearly etched on the stone. Later, I find out that this quiet piece of rock is likely to be 320 million years old.

I imagine throwing the rock back towards the sea that once covered Iveragh and that has left this indelible mark. I imagine myself throwing the rock back across eons of time, even before our planet came to be. Then I imagine throwing the rock forward, 320 million years into the future, beyond the 50,000-year time span during which, from the vantage point of the Earth, stars will form what we humans have called the Orion constellation, beyond the encounter our solar system will have with a travelling star a million years into the future. As far as my mind can imagine.

A week later, I return to my inner-city home. I keep in my mind the age of that unimaginably old beach. I sense that we need people who can relate to the Earth and universe in a new way. People who can comprehend that the Earth and the universe are alive. People who can move with confidence between the great age and splendour of our beautiful and ancient universe and the work needed to create better communities, and a healthy planet, in the here and now.

(Written with my daughter, Nora Kettleborough, 2013)

Our home planet and its inhabitants face an urgent crisis. Although we have the knowledge to tackle this crisis, it is only starting to become part of our everyday consciousness. It is not yet a deeply integrated part of mainstream economics, politics, communities or organisations. We urgently need new maps to guide us.

Starting off: Maps to help us see differently

Maps have been part of human civilization for millennia. Some of the oldest maps in existence are from Catal Huyuk, in Turkey and Nippur, in Mesopotamia (Dorling Kindersley, 2016), and date from the eighth and third millennia BCE, respectively. Maps shape how we see the world. The 1974 Peter's Projection map showed countries in relation to their actual surface area, and was a rejection of Mercator's projection, in which countries at higher latitudes appear bigger than those at lower latitudes, effectively making the continent of Africa appear much smaller than its actual size. Maps provide us with a sense of our changing place in the universe. Fludd's 1617 map places the Earth at the centre of the universe, with eleven rings rotating around the Earth, while a 2018 European Space Agency map shows background cosmic microwave radiation from the Big Bang (Benson, 2014). Maps help us to make sense of the enormity of the Cosmos, and they can combine physical journeys with journeys into the interior. For example, Peter Matthiessen's (1978) story *The Snow Leopard* includes a map of a physical territory of the mountains of Nepal, while his writing takes the reader on an interior journey of the spirit. Can maps help us deal with the problems our planet faces?

The challenges and the solutions facing humanity are interconnected, systemic, highly complex and time specific, and will require all our reflexivity and resourcefulness. Many of our current solutions tackle one problem or one area at a time. But this is insufficient to meet the task. Simply reducing plastic waste or pollution in the home is not enough. Addressing the climate emergency without tackling structural racism and white privilege will not create lasting solutions. Yet, when we put our current maps together, the enormity of the problem can feel overwhelming, leading to despair or the impulse to give up. Our current maps are not wrong. They are simply out of date. These maps give us tasks for action, but not the sustained energy for the challenges ahead. It is time for new maps.

For Thomas Berry, the story is more complex. The challenges we face are not only human challenges, but rather challenges for the whole Earth and Cosmos (1999). It is within this cosmological telling of our story that we can find the energy for the tasks ahead, to make the "unprecedented changes" (IPCC, 2018) that we need to meet these challenges.

One way to think about the present situation is to reflect on how we see the world in our daily lives. Although we care, we do not care enough to take wise action. At present, we are unable to create a renewable energy moon shot or to decarbonise society, both of which could produce zero carbon emissions and create thousands of jobs (King et al, 2015; Sachs, 2015). As a result, the species of our planet are silently dying as carbon dioxide levels increase daily.

Emerging cosmologies for humanity

One way to create new maps is to change the stories we tell ourselves. In Chapter 1, I explored the achievements of human development during the twentieth century. As the twenty-first century progresses, however, another story is emerging. Cultural historian Thomas Berry (1988) observed that our culture lacks a integrative story. Or, rather, that our predominant stories are about consumerism. Our lives might be summarised as "work, shop, consume, and die" (Swimme, 1996: 6). In the 1960s, Vance Packard (1957) traced the influence of marketing in our lives. In the 1990s, Brian Swimme referenced the thousands of advertisements that flood our television screens (1996). In the 2010s, philosopher Kate Soper (2020) described the avalanche of advertisements we see throughout our lives, so that every aspect of society is monetarised and for sale (Sandel, 2012). Benjamin Barber (1995) has traced the spread of the ubiquitous culture of global consumerism through the spread of McDonalds' as a global phenomenon against which communities around the world, often unsuccessfully, struggle to maintain their own local ways of life. The resources at the command of this growth paradigm, expressed in the development of airports, hotels, ever more extravagant shopping malls and private luxury goods, are vast. Challenging such development is extremely difficult, as it is linked to jobs and livelihoods.[25] The rise of unfettered capitalism and technology has become a global phenomenon (Piketty, 2014). If we perceive consumerism and growth as the cosmology and underlying metaphysics of our daily lives, we can understand why it is so hard to deviate from this map. Indeed, economist E. Schumacher suggests that changing the world is about how we see the essential nature of the world, and about our core values which determine our thoughts and actions (1973). Swimme suggests that marketers, who make advertisements, are the people who teach our babies, children and young people their cosmology. Cosmology, in this sense, refers to a society's creation myth or story and, based on that, a society's beliefs and values. It is, as Primack and Abrams put it, "a culture's Big Picture, its shared view of how human life, the natural world and God or the gods fit together" (2006:16).

Every society has its own cosmology, which provides a sense of meaning, offers guidance on moral issues and creates a sense of community. According to a society's cosmology, is the world alive or dead, a resource to be exploited or a living being? Are the barnacles and mussels my cousins or are they entirely unrelated to me and, therefore, not worthy of my compassion? Do I see all people as equal and worthy of respect or of differing worth depending on where they come from or the colour of their skin? If we have been between stories in the twentieth century, now there are emerging stories that offer us new ways to see and understand our place in the world, combining indigenous knowledge, ancient wisdom and science.

Windows and words onto our place in the Cosmos

How might we develop an understanding that we can perceive the world from multiple perspectives? Here I explore two possible ways, one through experimentation and the other through language. Thomas Kuhn (1962) suggested using gestalt images to understand diverse ways of perceiving the world. Many of you will be familiar with Figure 2.1, a gestalt image that, from one perspective, is a duck, and from another, a rabbit. This picture, and others like it, draw attention to the fact that we have the ability to see the same thing differently.

Figure 2.1: A gestalt figure of a rabbit/duck (Source: Unattributed Author "Kaninchen und Ente" ("Rabbit and Duck") from the 23 October 1892 issue of Fliegende Blätter, cited in Wikipedia, https://en.wikipedia.org/wiki/Rabbit%E2%80%93duck_illusion)

An alternative exercise is to observe how looking through a window frames and transforms a view. A striking example of this is the revamped Whitworth Art Gallery in Manchester, where the local park has been enhanced by being framed by the windows of the Gallery. The view through different windows is subtly changed according to the size and shape of the frame, reflecting the idea that facts are sometimes meaningless unless we frame (or contextualize) them. In workshops, I invite participants to put on and take off sunglasses, and to observe how the world changes through this simple act.

There are many terms to describe such changes in perspective. Most are already in common use and describe how we experience and discover the world. I invite you to find the one that fits you and your journey. By the end of the book, I hope you will have your own set of words that you are comfortable using and that convey the joy and excitement of seeing planet Earth afresh.

'*Mind-set*' refers to a way of thinking about an issue or problem. For example, mental resilience encourages us to develop a growth mind-set rather than a more limiting fixed mind-set. With a growth mind-set, mistakes and challenges are transformed into learning opportunities.

'*Worldview*' refers to our "views on life, the world and humanity" and can be created at the individual level or through organised systems of thought. According to van der Koolj et al. (2013: 217),

> "An organized worldview is a view on life, the world and humanity that prescribes answers to existential questions. In this way, organized worldviews aim to influence the thinking and acting of people. Organized worldviews contain moral values and aim to provide meaning in people's lives."

A personal worldview, meanwhile, "is a view on life, the world and humanity that consists out of norms, values, ideals that can be but are not necessarily moral and out of answers to existential questions" (ibid: 222). Worldviews are not static and, as we shall see, an emerging participatory worldview is integral to the action research at the heart of this journey.

'*Framing*' is a concept from cognitive sciences. Lakoff (2010:71) writes,

> "We think, mostly unconsciously, in terms of systems of structures called 'frames'. Each frame is a neural circuit, physically in our brains…. Frame systems are organised in terms of values and how we reason reflects our values and our values determine our sense of identity."

Framing helps people to identify how they see the world. Lakoff argues that if your thinking is not appropriately framed, you will be unable to process knowledge. For example, he explains that without a knowledge of the effects of heating, we cannot understand the catastrophic impact of a 2°C rise in global temperatures. If one's understanding of economics is that growth is the only way to run society, then the idea of 'no growth' is incomprehensible.

A *'paradigm'* is the totality of an understanding of the world that is widely shared and agreed upon. Kuhn (1962:175) defines 'paradigm' as "The entire constellation of beliefs, values, techniques and so on shared by members of a given community."

These perspectives of an entire community are of interest to us as we create a new story. The gestalt images that Kuhn used in his work represent a paradigm shift, from seeing the world one way (the image of a rabbit) to seeing it in an entirely different way (the image of a duck).

 Creative Learning Exercises

The following exercises will help you to appreciate seeing the world differently. Draw your responses to these exercises.

Do an online search for 'gestalt images'. Who or what do you see? Ask friends or family members what they see when they look at the same images.

Sit in front of a window and look out. Notice how looking through the window frames the view and makes it look different. Move to a different window of the same view (e.g., upstairs vs downstairs; two locations on the same floor). Sketch what you see.

Draw a number of rectangles representing window frames. In what ways do we need to sometimes frame the facts that we already know? Write the numbers '350' and '416' inside two of the frames. These numbers represent parts per million of carbon dioxide in the atmosphere in the 1980s and in 2021. Add any other facts to the rectangles that you think need to be framed.

Find a pair of sunglasses. Put them on and notice how your view of the world changes instantly. Try putting them on and taking them off in order to appreciate how differently the world looks simply by adding sunglasses.

Worldviews and paradigms in transition

The previous chapter traced the many environmental challenges facing the world and threatening humanity's social and political progress in the last hundred years. The origin of many of the improvements in the human condition can be traced back to the growth of modern science. Hand-in-hand with the scientific worldview has been the growth of a philosophical view that has led to dis-enchantment with the natural world and a view of the universe as a non-living mechanism, lacking mystery or spirit. This world view has taken hold even though many indigenous cultures in the Americas, Africa, Australia and Asia continue to perceive the Earth as full of spirit, alive and sentient. The Western scientific paradigm arose from Cartesian dualism, and both excluded the human spirit and the metaphysical nature of the rest of the world (Goff, 2019). Western philosophy began to perceive mind as restricted to humans and the laws of the universe as secrets to be discovered. Anything that could not be observed and measured was rejected by science. This reduction of nature to mere materiality coincided with an emerging capitalist economic order that enslaved, exploited and murdered indigenous peoples in Africa, the Americas, Australia and elsewhere in the non-Western world (Boff, 1997). The oppression of the natural world is also associated with the oppression of women (Griffin, 1984).

These philosophies and paradigms have led to the world we live in today, where the sole role of the Indonesian rain forest is production of palm oil for our consumer needs and where fish populations off the Atlantic coasts of Ireland and the UK are mere resources to be hoovered up by super fishing trawlers (Riegal, 2014; Carrington, 2020). The task on the journey ahead is to transform these paradigms and offer visions of hope.

⭕ Hopeful Companions

The origins of the modern Western mind set:

Books
Andrews, K. 2020. *The New Age of Empire*. London: Allen Lane.

Berry, T. 1988. 'The New Story' in *Dream of the Earth*. Berkeley CA: Counterpoint Press.

Shiva, V. 2020. *Reclaiming the Commons. Biodiversity, Indigenous Knowledge and the Rights of Mother Earth*. London: Synergeticpress.

Kuhn (1962) argued that a paradigm shift involves not simply a change of methods or techniques, but a fundamental change in how we see the world. It undermines our assumptions and understanding about how the world works.

For the scientist, Kuhn argued, a paradigm shift changes how data are interpreted and what they reveal, sometimes while still using the same tools of analysis as before. For example, while Chinese astronomers recorded the appearance of new stars in the sky, European astronomers before Copernicus did not, because in the latter world view, the composition of the heavens did not change. Similarly, in the eighteenth century, William and Caroline Herschel's detection of the disc and subsequent motion of Uranus enabled other astronomers to detect other "minor planets or asteroids", using the "same standard instruments" that they had previously used (Kuhn, 1962: 116; BBC News, 2016).

Linguist Mike Beaumont, in observing the process of creating paradigm shifts suggested by Kuhn, reflects on a combination of "periods of stability", followed by "periods of intense and heterodox experimentation" finally resulting "in the emergence of a new paradigm" (2008:61). A paradigm shift might start with only a small number of individuals, with different motivations.

"Nonetheless, if they are competent, they will improve it, explore its possibilities and show what it would be like to belong to the community guided by it. And, as that goes on, if the paradigm is one destined to win its fight, the number and strength of persuasive arguments in its favour will increase." (Kuhn, 1962: 159)

One notable paradigm shift relates to how society regards women. From ancient Greece to much of Western civilization prior to and during the twentieth century, customs, mores and beliefs existed to exclude women from participation in many aspects of society. Over time, a paradigm shift occurred, during which women achieved equality in law, marriage, employment and society in general. Customs and beliefs that once steadfastly barred women from full participation in society have now been replaced by customs and beliefs that steadfastly expect women to fully participate in society. Critical race theorist Kimberley Crenshaw (1991) developed the concept of intersectionality to explain how different forms of oppression, such as gender, class and race, interact.[26] In the United States, critical race theory and intersectionality integrate the struggle to end white privilege and police and other public agency violence against people of colour with the struggles of African-American women against male violence.

This integration has developed to challenge how other forms of oppression operate; including ablism, homophobia and class.

Here, I focus on paradigm shifts within civil society that shift our perceptions of and actions against biodiversity loss, the climate emergency and all forms of inequality and social injustice to situate them within our wider planet Earth and Cosmos.

◯ Hopeful Companions

Resources on paradigms shifts from diverse female voices.

Books

Llewelyn Davies, M. 1905/1978. *Maternity: Letters from Working Women, Collected by the Women's Co-operative Guild.* London: Virago Press.

bell hooks. 1984. *Feminist Theory: from margin to centre.* Boston: South End Press

Rowe, M. 1982. *The Spare Rib Reader.* London: Penguin.

Films

Crenshaw, K. 2016. *TED talk: The Urgency of Intersectionality* https://www.youtube.com/watch?v=akOe5-UsQ2o

Websites

UN Women 2021. In Focus: International Day of Worlds Indigenous People 9th August 2021 https://www.unwomen.org/en/news/in-focus/indigenous-women

---

Invitation to Reflect

Can you create a timeline from your own knowledge on the paradigm shifts which have occurred during the last century in society?

Can you 'mind map' how different forms of discrimination interact in your life and the lives of your family and friends – whether through racism, as a result of socio-economic forces, through migration or being a refugee, as a result of LGBTQ+ prejudice, mental health issues or as a person with disabilities.

Can you reflect on how these forms of inequality connect with each other?

Can you commit to recording your thoughts and observations as you journey to hopeful futures? This could be on a daily or weekly basis.

A family of approaches

To create our new maps, I wish to explore five interconnected paradigms that will contribute to the emergence of hopeful cosmologies for a living Earth. Each one arises out of emerging scientific and spiritual explorations of the last few hundred years. Each has a different history and focus. Over the past two decades of teaching, I have come to offer these paradigms as an interlinked family of approaches, appropriate for diverse audiences either on their own or grouped together. Together, they are part of emerging cosmologies for hopeful futures, to be explored through cycles of action and reflection, as illustrated in Figure 2.2.

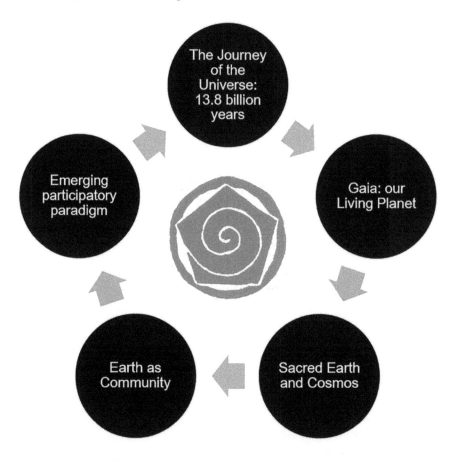

Figure 2.2: A family of approaches (paradigms) for hopeful futures: cycles of discovery and exploration. You can enter from your personal basecamp at any point. (Source: Kettleborough, 2023)

I offer these paradigms with humility. An important aspect of drawing new maps is being careful not to assume you are right or certain but to invite inquiry and learning. As I explore what it means to live these paradigms in our daily lives, I hope that you will find new maps for your life. I hope they will allow you to feel the grandeur of the universe, to understand its vast age and size and our potentially meaningful place within it.

First paradigm: The Journey of the Universe
The Cosmic dawn

You may be familiar with the Journey of the Universe Story, as it is the result of scientific discovery. It is a story that has been painstakingly put together over centuries by scholars and scientists.

This story builds on the work of early astronomers in ancient China, Greece and Rome, of Islamic mathematicians from the early and Middle Ages, and of scientists from the European Renaissance. Those centuries of scholarship are the foundation for contemporary scientific collaboration, such as at the Large Hadron Collider at CERN, where scientists are seeking to find the fundamental particles of the Cosmos.[27]

This emerging cosmological story begins with the birth of the universe at the great flaring forth 13,800,000,000 years ago and follows each irreversible transformation along the way. It is a magnificent story, and often a long way from everyday human understanding. How can we imagine or understand those first moments, when the universe expanded from a singularity containing all of the energy and matter that exists today? Parts of the story poignantly reflect our own experiences, such as the very first moment that the universe contained light that would be visible to the human eye. This is the *cosmic dawn*, which took place around 180 million years after the Big Bang, when the first stars in the universe were born from hydrogen and helium. Like the first glimmer of dawn in the east, the universe was filled with light (Devlin, 2018). Within these stars the lighter elements were created – carbon, nitrogen and oxygen, among others. The first galaxies began to form, maybe a billion years after the Big Bang, including our own Milky Way.

Tiamut

The Journey of the Universe story is one of life and death, in which we find mirrored our own experiences and can come to understand our part in this great cosmic drama. We find that stars, like us, are born and die. And, in their death, comes life. Seven billion years after the Big Bang, one of those early stars grew old and died. As it died, it turned into a glorious supernova. The dying star lit up the heavens and gave birth to new cosmic creations, which 7,000,000,000 years later, humans named as the elements heavier than iron, including cobalt, zinc and iodine. These elements, now found in our bodies and in the bodies of all life on Earth, are a common bond that make us cousins to all living and non-living things on Earth. Without that explosion, and others that followed, life on our planet could not have come into being. Swimme and Berry (1992) named this supernova Tiamut, after the ancient Babylonian mother goddess of creation.

This supernova was an extraordinary 'cosmic coincidence' that allowed for the creation of a cosmos suitable for complex life. Other such epic cosmic co-incidences include the Big Bang itself. If the universe had expanded just a little more, it would have grown too fast for galaxies to form. If it had expanded just a little slower, it would never have created the ripples necessary for galaxies to take shape. Billions of years later, Earth was formed from swirling clouds of dust and rock around our mother, the Sun, alongside the inner rocky planets of Mercury, Venus and Mars. Beyond Mars, Jupiter and Saturn were formed from gas. Through their interactions, they protected Earth from bombardment in the early million years of her childhood, allowing the conditions for life to arise from the rocks and seas (Cox & Cohen, 2011). Passing close to Earth in those early million years, Saturn pulled debris from the asteroid belt towards itself, thus protecting our fledging planet. All of these planets in the Solar System can be perceived as Earth's sisters and brothers. From a human perspective, the most wonderful occurrence came next – the birth of life. The oldest fossils, unicellular stromatolites, are about 3.5 billion years old and the oldest multicellular fossils have been dated to 1 billion years ago. However, some studies suggest that very early life may have begun as soon as 350 million years after the birth of the Earth (Lenton & Watson, 2011). It is almost impossible to imagine how sustained this journey has been and how long the universe laboured to give birth to simple life and then to the complex life of plants and animals. The Cenozoic period of the last sixty-five million years has seen a vast outpouring of life on Earth, underscoring how diversity is built into the fabric of our planet. By understanding the great age of the universe and the co-incidences and wonders that give birth to life as we know it, we understand the many pivotal points along the journey to where we are today.

Our place in the universe

In the twentieth century, physicists and cosmologists have continued their research into the origins and evolution of the universe. They have recently discovered that the visible universe accounts for only about 5% of the matter in the universe. Approximately some 27% of the universe is made up of invisible 'dark matter', which scientists can only observe "through its gravitational effects" (CERN, 2022).[28] In addition, approximately some 67% of the mass-energy of the universe is made of 'dark energy'. Even less is known about dark energy than about dark matter (CERN, 2022). This makes star dust, the carbon-based matter from which all known life is made, very scarce indeed (Primack & Abrams, 2006). One of the discoveries on this journey is how rare and, therefore, special are these materials that have created us and all other complex life (Gribben, 2011).

Immeasurable Heaven

Scientists are also busy mapping the universe. They have discovered that every part of the universe is also the centre of the universe. This means that we are not in some insignificant galaxy but are at the heart of the universe. The galaxies around the Milky Way have also been charted in great detail and the superstructure of galaxies in this part of the cosmos have been named Laniakea, the Hawaiian name for Immeasurable Heaven (Sample, 2014). This name bears a striking resemblance to the creation stories of many faith traditions. Chapter 6, verse 2.2 of the Chandogya Upanishad, for example, teaches,

"In the beginning was only Being/One without a second. /Out of himself he brought forth the cosmos /And entered into everything in it. There is nothing that does not come from him." (translated by Easwaran, 2007).

This epic story convinced geologian Thomas Berry of the need to create societies that live in mutually enhancing ways with the Cosmos.[29] Rather than accepting that we are living through our self-made Anthropocene, Berry argued passionately for the creation of the *Ecozoic*, an era in which we live with social justice and in harmony with the planet and Cosmos. We need the energies of the cosmos to help us transform to a new world (Berry, 1999). Travelling back into the Cosmos to find new energies offers us a route, literally, to the stars. Berry's collaborator, Brian Swimme (1984), eloquently picks up this theme of the dynamic powers of the universe. He suggests that we can learn about and learn to find these dynamic powers in our experiences of the living Earth. In humans, the universe has created a conscious species, a part of herself able to reflect on and appreciate the wonders of our own existence and the existence of the Cosmos (see also Sagan, 1980; Davies, 2006). This remarkable story is extensively explored through multi-media by The Journey of the Universe Project.

○ **Hopeful Companions**

<u>Films</u>
A New Story for Humanity, by the Findhorn Community: http://newstoryhub.com/film/watch/.

Wisdom weavers of the world: https://www.wisdomweavers.world/

Thomas Berry tells the Great Story: https://thomasberry.org/the-new-story-1/

<u>Resources for Action</u>
JourneyoftheUniverse.org offers a wide range of resources, including curriculum material, film and podcasts

Free online courses at Yale University: Journey of the universe: A Story of Our Times - https://www.coursera.org/specializations/journey-of-the-universe

 Creative Learning Exercises

Imaginatively reflect, through drawing/writing/creating, your personal responses to the following questions:

Which parts of the Journey of the Universe story seem most important to you.

Imagine a New Universe story for children.

Reflect on ways to share the Journey of the Universe story with work colleagues, neighbours and family members.

Attach the creations you have made to your kitchen door or some other place that you pass regularly. When you pass, try to bring this and other emerging paradigms to your mind, so that they become part of your thinking.

Second paradigm: Gaia
The Earth is interconnected and alive

Out of the Journey of the Universe emerges the paradigm of Gaia, our home planet. Earth was born 4.5 billion years ago, created from great swirling clouds of dust and rock. With the Sun and her seven siblings, Earth roams through the Milky Way, taking 250 million years to make one revolution, longer than the length of time the dinosaurs roamed the Earth.

Since the Renaissance, our living planet has gradually been lost to Western science and philosophy. The knowledge of the indigenous communities encountered by colonialists was discounted as backwards and ignorant (Wangari, 2010, Primavesi, 2013). The oppression of Gaia can be mapped onto the oppression of women and women's knowledge (Griffin, 1984) and the oppression of indigenous and colonialized peoples (Andrews, 2021).

Over the past fifty years, our understanding of our planet has changed significantly, thanks, in part, to James Lovelock and Lynn Margulis. Lovelock was an English scientist who worked on the NASA space programme in the 1960s, designing an experiment for the Viking Lander to search for life on Mars. While working on that experiment, he realised that conducting an experiment on the surface of Mars was unnecessary. Rather, he could analyse the atmosphere of Mars from Earth. He found that the atmospheres of both Mars and Venus consist predominately of inert carbon dioxide. Earth's atmosphere, in contrast, is made up of nitrogen (78%), oxygen (21%) and minute portions of other gases (1%), including carbon dioxide, and is in unstable equilibrium. These are the tell-tale hallmarks of life (Lovelock, 2009).

Lovelock sought to understand the relationship between life and the planet. Four and a half billion years ago, the sun was cooler than it is today. Yet, across that vast stetch of time, Earth has remained capable of sustaining life. How could that be? Lovelock deducted from the 'young sun' problem that something was keeping the planet habitable (Gribbin & Gribbin, 2009; Lovelock, 2009). He realized that life itself maintained temperatures suitable for life. He called this the Gaia Hypothesis, arguing that not simply individual plants and animals, but the Earth herself is a tightly coupled superorganism, that maintains the planet's suitability for life. There are many ways that the Earth does this. To keep the planet cool, marine creatures draw carbon dioxide from the air into their shells, which fall to the ocean floor when they die. Rocks weather faster when life is present, also capturing carbon dioxide from the atmosphere.

Lovelock's neighbour, the writer William Golding, suggested naming this hypothesis of a self-regulating Earth 'Gaia', after the Greek Goddess of the Earth. As holistic Stephan Harding (2006) writes, at that moment, "all the molecules and atoms on planet earth danced with joy". Lovelock faced hostility from many scientists for using the name Gaia, but scientist Lynn Margulis became a strong advocate for the hypothesis. Margulis's lifelong research found evidence that, over two billion years ago, the earliest organisms consisted of two separate entities that came together through mutual co-operation (Margulis & Sagan, 1997). Her radical contribution was her hypothesis that interdependence rather than competition was crucial to evolution. She also discovered that early organisms learned together, and this influenced her hypothesis that learning is integral to Earth and not simply confined to humans and other complex animals.

Biologists disagreed with Lovelock, arguing that the Earth is not alive because it cannot reproduce and his hypothesis harked back to ideas of "the magical properties of living matter" and, thus, was contrary to 'rational science' (Lovelock, 2006). Geologists disagreed because they failed to see the interconnections between rocks and life (ibid.). However, Lovelock persisted in the face of hostility and ridicule. He wrote (2006: 128):

> "My reason in persisting in calling the Earth Gaia and saying it is alive is not a personal foible; it is because I see this as an essential step in the process of public as well as scientific understanding. Until we all feel intuitively that the Earth is a living system, and know that we are part of it, we will fail to react automatically for its and ultimately our own protection."

Mystics and New Age people responded instantly to Gaia. Through several conferences, a growing number of scientists came to accept the Gaia hypothesis. One effect of Gaia has been the emergence of the discipline of Earth systems science. Earth systems scientist Tim Lenton and philosophers Sebastien Dutreuil and Bruno Latour have suggested that the reason why Lovelock's theories were resisted for so long was that biologists and physicists failed to see Life hiding in plain sight:

"Lovelock's central contribution, aided by Margulis, was to discover a new living entity: Life. Too big and too foreign to be studied by biologists, too hard to spot in the energy balance to be detected and taken into account by early climatologists; too living to be embraced by Earth system scientists. Yet Life massively alters its global environment. So much so that it becomes hard to separate Life's boundaries from its environment, hence the name given to the complicated entity which results from these interactions: Gaia." (Lenton et al, 2020)

◯ Hopeful Companions

Books
Lovelock, J. 1979. *Gaia: A New Look at Life on Earth.* Oxford: Oxford University Press.

Films
James Lovelock talks about his book *The Vanishing Face of Gaia* at the RSA on 8 March, 2010: https://www.youtube.com/watch?v=6eixcaTVd_c

Stephan Harding reflects on 30 years of teaching about Gaia, 31 July 2019 at the University of Exeter: https://www.youtube.com/watch?v=JpQTPD5wF4E

Symbiotic Earth explores the contribution made by Lyne Margulis's ideas, including the importance of co-operation for the evolution of life and the microbial world: https://hummingbirdfilms.com/symbioticearth/margulis-revolution/

Creative Learning Exercises

As you research the story of Gaia, think about how it helps you to feel part of our living planet.

Take a pen and paper and go to a favourite place in Gaia. Sit and reflect on our planet's 4.5-billion-year history. Close your eyes. Breathe deeply. Remembering the Invitation to Reflect that you undertook at the end of chapter 1, through your senses, feel yourself part of the planet and not separate from her.

Touch a plant and wonder at its ability to turn sunlight into energy. Feel yourself breathing in oxygen and breathing out carbon dioxide and participating with the plant which, through the amazing process of photosynthesis, is breathing in carbon dioxide and breathing out oxygen.

Using a few simple lines, draw yourself as part of Gaia. Place this drawing next to your picture of the Journey of the Universe.

Third paradigm: Sacred Earth and Cosmos

One of the drawbacks of the current dominant Western paradigm is that there is no room for the sacred. We live on a planet which is dead in an insignificant corner of an ordinary galaxy, amongst billions of other galaxies, in an inert cosmos. We live among beings that are merely to be used as resources, and then discarded. We might make exceptions for favoured species, but not for life as a whole. Such is the materialist or mechanistic worldview. But this is a very recent way of perceiving the world and not the dominant worldview for most of history, nor the dominant worldview for many faith communities and indigenous communities today, where spirit and spirts are integral to the planet.

Indigenous communities all over the world offer an understanding of the world of spirit and more-than-human persons. In the late nineteenth century, Oglala Sioux holy man Black Elk gifted humanity with his encounter with the Cosmos as interconnected and holy (Neinhardt & Black Elk, 1932/2000). Or, as Chief Oren Lyons, faith keeper of the Turtle Clan of the Onondaga Nation reflected when asked to gather indigenous spiritual leaders to attend an international gathering of faith leaders:

"The message we were going to give [the United Nations] was

that the ice is melting, that this is indeed a spiritual event, that it is caused by human beings, and that there is a consequence to all our activities."[30]

For Berry, the Journey of the Universe story is a spiritual story, and he argues that those who tell the story simply as one of physical matter only tell half of it. A more complete story opens up the world as spiritual and a place of love. Swimme (2001) explains the short history of the universe:

"You take hydrogen gas, and you leave it alone, and it turns into rosebushes, giraffes and humans."

This statement has a dual purpose. If humans emerged from hydrogen gas and have a knowledge of the sacred, then the universe does too, right from the beginning.

But appreciating the role of faith communities around the world and their defence of the planet is not enough to stop the plunder and destruction of the natural world. This can only be achieved, Berry and Tucker (ed) (2006: 57) write,

"...by a realisation that the universe from the beginning has been a psychic-spiritual, as well as a physical-material, reality.... The New Story of the universe is a biospiritual story as well as a galactic story and an Earth story."

Rather than seeing the Earth as something to be trashed, we start to see it as sacred and to be venerated. When we perceive the world as sacred, we enter a mutual relationship with the other species that share our planet, with the rocks and with the climate. Our relationship becomes one of gratitude from which awe and wonder become the predominant views of the planet. Our understanding of the Earth as sacred is embedded in the wisdom of many Indigenous traditions that understand that the land is alive and that the animals are full of spirit.[31] This knowledge and understanding underpins Indigenous interactions with the Earth and, in those places where Indigenous people retain autonomy, flora and fauna have been found to thrive.[32]

If the Earth is sacred, then all beings on the Earth are sacred and the wanton killing of plants and animals, and the pollution of the oceans and the air become crimes against the sacred nature of the world. Extinction becomes not something that takes place silently, but a tragedy within the history of the Cosmos. Berry (1999:196) argued that our present era is one of grace.

"There are cosmological and historical…as well as religious moments of grace. The present moment is one of those moments of transformation that can be considered…[a] moment of grace."

But these periods of grace are short. The IPBES (2019) has warned that humanity has a maximum of one to three decades to prevent catastrophic biodiversity collapse and limit global warming. António Guterres (2020), General Secretary of the United Nations, said, "Making peace with nature is the defining task of the twenty-first century. It must be the top, top priority for everyone, everywhere." A sacred worldview allows us to see the planet afresh and to frame what we do, how we act, what we perceive to be sacred and what we perceive as living and dead. Perceiving the Earth as sacred can be pan-psychic in scope, where consciousness is inherent in the whole universe (Skrbina, 2007). Gregory Bateson (1972) also saw Mind as part of the living systems of the Earth and, towards the end of his life, began searching for an epistemology of the sacred. Even current mathematical theory suggests that "inanimate matter could be conscious, maybe even the universe as a whole" (Brooks, 2020).

⭘ Hopeful Companions

Films
The Awakening Universe: http://thomasberry.org/publications-and-media/the-awakening-universe

Conversation with Leonardo Boff: https://www.youtube.com/watch?v=C4srb2h0daY

Resources for Action
Books, videos and audio resources concerning the work of Thomas Berry can be found at: https://thomasberry.org/

Yale Forum for Religion and Ecology resources concerning the sacred nature of the Earth from major World Religions: https://fore.yale.edu/World-Religions

---

<u>Websites</u>
One hundred and thirty-five faith leaders from 12 faiths discuss their
common purpose: https://www.unep.org/news-and-stories/video/
introduction-faith-earth

Fourth paradigm: Earth as Community

These other paradigms bring us to a new perspective of Earth as Community,
in which all things are related and all beings participate together: the rocks,
the oceans, the climate and all the beings of the Earth, including humans.
Such an expression of life is a direct challenge to the dominant paradigm of
inert objects on the face of the Earth.

Earth as Community enables us to bring together and combine social
justice and ecological justice, in which the struggles for human and civil
rights are also the struggles for nature.

Earth as Community requires change in all areas of society. Human-
centred laws must be transformed to encompass the rights of the Earth. Polly
Higgins and, since her death, the Stop Ecocide International Institute, have
worked to criminalise the excessive and wanton killing of species through
practices such as industrial fishing and palm oil and soya monoculture, by
creating the crime of ecocide – the destruction of ecosystems.[33] The Earth
Charter 2000 gives natural rights to the Earth and all her inhabitants, and
seeks to legally enshrine the perspective that all of Earth's beings deserve
compassion and respect.[34] In addition to the law, health care needs to
encompass the health of the whole Earth community, capturing the reality
that "we cannot have healthy humans on a sick planet" (Swimme & Berry,
1992: 257). The economy must also move from being human-centred
to becoming a sub-system of the Earth and the flourishing of the whole
Earth must be the objective of all economic systems. The energy to power
Earth as Community will come from the sun and other renewable energy
sources. Justice for human communities will encompass the rights of all
communities, with a particular focus on indigenous communities who live
in closer harmony with the planet, who have been rigorous in her defence
and who hold valuable knowledge for living sustainably (Shiva, 2022). Earth
as Community tackles the structural inequalities built into Western society,
including the predominance of white privilege, and seeks a just and egalitarian
society. It also seeks to end structural violence to black communities around
the world. Earth as Community seeks to establish an Earth Democracy,

where all humans have the right to participate and the Earth herself has rights.[35] Earth as Community means incorporating Indigenous wisdom into the legal systems of every society. It means transforming education, so that children learn from a very young age, and throughout their formal education, that they are part of a self-organising, self-regulating whole Earth system, and that their responsibilities as humans are to ensure that we maintain the Earth for all life, and not simply our own (Berry, 1988; Worldwatch Institute, 2017). Education must become collaborative and transformative for the mutual good of individuals and the whole Earth community. Berry (1988:12) wrote,

> "To learn how to live graciously together would make us worthy of this unique, beautiful, blue planet that has evolved over billions of years, a planet that we should give over to our children with the assurance that this great community of the living will lavish upon them the care that it has bestowed so abundantly on ourselves."

○ Hopeful Companions

Books
Alastair McIntosh explores his experience of community and spirituality in the Western Isles of Scotland in *Soil and Soul* (2001) and in *A Poacher's Pilgrimage: An Island Journey* (2016).

Kapoor, A., Hood, S., Yousef, N. 2022. *Confronting Injustice: Racism and the Climate Emergency.* London: Greenpeace UK and the Runneymeade Trust: https://www.greenpeace.org.uk/wp-content/uploads/2022/07/Confronting-Injustice-Report_2022.pdf

Films
Vandava Shiva speaking on Earth Democracy at Naropa University, 2015, a Buddhist inspired, ecumenical and non-sectarian institution: https://www.youtube.com/watch?v=ePCqDOLUTvU

Resources for Action
The Earth Charter entered a Partnership with the Deep Time Walk to encourage understanding of the Earth's history: https://earthcharter.org/partners/deep-time-walk/

Earth as Community: http://emergingearthcommunity.org/journey-of-the-universe

---

Creative Learning Exercises

On a large piece of paper (or several smaller pieces of paper stuck together), draw a big circle, covering as much as the paper as possible.

Inside the circle, draw animals, rocks, plants and trees. Join them together.

Add humans. Use this drawing to help you visualise them all as one Earth Community.

To this drawing, add all of the social, economic and ecological questions that you think are important.

Think of as many ways as possible to create Earth as Community and to reverse our present destruction. Add these to the drawing.

Place this picture next to the other drawings you have done and use this as a reflection point.

Fifth paradigm: Emerging participation

An emerging participatory paradigm embraces humans and the more-than-human in countering the rise of ideologies that seek to limit public participation and democracy (Monbiot, 2020; Penny, 2022). It also offers a bridge between emerging paradigms and the current dominant paradigm. It achieves this by focusing on a participatory ethos as a key ethic for human society, expressed through action research and participatory learning, and offering a route to transformative learning.

To illustrate its importance as a different way of framing the world, it is necessary to go back to 1997, when a small but dedicated group of academics at Bath University UK School of Management set up a Master's programme in Responsibility and Business Practice in partnership with the ethical business The Body Shop. The Master's programme was framed to include radical content, including the study of new economics, ecology, diversity and inclusion and global strategy. However, the truly innovative aspect of the programme was its underlying methodology of action research. The Master's degree was firmly anchored in understanding that the world needed to be framed differently, and to be based on a wider, participatory and cosmological worldview. The programme organizers agreed that a process of participatory transformational learning was required to enable students to understand that our present paradigms of utilising perceived dead resources within a discriminatory patriarchal and racist system was not conducive to creating flourishing societies. Instead, business students needed to be offered the opportunity to learn to understand the world through an emerging participatory paradigm offered in a way that respected the students' existing worldviews (Marshall et al., 2011). The result of this emerging participatory paradigm – the action research methodology – defined the teaching. Action research offers a tool kit to explore emerging and current paradigms and offers a link to the social sciences. The emerging participatory paradigm acts as a bridge between emerging and dominant paradigms.

Reason and Bradbury (2001: 6) define this emerging participatory paradigm

"...as systemic, holistic, relational, feminine, experiential, but its defining characteristic is that it is participatory: our world does not consist of separate things but of relationships which we co-author."

Heron and Reason (1997) argue that other paradigms are inadequate to the task of enabling humanity to see itself as an integral part of the planet. Instead, they argue for (p. 292):

"The participatory worldview, with its emphasis on the person as an embodied experiencing subject among other subjects; its assertion of the living creative cosmos we coinhabit and its emphasis on the integration of action with knowing..."

This emerging participatory paradigm integrates mind and matter in an interconnected and living cosmos. Many concepts contribute to this, including Skolimowski's (1994) participatory mind, the philosophy of participatory community development (Gilchrist & Taylor, 2011; Tam, 2021) and community participation to tackle climate change, biodiversity loss and inequalities (Craig, 2017; Nakate, 2022).

The emerging participatory paradigm must arise from lived experience (Heron & Reason, 1997) and encompass all aspects of life. There is no single way to understand, no fixed ideology. Peter Reason (2005)[36] suggests nine ways in which participation manifests in our lives:

Participation as method: Researchers are integral to the research they undertake.

Participation as power and democracy: The rights of different members of communities to have a say, participate in their own lives, address injustices and include the more-than-human in their deliberations.

Participation as education and transformation: The co-creation of knowledge, as people individually and together transform their lives and communities.

Experience of the participative nature of the world: The interconnections and interrelationships of everybody and everything in the world.

Participation in knowing and acting: The flourishing of all communities and multiple ways of knowing and acting.

Participation, systems and our place in ecology: Understanding the systemic nature of ecosystems, of which we are a part.

Participation and beauty: Living as part of the whole, in which we relate with awe to the wonder of the universe.

Participation and spirit: Understanding that we live as part of the whole, and can start to heal divisions when we perceive ourselves as part of the planet and perceive the Earth as living.

Participation in a cosmological timescale: Understanding that we have been part of the Cosmos since the Big Bang, 13.8 billion years ago.

These qualities evoke a different way of being in the world. They suggest co-operation, openness to wonder and beauty and participation in our planet and Cosmos. They suggest that we can learn by ourselves, with each other and with the planet and Cosmos.

Qualities of participation can be seen all over the world, for example in the Black Lives Matter movement following George Floyd's murder and in Indigenous peoples working with nature to save local threatened species.

The United Nations Development Programme advocates for solidarity to meet the current challenges facing the planet, so that humanity works together to systemically address these challenges rather than addressing individual challenges (UNDP, 2022). The development of participation at every level of society and within every institution will contribute to the development of solidarity.[37]

 Creative Learning Exercise

Watch Beyoncé: United Nations World Humanitarian Day Performance Video 2014: https://www.youtube.com/watch?v=i41qWJ6QjPI

Create a drawing, a map, a chart, or some other visual representation of how the various aspects of your life – community, friends, neighbours, work – are connected.

List or draw all the ways you participate with others and with the planet, including such activities as breathing, eating, using water, creating warmth and shelter.

Draw or list all the ways you participate in learning with others and with the planet.

Write or draw all the ways you participate in the universe through planet Earth.

Add these drawings and lists to the emerging cosmology on your kitchen door or elsewhere.

Reflections

What we now need are emerging cosmologies to embed novel technological, biological and economic ideas as possibilities in our societies, our universities, our communities and our businesses, and in our governments and legal systems.

Each of these five emerging paradigms point to a world beyond consumption and growth, to a world of joy and ecological and social justice. These paradigms represent powerful stories that, when shared, can inspire and motivate. However, we must also be aware of the dangers of stories so that we always continue to seek the truth.

Critiques

Some stories can be dangerous however. Consider the nationalist or religious stories deployed to subjugate 'outsiders' under a dominant narrative. Think of the terrible power of the story of Europeans who went to the Americas convinced that they were in the right. Throughout his life, Black Elk remained haunted by the massacre of his people by white settlers fuelled by their story of Manifest Destiny. In Amazonia, indigenous peoples have been murdered by representatives of corporations and governments in pursuit of the region's natural wealth and driven by a mechanistic story of progress (Boff, 1997). In recent years, the story of the threat of the other, the migrant and the refugee, has been used to discriminate against people fleeing violence, poverty, drought and the climate emergency (UNHCR, 2020). Stories can be used to create a single grand narrative, in which there is only one right way. The dangers of such an approach are evident from history, leading to exclusion and division and, at worst, atrocities such as the Holocaust. The advertising industry currently misuses stories to lure us into buying products, even appropriating spirituality and music to that end (Barber, 1995). Such mis-use of stories by those who seek to divide communities and create discord and hate, and those who seek to sell products, teaches us the need to continually reflect on the stories we create to ensure they remain open to all. Together with the stories I have highlighted here, there are others that can be woven into our hopeful futures and holistic dreams. Each of us has our own perceptions of self and our own personal experiences, meaning that we relate and react to stories differently. The stories we need now must run counter to mainstream media and culture. As such, they are important as they tell the story of other possible futures.

Growing beyond ourselves: coming home to the universe

As discussed in Chapter 1, we are so used to seeing ourselves at the centre and ignoring the Cosmos (Figure 1.4 page 53), because our dominant paradigms are so overwhelmingly powerful. As my students have observed, challenges to consumerism do not often appear on social media.

However, the Club of Rome's 1979 seminal report concluded that material growth is limited, but learning is unlimited (Botkin et al., 1979). The UN Development Programme, in the face of the challenges facing the environment, social justice and human health, calls for greater solidarity in human societies and that we work together (2022). As we mobilise to challenge dominant paradigms, we are reminded that we can orient our resources differently, following an emerging participatory ethos. Those resources include ourselves, our families, our neighbours, our communities, our workplaces, our learning institutions, our hospitals and public health services, our libraries and museums, our archives, our cultural and theatrical centres, our musical centres and our faith communities. These open our emerging paradigms to the whole world, transforming our institutions and organisations. As adherents to these new paradigms, we can improve these institutions, show their possibilities and how they belong to all communities, including the more-than-human and the Cosmos.

 Creative Learning Exercise

For this exercise, you will need paper, pens, a large sheet of paper and some time outdoors.

Find a favourite place in Gaia, weather permitting.

Draw the largest circle you can on the paper. All the instructions that follow fit inside this circle.

Draw the outline around both your hands and colour in the shape. How old are your hands? Write their age.

Draw a picture of the birth of our planet 4.5 billion years ago. Add animals, rocks, the climate and carbon dioxide molecules to your drawing to depict how life kept the planet habitable as the sun grew hotter over time. Think about Gaia.

Write a list of qualities, such as compassion, love, kindness, participation, tolerance, patience, determination. Add the words 'awe-inspiring' and 'sacred' to your picture.

Add humans to the picture and some images for community actions that connect humans and nature. And symbols of struggles for social justice, equality and ending structural inequalities built into society.

Draw symbols representing participation, such as images of people and animals, all the way around the circle.

Are you in any way critical of these five emerging cosmologies? If so, add these criticisms to your drawing.

You have now made a visual representation of the five emerging cosmologies. Add this final summary diagram to the others and use them as a source for reflection.

Notes

[25] Four-part series on the rise of unfettered capital in Manchester: https://www.theguardian.com/tv-and-radio/2020/aug/18/manctopia-billion-pound-property-boom-review-the-price-of-gentrification

[26] See NASA research mathematician Katherine Johnson's autobiographical account of growing up in America in the early twentieth century and the struggles of the Black community against segregation, racial violence and inequality (Johnson, 2019).

[27] The CERN (European Agency for Nuclear Research) 2022 website contains an accessible account of the research conducted there and explores understanding of our universe: https://home.cern/science/physics/early-universe

[28] CERN 2022: https://home.cern/science/physics/dark-matter

[29] Berry referred to himself as a geologian, as his spiritual ideas were embedded in the billions of years of universe history.

[30] Oren Lyons address to the E. F. Schumacher Society Annual Lecture in 2004: https://centerforneweconomics.org/publications/the-ice-is-melting/

[31] For example, the Aboriginal view of land: https://www.creativespirits.info/aboriginalculture/land/meaning-of-land-to-aboriginal-people.

[32] https://stories.undp.org/10-things-we-all-should-know-about-indigenous-people

[33] For a video about the need for such a law see: https://www.stopecocide.earth/watch The Stop Ecocide Institute: https://www.stopecocide.earth/polly-higgins

[34] Earth Charter in Action: Powering a global movement: https://earthcharter.org/the-movement/

[35] For a critique of approaches to conservation, land and development which does not include the concepts of Indigenous rights and Earth Rights, see Harrop et al. 2022.

[36] Words in italics from Reason (2005) pages 36 – 39.

[37] See chapters 7 and 12 for resources for developing participation within human societies, and with the planet and Cosmos in chapters 8, 9 and 11.

Second Cycle: Opening the Tool Kit

Let us begin the journey by unpacking the tools that will help us to address the challenges we face and put these new paradigms into action. We will explore the potential of education and learning and the green shoots in education currently working towards environmental learning and sustainability. Learning is a lever for societal transformation that will guide us on our journey. Much of our current education system is human-focused, growth-orientated, individualist or narrowly discipline-centred and, therefore, unable to encompass these essential new paradigms. What we need, instead, are educational approaches that embrace transformation. Our journey must be both internal and external and this can be facilitated through values-based learning approaches.

One key educational approach is *action research*, a learning method that helps individuals and groups transform how they learn. It will be the methodology underpinning the journey ahead. It liberates ideas and methods from the ivory towers in which they have been too long imprisoned.

One form of this methodology is first-person action research, which enables us to delve deeper into our daily lives through a range of creative, investigative and reflective practices. First-person action research embraces the practice of bearing witness to what is happening to our planet, allowing us to engage fully with our home as we journey.

Chapter 3: A participatory and value-based approach to learning

*"Human potential is being artificially constrained and vastly
underutilised, so much so that for all practical purposes there
appear to be virtually no limits to learning."*
James Botkin, Mahdi Elmandjra and Mircea Malitza (1979: 9)

*"We must learn that ecosystems are so complicated and
interconnected that almost no action is isolated. Our motto
should be 'We can never do merely one thing.' We should
continuously ask: 'And then what?'"*
Lester Milbrath (1989: 86)

*"One child, one teacher, one book and one pen can change
the world."*
Malala Yousafzai (2015)

In 2011, the European Appreciative Inquiry Network met in Manchester. Network delegates offered free appreciative inquiry sessions to local groups in the host city. One such group was in Rusholme, a diverse inner-city neighbourhood. Two facilitators from the European Network met a group of ten local residents at the Lakeside Centre in Platt Fields Park to explore ideas of appreciative inquiry. The meeting generated great interest and ended in agreement to convene a larger community summit. And so, the community dreaming initiative Imagine Rusholme! was born. Four locally based European AI Network volunteers acted as facilitators. The group met over several cycles of planning, debating and learning. The key challenge in planning the structure of the summit was how to help local people to be positive about what they would like to see happen in their community and identify the systemic changes needed to fulfil their dreams. Only then could action steps be taken to make these changes happen. The city council provided funding for refreshments and workshop resources. Over 70 people attended the summit, including local council officers, public sector workers, local councillors, the local MP and local residents. Participants were asked to consider 'what gives life' to the community and to share examples and stories of what works. The room was soon abuzz with multiple excited voices. As sunlight poured through the high windows, the participants were asked to dream a new Rusholme. In the silence, seventy people together dreamed a new vision for their community.

At every step, the facilitators encouraged reflection and positive thinking. Some aspects of the summit were difficult, such as encouraging individuals to voice positive ideas of what they would like rather than voice the many challenges facing the area. One facilitator, an artist, provided an ongoing line drawing record of the day, while another filmed the event. By the end of the summit, seven work streams had emerged, each with potential facilitators to take the ideas forward. A few months later, a second community summit reinforced the process. Out of these workstreams, Creative Rusholme eventually developed as a creative vision for the area, including a series of local postcards, a calendar and a book.[38] From this positive mindset, a community organisation, Upping It!, was born two years later, which aimed to "clean and green alleys, reduce fly tipping and improve our environment."[39] These community summits demonstrate what local residents can achieve with the support of transformational learning methods.

Introduction

As early as 1979, Botkin et al. argued that, while humanity has reached the limits of growth, its capacity to learn is limitless. Learning and education offer a way to grow new paradigms and address the challenges facing our planet. But the type of learning we need is not that which maintains the status quo; rather it should reflect on and change the status quo. This learning needs to be participative, reflective, holistic, interdisciplinary and creative. We need internal and external values-based learning to meet the challenges head on.

'Wicked problems' require transformative approaches and critical thinking

Together, these create a whirlwind of challenges that require lateral thinking, creativity and good will. In 1973, Rittel and Webber used the word 'wicked' to describe the planetary challenges identified in Chapter 1. Such problems range from the displacement of peoples through war, famine or environmental catastrophe through to the need to share water supplies and protect our soil in the face of climate change. The linear thinking so long applied to growth, to nationhood or to individualism cannot cope with the 'wicked' problems our planet and its inhabitants face. In addition, an increasing number of technological developments give cause for concern, including genetically modified food, nanotechnologies, drone surveillance technology, biomedicine and geoengineering. Lovelock (2009) cautions against the use of geoengineering because we inhabit a living planet and do not know the consequences of what we do. Sadly, such is the effect of humanity on nature and ecosystems, that Elizabeth Kolbert (2021) finds herself sympathizing with the scientists developing technology to solve the mistaken technological fixes of the past.

'Wicked' problems are complex, systemic and enormous in scale and the solutions to these problems have the potential to create further challenges. 'Wicked' challenges need to be tackled all together, but in such a way that achieves positive societal transformation. Learning and education are essential to both challenging and transforming the status quo.

Potential of learning

Since at least Plato's *Republic*, we have been aware of the potential of learning to transform society. In 2000, when the member states of the United Nations came together to set out the ten United Nations Millennium Development Goals, top of the list was "Achieve universal primary education" and "Ensure that, by 2015, children everywhere, boys and girls alike, will be able to complete a full course of primary schooling". In 2015, when the UN created its 17 sustainable development goals to be reached by 2030, "Quality Education" was listed fourth on the list. This was only preceded by ending poverty and hunger and improving health and well-being. Since the UN SDGs Inaugural Progress Report in 2016, progress and challenges have been recorded annually. The 2020 report highlighted the global disruption to education caused by the COVID-19 pandemic as a threat to ultimately achieving the goal. However, one notable result of SDG 4 has been the steady rise in the number of people in tertiary education, and attaining degrees and higher degrees (UNESCO, 2021).

Not only is access to formal education rising but, through computer technology, there is unprecedented access to knowledge and learning. Fifteen years ago, the idea that much of the world's population would have instant access to most of human knowledge at the touch of a screen would have been the stuff of science fiction. Today it is a reality that is rapidly spreading across the world, serving as a tool for literacy and empowerment (UNESCO, 2015). As a result of changes in technology, globalisation, the widespread privatisation of public sector services, diversity, emphasis on the individual and the rise of postmodern thinking, there has been a move away from the concepts of education and training to the emergence of the concept of learning (Mayo, 1997). Prompted by UN agencies and member states, there has been a worldwide move to lifelong learning and learning outside of educational institutions, opening up potential opportunities for people who would not previously have had the chance to access learning (Jarvis, 2006; Osborne, 2014).

Critiques of mainstream education and learning

Despite these developments, theoretical debate continues on the instrumentalist and emancipatory purpose of education (Cranton, 2006). A managerialist approach argues that the purpose of education is to equip workers for employment in an increasingly global marketplace, while a humanist approach argues that the purpose of education is to develop full human beings (Hutchins, 1968; UNESCO, 1997; UNESCO, 2015). In the UK, the purpose of education is increasingly defined in terms of the former (Joseph-Salisbury & Connolly, 2021). Learners are taught in a linear fashion for a market-orientated world (Blincoe, 2009). For many of us, as community activists, students, business people or NGO workers, even if we want to journey beyond the current paradigm towards an ecologically sustainable society, accessing education and learning that helps us on our journey is not always easy.

Much of mainstream education and learning fails to meet the requirements for creating an ecologically sustainable society (Sterling, 2001; Black et al., 2017; Lewis & Shore, 2019). Indeed, Berry suggests that mainstream education, like society's other major institutions, plays a part in driving the devastation that we are inflicting on the planet. David Orr (2002: 1458) reflects on the importance of Berry's call for the "Great Work", which, he argues, will help us to understand the "interconnectedness of the web of life" and the need for a broader education which encompasses spiritual qualities. A key path into the future is through social learning. Milbrath (1989) argues that what is most important is that "we deliberately design a society that encourages social learning."

Meanwhile, Fritjof Capra (1996) calls for the creation of an "ecologically literate society". Education currently plays a crucial role in continuing and deepening the devastation of the planet, and obscures understanding of the structural causes of societal problems (Freire, 1973). It supports the education and training of those who enter professions and organisations that, separately and together, collude in the exploitation of the planet and the destruction of eco-systems. It divides investigation and understanding of the world into separate disciplines, thus obscuring the whole. Furthermore, education continues to foster the destruction of the planet through the promotion and development of certain skills: "Education [in recent history] became more an external conditioning than an interior discipline, more a training in manipulative techniques than initiation into religious rituals. The skills to be mastered [are] not the contemplative skills or imaginative capacities for dealing with numinous presence or with the aesthetic insight into the inner structure of reality; they [are] rather the skills needed by industry…" (Berry, 1988: 94). Alongside this, it can be argued that current pedagogical methods encourage a culture of consumerism among children (Illich, 1971).

Thus, while formal education teaches about (astro-)physics, it rarely captures what we can learn from the universe in relation to our own purpose as a species. Nor does education emphasise the wonder of the Universe in which we live and, despite the attempts of inspirational teachers, such wonder is unlikely to secure high examination marks or school inspection grades. Teaching from within a mechanistic worldview, education fails to teach that we are part of a whole, nested within cosmic, planetary, societal and bioregional systems and patterns (Bateson, 1972; Berry, 1988; Stirling, 2010).

Pedlar and Trehan (2009) argue that a key failure of management education is that, rather than concentrating on the huge challenges facing humanity, it concentrates on the single career journey. Indeed, higher education in Western universities can be seen to be in the grip of a philosophy of hierarchical management and the pursuit of higher numbers of students to maximise financial gain. This has resulted in a loss of staff and a poorer student learning experience (Boden et al, 2015). Erik Assadourian (2017), the Director of Worldwatch's *Earthed* project, concludes, "The gap between Earth Education and where schools are today is about as wide as the gap between human civilisation's current climate change policies and what science requires of us to get to a sustainable future."

 Invitation to Reflect

Write or draw how you see learning in society today.

Reflect on how you learned at school and in other educational institutions.

Do you think that education today helps to meet the challenges identified in Chapter 1?

Do current educational practices help to build new paradigms for society?

Where else in society do you see learning taking place?

What sort of learning would you like to see for hopeful futures?

Exploring learning

Extensive research has been undertaken into the ways that people learn. Knud Illeris (2009) identifies four types of learning. Mechanical learning is the learning of simple facts, for example, times tables or the physical features of a country. Assimilative learning, or learning by addition, is building on what is already known, for example, learning to read, in which we build on the words we already know to grasp new and more difficult meanings. Accommodative or transcendent learning is when the learner deconstructs what they are learning and puts it back together again, for example, when learning about the carbon cycle or how different gases heat up the atmosphere. The fourth type of learning is deep learning, which questions assumptions and challenges the status quo.

Learning that maintains the status quo

Jarvis et al (2003) have devised a list of types of learning based on whether they are reflective or non-reflective, and whether they challenge or support the status quo. Learning that does not challenge the status quo is preconscious learning, skills learning and memorisation. Memorisation is commonly used in schools and colleges. Information is given, the learner memorizes it and reproduces it in exams or assignments. Skills development can be easy or difficult, and includes such common examples as learning to ride a bike or play a sport or learning to cook or sew. Preconscious learning takes place at the boundaries of all learning when we are unaware that we are learning.

Non-reflective learning has been described as single loop learning (Schön, 1983), in which we learn something but do not think about the values or assumptions underpinning it. Paulo Freire (1970) used the term 'banking learning' to describe the process of regurgitating facts without thinking, a process of storing or 'banking' information for future use. Botkin et al. (1979) argue that often we learn to simply maintain the status quo, without learning to question whether change is needed. They refer to this as 'maintenance learning'.

An appreciation and critique of maintenance learning

Clearly learning to play a sport, to cook, or to play a musical instrument are skills that contribute to society. We need a range of skills that we can deliver well, with little change or deviation. However, in our education system, this type of learning tends to be prioritised. For example, the dominant force behind the UK National Curriculum is to equip individuals as consumers and employees. Introducing a 'tougher' version of the curriculum in September 2014, the Department of Education justified the changes thus: "[the government requires] all children to learn the core knowledge in key subjects – the ones universities and employers value the most" (Richardson, 2014). It is important to critique such an approach to learning. It does not teach students the skills they need to tackle systemic planetary challenges. Nor does it encourage students to think about and reflect on the values underpinning their learning, or to learn to anticipate future challenges and how they might be addressed. With 'maintenance learning', shock learning comes about only in the face of crises (Botkin et al., 1979). This, however, does not help the planet when it faces such a variety of systemic challenges.

 Creative Learning Exercise

Draw a picture of a time when you engaged in learning that did not challenge the status quo or that was non-reflective.

Draw or sketch what you learned from that experience.

Describe the learning process at that time.

What are the benefits of this form of learning?

What are the limitations of this form of learning?

Write or draw your reflections in your journal.

Learning for the future

Much of mainstream education focuses on a mechanistic paradigm that follows conventional, rational, linear wisdom. However, there are many other learning approaches that can lead us to change the way we think and act.

In 2019, the Intergovernmental Science-Policy Platform on Biodiversity and Ecosystem Services (IPBES) reported that, to live in a fairer and more ecologically just planet, we must change our habits and ways of life through transformational change, including transformational learning. This type of learning builds on the legacy of a number of educational visionaries and movements for change. Basil Yeaxlee's book *Lifelong Education,* published in 1929, envisioned learning beyond school and a quest for spiritual meaning for every member of society (Smith, 2020). In 1968, humanist Robert Hutchins called for the creation of 'Learning Societies' where learners could acquire wisdom that would help them to change the world around them.

Learning visionaries Botkin et al. (1979) concluded in their Club of Rome report that, in order to achieve an ecologically sustainable world, we must develop innovative learning, which includes participatory and anticipatory learning. A decade later, in 1992, the concept of Environmental Learning emerged out of the Rio Earth Summit leading to the development of the Foundation for Environmental Education's Eco-Schools Programme which now operates in primary and secondary schools in 70 countries. Education for Sustainable Development has emerged from the United Nations Millennium Development Goals and the UN SDGs (Wals & Corcoran, 2012). Higher education institutions around the world have seen the creation of centres for transformational learning, including the Centre for Alternative Technology, the Findhorn Foundation and Schumacher College in the UK and the Esalen Institute in California, while initiatives such as forest schools are transforming primary and secondary education. More recently, Erik Assadourian (2017), from the Worldwatch Institute, has called for education to "teach students their dependence on a living planet and [provide]…them with the skills to live restoratively." Filho et al. (2018) have called for the development of integrated sustainability initiatives centred on the UN SDGS, on best practice within universities, and in collaboration across different sectors.

⭘ Hopeful Companions

Education and Training
The Centre for Alternative Technology in Wales, Graduate school, short courses and Zero Carbon Britain events and training: https://cat.org.uk/courses-and-training/

Schumacher Institute short courses and the Pale Blue Dot leadership course: https://www.schumacherinstitute.org.uk/learning/

Eco Schools: empowering children and teens to improve our environment: https://www.ecoschools.global/

Forest Schools – nature based communities for learning, wellbeing and growth: https://www.forestschools.com/

Filho, W. (ed.) 2018 to present: *World Sustainability Series,* series of edited books exploring different aspects of sustainability including supporting the implementation of the UN SDGs (2021) and university education (2022): https://www.springer.com/series/13384

A recognition of the importance of learning is spreading within sustainability policy. The 2019 IPBES report suggests a model of transformative change with learning as a key lever which it defines as "fundamental system-wide reorganisation across technological, economic and social factors, including paradigms, goals and values." It extends Botkin et al.'s (1979) "unlimited potential of learning" to all sectors and to participatory and anticipatory forms of learning. Figure 3.1 models how such learning might take place. It includes "multi-actor governance interventions" on policy, collaboration and actions to leverage learning in society that includes "embracing diverse visions of the good life, unleashing values and actions and promoting education and knowledge generation and sharing" (IPBES, 2019). Transformation can be achieved by the participation of a wide range of actors including Indigenous peoples, local communities, businesses, NGOs, trade unions, the scientific community and government.

For humanity to achieve such transformative learning, the way we currently deliver formal education must be changed so that we deliver education in every community and institution that helps people change the way they think and act.

Jarvis et al (2003) notes three types of change: 1. The learner may be changed, 2. The learner may accept or reject what they have learned, and 3. The learner may act to change the situation within which they function. Learning that seeks to transform the status quo contains some element of changing the assumptions and worldviews that underpin the subject being studied. Furthermore, such learning needs to be set within a wider context of love and understanding that inspires action and provides the tools for action. There also needs to be recognition that failure is a part of learning and growth and, after failure, we need to pick ourselves up and start again.

The qualities of learning beyond the status quo

Transformational learning requires the paradigm shifts described in Chapter 2. Different learning approaches are relevant and useful in different times and places. I invite you to consider which of the approaches below speak to you the most.

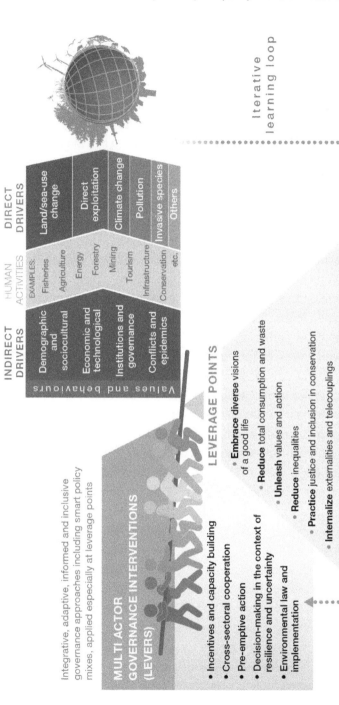

Figure 3.1: Recommendations from global scientists on ways to achieve transformational change. (Source: IPBES. 2019 Summary for policymakers of the global assessment report on biodiversity and ecosystem services of the Intergovernmental Science-Policy Platform on Biodiversity and Ecosystem Services, page 40. https://doi.org/10.5281/zenodo.3553579)

The world as an interconnected whole

Integral to learning beyond the status quo is understanding the world as a single interconnected whole. Such understanding can often occur through profound and transformative experiences. I recount three examples of such experiences from key figures in the ecological movement.

As a child, Thomas Berry moved to the outskirts of Gainsborough. Early one morning, when he was 11 years old, he walked into the meadow beside his house and saw lilies through the mist that cloaked the meadow. He experienced the utter righteousness of the meadow, and the image of the lilies in the mist stayed with him forever and became his touchstone: whatever was right for the meadow was right, whatever harmed the meadow was wrong (1999).

Alpo Leopold was a wildlife ranger in 1930s America. His job was to protect deer from wolves, so that the deer could be hunted for sport. One day, as he sat on a cliff overlooking a river, in an area surrounded by mountains, a mother wolf and her cubs appeared in the river valley below. Leopold shot the cubs and badly wounded the mother. He descended the cliff face to where the wolf mother lay, to kill her. He recounts, in *Sand County Almanac* (1946), how, as he took aim and shot her, he saw a "fierce green light dying" in her eyes. Leopold suddenly understood that "neither the wolf nor the mountain agreed with what he had done." At that moment, the course of his life changed and he became committed to an ethic that protected the environment and the ecology of the area.

Chemist Rachel Carson's moment of transformation came when she became aware of the absence of birdsong. The profoundly sad silence drove her to discover what was killing the birds, resulting in her influential environmental classic *Silent Spring* (1962) which first drew attention to the effect of pesticides on wildlife.

Such inspirational stories allow us to think about our own moments of transformational learning. They suggest the need for deep experiential learning that takes us outside of our normal learning experiences. These experiences suggest the qualities of a new way of learning, such as shifting our focus away from human concerns to nature and engaging with nature through our senses. They suggest learning to see nature as she exists, in her own right, with her own beauty and coherence. They suggest a long time-frame for self-reflection that incorporates the geological time needed to create the ecosystems in which we live.

Systemic thinking

In the 1960s and 1970s, systems thinker and cyber scientist Gregory Bateson (1972) analysed the challenges facing contemporary ecology and argued that linear thinking reflects neither how society nor natural systems function. He argued that a society that sets itself up in opposition to the environment − that cuts down forests, pollutes, overexploits, that thinks it can win against other societies and against the environment is, quite simply, mad. His solution was a systemic approach to tackling social and environmental problems through transformational learning. He suggested four levels of learning. Level I is learning with a set array of choices and accepting the choices given. Level II is the ability to think about the parameters within which choices are made. Level III is learning the ability to understand ourselves as part of the greater cosmic whole. According to his biographer, Noel Charlton, Bateson believed Level IV comes around through the process of evolution "…[by] adding the learning (which includes their growth and life process) of some organisms to the whole process of their evolutionary development" (2008:59). Engaging with Level IV learning encourages us to think far beyond the focus of current educational systems, and to re-imagine learning as part of all organisms and elements of our planet, allowing us to interact together as interconnected systems.

In recent decades, there has been a growing emphasis on learning together. Peter Senge (1990) introduced the concept of the learning organisation, one of the characteristics of which is systems thinking. Lovelock describes Gaia as a self-organising living system, where the rocks, climate, oceans and life are in a tight coupling that maintain the planet's fitness for life. Our learning needs to help us see Gaia as such.

Learning beyond the status quo in our daily lives

The experiences of learning beyond the status quo can be simple and part of daily life, such as Thomas Berry's experience in the field of flowers or Rachael Carson's awareness of the absence of birdsong. These experiences can be part of our work, as with Alpo Leopold, when we carry out an action that is expected of us but realise that it is not the correct choice for our planet. We all have moments of learning in the daily run of life: going on holiday, walking, learning with neighbours and friends, thinking about our wellbeing and health, being a student. Within these daily experiences, we can learn to use our senses more, so that we engage with nature, Gaia and our wonderful Cosmos. We can reflect on and learn from the experiences of others. Through reading, watching and reflecting, we can stand on the shoulders of others as we learn.

The tools in this kit – Hopeful Companions, Creative Learning Exercises and Invitations to Reflect – will guide you as you become more aware of the world around you, helping you to reflect on and put what you have learned into practice.

 Creative Learning Exercise

Think about the types of learning that you most enjoy. Reflect on how you can maximise these learning opportunities.

Do you like reading? If so, what materials do you prefer? Books? Short articles? Etc.

Do you find it easier to listen?

Do you like watching educational and informative programmes on the television or internet?

Do you most like learning with other people?

Do you like being practical and learning by doing?

Research some learning resources for change, locally and nationally, that interest you.

Create notes for yourself concerning how you plan to learn.

 Hopeful Companions

Organisations
Infed.org is an independent, not for profit education and community building organisation: https://infed.org/mobi/aboutus/

UNESCO Institute for Lifelong Learning: https://uil.unesco.org/unesco-institute

---

Listening to feedback from the living Earth

Meadows et al. (2004) argue that we need to listen to feedback from the planet. Such feedback comes from both science and our senses. In many ways, we know that something is wrong, but we do not allow that knowledge into our conscious minds. Learning to listen to the planet allows us to hear what we are doing. We can do this by being outside in nature and by engaging with science.

Participatory and anticipatory innovatory learning

When we see the world as an interconnected living whole, we can engage in profound learning. Botkin et al. (1979) propose innovative and anticipatory learning, such as the dreaming used in the *Imagine Rusholme!* appreciative practice. "[Anticipatory learning]," they write, "encourages [people] to consider trends, to make plans, to evaluate future consequences and possible injurious side effects of present decisions, and to recognise the global implications of local, national and regional actions.... It emphasizes the future tense, not the past, it employs imagination but is based on hard facts. The essence of anticipation lies in selecting desirable events and working towards them, in averting unwanted or potentially catastrophic events and in creating new alternatives" (ibid.: 13). Botkin et al. propose that all learning be participatory, involving all sectors of society. Learners must be taught and must experience how to participate, and learning and societal systems need to genuinely address participation and not treat it as a box-ticking exercise. Learning must be values-based and should be communicated through a combination of visual images, language and the relationships between people.

Everyone is a problem solver

Learning to listen to feedback from the planet is a job for everyone. Maslow (1962) argues that, irrespective of skills or experience, we can all contribute to creating a better world. Such an inclusive approach is not often part of formal education, where students can all too easily see themselves as failures or with skills that are not essential. Learning, in this instance, is about developing an understanding of the problem and creating solutions.

Social learning

This approach to learning leads to the creation of a whole society approach. At the end of a long academic career as a political theorist, Milbrath pondered what constituted a sustainable society and concluded that society must be based on ecological values and social learning. His ideas had more in common with Thomas Berry's cosmological learning than with the models for learning offered by formal education. Milbrath (1989:88) defines social learning as something that,

> "Takes place in several different ways…. Thomas Berry's phrase, a 'self-educating community', comes close to what I mean; but even that phrase needs explanation. In a community, we learn from each other and from nature. It is meaningful to speak of a 'learning community' or that 'a community makes up its own mind about something', even though a community does not have a mind."

Interdisciplinary learning

Transformational learning occurs when people from different professional, intellectual or social backgrounds work together. The challenges identified for the planet cannot be addressed through a silo mentality. The Gaia hypothesis led to the establishment of new disciplines in the Earth sciences. Jonathon Porritt (2013) imagines a route to a sustainable future through collaboration, where every discipline and profession in society works together. Sachs (2015) calls upon all disciplines to work together to achieve the UN SDGs. A transdisciplinary approach allows us to tackle the challenges our world faces and academics must be critical and open to this. Such an approach will not be easy, and must overcome many barriers (Aslin & Blackstock, 2010). In a demonstration of the holism encountered when working beyond the status quo, Brown et al. (2010: 6) suggest we need "transdisciplinary imagination". The qualities of imagination – "creativity, insight, vision and originality…memory, perception and invention" – will contribute to changing the world in hopeful ways.

Reflective individual and group learning

One way to learn to see Gaia is through reflection. Reflection involves both reflection-in-action and reflection-on-action (Schön, 1983). Reflection-in-action raises the possibility that we can change our actions in real time, while reflection-on-action entails looking back at actions already taken. Argryis and Schön (1974) use the concept of double and triple loop learning, in which we reflect on an experience by returning to the values and assumptions behind our actions. Triple Loop learning involves reflection on our worldviews or paradigms. We need to learn more deeply as individuals, in groups and beyond into wider society, the last of which is increasingly facilitated through social media.

Slow revolution

For Maslow (1962), a critical element of learning is making time for reflection. He advocated for slow revolutions and building new societies over time. We can be like the cathedral builders of the Middle Ages, who never saw their cathedrals completed, or the gardeners of the eighteenth century who planted trees they would never see grow to maturity, bequeathing their beauty to future generations. Such movements for 'slow science' and 'slow learning' can be seen emerging within education (Honore, 2004; Stengers, 2018). Our learning needs to take place over years, and not simply hours or days. It is the learning glimpsed by Aldo Leopold, when he came to the understanding that "neither the wolf nor the mountains" agreed with what he had done. He had a sense of the immense time span of the mountains and of his participation in that landscape.

Extending learning through time and place

The concept of learning must be extended beyond formal education to whole life experience, in which we learn in everything we do. The United Nations now advocates for lifelong learning, from cradle to grave and from educational establishments to all parts of society. Indeed, UNESCO promotes such concepts in its support of learning streets and learning cities.[40]

Self-organising learners in a self-organising universe

The possibility that learning can blossom at all levels of society requires that individual learners have the ability to shape their learning to their own interests. Zimmerman (2002) argues that we need to identify how some learners become self-regulated and take charge of their own learning. To understand ourselves as learners, we must reflect and plan and think positively about ourselves. Such self-belief in the power of our own learning is a powerful motivator to learning and development. This approach puts students in control of their own circumstances, so that they can develop strategies to learn better. Learning is not framed by failure, but by the ability to think, reflect and learn positively. Teachers play a key role in developing learning that enables students to become fully involved, learning how to become 'knowledge-able' (Elder, 2012; Randles et al, 2023). Self-organised learning is nested within Thomas Berry's concept of a self-organising universe and education that encourages students to be part of a self-organising planet and to act in harmony with such a planet is essential.

 Creative Learning Exercise

Consider a time when you learned for change.

What was the occasion? Draw or sketch it.

Did this learning take place in an informal or formal setting?

Using colours and shapes, illustrate what you learned.

Were you conscious of changing your perceptions?

Record your reflections of this learning experience in your journal.

Values-based critical thinking

Botkin et al. (1979) argue that values should be inherent in innovative learning and are an important element of learning. At each crossroads of societal development and change, we must question our learning, values and ethics.

In a 2015 editorial, *New Scientist* explored the need for ethical and systematic questioning, and for the development of the ability to combine "scientific literacy and critical thinking" in our approach to science and technology. It cited such developments as genetic engineering and geoengineering as fields that make values-driven choices crucial. The need for ethics is explored further by Azeem Akhar (2021) who argues for the importance of values in the face of the threats posed to society by the current exponential growth of technology.

Our values impinge on all our decisions. They are what lead us to make decisions that protect or destroy every tree, rainforest, bird, and insect on this planet. Therefore, our values must change. The Earth Charter, launched in 2000, following the 1992 Rio Earth Summit, contains an ethical vision and strong values to frame the way we live.[41] The charter asserts that we should respect and care for all life on Earth and care for the bounty and beauty of all life for now and for future generations.

Calls for a transformation in values are not, as yet, part of mainstream political or economic action and are mostly honoured in the breech. It is imperative that we craft learning that can help us to identify and integrate these values. We can start with an understanding that our values come from the inner journeys we undertake.

An inner and outer individual journey

Ecological and social justice-based values require that we embark on inner and outer journeys. Developing our own individual values within our own traditions or moral systems must be integral to the journey. Only when our values are internalised can they consistently guide us as we carry our own sense of "true north" within (Covey, 1989). All wisdom traditions teach of the need for inner and outer journeys. However, in modern times, many of us have rejected those teachings along with the notion of the divine. The First Millennium BC Tao Te Ching suggests that our lives reflect on the inner way or Dao and it offers verses or commentaries to help us. Inspired by the Bhagavad Gita, Satish Kumar (2007) suggests that we create our own spiritual compass, using the ancient concepts of sattvic, rajasic and tamasic, which Kumar translates as "elegant and simple..., shining and exciting... [and] fearful and depressing", respectively (p.21). We can live a good life in the knowledge that these qualities interact with each other, seeking the harmony and simplicity of the *sattvic* way of life.

Pope Francis's encyclical, *Laudato Si' On care for Our Common Home* (2015), calls for a spiritual change in our inner lives that will lead to action in the outer world, across humanity. As I explore further in Chapter 10, other expressions have arisen, which also reflect and teach the values of inner journeys. People of other faiths or no faith have also developed inner journeys and values for such inner journeys (see Bloom, 2011). The Alcoholics Anonymous (AA) self-help programme, for example, encourages inner transition. Addictions counsellor Albert LaChance worked with Thomas Berry to develop a 12-step programme to combat humanity's current addiction to consumerism and the destruction of the planet (LaChance, 2001). An inner journey can begin as a response to grief, bereavement or unhappiness. Susan Jeffers (1987) suggests that each of us create nine boxes for our inner lives, with a higher power, or one's own sense of God, inhabiting the central box (see Chapter 6).

◯ Hopeful Companions

The inner journey.

Books
The Bhagavad Gita. 1985/2007. Introduced and Translated by Eknath Easwaran. California: Nilgiri Press.

Hanh, N. 1991. *White Clouds. Old Path. Walking in the Footsteps of Buddha.* California: Parrallax Press.

Films
Satish Kumar, The Spiritual Compass, the Three Qualities of life
https://www.youtube.com/watch?v=Gb7lBdtGBjo

Tao Te Ching (audio): https://www.youtube.com/watch?v=o2UYch2JnO4

Organisations
The AA Twelve Step Programme: https://www.alcoholics-anonymous.org.uk/About-AA/The-12-Steps-of-AA

Invitation to Reflect

Starting from resources in the Hopeful Companions above and the section Sacred Earth and Cosmas in chapter 2, conduct some online research into the spiritual underpinning of different religious beliefs.

Choose three faith traditions and consider how they:

describe how we should treat each other?

suggest we should do in relation to social justice, equality and diversity?

describe their relationship with the Earth?

describe how we should treat the planet, the environment and each other?

What can the different faith traditions teach you about your own values and ethics?

Values based inquiry – finding 'true north'

Without values-based learning, we are unlikely to challenge the status quo or to make substantive progress towards a sustainable future. But what is the purpose of this value-based learning and inquiry? The following are some key interconnected concepts.

Social and ecological justice: Joint goals and the direction of travel must include both simultaneously. A Swedish organisation, The Natural Step, lists four "system conditions" to achieve a sustainable planet. The first three are connected with the Earth's ability to cope with the extraction of natural resources faster than they are replaced, the build-up of waste from human activity and the destruction of natural systems faster than they can regenerate. The fourth states, "We cannot do things that cause others to not be able to fulfill their basic needs."[42] A society that is not socially and economically just, to the point that everyone can meet their basic needs, is a society locked into destruction and over exploitation. Hawken (2007) points out that there is only one bus for humanity, and we all need to be on it, and that bus must combine ecological and social justice. Bringing these ideas together, economist Kate Raworth developed 'doughnut economics', an "economics for the twenty-first century" which combines Rockström's nine planetary boundaries with the needs of all people to live decent lives. This model offers a simple yet dynamic new form of economic theory and practice. (Figure 3.2 overleaf)

A participative approach: Humanity will not solve the challenges facing the world with the business-as-usual approach of identifying a problem

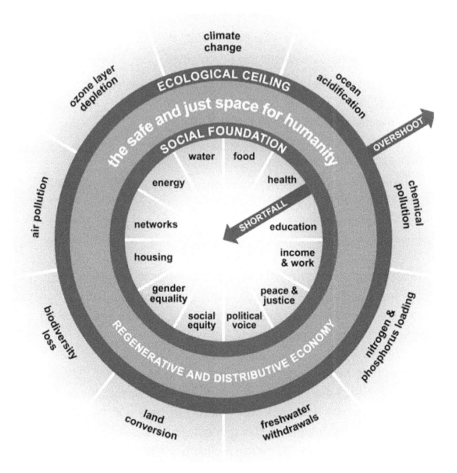

Figure 3.2: The Doughnut of social and planetary boundaries. (Source: Kate Raworth & Christian Guthier, 2017. Doughnut Economics Diagram, https://doughnuteconomics. org/about-doughnut-economics: Creative Commons-BY-SA 4.0)

and studying it. We must first recognise that the challenges we face are nested within larger, complex and uncertain systems. Nor can we stick to the tramlines of a traditional research approach with a single objective researcher studying discrete objects under controlled conditions.

Rather, we must shift to a participative approach that is active, practitioner-led, collaborative, cooperative, feminist, antiracist, inclusive and holistic and that incorporates communities and organisations in action learning, appreciative inquiry, citizen's assemblies and juries and participatory budgeting (see Cycle 3).

Self-organised learning: If, as Berry argues, the Universe is self-organising, then human learning must be modelled on this. We cannot depend on 'leaders' or others 'out there' to shape our learning. Each one of us can be responsible for organising our learning, for initiating action and for organised participation with others. The internet is a vast source of knowledge offering videos, podcasts, and the growth of massive open online courses (MOOCs) providing free university-level education to all. It offers some of the potential of Ivan Illich's (1971) educational web, with its different learning networks. The COVID-19 pandemic has stimulated growth in online learning, which is likely to continue alongside face-to-face learning in different blended forms. Such initiatives for self-organised learning, however, need to incorporate social and ecological justice, diversity and inclusion. The 2020 UN SDGs Progress Report emphasises that internet access in the home and the computer skills of parents and teachers vary greatly around the world.

Diversity and inclusion: Learning must be premised on the values of disability rights, gender, ethnicity, sexuality, religious, age and socio-economic diversity and inclusion, and encompassing global voices. It must also expand beyond to include the more-than-human and have an overarching intrinsic value of the right of all to habitat and life. Action to make such values real within education are continuously required (Donald et al., 2013; Arday & Mirza, 2018; Karpf, 2021).[43]

Self-reflection and awareness: As learners, we must be aware of the bias and cultural context of our learning and actions. Furthermore, we must be aware of the urgency of the crisis facing humanity and the Earth as a consequence of current economic, legal, religious, political and media institutions and practices. We must also urgently address the effects of injustice resulting from patriarchy, colonialism and racism.

Awe and wonder at life and our cosmos: Children often experience a sense of kinship and belonging with animals. Encounters with nature can create a sense of wonder at the beauty and diversity of life. When we can look up at the stars and experience a sense of awe, we are part of something bigger than ourselves, within which we can find meaning. This sense of awe, wonder and belonging must be central to our learning as it gives purpose to our lives.

Developing a sense of meaning: In the twentieth century, the Universal Declaration of Human Rights laid the foundations of a planet-wide basis for meaning in our lives.[44] For many people, the definition of leading a happy or successful life consists of a combination of earning enough money to meet basic needs, living free from fear, discrimination and inequality, having family and friends, having a meaningful purpose in life, and, for some, having children. Indeed, several influential writers and activists endorse this. Korten (2006) suggests that the desires of people in the middle of the political spectrum around the world are similar. These desires include healthy communities, the environment and children. Hawken (2007) discovered a vast network of individuals and groups around the world working for the common good. Archbishop Desmond Tutu writing with his daughter, the Rev. Mpho Tutu (2015), refers specifically to apartheid, envisioning a just and ecologically sustainable world and believing in the power of forgiveness to address the terrible wrongs that have been committed. In 2015, Pope Francis issued a clarion call for a world that values the environment, the climate and social justice. Finding a sense of meaning that is bigger than our individual selves gives us a deeper purpose by which to gauge our actions.

 Creative Learning Exercise

There are websites available with books for young people and children that represent Black, Asian and Global Majority main characters and that focus on anti-racism and inclusion for diverse groups of children. See for example: https://uk.bookshop.org/lists/children-s-books-featuring-black-asian-and-minority-ethnic-main-characters or https://newsfromnowhere.org.uk/books/DisplayBooklist.php?BookListID=1536

Find and spend some time exploring these resources. Research the books offered in Hopeful Companions. Draw the front covers of any books you particularly enjoy.

Can you create mind maps of these resources to use in your journey?

For over 50 years there has also been a growing citizen-led movement for change, including civil and human rights, the environment and global social justice. More recently new movements have emerged, including the young climate strikers inspired by Greta Thunberg, the climate campaign 350.org, the Black Lives Matter movement, the #MeToo movement, the #UN4refugeemigrants movement, the global fight for LGBTQ+ rights and for human rights within totalitarian states. Such participative movements demonstrate the potential to address the multiple challenges facing the Earth. Such movements underpin the emergence of new forms of learning.

◯ **Hopeful Companions**

The need for a different ethics.

Articles
MacRae, D. 2022. Azeem Rafiq: The England & Wales Cricket Board Needs a Reset of its morals and values. Morals. Interview with Azeem Rafiq. The Guardian, 2 January: https://www.theguardian.com/sport/2022/jan/21/azeem-rafiq-cricket-ecb-needs-a-reset-of-its-morals-and-values-simple-as-that

Melissa Parker. 2022. For disabled environmentalists, discrimination and exclusion are a daily reality. Greenpeace, 27 January: https://www.greenpeace.org.uk/news/disability-environmental-movement-exclusion/

Resources for Action
The Doughnut Economics Action Lab offers ideas, models, theories, practical examples and free accessible materials to take this model forward. It also offers a free community for learning and sharing ideas: https://doughnuteconomics.org/

The UN General Assembly adopts a clean and healthy environment as a basic human right. 2022: https://news.un.org/en/story/2022/07/1123482

Creative Learning Exercises

Engage with nature and begin to create your own sense of 'True North', containing your own inner values and moral compass. For example:

Go outside early in the morning. Find due east. Listen for the dawn chorus. Note the colours in the sky.

Go outside at midday when the sun is overhead. Find due south. Note the insects and flowers that can you see.

Go out at dusk. Find due west reflecting on the ending of the day.

Go out at night and find the Pole Star in the Northern Hemisphere. The southern hemisphere Pole Star, Polaris Australius, is much dimmer. Meditate on your own version of true north.

Draw your own version of your personal inner values and your True North.

Identify which of these inner values feel most relevant for growing a sustainable society.

Reflections

What is needed right now is learning that transforms the status quo. By adopting a participatory and values driven learning approach, and by understanding the systemic nature of the planet, we can begin to rise to the challenge. We also need to develop a learning method that will help us on the journey ahead.

Notes

[38] The projects are detailed on the website https://creativerusholme.c4cp.net/

[39] https://mosssidestory.uk/community-projects/upping-it/upping-it-about/

[40] For examples of 200 learning cities in 40 countries around the world, see: https://unesco.org.uk/learning-cities/

[41] For the text of the Earth Charter and how to support its development, see: http://www.earthcharterinaction.org/content/

[42] Details of the Natural Step approach with clear accessible visuals and the 'ABCD' Back casting solutions process available here: http://www.thenaturalstep.org/our-approach/

[43] There is a growing focus on animal and inter-species rights and justice explored, for example, by Peter Singer (1975/2015) and Helen Wadham (2021).

[44] For the full text, including an illustrated version, see: https://www.un.org/en/about-us/universal-declaration-of-human-rights

Chapter 4: Action Research

"...there is broad agreement that the purpose of human inquiry is the flourishing of life, the life of human persons, of human communities and increasingly of the more-than-human world of which we are a part."
Peter Reason and Hilary Bradbury (2001: 10)

"Action research is emancipatory; it leads not just to new practical knowledge but to new abilities to create knowledge. In action research, knowledge is a living evolving process of coming to know rooted in everyday experience; it is a verb rather than a noun."
Peter Reason and Hilary Bradbury (2001: 2)

In 2000, I registered for a Master's degree at the University of Bath School of Management, a leading UK business school. The programme consisted of eight residential weeks, spread over two years. The first week was at a venue I knew. Held on the lower floor of a modern university block, the room was mostly monochrome and angular, white tables surrounded by grey chairs, and bland cream-coloured walls. There were no plants or flowers in the room. The first shock came when we were asked to sit in a circle and introduce ourselves. We were asked to think about how we see the world, to consider our worldviews and perspectives. Gradually, I came to the realisation that this was not the sort of teaching and learning with which I was familiar. The second week took place a few months later at a residential college in the Devon countryside. We were encouraged to spend time out of doors, sitting by the river, tuning in to what the water was telling us, walking in the dark and listening to the sounds of nature. We were invited to participate in a Council of All Beings (see Chapter 11), to take on the spirit of another creature and to speak from that creature's perspective. During the third residential week, we met a retired civil servant who had spent his working life trying to change the economic system, one step at a time, to meet the needs of all. I was presented with the concept of researching myself and my motives, and of co-researching with others as collaborators rather than subjects. This type of learning was transformational and I set about bringing it into the local authority department where I worked and into the neighbourhood training we offered to communities.

Introduction

Transformational learning challenges and changes the status quo. It is participatory, innovatory and anticipatory. Action research is a transformational learning methodology that will help us on our journeys to tackle the 'wicked challenges' our planet faces.

Research as learning and inquiry

The word 'research' conjures images of scientists and other academics working on problems in their laboratories, libraries or research sites. One thinks of surveys and hypotheses, graphs and tables and journal articles. However, the concept of research is much broader than that. We all conduct research in our everyday lives. If you want to visit a friend on the other side of the country, you might research multiple public transport options to find out which offers the best value for money, which takes the least time or which offers the greatest convenience. If I want to reduce my plastic footprint at home, I research ways that I can make that happen. If my community wants to create a sustainable garden where elders and young people can learn and work together, we research the how, why, where and when of making it happen. In other words, 'research' refers to any inquiry or learning that leads to enhanced knowledge, participation and action. Research might take the form of internet and library searches, seeking out and learning from people with more skills and experience, learning by doing, and self-reflection on goals, motivations and subjectivity, as well as skills and limitations. Action research, which is central to this book, is both a way of examining a problem or an issue and a reflective orientation towards inquiry.

Action research is not only an individual undertaking. Perhaps a faith community is trying to reduce its carbon footprint. It will have to conduct research and inquiry to find out how to do this. Perhaps a residents' group wants to grow more of its own food, so it needs to research how it might plant vegetables and fruit trees together, or establish a communal garden for residents who lack space for gardening at home. But research is not only about action. It also provides an opportunity to reflect on what we are doing and why we are doing it, to be aware of the forces that conspire against our success, and to evaluate and choose one of myriad ways forward. This chapter explores research as inquiry, learning and reflection from the individual learner through to the community, the wider planet and the cosmos.

Choosing to inquire

McNiff and Whitehead (2011: 13) describe action research as

> "a rich tapestry of people, all working with the same purpose of finding better ways of creating a better world, from their different values, perspectives and methodological commitments."

Action research is a more participatory approach than traditional research that involves a researcher and an object of that researcher's interest. It seeks, instead, to involve people as equals in the research process and to produce results that are of value to communities and organisations. Reason and Bradbury (2001) note a wider purpose that includes the simultaneous flourishing of human communities and ecological or more-than-human communities.

A distinguishing feature of action research is the "action turn", or the call to action that goes beyond the mere advancement of academic knowledge (Reason & Torbert, 2001; Raelin, 2009). A key characteristic is that theory emerges from the experience of undertaking action research and practice remains central to theory (Dick et al., 2009). Action research uses a variety of different mediums, including writing as inquiry, theatre, performance, visual art and photography (Seeley, 2011).

Action research is not a particular research method, but rather an "orientation towards inquiry" (Reason & Bradbury, 2008) or a particular way to approach research. It is, as Bob Dick writes, "a mental framework and mindset" (in Zhao et al., 2012).

Reason and Bradbury (2001:1) offer a working definition:

> "Action research is a participatory, democratic process concerned with developing practical knowing in the pursuit of worthwhile human processes, grounded in a participatory worldview, which we believe is emerging at this historical moment. It seeks to bring together action and reflection, theory and practice, in participation with others, in the pursuit of practical solutions to issues of pressing concern to people and more generally the flourishing of individual persons and communities."

Action research has blossomed in the social sciences, including in the fields of management, organisational development, health, youth work and social care, wherever the principles of researching *with* people are embraced. It has grown within the fields of community development and within learning in higher education (Dick, 2010). Action research methods have flourished internationally in a wide variety of community and voluntary sector settings and there has been particular growth in the field of educational action research.

The action research family includes a diverse range of approaches to undertaking research in the field, including action inquiry, action science, action learning and appreciative inquiry, participatory action research (PAR), cooperative inquiry, feminist action research, and antiracist participatory action research.

This approach has a number of advantages. For example, Argris and Schön (1974) found differences between the theories people espouse and what they actually do within organisations. Building on this work, Torbert (2001) developed the concept of "action inquiry" to explore how four areas of experience reflect on our behaviour. These four areas are "the outside world, our own behaviours, our thoughts and our intention or vision" (p. 241).

Participatory action research is a strand of the action research family that originated in the Global South. In the 1970s, Orlando Fals Borda and colleagues in Colombia and elsewhere in Latin America wanted to better understand movements for social justice. They saw the need for researchers to practically help people, by working alongside the rural and urban poor (Fals Borda, 2006). They wanted to combine knowledge and action to transform the communities they worked in. Power and intersectionality scholarship (see p 70) contributed to this approach, giving rise to forms of feminist and anti-racist participatory action research. Meanwhile, co-operative inquiry is a form of action research in which researchers and communities are co-researchers in business, organisational, academic and community settings, jointly identifying inquiry questions and using a series of inquiry cycles and extended ways of knowing in the research process (Heron, 1996). Action learning is yet another part of the action research family, developed in the 1950s and 1960s by Reg Revans, at the National Coal Board and at University of Manchester (Cunningham, 2003). He sought to encourage reflection on what people actually did when they undertook business activity and to use their actions as the basis for learning. Finally, appreciative practice, developed by David Cooperrider, amongst others, begins with the power of the positive question to lead to transformative learning (Grieten et al., 2018).

◯ Hopeful Companions

Examples to help develop a deeper understanding of action research.

Articles
Johns, T. 2008. 'Learning To Love Our Black Selves: Healing From Internalised Oppressions'. in Reason P. and Bradbury, H. (eds). *The Sage Handbook of Action Research.* (2nd edition). London: Sage, pp. 553 – 563.

Larrea, M. (2022). Love as an energizing feature of action research for territorial development. *Action Research, 20*(3), 295–312. https://doi-org.mmu.idm.oclc.org/10.1177/14767503221107937

Scrine, C., Farrant, B., Michie, C., and Shepher, C. 2022. Implementing genuine participatory action research with Aboriginal elders: The Ngulluk Koolunga Ngulluk Koort project. *Action Research Journal.* 2022. Vol. 20(2) 144–161: DOI: 10.1177/1476750320932974

Siu, K., and Xiao, J. 2020. Public facility design for sustainability: Participatory action research on household recycling in Hong Kong. *Action Research Journal.* 18(4):448–468: DOI: 10.1177/1476750317698027

> **Films**
>
> Institute of Humanities and Global Culture, 2019: Joanne Rappaport: Cowards Don't Make History: A Discussion on Participatory Action Research and Orlanda Fals Borda: https://www.youtube.com/watch?v=vDEeCsR92rY.

Characteristics of action research

The action research family of methodologies shares a number of dynamic and interconnected characteristics. Reason and Bradbury link these to an emerging participatory worldview and to standards of quality and validity (2001).

These nine characteristics offer hope for the journey ahead and provide us with clear directions and signposts for reflection, action, understanding and working together set out in the nine boxes below.

Reflection 'unlimited learning'	First, second and third person action research 'I, We and Bigger We'	Emergent developmental form 'the whole is greater than the sum of the parts'
Cycles of action and reflection 'continuous loops of learning'	Emerging worldviews and paradigms 'Cosmological, Gaian, spiritual, holistic and participatory worldviews'	Worthwhile purpose 'flourishing of human and more-than-human communities'
Participation, power and democracy 'bringing equality and participation together'	Action-in-Knowledge and Knowledge-in-Action 'knowledge is power'	Extended ways of knowing 'experiential, presentational, propositional and practical ways of knowing'

Figure 4.1: Create your own tools for learning and inquiry with the Action Research Tool Kit. (Source: adapted from Reason & Bradbury, 2001; Marshall 2016)

Reflection as a daily practice

Finding the time to reflect is essential to action research. From the meta level of planetary and human systems to the micro level of our daily lives, a multitude of issues require our attention. We all live very busy lives. It is not that we intend to cause the destruction of our planet and more-than-human systems. Rather, these bigger issues are crowded out by the immediate, the local and the dominant world view. As we prepare for a journey towards a new, happier future, we must be kind to ourselves and understand the pressures we are under. When I once asked a sympathetic fellow traveller why we are not doing more for the environment, he replied, "life happens and the roof is leaking."

As far back as Ancient Greece, reflection has been considered an important aspect of life. Indeed, the Oracle at Delphi reminds the visitor to "Know Thyself". This is a message central to all faith traditions, a major strand within the social sciences and an important theme within this inquiry. We can distinguish between many different strands of reflection. Here, I highlight those that will be useful on the journey ahead. Schön (1983) identified two reflective qualities of experienced professionals – reflection-on-action and reflection-in-action. The former refers to reflection on actions or events that have occurred in the past. Reflection-in-action, however, occurs in the moment, while we are carrying out the action. Schön argued that the skill of reflecting-in-action is very important, using intuition, our creative senses and making technical judgements to create space for questioning, uncertainty and doubt and, thus, change direction or approach. Reflection-in-action can change the present while reflection-on-action can change the future.

Self-reflection enables us to think about ourselves and who we are and, as enquirers, to reflect on our motivations, our privilege and our expected outcomes. By reflecting on ourselves, we can identify 'upstream' issues that might affect our practice. Torbert (2001) identified challenges that we need to reflect on, such as psychodynamic issues that might stem from childhood or experiences of abuse, and awareness of archetypal patterns, such as the influence of key societal myths and awareness of unconscious racist or sexist bias. Throughout the book, I include the insights of a range of writers on ways to reflect on such challenges.-

When we undertake self-reflection, we identify the particular perspectives through which we carry out our research. Shulamit Reinharz

(2010) argues that we bring three selves to our research – the self who adopts particular research methods and values, the self created by our individual upbringing and society and the self who arises from our particular personal circumstances.

Reflexivity refers to reflection on the self and the development of awareness of one's motives, assumptions, and ways of acting in the world (Allen, 2017; Vu & Burton, 2019). Lather (1991:150) calls for "a kind of self-reflexivity that will enable us to look closely at our own practices in terms of how we contribute to dominance in spite of our liberatory intentions." For example, we might reduce our meat consumption or become vegetarian but not investigate the damage caused by the production of palm oil or soy beans. We might feel good about recycling our plastic bottles but not investigate what happens to them once they are in the recycling bin or consider how to reduce our plastic use.

A further stage in the reflection process is critical reflection. In contrast to simple reflection as an element of problem solving, Reynolds (1998) argues that critical reflection leads to emancipatory learning, and asks questions about power, social inclusion, diversity, participation and democracy.

Reflection must be active, rather than passive, and, through it, we must actively engage in creating reality. In other words, we must consider our own subjectivity and how we act in the world (Taylor et al., 2015). Furthermore, we are not simply individuals acting alone in the world. We constantly relate to others in what Ann Cunliffe (2010) calls "an embodied and intersubjective knowing", as we know the world through our own physical bodies and through our relationships with others.

Critical reflection must extend beyond the human to the wider planet and Cosmos (Swimme, 1984). In *The Great Work*, Thomas Berry (1999: 159) sets out the challenges facing humanity:

"The historical mission of our times is to reinvent the human – at the species level, with critical reflection, within the community of life-systems, in a time-development context, by means of story and shared dream experience."

Therefore, in order to reflect we must also be aware of nature, of the history of the planet and the journey of the universe. It is imperative that we learn and practice how to do this.

In my own journey, I have sought to reflect on my 'three selves', as suggested by Reinharz (2010). As a child of the British welfare state, I am educated, relatively free and healthy. I live in a wealthy nation built on a history of colonialism, empire and slavery, which remains rooted in deep inequalities and racism that require continuous work to eradicate (Andrews, 2021; Sanghera, 2021). By adopting a participatory, reflective approach to my own practice I have sought to be open to learning and inquiry. I employ an action research methodology that recognizes the importance of power, as I seek to be aware of and continuously re-educate myself in relation to the imbalance between rich and poor, the empowered and the powerless, arising social justice and ecological issues, and to 'walk the talk' in my life (Gordon, 2007: 139 & 141). I have sought to become and live an awareness of being part of the planet and Cosmos, and to express this within my writing and practice. Such reflection is a regular and ongoing process.

Reflection is a key element of my practice and a key aspect of my teaching. I find the terms 'reflective practice', 'critical reflective practice' and 'cosmologically reflective practice' most useful, as they bring together elements of reflection and subjectivity.

○ Hopeful Companions

Books
Maathai, W. 2006. *Unbowed. One Woman's Story*. London: Arrow Books.

Creativity
Evaristo, B. 2022. They are totally smashing it. Bernadine Evaristo on the artistic triumph of older Black women. The Guardian, 28 April: https://www.theguardian.com/books/2022/apr/28/bernadine-evaristo-on-the-artistic-triumph-of-older-black-women?ref=upstract.com&curator=upstract.com

Resources for Action
Runneymede Trust: The UK's leading independent race equality think tank, challenging race inequality through policy, networking and leading debate: https://www.runnymedetrust.org/

Saad, L. 2020. Do the work: an anti-racist reading list. The Guardian. 3 June: https://www.theguardian.com/books/booksblog/2020/jun/03/do-the-work-an-anti-racist-reading-list-layla-f-saad

---

Creative Learning Exercises

The Hopeful Companion boxes signpost the increasing number of resources that help us think about diversity, inclusion, power and decolonising learning in our lives.

Spend some time gathering resources that will help you to understand your background and your relationship to these issues. This may require a visit to a library, a local bookshop or an online search, springing from the resources that I suggest here. As you find resources, keep them together.

Commit to spending time with the resources you have gathered. Do they prompt you to see yourself or to see learning differently? Record your thoughts.

Explore creative ways to reflect deeply on yourself and your background with regard to issues of power. Can you find music or art that expresses how you feel?

First-, second- and third-person action research and practice

There are three forms of action research. First-person action research involves the researcher thinking reflectively and deeply about his or her own practice, assumptions, values and methods, before, during and after taking action and conducting research. First-person action research can take place in a defined research setting, in the workplace or in daily life. Reason and Torbert (2001a) describe first-person research as "the ability of the researcher to foster an inquiring approach to his or her life, to act awarely and choicefully and to assess effects in the outside world whilst acting."

Fisher et al.'s (2002:17) four territories of experience (visioning, strategising, performing and assessing) help to reflect on behaviour. Figure 4.2 (overleaf) offers an example of first-person action and reflection in practice, through the use of triple loop learning.

First person action research will be explored in greater detail in the next chapter.

Second-person action research involves "speaking-and-listening-with-others" (Torbert 2001: 211) and researching together in mutually supportive and self-reflective ways, with an emphasis on participation. Second person action research normally takes place in face-to-face settings and in small groups, where all are of equal value and the research to be undertaken is

		Single	Double	Triple
Anya imagines a time when annual carbon emissions are falling locally and globally. She feels that systemic changes are needed and not the individual actions she has been co-ordinating so far. She gets agreement from the faith community to join in a campaign for a Green New Deal, which advocates for green jobs, renewable energy and support for refugees. With renewed energy, Anya seeks new volunteers for the Refugee Support Group to fundraise.	Visioning			
Within a few months, the subject of climate change has slipped down the agenda. Anya recognises that the climate emergency is bigger that her faith community and contacts the Council who have declared a Climate Emergency. At the same time, the Refugee Support Group is struggling for funds for the needs of the refugees.	Strategising			↑
All members of the community attend and make individual and group pledges. Anya feels that the carbon literacy training is a success.	Performing		↑	↑
Anya is active in her local faith community in a Refugee Support Group. From her reading she is worried about climate change. Anya gets agreement to organise carbon literacy training for every member of the faith community.	Assessing	↑	↑	↑
Inquiry loops		Single	Double	Triple

Figure 4.2: A worked example of single, double and triple loop inquiry across the four territories of experience. The table reads from the bottom up, but in practice you can cycle between the stages in any order.
(Source: adapted from Fisher et al., 2002)

jointly agreed. The inquiry often involves creative and non-hierarchical ways of working, aiming to develop trust between participants and deeper forms of understanding. I explore second person action research in chapter 7.

Third-person action research aims to "create a wider community of inquiry" (Reason & Bradbury, 2008: 6). It attempts "to create conditions which awaken and support the inquiring qualities of first- and second-person research/practice in a wider community" (Reason & Torbert, 2001: 15). Gustaven (2003) argues that the region is an appropriate geographical scale for third-person action research, and may involve the joining up or collaboration of a range of smaller projects, creating a systemic approach. Third-person research also takes place when practitioners widely disseminate their research findings via publications, presentations, social media and other media.

Certain qualities of third-person action research differentiate it from simply organising meetings or online events on a larger scale. It is concerned with involving all participants in the entire system, rather than only one part. For example, in a community setting, third-person research will include public sector officers, local residents, community groups and local councillors. Relationship-building is crucial and signals the difference between one-off events and longer-term collaboration. Third-person action research seeks to generate as many ideas as possible from all participants to encourage deeper learning (Marten, 2008). Increasingly, action researchers are engaging with wider audiences through writing and the use of a wide variety of media (Embury, 2015).

Torbert and Reason (2001) argue that the best research seeks to contain qualities of all three forms of action research. As part of larger social movements for change, we are all part of third-person inquiry (Marshall et al., 2011). Action inquiry is a revolutionary process (Fisher et al., 2002: 39), as it opens up "the possibility of transformation... [through reflective processes which allow for] shifting one's thought and action from a pattern where underlying assumptions go unrecognised and unchallenged" to patterns that challenge the status quo and accepted paradigms. Marshall (2008) argues that "being reflective is a radical act" and there is evidence for this in the outcomes of the Bath University Masters in Responsible Business Practice (Marshall et al., 2011) and in Riddiford's (2021) account of using action research to work with young people at the Global Generation Project in London.

In my own practice, I seek to engage with all three forms of action inquiry. My thirty-year journaling practice is a process of first-person action research; engaging in co-operative inquiry projects with colleagues is a practice of second-person action research; and my participation in online action research, community development and faith spirituality networks is an engagement with third person action research.

Emergent developmental form

Action research takes an emergent, developmental form, which characterises what it looks like, and the processes and methods it encompasses.

Ecological systems, for example, are continuously being born, growing, bearing fruit and dying (Capra, 1996). In his philosophical explorations of cybernetics and, later, ecology, Gregory Bateson (1972) suggested that nature never follows a linear path, but instead grows in an emergent manner. If we want to live in harmony with the ecology of the Earth, Bateson suggested we must abandon linear thought processes. Action research helps us to do this, through a variety of ways of knowing, acknowledgement of spirit and reflection *in* and *on* action (Reason & Canney, 2015). By tracing the emergence of galaxies within the Cosmos or life on planet Earth from 4.5 billion years ago to the present, we see the emergence of patterns within existing systems with new features and qualities that could not have been predicted. Action research techniques allow us to observe and follow such emergence, and the action research process itself allows new elements to emerge.

If the world is emergent, then action research is an appropriate methodology for mirroring and following that emergence.

Emergence can be understood through practices within the action research family of methods. In appreciative inquiry, the *questions* explored at the start give shape to the inquiry that follows. The community-based inquiry described in Chapter 3 started with the facilitator asking people to tell stories of "what gives life" to their streets and their neighbourhoods. From those stories, participants shared stories of the things that worked in the places they come from. Each story was specific to its own time and place. From that sharing emerged the next stages of the appreciative inquiry process (Mulhern & Emmanuel, 2010).

Although the methods for emergence are laid out beforehand, the results of the inquiry are never certain. At the beginning of an inquiry, it is impossible to tell what will be foregrounded, as this will emerge through the process (Marshall, 2004). As I developed my own first-person practices, I encountered many instances of emergence. One of these was journaling, which emerged as a first-person practice of inquiry into my life as I progressed to seek patterns in the journals and incorporated the use of visual materials. My experience working in my local community has been similar, with the outcomes of actions sometimes not evident until years later, such as the

Imagine Rusholme! summits of 2012 that resulted in the *Creative Rusholme* workstream and the creation of a book, *Stories of a Manchester Street*, in 2019.[45]

Cycles of action and reflection

Common to all action research is its cyclical nature, consisting of phases of action and reflection. Kolb (1984) describes the iterative processes of concrete experience, reflective observation, abstract conceptualisation and active experimentation. Critics argue that this cycle omits a host of important characteristics, including the person, emotional learning and the embodied nature of learning (Jarvis, 2006: 10). Nevertheless, the concept has been widely developed and Heron has integrated extended ways of knowing into this cyclical process (2006: 251).

A human-centred view of cycles of action and reflection might limit the period of time dedicated to the work. However, by expanding outwards to the scale of the planet and Cosmos, cycles of action and reflection become far longer. As we seek to create a sustainable planet, we learn from the nations of the Haudenosaunee Confederacy to think seven generations into the future, the Seventh Generation principle.[46] Unless we curb greenhouse gases now, the cycle of time to repair the planet will extend into hundreds and even thousands of years, way beyond the life span of any human civilisation to date (Stager, 2011).

To engage with this characteristic of action research, I started a cycle of action and reflection which involved collecting newspaper cuttings of biodiversity loss, which, through emergence, has lasted twenty years. In the time of the COVID-19 lockdown, I sought to spiritually enter into the cycles of the Cosmos, not to feel insignificant but, rather, to feel part of the whole.

Emerging paradigms

In Susan Jeffers' nine boxes of life visualization (which I will explore further in Chapter 6), spirit or a higher power is at the centre. Similarly, emerging paradigms or cosmologies are at the heart of action research. Each one of us must establish our own emerging paradigm, helping us to do that is one of the central aims of this book.

Human and ecological flourishing: Developing worthwhile purposes

A key distinguishing characteristic of action research is that it aims to create a flourishing world for humans and for the ecology of the entire planet.

From a traditional or positivist research perspective, a "values free" (Marshall & Reason, 2003) and objective approach to research is seen as methodologically advantageous. In action research, however, values are explicit and directed towards human and more-than-human wellbeing. For example, Gloria Gordon (2001) used first-person action research methods to explore her "life-world" experience as a "'Black British' woman of African-Caribbean descent" (2001: 314). Exploring the concept of bicultural competence, Gordon came to see how first-person inquiry could be used as a method to understand society's silence around racism and to grow in her own self-renewal. Engaging in cycles of action and reflection enabled Gordon to create links between action research and the 'Black' liberation movement in the African Diaspora (p. 315). Reed and Frisby (2008) have sought to integrate feminist research, participatory action research and action research into a Feminist Participatory Action Research Practice. They argue that guiding questions must start with "establishing issues of central concern to girls and women and how are they tied to their everyday experiences." In my own community and my exploration of appreciative practice, I was attracted to action research because it does not use a problem-solving approach, but rather "focuses on asking the unconditional positive question to ignite transformative dialogue and action within the human system" (Ludema et al., 2001). I witnessed the power of the positive question to make ripples of change through time.

An awareness of the explicit connections between human and ecological flourishing provides a powerful framework for the aims of action research.

Grounding action research in practice is evident in the work of early pioneers, such as Fals-Borda, who sought to find ways to enable communities in Colombia to research their own histories and present-day challenges and, in the process, gain a sense of agency over their futures (Rappaport, 2021). In my own work, I seek to contribute to the flourishing of human society that incorporates the ecological communities to which I belong (see Chapter 7).

Participation, power and democracy

Although we in the United Kingdom live in a democracy, the principle of community participation or community research is often not supported by those in power, such as organisations, businesses, local governments and universities (Gilchrist, 2004; Chanan & Miller, 2013; Tam, 2021). Individuals or communities that challenge power inequalities often experience a strong push back from those in authority, necessitating steadfast resistance (Ledwith, 2020). However, participation is central to action research.

In order to improve participation, the opposing tensions of autonomy, collaboration and hierarchy must be balanced (Heron, 2006). A challenge for the researcher is understanding and remaining aware of these three forms of authority throughout the research process. Action research is often used in the context of community development, where community participation is central (DCLG, 2006; Harley & Scandrett, 2019). Freire (2004) called for "co-investigation" rather than the more traditional roles of researcher and researched. Participatory action research can help us work with opposing views, and Kemmis (2001) argues that it is necessary to create spaces for discussion that can accommodate difference.

A key element of participation and democracy in action research is the awareness of power. Power relates to how communities and individuals participate in society and which forms of democracy (if any) are open to them. Power is even more crucial in relation to the more-than-human world as, at present, all power is seen to reside with humans. Lukes (2005) has analysed four dimensions of power to understand how power structures are held in place, often against the seeming interests of those involved: (1) *decision making* or *direct power*, when an individual or organisation holds power and can exercise it over others as an agreed and visible form, such as in the relationship between the local state and democratically run community groups (ibid, 19); (2) *indirect power*, in which concepts, knowledge or actions are removed from open decision-making processes. This often reflects the limited power of some groups in society (ibid, 24-25); (3) *hidden power*, in which society is organised so that people are unaware of power being exercised over them. Power, in this sense, can be exercised through meanings, stories, assumptions and norms, thus preventing people from recognising their own interests; and (4) *power of the system*, which is exercised through what Foucault (1979) called the *"multiplicity of force relations"*, often in the form of self-policing.

In any inquiry, these forms of power must be identified and made visible to participants. Such forms of power include the hidden power of advertising that encourages individuals to consume, the power of a system that promotes cheap air travel and makes train travel expensive, or the power of the oil industry to fail to acknowledge the devastating effects of its products.

However, it is also important to bear in mind that there are also positive aspects of power, such as power *from within* and power *with*, rather than simply power *over* (Haugaard, 2012; Gaventa & Cornwall, 2015). In addition, multiple forms of power can exist simultaneously. As Crenshaw (1991) demonstrates, intersectionality reveals how different forms of power interact. For example, scholar and teacher Ibram X. Kendi explores how a feminist and anti-racist analysis reveals where race, gender, class, poverty, sexuality and ethnicity intersect (Kendi, 2019). Intersectionality is a critical aspect of action research. The concept offers ways to re-imagine the future through emphasising continuous engagement with the interrelated effects of different forms of power.

In recent decades, many gender-, class-, ethnicity- and sexuality-related sources of discrimination and power have been named and challenged (Lincoln et al., 2011). Community development uncovers power dynamics between different groups and works to reduce discrimination through practical understanding and collective action (Gilchrist, 2004; Packham, 2008; Ledwith, 2020). Examples of such work include the UK 2009-2011 North West Together We Can Awards and campaigns that involved the participation of local people to secure a living wage and to secure community land trusts.[47] Awareness of different forms of power is crucial to the development of participation, democracy and tackling inequality, and is central to the work of action research that, in the words of the UN SDGs, "leaves no-one behind".

Power will be a constant theme of our journey, demonstrated through the power of humans over the more-than-human world and through the social justice challenges that communities and nations face (Boff, 1995; UN HDR, 2011 & 2019). In the Western tradition, the more-than-human world has no rights. This has led to the creation of the concept of wild law and the Earth Charter, among others, and campaigns for an Ecocide Law (Cullinan, 2002; Higgins, 2012). There are now the first hints of personhood and rights being granted to the more-than-human. The Whanganui River in New Zealand and the River Atrato in Columbia have been granted legal personhood (Benöhr & Lynch, 2018), Spain and other countries have granted personhood to all five great ape species, and Germany has guaranteed animal rights in its constitution.

O Hopeful Companions

Organisations
European Appreciative Inquiry (AI) Network: A European wide network for a better world using AI: https://www.appreciativeinquiry.eu/

Earth Conversations: Free online workshops on action research alongside visionary speakers on sustainability: https://sustainabilitypractitioners.org/category/earth-conversations/

Educational Action Research Group Ireland: http://www.eari.ie/neari-network-for-educational-action-research-in-ireland/

Knowledge-in-action: Knowledge within practice and practice within knowledge

Action research is emancipatory (Reason & Bradbury, 2001). An important element of emancipation, according to Freire (2004), is critical consciousness, or having the ability to intervene in one's own reality in order to change it.

In action research, the production of "practical knowledge which is useful to people in the everyday conduct of their lives" (Reason & Bradbury, 2001: 2) is essential.

This is exemplified in the work of action researchers and emancipatory movements around the world. From his origins as a teacher of literacy in Brazil, Paulo Freire (1979) sought to help the oppressed to liberate themselves and their oppressors through his methodology of *critical consciousness*. He developed methods to teach literacy through the creation of texts that helped students to understand their position in society and the injustices they faced, thus assisting them to become researchers in their own right.

This book is an example of knowledge in action and action in knowledge. It was inspired by Alan Shepard, a farmer-turned-librarian and founder of GreenSpirit books. In the 1990s and 2000s, through the simple practice of displaying books at conferences, he spread the ideas of Thomas Berry and others within the green spiritual movement in the UK.[48] In my own community development and regeneration work, I have sought to combine knowledge and action to work with people in local communities, with council officers, with front-line staff and with interdisciplinary professionals. One example of this in practice is the Living Archive for Community Resilience, located in Manchester Central Libraries, which shares pioneering local government practices to tackle inequalities more widely.[49]

Extended ways of knowing

The challenge of action research is that it can, at first, seem too much to understand. But it is based on an extended epistemology, suggesting not one, but many, way of knowing. As Reason and Bradbury (2001: 9) write, "we draw on diverse forms of knowing as we encounter and act in our world." Heron (1996) suggests that there are four ways of knowing, which combine to create a systemic whole.

Experiential knowing is the knowing of living, of experiencing daily life. It is akin to what Belenky et al. (1986) describe as "women's ways of knowing". Second wave feminists argued that the personal is political and that the life knowledge of women is crucial and important (Griffin, 1984). The importance of experiential knowledge is an underlying theme of this journey, in relation to how we conduct ourselves in the world (Leopold, 1946) and the embodied nature of our knowledge of the world emerges into action. In this way, we learn to listen to the voices of the planet speaking to us and we allow other, more-than-human, beings to come into presence with us (Berry, 1988). David Abram reflected on how he came to know the Earth through entering into a relationship with her, rather than studying in an objective manner. He described the experience of observing myriad spiders spinning webs, "I had the distinct impression that I was watching the universe being born, galaxy upon galaxy" (1996: 18), demonstrating how, in the words of Reason and Goodwin (1999), "perception itself it based on relationship."

Presentational knowing uses a wide variety of media, including art, photography, crafts, as well as more traditional media, such as writing as inquiry and journaling. Seeley and Reason (2008) describe presentational knowing as a "sensuous encountering" with the world. It involves suspending judgement and rational thought to allow the body and the imagination to directly know the world. This *"bodying-forth"* inspires and *"in-forms"* our understanding and actions in daily life.

Propositional knowledge is the knowledge more traditionally associated with higher education, think tanks and research institutes. This invaluable form of knowledge is scientific or positivist and only refers to what can be measured or observed. It frequently embodies a division between mind, body and spirit, with the latter either resident outside the world (dualist) or not present in the world at all (materialist). However, within action research, propositional knowledge becomes wider and more holistic, particularly when combined with practical knowing. So, when Greta Thunberg speaks about "following the science" and taking action to end the use of fossil fuel, she is linking propositional knowing about climate change to practical knowledge.

Practical knowledge, incorporating experiential, presentational and propositional knowledge, involves acting in the world. It is, as Heron (1996: 14) writes,

> "The consummation, the fulfilment of the knowledge quest.... It affirms what is intrinsically worthwhile – human's flourishing – by manifesting it in action".

In action research, practical knowing is integrated with the other forms of knowing through cycles of action and reflection.

 Creative Learning Exercises

On nine pieces of differently coloured paper, write out each of the nine characteristics of the Action Research Toolkit (see Figure 4.1).

Make a pattern of how your different characteristics are connected.

In what ways do these nine boxes help you to think about action research?

Identify the characteristics that are most helpful to your work.

Identify how you see issues of diversity, decolonisation and power fitting into these characteristics.

On a large piece of paper, draw what you have learned about action research, creating links between the different parts. Add the nine boxes. Place this poster somewhere visible in your home/office space.

Creativity and action research

Action research practitioners use a variety of methods to encourage and facilitate participative research and learning. Visual images and text are often used to engage participants in the process. During a Diploma in Action Research workshop at Bath University, participants were encouraged to use art and drawing to deepen their understand of action research. What emerged was a large diagram of bullet points, arrows and headings.

Figure 4.3: Flip chart exploring what is action research? From group discussion at the Diploma in Action Research, Bath School of Management, drawn by Chris Seeley, 2008. (Source: Estate of Chris Seeley)

By challenging different labels and through acts of creativity, the workshop participants were able to more clearly visualize action research. Such creativity is an emerging strand of action research, that grows out of extended ways of knowing. Indeed, Seeley argues that action research seeks to make and protect transformational spaces for ourselves, for the systems within which we work and for others to grow and learn. We might see ourselves, as Kaplan puts it, as "artists of the invisible":

> "That which we call 'art' is one way we can break away from the destructive norms of the Industrial Growth Society, and that which we call 'action research' is the research attitude needed for a more sustainable future. Together they make a kind of guide for living with curiosity, respect, meaning and gratitude." (2002:97).

◯ Hopeful Companions

Online and hard copy Handbooks offer helpful learning resources, including previous editions. Initial resources:

Books
Heron, J. 2006. *The Complete Facilitators Handbook.* London: Kogan Page.

Marshall, J., Coleman, C., and Reason, P. 2011. *Leadership for Sustainability*. London: Routledge. The first three chapters provide an accessible introduction to action research.

Bradbury, H. 2015. *Sage Handbook of Action Research*, 3rd edition. London: Sage. Reason, P. and Bradbury, H. edited earlier editions in 2001, 2006 and 2008.

Denzin, N., and Lincoln, Y. (eds.). 2015. *Handbook of Qualitative Research,* 5th edition. Thousand Oaks: Sage.

Zuber-Skerritt, O., and Wood, L. 2019. *Action Learning and Action Research: Genres and Approaches*. Bingley, UK: Emerald Publishing.

Critiques of action research

In keeping with the spirit of the hopeful journey we are undertaking, we must periodically check that we are going in the right direction, and using the right tools. As Marcus Aurelius expressed over two thousand years ago:

"Direct yourself to one thing only, to put yourself in motion and to check yourself at all times."

Action research has been criticised for consisting of individual case studies that are too small to address the global nature of the challenges facing humanity. But understanding the impact of macro global-scale processes at the local scale is very important. Statistics and quantifiable data do not reveal the human and more-than-human stories at the heart of action research.

In addition, small action research projects can be systemically linked to scale up research projects or research can be undertaken across larger areas, for example, a geographical region (Gustaven, 2003; Burns, 2007). As part of this, action researchers can create knowledge sharing networks to share with and learn from each other.[50]

A more damning critique is that action research co-opts individuals into the system and does not challenge existing power structures, thus diminishing the radical nature of this form of research (Cook & Cox, 2005; Gaventa & Cornwall, 2015). However, developing a critical, self-reflective voice is central to action research. When assessing the quality of action research, it is important that researchers ask probing questions about the ideas of power they work with in their practice (Kristiansen & Bloch-Poulsen, 2008; Pedler & Burgoyne, 2008). The visibility of research values is also important, particularly as values such as 'participation' and 'valuing diversity' are difficult to quantify (Podger et al., 2013). Action research must consistently be values-driven and reflective (Vu & Burton, 2019).

A more pervasive critique is that action research has not achieved its potential and gained widespread traction, as its early proponents had envisioned (Raelin, 2009; Dick, 2010). This critique may be linked to the proliferation of different types of action research and the use of overly complicated language (Bradbury, 2015). These issues can be overcome by improving the clarity of the language and methods. There continues to be a steady growth in the use of action research in different fields, including in higher education and in community organisations and workplaces.

A further critique, which is especially relevant during the climate emergency is whether action research methods can demonstrate outcomes and impact. The case studies in this book indicate the growing potential of action research. For me, seeing what action research can do in practice is what makes it such a powerful method.

Quality in action research

It is important to ensure the quality of the research undertaken. Reason and Bradbury (2001) developed a series of questions to guide action researchers, which have been developed and updated in the *Action Research Journal* (2020) to reflect the urgency of the climate emergency and the need to address social injustice (Bradbury et al., 2020). The following are some important guiding questions:

- Is the research to be undertaken worthwhile?
- How will the research be carried out? Will extended or multiple ways of knowing be employed?
- How will the researcher ensure reflexivity regarding themselves and their context?
- What research style will be used and will it consider the participation of all?
- How will the relationships between humans and nature be drawn out?
- What might the nature of the outcomes of the research be?
- Will the outcomes be long term and sustainable?

In my own journey, four quality criteria are important.

Quality as the ethics of action research

Ethics is a key part of all research and, in action research, general research ethics are combined with the characteristics of action research. General research ethics cover principles of not harming research participants, respecting participants' confidentiality and anonymity, ensuring the research does not exploit people, and considering how the data will be stored and used (Eriksson & Kovalainen, 2008). The transformative learning values introduced in Chapter 3 are useful for considering ethical questions related to "power, equality and participation" (Marshall, 2016). Ethical consideration must also be given to the outputs and outcomes of action research as they relate to the overall aims of human and more-than-human flourishing. What ethical concerns of social justice, global justice, racial justice, gender equality, and equality for different sectors of society need to be addressed? In thinking about the need to transform society, action research takes a 'critical view' asking: "for whom, from where, in what specific form, and with what permanency?" (Bradbury et al, 2020). Bryon-Miller et al. (2015) suggest adopting a questioning approach to all aspects of the research, including the research outcomes and the researcher. As researchers, we must think about who we are, our privilege, our values, our ethics and our different identities. Research is not neutral, but rather takes place within the context of different power relations. Based on aspects of our identities, do we have an understanding of the power relationships of which we are a part?

Creating an ethical framework is one way to chart the ethics of the research undertaken (Bryon-Miller et al., 2015). Engaging with the ethics of the research has important implications for the quality of action research.

Quality as multi-layered

Marshall (2011) has called for a dynamic, multi-layered approach to quality that reflects on ourselves as individuals and the situation we are in. Quality is found in relation to systemic thinking, in relation to how human society works, how human society relates to nature and how nature works. Of key importance is being aware and reflective of power issues relating to the self, one's community and the planet. What ethical questions drive us?

Quality as awareness of beauty

Beauty is an important quality criterion of action research (Reason, 2007; Cunliffe, 2010). As Keats wrote, "Beauty is truth, truth beauty. That is all on earth you know and all you need to know." For example, the images in Michael Benson's *Cosmigraphics* (2014) show humanity's efforts to understand and draw the Cosmos and our place within it and to illuminate the wonder around us. Beauty emerges within this research in a number of ways. It fills us with awe and wonder when we look up at the night sky, or at the photographs taken by astronauts or from the Hubble telescope, or from close-ups of lichen, moss and leaves (Kelley, 1988). Beauty can help us to visualise the way ahead. My daughter, for example, drew a map that sought to capture the beauty in the journey ahead (see page 258). Beauty can also be found in the processes of action research. Does the writing, for example, contain beauty, or hint at beauty? Is there beauty in the social processes of working together?

Quality and the more-than-human world

Quality research must consider the more-than-human world. It is important that we ask the following questions of our research. Whose voices are heard? Am I paying attention to the voices of indigenous communities and marginalised communities? How am I, in the words of Abram (1996: 273), "taking up the written word, with all of its potency, and patiently, carefully, writing language back into the land?" Do I take words and help them to take root in the soil and in my soul? Can the methods of participatory action research help us to hear the voices of the more-than-human world?

As I research my conduct and that of others, how can I capture participation in the Cosmos in such a way that I can articulate and explain it (Swimme, 1996)? How can I use first-person research methods to understand being and living in the universe and express the presence of the more-than-human? Following Thomas Berry (1999: 20), I repeatedly ask myself whether I am "participating in a symphony or as renewed presence to some numinous presence manifested in the wonder world around us?" As I stand and experience dusk in my back garden, can I become part of the world around me, see it as sacred and participate in it with other beings?

 Invitation to Reflect

Identify one challenge you face.

Identify a challenge your community faces.

Consider one ecological challenge identified in Chapter 1.

Consider one challenge facing the whole of planet Earth.

Mind map how the characteristics of action research might help you to investigate these challenges.

Notes

[45] For the origins of Creative Rusholme see: https://creativerusholme.c4cp.net/about/

[46] For an exploration of the work, community, and values of the nations of the Haudenosaunee Confederacy see: https://www.haudenosauneeconfederacy.com

[47] Descriptions of community organising in England can be found in Tam et al., 2021. For examples in Scotland see: https://www.scdc.org.uk/who/. International examples include the International Association of Community Development Practice Insight publications and the Community Development Journal: https://www.iacdglobal.org/publications/

[48] For an account of Alan Shepard's contribution, see: https://www.greenspirit.org.uk/alanshephard/

[49] Due to the COVID-19 pandemic, work on cataloguing this collection was delayed and it is intended will commence in the mid-2020s.

[50] Two networks to explore. First, The Action Research Group Ireland's annual international event: ActionResearchColloquium@TUDublin.ie. Second, connect globally through AR+ Helping Sustainable Transformations Happen: https://actionresearchplus.com

Chapter 5: First person inquiry

"In the end we will conserve only what we love; we will love only what we understand; and we will understand only what we are taught."
Baba Dioum (1968)[51]

It is July 2008 and I am on a train heading to the southwest of England and a workshop at the Centre for Action Research in Professional Practice at Bath University. The sun is setting to the west over the Malvern Hills, and the sky is orange. I am reading Thomas Berry's The Great Work, when I get the sense that this is where my work is placed, drawing on the ideas in this magnificent book. As I gaze at the setting sun, at the rolling landscape and the majestic clouds, I understand that all of this is placed within me, within Gaia and within the Cosmos, all at the same time. Thomas Berry's words help me to understand that it is the curvature of space that holds me on the Earth, that holds the Earth within the Solar System and the Solar System within the Cosmos.

It is a mystery of the universe that it is simultaneously open and closed — open so that it can continue to be creative, closed so that it holds together. I open my reflective journal and transcribe some of The Great Work, all the better to remember it:

"Only Earth held a creative balance between the turbulence and the discipline that are necessary for creativity.... The Universe solved its problem by establishing a creative disequilibrium expressed in the curvature of space that was sufficiently closed to establish an abiding order in the universe and sufficiently open to enable the wild creative process to continue" (Berry, 1999: 52).

My personal challenge is to hold onto the glorious infinity of space and Cosmos which surrounds me, the integrated Earth in which I live, and to find the work I can do, held together in this curvature of space.

First-person inquiry

In this chapter, I explore the practices of first-person action research and I encourage you to begin to practice paying attention, journaling and free fall writing. I will explore different contexts for first-person action research and different sources of research material. I will also critique this form of research and consider some of its ethical implications. Some form of first-person action research is essential for the journey to hopeful futures. Therefore, I will provide you with a route map of the journey ahead and encourage you to create your own map.

The inquiry practices described in this chapter arise from my personal experiences of learning first-person action research over the past twenty years. I have learned and experienced many of these practices in small and large learning groups, and I have taught and shared these with others, developing my understanding through iterative cycles of action and reflection.

Living life as inquiry

One of the most expressive phrases to describe first-person action research is 'living life as inquiry'. In the 1980s, Judi Marshall explored the lives of women managers in the workplace and described her first-person practice as "living life as inquiry" (1999) and "inquiry as life process" (2001). Living life as inquiry offers us a route map for our journey to hopeful futures. It suggests that everything is open to investigation, exploration and questioning, and not just the research that takes place in academic or work contexts. This means accepting that we cannot know everything, we cannot know the outcomes of our actions, and our beliefs are open to questioning and critique. It suggests being tentative about the approaches we take, not always being certain, and seeking to be open and to question on a daily basis. Marshall (1999: 156) writes, "By living life as inquiry, I mean a range of beliefs, strategies and ways of behaving which encourage me to treat little as fixed, finished or clear-cut." Marshall (2016) explores the principles and practices of living life as inquiry, and with Gearty, reflects on how the concept had gained traction in practice, research and teaching over the past twenty years (Gearty & Marshall, 2021).

Living life as inquiry encourages us to live values-based lives. It is not always possible to steer to our values but, by living thus, we can notice the world around us, enabling us to get back on course. Perhaps we want to be less driven by consumerism, but it is hard not to be influenced by advertising. Perhaps we want to show our support for refugees, but are uncertain how to start. By living life as inquiry, we can continually question our motivations and correct ourselves. It helps to appreciate that there are multiple worldviews, and that ours is neither the only nor the best one. Living life as inquiry allows us to live as we are, while seeking a better world. Marshall (1999: 157) describes her own process thus, "I seek to live with integrity, believing in multiple perspectives rather than one truth, holding visions of a more equal world."

Self-reflective inquiry practices

There are a range of self-reflective inquiry practices, that Marshall (2001) refers to as "attentional disciplines," through which she seeks to deepen her inquiry. We will each have a distinctive inquiry approach that cannot be copied or cloned; however, we can use Marshall's disciplines as guidelines for our own journey. The things we pay attention to vary over time and the skills required to pay attention are developed over years. We might pay attention to what we are doing, how we are participating with other human beings and how we, individually or in groups, interact with the more-than-human world around us.

The first attentional discipline is developing cycles of action and reflection. Marshall refers to these cycles as framing processes that in her own life, took place over a period of a few days at a management conference (2001) or over a few years as she assisted her mother in her care home (2016). Inquiry became a dynamic process of being alert to what was internal to herself and to what was happening in the world around her. When we simultaneously think about "inner and outer arcs of attention" (2001: 433), we reflect on our thoughts in the present moment, while paying attention to what is going on around us or participating in tasks to be completed. This requires us to be attentive and in the moment. For example, often, while we outwardly appear to be paying attention, internally we are thinking about work, or friends, or what we will do at the weekend.

The second discipline is noticing when we are actively participating in the world, and when we are being receptive to what is going on. Marshall chose to capture these experiences by writing them down. Other ways to capture and reflect on lived experiences and living life as inquiry are through painting, drawing, music or other forms of creativity.

When incorporated into first-person practice, cycles of action and reflection are the simplest way to remain on the journey of inquiry. When combined with other action research characteristics, they become powerful tools for inquiry. I learned to combine cycles of action and reflection, living life as inquiry and writing as inquiry, and I repeated this research process for each of the main cycles that I undertook on my journey. Mindful of the emergent nature of action research, I reflected on each part of each parallel cycle, and a number of smaller cycles emerged. These generated further data and were incorporated into the process.

After researching the threat of extinction faced by so many species, I sought to understand how we could change the world and I felt that the forces against us were very powerful. However, I remembered my early involvement in the women's movement and my work as a women's officer in a local authority. This led me to research how women had successfully challenged patriarchy, racism, poverty, homophobia and ablism and had won resources to address these inequalities in public policy and services such as local government, employment, health and education. Through this research I realised that a similar society-wide movement could, at the local scale, tackle biodiversity loss, climate change and social injustice.[52]

'Learning edges' as first-person inquiry practices

When developing cycles of action and reflection, it is important to try to understand where you are at each point in the learning journey. This involves identifying your 'learning edges', or the focal points for our learning as you go along. Such a practice means that, at each stage of the learning journey, the focus is as much on 'what do I want to learn at this point?' as it is on the ultimate research objective. As I journeyed into my hopeful future, I found that at different 'focus points' (in the journey analogy, perhaps best described as 'signposts'), I needed to learn more about particular subjects. For example, at one point I needed to understand the meaning of 'parts per million CO_2' and why over 350ppm threatens the oceans with acidification. Another time, I wanted to know how I could enter into a new way of seeing the world, of living a new paradigm in my daily life. I had reached a learning edge in my inquiry and it followed a new route from the focus point incorporated into the major research cycles.

Interrupting daily habits

Many first-person practices can be developed to interrupt habitual daily patterns, such as, for example, an 'impromptu holiday' at work or at home. This goal-free period allows you to simply notice what is going on around you. It could be as simple as taking the time to make a coffee, walking out to buy a sandwich, talking to a colleague or pausing to reflect (see Fisher et al., 2002 for ideas). Berners-Lee and Clarke (2013) argue that we need such a process of 'waking up' to become aware of the climate emergency. A more internal practice is to use double loop inquiry to examine a challenge at work or at home (see Figure 4.2).

Meanwhile, a more reflective approach is to participate in meditative practices, such as Tai Chi or gestalt awareness. These practices might become part of a daily routine or part of a practice at work. For example, as part of the postgraduate programme at the Centre for Professional Practice, students were encouraged to attend a week-long silent Buddhist retreat in the Welsh countryside and to engage in reflection with themselves and with nature.

Cosmology and first-person inquiry practice

There are some situations in which reflective first-person practice is clearly problematic. For the purposes of this journey, the most relevant of these is the Cosmos itself. To date, twenty-four people have journeyed into lunar orbit, twelve have walked on the Moon and six hundred and one have been into space. Of these, only 65 have been women.[53] As far as I am aware, none of those who have so far travelled beyond Earth's atmosphere have been students of action research. However, it is clear from reading their accounts that travelling to space and seeing the Earth in its entirety has led to deep reflection. Kalpana Chawla (in Jackson, 2017: 96) reflected from the Space Shuttle,

> "When you look at the stars and the galaxy, you feel that you are not just from any particular piece of land, but from the solar system."

For some, the experience is so transformational that it leads to the re-examination of personal perspectives and the place of humanity in the Cosmos; in effect, these astronauts engage in first-person inquiry, even if they don't name it as such. During a leadership talk in 1972, Rusty Schweickart, who flew on Apollo 9 and was the first human to undertake a spacewalk, said that the voices of the astronauts belong to all of humanity (in Senge, 1990: 370):

> "And you realise that that perspective…that you've changed, that there's something new there. That relationship is no longer what it was…. Because now you're no longer inside something with a window looking out at the picture, but now you're out there and what you've got around your head is a goldfish bowl and there are no boundaries. There are no frames, no boundaries."

Nearly 50 years later, astronaut Leland Melvin (2018:63) reflected on how being in space changed his perspective.

> "I saw the planet for the first time without borders. I thought about all the places on Earth where there is unrest and war and here we were flying above all that working together as one team to help advance our civilization. That was an incredible, incredible moment for me."

This is not a change of perspective that I, or most of you reading this, will ever experience. However, I can take the written and spoken reflections of those who have travelled to space and incorporate them into my first-person practice. Those privileged individuals are, as Schweickart called it, "my eyes and ears" onto the space beyond Earth, allowing me to reflect on my place in the Cosmos.

Creative Learning Exercises

Delve into the idea of living life as inquiry. Think about how practices of self-reflective inquiry might apply to your life. The following are some creative ways to help you do this:

Draw in your journal what living life as inquiry means to you.

Outline some practices you might use to undertake first-person inquiry.

Take a short break and go outside. Simply walk for a few minutes without consciously deciding where you are going. Reflect on how this makes you feel.

Imagine always living with uncertainty and always questioning. Reflect on how this makes you feel.

Think of a situation in your life when first-person inquiry might be helpful. Sketch out potential inquiry steps.

Imagine being an astronaut and looking down on the Earth from space. Draw what you see.

Writing as inquiry

First-person inquiry practices take many forms. Writing as inquiry "provides a research practice through which we can investigate how we construct the world, ourselves and others" (Richardson, 2000: 924).

Richardson explores the many forms of writing that can contribute to inquiry in diverse ways, creating a starting point for the journey into hopeful futures. She draws attention to what she calls evocative writing, which helps us to understand the world through the written word and through our bodies, as it is through the latter that we experience the world.

Many forms of writing can be used in first-person inquiry. Each offers a different level of reflection and none should be considered superior to any other. Using these, it is possible to simultaneously work with different levels of reflection.

Free fall writing

Starting to write and maintaining that practice is not always easy. Free fall writing (Turner-Vesselago, 2013) is a way to get started. It involves writing whatever comes to mind for a period of time without self-censorship or judgement. It can be a fruitful inquiry method, allowing your writing to flow without conscious editing or stopping. Natalie Goldberg (1986) describes the process as "writing down the bones". The "art of free fall", according to Turner-Vesselago (2013) is the production of writing that enables deeper themes to emerge by paying close attention to daily circumstances.

A helpful way to get started is to use writing prompts, choosing those that most speak to you. By using prompts, you can quickly get beyond the self-censorship that our propositional brains so frequently impose. Another helpful technique is to set a timeframe in which to write. If you find the prospect of writing daunting, this could be for as little as one or five minutes, or it could be more, if that works for you. Over time, you might find that you want to write for longer. Simply set a timer and write what you can, uncensored, during that time. You can then adapt these techniques to develop your own unique style.

Starting the journey with free fall writing

Free fall writing can become a journey into many different worlds. Students are encouraged to practice free fall writing to develop their writing skills for higher education. The method can help you get started on a writing assignment, to get thoughts flowing (see Murray, 2013). Free fall writing can be used in workshops to change the emotional mood of a room, or to enable participants to access deeper parts of themselves, if they so desire. It can also take us into deeper honesty and truth. I will return to these themes at the end of the chapter.

 Creative Learning Exercises

Simply start writing. Take a pen and notebook. I advise against using a laptop, unless it is completely necessary. Without self-censorship, answer some or all of the following questions. These will help you to begin the practice of free fall writing. You can use these questions as a model to answer other questions that are important to you.

When I think of a sound from my childhood that made me happy, I think of....

When I look out of my window today, I can see....

> When I imagine what needs to be done to create a fairer world, I think the first steps are....
>
> When I think of the spiritual qualities needed to create a fairer world, I think....

Writing and stories as first-person inquiry

Another writing practice is the creation of short stories as a form of inquiry. In this sense, 'story' refers to both fiction and non-fiction. Stories, both those we invent and those that emerge from real events, resonate in being shared with others, in teaching and in workshops. Think about how you might transform a real-life event into a story. In *Animate Earth,* Stephan Harding (2006) offers some evocative examples, using stories to trace the emergence of a new paradigm out of historical events, such as the story of Aldo Leopold and the wolves and that of James Lovelock's friend William Golding coming up with the name Gaia.

Storytelling can become a means of inquiry into practice and a way of finding the 'mountain behind the mountain' (Raine, 1981). When Fr. Noel O'Donoghue sought to explain how one can find the spirit of a mountain, he realised that one first needs to know the place in a physical sense; one needs to understand that it is a place of peat and streams, of sheep and wild deer, of dragonflies and heather. Only with this understanding can one begin to understand that the mountain is also "a place of Presence and a place of presences" (O'Donoghue, 1993: 30). In my own life, to try to understand living in a new paradigm, I took the simple experience of being at work and completing the targets established by the workplace, such as teaching students at set hours while, at the same time, holding in my mind the belief that I was trying to live in the Cosmos, to understand that if our atmosphere warms by more than 3°C, the effects on the planet will be on a cosmological timescale (see Chapter 12).

One story method is to use the primary data of experiential knowing, "sensuous encountering", as Seeley and Reason (2008) call it, to explore which elements can be transformed into story as a way to give the encounter substance, "bodying forth", as it were, to share with others. I recall sitting next to a rock pool, and noticing the intricate beauty of a sea anemone waving in the water, tiny creatures scuttling across the lichen-covered rock pool floor and tiny fish darting here and there. When I lifted my head, I saw the shadows of the mountains of the Dingle Peninsula, and the clouds playing across them. Later, I sought to shape this experience through the story of Leopold and the wolves, to give meaning to this encounter and to see it as an example of sitting like a mountain, conscious of the rock pool's uniqueness, of which the sea and the mountains approved. Working through these ideas in my journal writing, I became aware of how stories and scientific discourse create reality in different ways (Bruner, 1968). The purpose of the story was to see the world from a cosmological, rather than human-centred, life span. First-person inquiry helps to make the creation of new stories a democratic and participatory process. We can each learn to tell stories of what a socially and ecologically just future will look like and share these stories with the world to replace the neoliberal stories that currently fill our airwaves and social media.[54] Stories – fiction, non-fiction or a hybrid of the two – make use of one of the characteristics of action research – extended ways of knowing.

Forms of inquiry
Autoethnography

Tony Adams (2008) uses the term 'narrative' "to describe the life writing-related genres of auto-ethnography, auto-performance, autobiography, personal narrative, memoir, and so on." Ethnography is an approach that sets out to understand people's experiences by taking a long-term approach and studying their lives in context. In this way, individual lives are placed within wider socio-political and cultural frames.

Autoethnography is a qualitative research method based on first person inquiry that arises out of ethnography. Ellis and Bochner (2000: 739) describe autoethnography as

> "An autobiographical genre of writing and research that displays multiple layers of consciousness, connecting the personal to the cultural."

According to Muncey (2010), autoethnography should "attempt to subvert" dominant discourses and, thus, address the power relationships involved in encounters. Different forms of writing can help in the understanding of individual experience.

○ **Hopeful Companions**

Starter resources for first person inquiry.

Books
Goldberg, N. 1986. *Writing Down the Bones.* Boston. MA: Shambala.

Melvin, L. 2018. *Chasing Space: An Astronaut's Story of Grit, Grace and Second Chances.* London: Harper Collins.

Muncey. T. 2010. *Creating Autoethnographies.* London: Sage.

Articles
Gearty, M. and Marshall, J. 2021. Living life as inquiry: A systemic practice for change agents. Systemic Practice and Action Research. 4: 441–462, https://doi.org/10.1007/s11213-020-09539-4 And: https://www.jmarshall.org.uk

Frankham, J. and Edwards-Kerr, D. 2009. Beyond 'technologies' of knowing in case study work with permanently excluded young people. *International Journal of Inclusive Education*, 13: 4, 409-422 DOI: 10.1080/13603110802242108

Journaling: A physical and embodied practice

The principal form of my inquiry practice writing is journaling. It is a simple practice that does not require expensive resources or tools. All you need is a notebook and a pen, and a place and time to write.

Journaling is a physical and embodied practice that I have undertaken for many years. At 5.30am on 1 December 1987, I got out of bed, picked up a pen and a small green notebook barely larger than my hand, sat down and started to write. More than 30 years later, I have filled more than 100 journals.

At the beginning, there was no sense of it being something special. I simply started to write. And I kept on writing. Thirty years on, the journal is different, but everything else is the same. I still write with a pen, filling in blank pages. I write in different places. Wherever I can. I used to write at home. Then I liked to write in coffee shops, and always sought out different coffee shops when I was in a new city. I remember once writing on the third floor of the Harvard University Coop bookshop, next to the ecology, climate change, animals and environment section. I had gone there to look at the books and also to write alongside those books in their existential space.

During the COVID-19 pandemic, I once again started writing at home, only to shift again as society opened up.

The notebooks I use have varied in size over the years, from small notebooks at the start, to large A4 ring-bound eco-journals, which took longer to fill and often contained visual records as well. Now I am back to using smaller journals because they are less heavy to carry. In the beginning, I used black and blue pens but, over time, started to use more colour. Some pages are filled with colours and drawing, others are filled with text. At present, I enjoy writing with a Lamy ink pen, filling the pen from an ink bottle, careful not to stain my fingers. I keep an eraser and a pencil sharpener in a tin with my pens.

The final ingredient to writing is finding the time. Some people write morning pages (Cameron, 1995) attempting to write even a few lines every morning. I take a more emergent approach, seeking to write at different times in the day, when time allows.

The physical act of journaling involves ongoing cycles of action and reflection, both for each daily entry and for each completed journal.

By their very nature, the beginnings, middles and endings of journals are a process of inquiry for the writer. By completing a journal, a certain period of one's life has come to a close. There is an end point. By starting a new journal, a new period begins, with a fresh clean page and every other page still clear and blank. Their physical presence invites the writer to see that life begins again, with new possibilities. Life begins anew. These cycles continue with each new journal.

The physical nature of journals encourages reflection. They do not allow you to lie. You cannot unwrite what you have written. Even if you cross words out, the marks remain on the page. The physicality of a journal pulls you into honesty and reflection.

Patterns and inquiry

For many years, I simply wrote in my journals. When I began a Master's degree at Bath University, I discovered there was a name for what I was doing: first-person inquiry practice. When it came to writing my dissertation, I realised that I had a great source of data – fifteen years' worth of journaling.

There are many ways to use the materials you record in your journals. Even if you only write intermittingly over a period of months, going back and reading over what you have written can be powerful. One inquiry process is to identify the types of writing you use in your journals. I discovered that I had used many different forms of writing, without giving names to them. I commonly engaged in free fall writing, and drew pictures, diagrams and shapes. In the next chapter, I will explore the process of taking notes while re-reading journals to try to find patterns and themes.

Seeking and finding patterns may provide insight into your state of mind. You may find that you are unhappy or depressed, or are becoming addicted to an unhealthy behaviour or relationship. Re-reading a journal and finding those patterns may be the trigger to affect change. Or you may be on a journey of inquiry into hopeful futures and wish to understand what you are doing.

Reading journal entries can uncover changes that are taking place beyond conscious awareness. Poet John O'Donohue (2007: 32) writes,

"In the out-of-the-way places of the heart,
Where your thoughts never think to wander,
This beginning has been quietly forming,
Waiting until you were ready to emerge."

Writing as a journey to spirit

If faithfully maintained, journaling can become a way of understanding the challenges in our lives. Over time, this can become a source for the development of a reflective and inner spiritual life. Writing regularly can become a way of connecting with spirit (England, 1991). MacDonald (1984: 136) writes,

"When I first began to journal, I felt self-conscious.... But slowly my reluctances lost their hold on me and I found myself recording in the journal, more and more, the thoughts that flooded my inner spirit."

However, such an outcome of writing practice cannot be willed or made to happen and requires faithful writing or visual practice.

Visual first-person inquiry methods

You may be more comfortable with other forms of creativity, instead of or in addition to writing. Over the years, I have developed an emergent practice of using diagrams and visual exploration. I have also gradually included personal and professional mementos that have become first-person data. Such methods have grown out of explorations of creative visualisation, where practices such as collage and drawing can help us to better visualize our personal futures (Gawain, 1978).

Over the years, I have used methods such as collage, craft models and drawing to explore work progress during professional community development team meetings. I have also developed the use of creative practice in higher education teaching, encouraging students to use drawing and making to reflect on ideas. An example of such work is a visual representation of a sustainable supply chain (Wozniak et al., 2018).

A crossover has now emerged between the personal and the professional in the exploration of life challenges through art and craft approaches. Seeley, for example, traced the development of what she called her own "visual journaling" and used this as a teaching tool (2011). This use of visual sources and artwork develops forms of presentational knowing and creative knowing (Seeley & Reason, 2008; Keremane & McKay, 2011; Bergland & Wirgen-Kristoferson, 2012). Indeed, Botkin et al. (1979) and Raworth (2017) argue that visual images are key to embedding new learning, with the latter citing the example of learning about different forms of sustainable economics through the illustration of ideas. A further development of visual inquiry methods includes the development of alternative mediums, such as knitting, to express inquiry. Neal (2015) explores the use of community art to explore issues of sustainability.

Finding landmarks for our journey: creating different forms of inquiry records

You might ask, "What do I inquire about?" There are many aspects of our lives that are open to different forms of inquiry. I have used a range of different inquiry methods, drawn from my work in the local community, my professional life, a range of academic disciplines, my own spiritual development and reporting on what is happening to the planet. The content of Chapters 1, 2 and 3 might offer questions for the journey ahead. In recording the journey, there are a variety of different ways to draw together your first-person inquiry practices, your writing and your drawing.

Creating multiple inquiry records from writing and reflection

I have recorded writing as inquiry in a number of different ways. I hope my explanations of these will help you to begin to identify your own recording method or methods.

Personal Journals: The personal journals I have kept since 1987 have been particularly important in helping me to track my reflective and spiritual journeys and to envision ideas for creating hopeful futures in our planet and Cosmos out of my management and leadership practices (see Chapter 12).

Field notes: I have hand- and electronically-written observations of situations I have observed or participated in. These usually refer to professional work or research situations.

Embodied observations of time and place: These are short, hand- or electronically-written pieces of writing attuned to embodied place, ecology and Cosmos. I started recording embodied observations in 2001, when I first developed the practice of 'sitting like a mountain' (see Chapter 9).

Visual material: These include illustrations, diagrams and photographs from a variety of sources, stored in journals, folders and drawers.

In addition to these practices, you might be comfortable using social media resources to keep records. For example, certain social media apps allow the sharing of photographs or reflections on the parts of your life that are meaningful to you, and allow for interaction with others. Creating art, and creating and playing music also offer opportunities to express how you feel and can be shared in whatever way you feel comfortable.

Figure 5.1: The United Nations Sustainable Development Goals (SDGs) adopted in 2015. (Source: United Nations, 2022: https://sdgs.un.org/goals)

Inquiry sources

There are many inquiry sources from which to draw ideas. Below are some of the sources I have used. These might inspire your own inquiry and journey into hopeful futures.

Newspapers: Over the years, traditional and online newspapers have been a source of inquiry for me on themes of biodiversity loss, climate change, local and global social justice, science and our universe. These can become very important over time as stories weave together. However, it is important to reflect on a newspaper's editorial stance when considering such stories. This can become an inquiry in itself. The COVID-19 pandemic was a recent illustration of how debates can change rapidly over a short period of time.

NGOs, think tanks, policy institutes: These organisations exist for the purposes of creating a better world. They also offer critiques of businesses and organisations, present more holistic visions of the future, and offer hope.

◯ Hopeful Companions

Organisations
New Economics Foundation, which works to change economics to be for all: https://neweconomics.org/

Ellen MacArthur Foundation: a mission to accelerate the transition to a circular economy: https://www.ellenmacarthurfoundation.org/

Working for social justice in communities: NGOs, trade unions, governments, the United Nations and other institutions and organisations work to serve communities and neighbourhoods, from local to national and global scales. Online resources demonstrate what communities, businesses, councillors and officers can achieve by having adequate resources to work together for social justice.

○ **Hopeful Companions**

Organisations - NGOs
Médicin Sans Frontières: an international medical humanitarian organisation: https://msf.org.uk/who-we-are

Southall Black Sisters: secular and inclusive organisation to meet the needs of Black (Asian and African-Caribbean women) and challenge all gender related violence: https://southallblacksisters.org.uk/about/

Unconditional Basic Income Europe: a network of 20+ countries which campaigns for basic income to be a human right: https://www.ubie.org/

Water Aid: making water, toilets and hygiene normal for everyone, everywhere: https://www.wateraid.org/uk/our-global-strategy

Organisations – International
The United Nations and many sister organisations: https://news.un.org/en/news

United Nations Sustainable Development Goals up to date information: https://unsdg.un.org/latest

Inspirational thinkers: Key figures from faith communities or from social and ecological history can inspire you as you start and progress on your journey. I have already referred to many such individuals in the preceding chapters, or you can find inspiration through online or library searches.

Living life as inquiry and action research: This can be as simple as finding a book, or an open access article or following action research websites.

Workers' rights, civil rights and global emancipation movements: Historical accounts such as eye-witness reports, primary sources and academic and popular literature relating to historical movements, or to figures or events can be inspirational and can inform you of different ways that social justice was won in the past.

○ **Hopeful Companions**

Organisations
LGBT Foundation: supports the needs of a diverse range of people who identify as lesbian, gay, bisexual and trans: https://lgbt. foundation/

Reclaiming our Future Alliance: alliance of disabled peoples' organisations to defend disabled rights and campaign for an inclusive society: https://www.rofa.org.uk/who-we-are/

Films
Small Axe: Five short films by Steve McQueen: https://www.bbc. co.uk/programmes/p08vxt33

Earthrise by Amanda Gorman: https://www.youtube.com/ watch?v=xwOvBv8RLmo

Films for the Planet: https://filmsfortheplanet.com/

Academic journals: Many peer-reviewed academic journal articles are now available open access, meaning that anyone can read them. Articles that are not open access can be read by those in higher education, or by joining the British Library or Research Gate.

○ **Hopeful Companions**

Finding open access resources.

Articles
The Conversation is a free online newspaper in which academics write about current affairs from the perspective of their area of expertise. The site invites courteous debate: https://theconversation. com/uk/

Proceedings of the National Academy of Sciences of the USA: many online open access articles: https://www.pnas.org/content/118/6

Individuals
Many individuals have open access resources on their personal websites or on their staff listing at the University where they are based.

Organisations
British Library: open access and online articles are available to anyone with a permanent UK address: https://www.bl.uk/help/open-access-resources-for-research

Research Gate: individuals can access academic papers by requesting them directly from the author: https://www.researchgate.net/

Creative Learning Exercises

Think about your sources of inquiry and the methods of reflection you will use. Gather together the materials you need. These may include, but are not limited to, pens and paper, craft materials and glue.

Create a visual record of how you will inquire.

What do you want to inquire about?

What sources will you start with?

What type of first-person inquiry methods will you follow?

Make a collage of these ideas.

My personal reflective cycles of action, learning and reflection: Working towards an anti-racist paradigm

To illustrate the first-person methodology, embedded cosmological perspectives and reflective cycles of learning upon which this Handbook is based, I wish to set out a recent example of one of my own reflective cycles. It was initiated by my experience of taking the knee for eight minutes forty-six seconds in Manchester's St Peter's Square at the height of the first COVID-19 lockdown in June 2020 at an open invitation protest event.

Strongly influenced by being raised between the mountains and the sea on what is now known as the Wild Atlantic Way, my mother and her five sisters all won state scholarships to Irish universities in the years after World War II. My mother graduated with a bilingual (English and Irish) history degree from University College Galway and then emigrated to England. My white working-class father was born into a family in an interwar council house in Newark, Nottinghamshire. Born before the 1944 Education Act, he never went to university. My parents raised me with a strong belief in social justice, education and the values of love and compassion.

Being brought up in the Roman Catholic faith in England and in Ireland shaped my thought and spirituality. I respect the teachings of other great faith traditions – Buddhism. Confucianism, Indigenous, Hinduism, Islam, Judaism, Sikhism and other Christian churches – as well as humanist and pagan traditions and have sought to draw upon them in my research. However, I recognize my own shaping in the Roman Catholic tradition.

I attended university in the 1970s and was schooled in a predominately white Western canon of history literature, which is no doubt reflected in these pages. I have been privileged to be in continuous employment all my life until I was made redundant in 2011 following the UK Government's austerity policies and reduction of the (local) public sector. My early career was in the women's movement (see Hopeful Companions in chapter 2) and my career since then has been within the movement for social justice and change, including working in neighborhood regeneration and community development in North West England.

The creation of this book has been a journey of inquiry, study and research, where I have sought to continue to 'walk my talk'. In 2020, George Floyd was murdered by police in the USA, sparking protests around the world. His death brough the Black Lives Matter movement to renewed prominence, focused on exposing and challenging the depth of racism still existing in our society.[55] It has also led to an exploration of the effects of colonialism and racism in the world today, alongside the lack of value given to indigenous communities. One result is the decolonisation movement in educational and other institutional settings. Joining hundreds of others in taking the knee in St Peter's Square led me to a deeper cycle of learning and reflection on racial inequality and decolonialisation.

Addressing these issues has led me to consider in what ways I can respond more actively to the racism that still persists at all levels of society and how colonialism and imperialism have shaped knowledge, learning and our entire society. I have sought to respond to the movement through educating myself in relevant issues and examining my own scholarship. I am indebted to the many members of the Black, Asian and Global Majority communities who write on these issues and who have shared their thoughts and wisdom. Some are referenced within this book. I am indebted to colleagues and students at the Science and Engineering Faculty at Manchester Metropolitan University who have produced an open access interactive resource, with extensive examples and stories from academics and students into their understanding of decolonising the curriculum. In examining my research, I identified my roots in a canon of work associated predominately but not exclusively with a white UK/US perspective. As I have developed my own scholarship, I have explored how I can strengthen the anti-racist perspective and I now offer a more diverse range of Hopeful Companions resources, than I did in earlier drafts of the book.

⭕ **Hopeful Companions**

Starting resources on anti-racism and decolonisation.

Articles
Arshad, A. 2021. Decolonising the curriculum. How do I get started? *Times Higher Education Campus Resources for universities and academics.* 14 September: https://www.timeshighereducation.com/campus/decolonising-curriculum-how-do-i-get-started

Creativity
Angelou, M. 1986. *And Still I Rise.* London: Virago and 'Still I Rise' Poem (Live Performance): https://www.youtube.com/watch?v=qviM_GnJbOM

Resources for Action
The MMU Science and Engineering Decolonising the Curriculum Toolkit: https://www.mmu.ac.uk/about-us/professional-services/uta/reducing-awarding-gaps/decolonising-the-curriculum-toolkit

University College Union Report for Colleges and Universities to Decarbonize and Decolonize by 2030: https://www.ucu.org.uk/media/11630/COP26-campaign-decarbonise-and-decolonise-2030---quick-guide/pdf/Decarbonise_Decolonise_quick_guide_Jun21.pdf

University of Salford 2022: https://www.salford.ac.uk/library/find-resources/reading-lists/reading-lists-staff/decolonising-your-reading-list

---

Challenges of first-person action research

First-person action research is often compared unfavourably with other research methods. Perriton (2001) argues that it is neither as relevant nor as robust as quantitative research methods. While it is true that a reliance on numerical data provides a form of accuracy, it can also hide the values and perspectives from which the research is undertaken. This is nowhere more evident than in oil company research to discredit climate science (Hall, 2015). All research is enhanced by the honesty and rigour of individual researchers who are clear about their values and ethics. A great deal of inquiry is deepened through detailed experiential stories.

First person action research has been critiqued as being part of a wider 'confessional' turn in the media, public life and academia. Elaine Swann (2008) considers this critique and is concerned that the power and privilege inherent in any situation can get lost in a confessional style of writing. However, Swann argues that the consciousness raising of second wave feminism allowed for both first-person reflection and action throughout the world. Therefore, her concern is about ensuring that the "social is not collapsed into the self but rather the self is a social and historical event" (ibid, 396). This reference to second wave feminism reflects that movement's central tenet that the "personal is political" (Hanish, 1972). Swann's concerns are related to a further critique that this form of writing is self-indulgent and centred only on the individual. A response to such critiques lies in the faithful use of first-person writing to help the writer to delve deeper into their world, gradually moving beyond the self to the community, the planet and the Cosmos. First-person writing at its best enables engagement with who one is and the world one inhabits, finding patterns and meanings over time where none were seen before. First-person writing can become a means to engage with discrimination and power in the world, as suggested by Gordon (2001) and Saad (2020). They examine how writing helps explore the deepening and widening of self-knowledge over time to understand the effects of racism on individuals. It can also help when working towards anti-racist societies and what Gordon (2007: 162) calls a "re-humanised British culture". First-person inquiry engages with other forms of inquiry – books, websites, films, poetry – helping us to find meaning in our relationship to the wider world. It encourages us to tell the stories of what we find, to share those stories with others, as friends, fellow activists and colleagues. In this process, it is not necessary to share the actual writing or visual journaling. The deeply personal can remain private to the individual.

A further critique of first-person action research is lack of awareness of the privilege of being able to undertake such an inquiry in the first place. When working with first person inquiry material, Gearty and Marshall (2021: 446) continuously sought to be aware of "what or who is missing here?" as an integral part of the inquiry process. Through an ongoing reflection on my privilege, as discussed in Chapter 4, I seek to contribute, as a community activist, to ecological and social justice movements.

 Creative Learning Exercises

In reflecting on first person practice, if you are a person of colour, consider and record how racism and colonialism has affected your life.

If you are from a white background, consider and record how racism and colonialism has given you certain privileges in life and how they affect the whole of society.

Can you make some time to follow a structured course of first person reflection on inequalities? For example, Layla Saad (2019) provides structured exercises for white people to understand their privilege and ensuing racism, requiring deeper work to become good ancestors. The exercises are in: *Me and White Supremacy How to Recognise your Privilege, Combat Racism and Change the World*. London: Quercus.

Can you commit to any actions to help grow diversity and decolonisation as part of your journey to hopeful futures? Can you draw these actions?

Quality

Creating quality first-person action research is dependent on some of the qualities referred to in Chapter 4. Writing as inquiry leads to questions concerning the quality of that writing. Reflexivity is a key quality when writing (Richardson, 2000; Sparkes, 2020). In other words, does your writing demonstrate that you are aware of yourself and what you are doing? How do you express and reflect on the emotions you have observed and experienced? Does your writing feel true? Does it feel embodied? Do your stories contain complexity and what Geertz (1973) called "thick description"? Does the narrative open up new possibilities (Ellis & Bochner, 2000)? Stories have a liminal quality that "takes us from the threshold of one experience to another" (Mead, 2011:18). Quality can also be observed in how stories make the reader feel about a situation. Mead argues that by creating mythical stories out of our own lives, we can engage with the healing properties of those stories (ibid: 44).

Drawing on years of living life as inquiry, Gearty and Marshall (2020) suggest a range of questions to draw out quality processes. One of these is maintaining ongoing curiosity in the inquiry. Another is asking yourself if the inquiry has life? They suggest seeing inquiry as a "dynamic and reflective process" (p. 452) which cannot be divided into sections, but needs to be seen as an integrated whole, returning us to the holistic nature of the universe herself.

Invitation to Reflect

Create the time to reflect, perhaps in your garden or in a park, on the following ethical questions.

What are the most important ethical questions for you?

What can you do to ensure that your work and inquiry are conducted according to your ethical values?

Is there someone who can support you as you make this ethical journey?

Route planning: Which way to hopeful futures?

We travel in a Cosmos some 13,800,000,000 years old, with an almost infinite number of choices on a long journey which has led to this planet with its complex and sentient life, and one species – ours – that is conscious of that history. So, it is no surprise that there are many route choices for each of us as we make the journey!

Create your own map of first-person practices

The ways forward are multiple. I hope you will reflect on and chart your journey of discovery and share it by whatever means seems most appropriate to you. I encourage you to think about all the ways you might share your journey of discovery. These might include social media, performance or sharing with your family, community or faith group. In any event, as a self-organising process, you will find that, as you start to work with the material, emergent properties of the inquiry will emerge.

 Invitation to Reflect

Consider creating your own journey, with your own questions to explore. Start by creating your own map.

Subdivide a sheet of paper into sections, each one representing part of the journey of exploration. You may choose to create a hand-drawn map or an electronic map on your mobile or laptop.

Fill in each of the sections with ideas of what questions you might explore and when. Are there friends, family, colleagues who might travel with you?

Come back to this map as you continue on your journey of exploration. Has it changed from your original ideas? Capture any new directions.

Reflections

I use first-person action inquiry for a number of reasons. First, it changes my view of life, transforming life into a journey of exploration and curiosity, rather than one of success or failure. It has allowed me to begin to understand how I act in the world and, as a result, how I can contribute to creating the world anew. A journey of inquiry rooted in the methods and ethics of action research explains the world as participatory and whole, and helps me to experience living in a world and Cosmos that are both physical and spiritual. Action research has invited me to think about myself: What are my stories? Where have I come from? What pain or wounds do I carry with me? It helps me understand if I am depressed or if I need to seek help from others. Such a journey helps me think about my privilege and how I need to address that privilege to bring about a more just society. A journey of inquiry encourages me, when I fail, to pick myself up and start again, renewed every day. Action research encourages me to communicate with others on a deeper level, using writing, story, or telling my story through performance or painting. Action research can do these things for you too.

You are now ready to go forth, with your new toolkit to create a new paradigm of our place in the world.

Notes

[51] Baba Dioum, a Senegalese ecologist, spoke these words to the Third Triennial IUCN General Congress in 1968 in New Dehli. See Dioum's profile in Modernising African Food Systems: http://www.mafs-africa.org/baba_dioum/

[52] See, for example, the Greater London Council Women's Committee Bulletin 1983-1986 in the TUC Library collection, London Metropolitan University: https://archiveshub.jisc.ac.uk/search/archives/7b664d79-a6fb-335f-8f47-04af373301a7

[53] The number of individuals who have travelled to space varies depending on how space is defined. These data are based on the US Air Force definition of space as above 80 kilometres. This number is accurate as of 13 November 2021. For women in space, see Alice Gorman's 2020 account: https://phys.org/news/2020-06-astronauts-men-future-space-female.html. See also NASA's history section for the names of those who have travelled to and walked on the moon: https://solarsystem.nasa.gov/news/890/who-has-walked-on-the-moon/. For details of all astronauts and cosmonauts, see https://www.nasa.gov/specials/60counting/spaceflight.html and https://www.worldspaceflight.com/bios/stats1.php

[54] See Green Stories Writing Competition, run by Southampton University, for the opportunity to be part of creating new stories: https://www.greenstories.org.uk/

[55] Wesley Lowery. 2017. *They can't kill us all: The story of Black Lives Matter.* London: Penguin

Third Cycle: Learning to use the tools

The maps that guide our lives at present are causing us to destroy the pale blue dot that is our one and only home. But we have now unlocked some of the tools we need to create new maps, including participative pedagogies, action research and first-person inquiry. Now, we can unpack the action research tool kit and put it into practice. We will do this by experiencing how we can learn to live in the Cosmos in our individual lives and in the company of others.

We will explore how to use first-person inquiry to engage, as individuals, with Gaia, community, and the Cosmos. By exploring deep time, and engaging with the ancient nature of the planet, we can learn to contemplate being part of the universe. Using the action research cycles of action and reflection and extended ways of knowing we can explore how to live within the intersections of Cosmos, Gaia, self and community.

But none of us is alone, and action research methods can help us to undertake journeys to hopeful futures in the company of others. Using the participatory methods of second-person action research, together we can explore the challenges we face and begin to find solutions. The challenges begin with finding the community energy to engage in shared learning and address the tasks ahead. We face the challenges of working together despite different paradigms and worldviews and developing a sense of scale beyond the street or organisation to the wider world of the neighbourhood, the city, the region, the nation and beyond.

Chapter 6: Exploring our conduct
Living within the Universe in our daily lives

"Such a fantastic universe, with its great spiralling galaxies, its super-novas, our solar system, and this privileged planet Earth!"
Tomas Berry (1988: xv)

"Cosmic perspective is the greatest gift that modern cosmology gives us."
Joel Primack and Nancy Abrams (2006: 269)

It is 1994 and I am in the Malvern Hills, in Gloucestershire, attending a Green Camp with my younger daughters. Nora, aged two, runs through the grass, picking up speed as she goes. She hurls herself at the ground, picks herself up without a sound and keeps moving. The object of her attention is a pen full of chickens in the middle of the field. Delighted, she stops and holds the side of the pen, fascinated by the chickens scratching and pecking at the grass. After a few moments, she whirls round and starts to run up the field again. Running. Happy. Free.

Her sister, Ita, four and a half, sits in the awning of a tent, intent on using cardboard and paper to make doll's furniture. With immense and focused effort, she twists the cardboard to create a chair. Annette, who is in charge of the children's tent, declares her intention to go for a walk in the woods. We follow her – three mothers and six children, stomping our feet, imagining we are warding off the wild animals who live in the bushes and just beyond our view. Under the trees, we sit on a fallen log and drum our feet on the ground, urging the wild animals to run away from us. Our voices rise in a crescendo and fade away, as we sit and listen to the birds in the wood.

Back in the main field, as I drink a cup of tea, I watch the children racing up and down the field. I talk to Annette about spirit, God, love. I tell her I am exploring Buddhism. "Why don't you explore your childhood spirituality," she asks? Why not? Next morning, at 9am, I meditate with the other campers. We sit cross legged in a field, the dew on the grass, the sunlight glinting through, sending sparkles of light across the field. Soaked in warmth, I resolve to explore my spirituality and I sense it will have something to do with the open fields where we are. In later years, on train journeys, I see the Malvern Hills shimmering and mysterious in the distance, reminding me of that immersion and happiness in nature.

Introduction

You are about to set off on an exciting journey. You will learn to create maps connecting your life as you live it within the wider Cosmos. What an invigorating and compelling thought, both simple and revolutionary. This wider cosmological perspective offers a way to simultaneously address destruction to our planet and to our human communities. First-person action research helps us to explore how to experience these perspectives in our lives so that we can come to live them in the heart rather than merely in the intellect. As I reflected on how we might undertake this practice, I was reminded of the joy of my three grandchildren going outside after weeks spent inside during the first COVID-19 lockdown. They joyfully jumped in puddles, creating the biggest splashes they could. They fell down, jumped up again, got soaking wet and delighted in wringing the water out of their socks when they returned home. Can we too learn to jump into the universe with childlike abandon and wonder?

Jumping up and down: exploring our place in the universe

The Journey of the Universe story places us as part of the universe all the way back to the Big Bang and stretching across space to the furthermost galaxies. It encourages us to live as part of this beautiful and awe-inspiring universe and not as separate or detached onlookers. In *The Dream of the Earth*, Thomas Berry laments the loss of our sense of place in the Cosmos over the past four hundred years of the dominance of the Western worldview. We have narrowed our focus down to ourselves as individuals and our human concerns. For the sake of our own and the planet's well-being, we must understand our place within the wider universe again. Berry (1988: xv) suggests, as a point of departure,

> "The greater curvature of the universe and of the planet Earth must govern the curvature of our own being. In the coincidence of these three curves lies the way into a creative future."

I meditated on these words when I first read them, reflecting on what they meant to me as an individual, in the context of my family, from my position as a Neighbourhood Regeneration Manager and as a volunteer worker in my community. According to Berry's vision, my journey into the future had to include community. And humanity's journey had to be a holistic journey of self, community, Gaia and Cosmos.

Using first-person methods to help us live in the Cosmos

How can we live in the Cosmos, when the dominant paradigm tells us that the universe is devoid of spirit and meaning? If we live life as inquiry, inquiring into everything with curiosity and generosity of spirit, we can find ourselves somewhere new. We can let go of our old thought patterns and live by asking questions and allowing the answers to emerge. We can pay attention to our thoughts and what is going on in the world outside, taking the time to meditate, so that our own thoughts become silent for a while. We can reflect or pray to become conscious of something greater than ourselves. We can read poetry about the universe, or about the Earth and nature. We can listen to the wisdom of indigenous communities around the world and learn from them. We can listen to music and reflect. We can find a way to record what is happening, in writing, drawing or photography. We can create visual images to guide us. We can create new metaphors to live by. We can participate in activities and events and simply observe what emerges, without judging the outcomes. Each one of these is a first-person method. Together, they are more than the sum of their parts. They are a process of emergence. When we use these methods, we are on a journey to cross the threshold into another paradigm, to another way of living in our Cosmos.

Finding your way: visual images and stories to re-imagine yourself

As I reflected on these curves to which Berry referred, I began to imagine and draw the point at which the self, the community, the planet and the Cosmos meet. The four points seemed to be a focus for every individual human life.

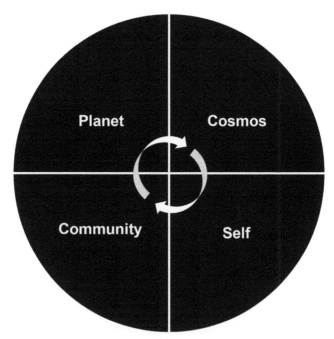

Figure 6.1: Imagining our way into living in the Cosmos: joining together
Self, Community, Planet and Cosmos – a first attempt.
(Source: Kettleborough, 2023)

Figure 6.1 was an attempt to visualise how we might see ourselves living in the whole. Each segment is equally important. The journey to self, the focus of so much struggle in past centuries, is too important to lose. The journey to community is a key element of living co-operatively with others. The journey to the planet must include the restoration and healing of biodiversity and the climate and tackling the structural causes of social injustice. Each of these is cradled within a meaningful Cosmos. Humanity is inextricably joined to the planet and Cosmos. Yet, the image I visualised suggested that the Cosmos is part of the whole, rather than the overarching whole. So, I imagined the four segments meeting one after the other:

This also failed to capture the sense of our lives meeting at a point and simultaneously held within the Cosmos. A further attempt to visualise the way forward involved a series of concentric circles, joined at a single point, all contained within the Cosmos (overleaf).

This suggests a way of being in ourselves, our communities, our planet, and our Cosmos unlike our current consumerist paradigm. Upon further reflection, I became interested in how I interacted with Gaia, Cosmos and community in my daily life at home, in my professional life and in my community work and in reflection; how Gaia interacted with community, self and Cosmos; and how Cosmos interacted with self, community and Gaia. Could I find evidence of these intersections in my journaling practice?

Periodically, I explore my journal material to search for

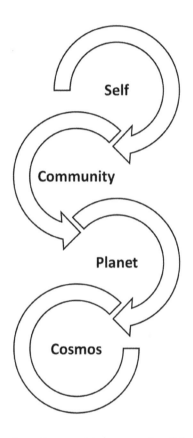

Figure 6.2: Imagining our way into living in the Cosmos: dancing between Self, Community, Planet and Cosmos – a second attempt. (Source: Kettleborough, 2023)

patterns that might reflect new insights into where I am living within the Cosmos and Gaia. As I traced back through the material in my journals, certain incidents appeared to illustrate these four segments. I worked on these pieces of journaling, configuring the experiences I had recorded with ideas from the relevant literature. Although I conducted separate research

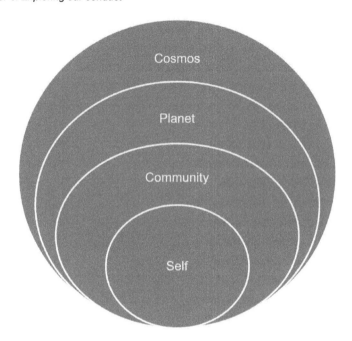

Figure 6.3: Imagining our way into living in the Cosmos: at the intersection of Self, Community, Planet and Cosmos. (Source: Kettleborough, 2023)

around the different narratives, all were interwoven. I referred to each piece as a story, as it was a retelling of a meaningful event in my life (see Sparkes 2002; Muncey, 2010). These stories recounted events or incidents in my life, and followed first-person inquiry methods (Goldberg, 1986; Turner-Vessalago, 2013; Marshall, 2016). The reflection, research and writing of each story was a learning experience, helping me to understand something profound about living in the Cosmos which I crystallised into something palpable that I could share with others (Richardson, 2000). Some of the stories seem unfinished because they relate to an unfolding journey. Significantly, the stories are an attempt to capture, from the inside, my experience of living within the Cosmos, not as a detached observer, but as an integral part of it. As the planet becomes a breathing place in which I reside, I seek to create stories to make the journey accessible.

Creative Learning Excercise

Creatively capture (through writing, drawing, etc.) experiences from your own life. This is a powerful tool for opening up the possibilities for reflection and analysis, helping you to identify insights and patterns as you seek to make the journey to hopeful futures.

I include some of these stories here, to express the journey that I undertook. I have chosen to share these particular stories because they reflect instances in my life when I intersected with a transition to a new, participative paradigm. They reflect my experience of living in a wider Cosmos and how this journey has become embodied in my life, learning and practice. I have shared these stories with my family, at community workshops and in my teaching practice. I remain inspired by Stephan Harding, who uses mime and storytelling to bring stories to life and into participative relationships with others (Hamera, 2011).[56]

The method you choose to capture these learning experiences must relate to you. The key element is to continue capturing and recording those experiences over time. Think of it as a family photograph album, except this album is of a journey into the wider Cosmos.

 Invitation to Reflect

Take the time to visualise the mental leaps and metaphors in this chapter.

Draw and write them from your imagination.

This journey took me over three decades to live into. I hope that, by following these learning paths, you will make this journey more quickly to meet the ever-tighter deadlines for action that we, as a species, face.

Living into the intersection of Cosmos with Gaia, self and community

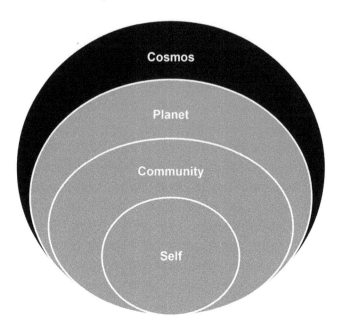

Figure 6.4: From Cosmos to Self, Community and Planet (Source: Kettleborough, 2023)

We can understand living in the Cosmos in our daily lives by using the first-person method of *living life as inquiry* and remaining curious and open to learning about the Cosmos. Using metaphor to better understand our Cosmos (Primack & Abrams, 2006), I have sought a shift from a human-centric to a cosmos-centric perspective (Swimme, 1996). Using extended ways of knowing, I read scientific books and journals to improve my knowledge of the universe.

Six leaps (2000)

It was the Millennium. The post softly thudded to the floor beneath the letterbox. The girls ran to the door and scooped up the mail, handing me the National Geographic Millennium special. Inside was a colourful A3 map of our neighbourhood, our cosmic neighbourhood. The map makers recommended taking "leaps of scale" around our neighbourhood.

I imagined taking these leaps. From our solar system to the nearest star, Alpha Centauri, 4.3 light years away. From there to the local group of stars, including Orion and all the bright stars we know and love. From there to the Milky Way galaxy herself, our neighbourhood. From our home galaxy, a leap of 2.5 million light years to our nearest neighbouring galaxy, Andromeda, which pin-wheels around the Milky Way every 250 million years. From Andromeda to our nearest group of galaxies, the Local Group. And finally, from there to the Cosmos beyond. I have mentally followed this path many times. Over the past 20 years, during occasional visits to university science departments, I have always felt a thrill of recognition upon seeing that cosmic map on the wall. [57]

These leaps around the Cosmos take place in my imagination. While my outer arc of attention might be the street in Manchester where I live, my inner arc of attention is jumping around the Cosmos. Such a practice, repeated regularly over two decades, enables me to get a sense of being part of a vast and mysterious universe.

Deep Time (2006)

Chapter 2 opened with *Deep Time*, a story to draw you into the great age of the universe. When I came across the remains of an ancient beach on top of a mountain path, I was staggered to find that the rock I held in my hand was 320 million years old. Yet, even this unimaginably long time, in human terms, from a time even before the dinosaurs, was only one forty-third (1/43) of the way back to the start of the universe. I was filled with a sense of wonder at the time it had taken to create that ancient beach and the time it had taken to create complex life. As an understanding of these unimaginably long time periods crept in, I began to feel an ethical sense of responsibility not simply for human life but for all life. Seeking to live within deep time offers a small glimpse of the effects of the climate emergency on the Earth. Such is the duration of carbon dioxide in the atmosphere that the effects of human activity over the past 200 years are likely to last for thousands, or even hundreds of thousands of years (Stager, 2011). Disbelief gave way to the gravity of the situation, as such a timeline is beyond the life span of human civilisation. A sense of urgency that began as a desire to understand the deep age of our planet and universe has remained a motivating force. The size of the universe and the age of our planet give me some sense of the length of time it took for our planet to be created. I now feel an emerging understanding of how special our planet is within this ancient universe.

Our one and only home (2010)

In autumn 2010, our youngest daughter left for university. During Fresher's week, she visited the Astrophysics Society stall and was given a picture of the Earth taken from the Cassini spacecraft, at a distance of nearly 930 million miles. Nora asked for a second copy, which she gave to me when we met two months later. I stared at the picture, mesmerised. It was a glorious full-colour portrait of Earth, our home planet. The spacecraft had turned back from farthest reaches of the Solar System to look towards the Sun and the planet from which it had come. With the light of the Sun blocked by Saturn, Cassini captured an image of Earth. It is not Earth as we normally see her, with her beautiful swirling white clouds and vibrant blue skies. Instead, she is a tiny pixel, barely a dot outside one of Saturn's rings. Staring hard, it is possible to see Earth as a tiny pale blue orb of haunting beauty. As cosmologist Carl Sagan (1994: 7) wrote, this tiny point of blue light is "the only home we've ever known." [58]

This photograph has great significance for me. It is shorthand to experiencing not simply the size of the Cosmos, but the extraordinary importance and significance of our home planet, the only place we know that harbours life and brings forth complex life. The photo was used to open our Pilgrimage for Gaia workshops and later for the Centre for Connected Practice logo (see back cover). As an extended way of knowing, the photo became a way to see our planet within the wider Cosmos. Sometimes, when the image is copied, the pixel of Earth vanishes. On computer or video screens, the pixel of light which is our planet home, stands out clearly – when you know where to look for it. Searching for Earth with people who have not seen the photo before is always a poignant exercise.

Together, these stories have helped me to articulate living in the Cosmos. I use them to invite you to explore living your own life in the Cosmos. Such a perspective opens us up to a more holistic understanding of where and how we live.

Creative Learning Exercises

Take the time to explore the idea of living in the Cosmos. Write or draw your thoughts.

Think about moments or stories from your life when you glimpsed living in the Cosmos?

Look back at NASA photographs of our solar system and beyond. In what ways do you feel that you are part of those pictures?

Draw a picture of yourself as part of the Cosmos.

Think about poetry or music that can bring you closer to the Cosmos.

 Hopeful Companions

Books
Harding, S. 2006. *Animate Earth, Science, Intuition and Gaia.* Cornwall: MPG Books

Films
Deep Field, the Impossible Magnitude of our Universe by Eric Whitacre: https://www.youtube.com/watch?v=yDiD8F9ItX0

Resources for Action
The National Geographic Universe Map is a helpful tool to visualize the size of the cosmos and to start taking leaps. It can be purchased from: https://www.natgeomaps.com/re-the-universe

The Story of our Universe: NASA Illustration: https://www.nasa.gov/mission_pages/planck/multimedia/pia16876b.html

The Emergent Universe: Books, storytellings, programmes, retreats: http://www.universestories.com/ including Jennifer Morgan's *The Universe Story Trilogy*, aimed at children

Living into the intersection of Gaia with Cosmos, self and community

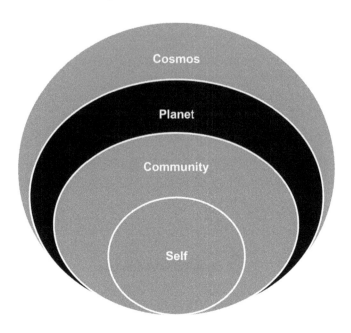

Figure 6.5: From Planet to Self, Community and Cosmos
(Source: Kettleborough, 2023)

The next three stories are meditations on meeting Gaia. These encounters emerged from structured or taught situations and they illustrate the openness to experiential learning that is at the heart of living life as inquiry.

Green Camp (1994)

The camping experience recounted at the start of this chapter was run by a not-for-profit organization, Green and Away,[59] which teaches about green camping and enables children to play in nature in the absence of consumerism. Being outside all day in the fresh air, with the mystery and excitement of going for walks in the woods, and reacting to hens roaming freely on the grass was, for me, an emergent meeting with Gaia. It taught me the joy of children experiencing nature at a deep level. Studies have found that urban children miss nature (Louv, 2011) and relish learning outside.[60] An unexpected outcome of the COVID-19 pandemic was a reduction in traffic, allowing children and adults to experience nature to a greater extent than before. Green Camp was a lightly structured family immersion in nature; a preparation, in part, for another learning experience six years later.

Deep Ecology – The day I was "Gaia'd" (2000)

Schumacher College is an educational institution dedicated to teaching about living in the world according to principles of social and ecological justice. The courses combine academic teaching with experiential learning in the college grounds and surrounding countryside.[61] The learning week was an integrated part of my Master's Degree in Business, and was the second of eight residential weeks over the course of the degree. During that week we engaged in propositional learning about nature and the planet, both in the classroom and outdoors, and we engaged in experiential learning outdoors.

The River Dart, Totnes, Devon. Twenty-four students sit by the river, watching it swirl and eddy, the water deep and fast flowing. We are tasked with appreciating the river. From the river bank, I carefully watch, with ceaseless delight, the bubbles and the patterns made by the swirling water. There is no sound except the swish and tinkle of water. Our teacher, Stephan, leads us on a walk in a wood. "Look!" he says, "Watch carefully. See the wood, tell me about the wood." We stare at the wood, puzzled – trees, shrubs, undergrowth and more trees. We walk a little further. "Look," he says again, "watch carefully!" Again, we stare, puzzled. Trees, more trees. Stephan watches our puzzled faces and smiles, explaining that the first wood had no sheep and was growing freely, full of undergrowth, new plants. A happy wood. The second wood, grazed by sheep, had no new growth, a sad wood.

The next day, I sit down with three other students and we reflect on our experiences. What is deep ecology? What does it mean? What have we learned about deep ecology from trying to get close to nature? One of us suggests it's like eating rocks, to be met by much merriment and laughter. We talk late into the night. Early the next morning, I get up and write in the beautiful library. I write about re-covering England with trees, of growing organic food, of creating green corridors. The experience of sitting next to the river and listening to the water stays with me. Gaia starts to move from words on a piece of paper to a sense of wonder. The experience of talking with colleagues shows me how hard it is to express this understanding in words. The residential learning week demonstrates the power of learning to change how we see the world.

The week was framed as a co-operative inquiry into deep ecology and Gaia. We were asked to reflect, as far as we could, *with* nature. Sitting by the River Dart and listening to the sound of the water, we were being asked to experience Gaia directly. As we walked in the woodland and noticed what was happening to the undergrowth and trees, we were being asked to see the woodland as a being in her own right and to experience her as worthy of respect. When we touched plants, we were asked to sense their essence and appreciate that they were touching us back. Later, on a night walk, we listened to sounds magnified in the darkness, and we were being asked to participate directly with nature. As we undertook this learning, we also took part in structured learning about Gaia, about her carbon, nitrogen and water cycles.

Teaching in an ancient woodland (2017)

Two colleagues and I are exploring creativity in higher learning. My area of interest is how creativity can help students more keenly understand the plight of the planet and inspire them to act. One of my colleagues works at our sister campus at Crewe, which has sadly been selected for closure by the university. The staff at Crewe would like us to run one of our workshops there before it closes. There is an ancient woodland on site and I suggest that we offer one of our sessions outside. My colleagues are open to the challenge.

I catch the train from Manchester, walk to the campus and sit in the classroom. The buildings are brick and concrete and there are no plants. When facilitators and participants have gathered (eight of us in total), we have coffee and walk out of the classroom in good humour, entirely uncertain about how the session will be received. We walk into the woodland. It suddenly feels very different. The trees are beautiful with moss and leaves underfoot. We facilitators explain to the participants that we have come here to learn about nature that is deeply threatened. We ask the participants to seek patterns in the nature around them. The students are immersed by simply being with the woodland, and quickly find patterns and shapes in leaves, soil, plants, bark and wood on the ground. We bring the shapes together and place them on a blanket. We talk about what we have found and why it called to us. Hearing how each person has responded in a unique way is moving. The light through the trees is dappled, making the place feel even more special. We say goodbye and walk out of the woodland. I hope the new owners will take care of it; my inner-city experience tells me that trees are vulnerable to developers. During the morning, we record a video of the trees and when we run our afternoon session in the classroom the woodland comes inside to join us.[62] Returning home, I reflect on how working together and the support of colleagues helped bring Gaia into the classroom.

This learning experience involved both first- and second-person inquiry. Taking a risk and teaching in an ancient woodland encapsulated trusting the experience of working with nature and how nature speaks to people when they give it a chance.

 Invitation to Reflect

Draw or write about a time when you experienced Gaia.

Make a list of ways that you can learn more about Gaia.

Make a list of ways that you can share these ideas.

Imagine a time when you see yourself as part of the planet Gaia in the Cosmos. What will that feel like?

Living into the intersection of Self with Cosmos, Gaia and community

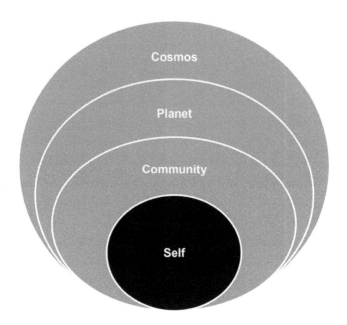

Figure 6.6: From Self to Community, Planet and Cosmos
(Source: Kettleborough, 2023)

The following three stories express the importance of time when searching for a new paradigm or worldview.

Nine Boxes

Susan Jeffers' (1987) notion of self has influenced my spiritual practice. She writes about moving from pain to power in one's life, from being trapped by circumstances to understanding those circumstances and developing agency. Jeffers uses the concept of nine boxes to represent moving from pain to power. Different aspects of our lives can be placed into these boxes, creating a holistic approach to life. One's life is not dependent on any one of those nine boxes. Furthermore, rather than simply imagining a different life, the boxes represent taking action. This approach has enabled the emergence of a widening sense of possibility in my life, expanding outwards from developing responsibility towards myself. It has become a technique to enact how I think about organising my life as part of the wider Cosmos.

Jeffers relegates work to only one box, while time for friends, for leisure and for being alone figure strongly. *Personal contribution* or doing for others is at the centre of the nine boxes. When I first encountered the nine boxes concept my life was dominated by my work and the life that Jeffers prescribed was a long way away for me. However, the nine boxes outlined a way of life to which I could aspire.

Hobbies	Relationship	Alone time
Home	Personal contribution	Family
Work	Leisure	Friends

Figure 6.7: Journal extract, 15 April 1989, 'My whole life'
(Source: Adapted from Jeffers, 1987: 70)

As Jeffers has developed this model, she suggests replacing 'personal contribution' with our Higher Self, which she describes as "the place within that is loving, kind, abundant [and] joyful," (ibid, 213). She recommends that this remains as the central box.

Higher self, therefore, should be at the centre of our lives. It can emerge from our own experiences of the spiritual. Following the Al Anon tradition, I have translated this concept into a Higher Power.[63] Over time, I used my journals to play around with and rearrange the contents of the nine boxes, through an emergent method of reflection and learning. The boxes have come to represent not simply how I organise my life, but of holding my life to areas of action that I deem important and relevant. Gradually, a sense of living in the Cosmos became part of my version of the nine boxes.

By 2008, nineteen years after I first transcribed Jeffers' nine boxes into my journal, the following arrangement had emerged:

Family	Home	Exercise
Prayer	Cosmos Love	Prayer
PhD	Work	Admin

Figure 6.8: Journal Extract, 11 January 2008, 'Nine Boxes'
(Source: Kettleborough, 2023)

The boxes in the top line centred around my home and my health. Exercise was a particular struggle in my life, and deserved a box of its own. The middle line focused on my commitment to spiritual qualities. Despite its importance in my life, making time for prayer was a particular challenge for me, so the practice of prayer merited two boxes. The bottom line related to work and study. Organising myself and administration, both at home and at work, kept slipping off the edge of my 'to do' list and, therefore, merited its own box. At the centre of the nine boxes were Cosmos and love, representing the Higher Power. This box contained my continued struggle between belonging to a particular faith community and feeling part of the

Cosmos, where discreet faith communities are consumed by the bigger whole. The PhD box served as a shorthand encompassing nature and the planet, central research themes, while the work box related to the issues of community, social justice and management central to my professional career.

Seven years later, in 2015, my circumstances had again changed. Time had now become the great pressure in my life, as I attempted to balance commitments to teaching, to setting up an independent Centre for Connected Practice[64] and to writing. This pressure was reflected in the top line of my nine boxes, which now emphasized care in all aspects of my life. Administration, still a challenge, was joined by financial care. The middle box had become more detailed, expanding from prayer to prayer and meditation and the practice of gratitude. Higher Power remained firmly in the middle box. The bottom line captured the issues of ecology, social justice and responsible enterprise at the heart of my teaching and writing practice, and at the heart of the Centre for Connected Practice.

Self-care	Home Care	Admin and Finance Care
Gratitude for family	Higher Power	Prayer and meditation Family and friends
Teaching	C4CP	Writing

Figure 6.9: Journal Extract: 19 February 2015, 'Nine Boxes' (Source: Kettleborough, 2023)

Visualising one's life with a Higher Power at the centre opens the door to a more ecological sense of life, planet and Cosmos. Taking a holistic approach to ordering one's life allows for spiritual practices such as meditation to emerge and have time to flourish.

 Invitation to Reflect

Work with the concept of the nine boxes in relation to your own life.

Arrange the boxes in a way that is appropriate to you. This may take some time and reflection.

Try to rearrange the boxes as you remember your life 20 years ago.

Look ahead to how the boxes might be arranged 10, 20 or 50 years from now in such a way that will create hopeful futures.

What action, spirit and reflection do you need to participate in to make these tasks happen?

Meditation

First-person inquiry includes meditative practices such as Tai Chi, meditation and reflection. Meditation is a way to bring oneself out into a wider concept beyond the self and, sometimes, within the planet. The setting for the next story is my neighbourhood faith community and local church in Manchester.

When my children were small, a neighbour from church gave me a taped talk on meditation. I listened to the speaker discuss meditating with utter faithfulness, every morning and every evening for twenty minutes, while saying the mantra "Maranatha". In this way, we can come to the Cloud of Unknowing between ourselves and God and, one day, come to know God. I listened to the tape many times and it permeated my consciousness. Over the years, I tried to meditate, with varying degrees of success. I would sit cross-legged on the floor in the same place. Once, I managed to maintain this practice for over a year. And then another year. I briefly reached the magical recommended 20 minutes. I do not know whether I will ever reach the Cloud of Unknowing which merges, in my mind, with the Oort cloud, but I sense the embedded spiritual value of the practice. Some years passed and my meditation lapsed. When COVID-19 struck and lockdown was imposed, I returned to meditation, finding comfort in breathing in and out on the ancient words. My practice continues.[65]

This relationship of self into community, Gaia and Cosmos is an account of the challenge over many years to make meditation a part of my life.

○ Hopeful Companions

Books
Christie, D. 2013. *Blue Sapphire of the Mind, Notes for a Contemplative Ecology.* Oxford: Oxford University Press. An account of the spirituality of the Desert Fathers.

Thich Nhat Hanh. 1987. *Being Peace: Classic Teachings from the Worlds most Revered Meditation Master* London: Rider and by the same author 1993. *Present Moment, Wonderful Moment.* London: Parallax Press.

Resources for Action
The Plum Village App: guided meditations, deep relaxation and other practices offered by Thich Nhat Hanh and his monastic community: https://plumvillage.app/

The NHS offers tips and support on mindfulness and access to a short video: https://www.nhs.uk/mental-health/self-help/tips-and-support/mindfulness/

Resources on meditation in the Christian tradition from WWM, a global community of over 100 countries, including live webcasts, videos, books and talks: https://wccm.org/

Creative Learning Exercises

What is your current meditative practice? Consider how you can deepen it to include the wider planet.

Seek space within your life for meditation. Make some time each day for silence.

Once you begin your meditative practice, explore or capture your experience in writing or drawing.

Journaling

For me, journaling is a way to make sense of the experiential ways of knowing that are integral to seeking to live at the intersection of Gaia, Cosmos, self and community. A recent journaling experience illustrates how this ongoing inquiry process helps me to understand living between these different spheres. In January 2020, I registered to participate in *Deep Cosmos*, a week-long residential course at Schumacher College which promised to be a co-operative inquiry into being part of the Cosmos.

Unfortunately, the course was cancelled due to the COVID-19 pandemic. One of the facilitators suggested I conduct my own first-person inquiry during lockdown. The following extract is from the first week of that inquiry, written on Easter Thursday, 2020:

So, writing down the bones...stopping a bit...sitting under the pear tree...the birds are singing like crazy. I think we are going to be in dangerous times until there is a vaccine...I wonder, I'm trying to live in the cosmos (not very successfully). But I'm trying. I'm reading The Universe is a Green Dragon and trying to learn it by heart. The other book I'm reading is The Quest for Gaia by Kit Pedler from 1979.... I could get all my Gaia books together...

These examples of self into Gaia, Cosmos and community lead to a number of learning reflections. A long-term quality of the nine boxes is that they bring action, spirit and reflection together in the same space. Meditation has been a long-term attempt to bring my attention to another way of being in the world. Reflective journaling facilitates an emergent process of sense making. These examples demonstrate that practice is an action not simply over a few days, but over years and decades. The stories refer to the long-term nature of the personal journey of development to experience being part of a wider whole.

Living into the intersection of Community into Cosmos, Gaia and self

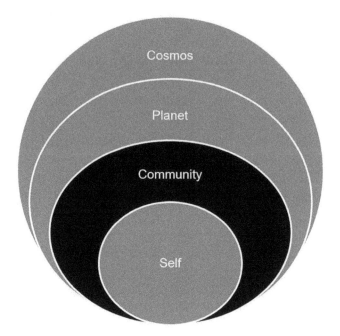

Figure 6.10: From Community to Planet, Self and Cosmos (Source: Kettleborough, 2023)

I used the first-person inquiry principle of attentional discipline to reflect on the final sphere, community. I focused on simultaneously noticing what was happening inside and outside, noticing when I was acting, when I was being receptive, and I engaged in cycles of action and reflection. I used journaling to record this process.

Our Cousins

This story takes place over decades.

My children are small. I take them down to the sea in Iveragh, County Kerry. The beach is deserted. We clamber over the rocks by the seashore. "Come and meet your cousins," I say. Perplexed, they stare at the rocks. Triumphantly, I point at the rocks. "The barnacles! They are your cousins! Say hello!" Delighted, and finding the concept funny, they crouch down beside me and noisily say hello to our cousins. It's a practice I continue. Each new child, each new member of the family, on the beach with me in Iveragh, is solemnly introduced to their cousins. It becomes a game, understanding barnacles as our cousins. The years pass.

Now, more than two decades on, these precious cousins are threatened. My adult cousin mussels have vanished in our little bay. If my human cousins were to vanish there would be an outcry, an investigation. But these cousins go silently. My 12- and 9-year-old human cousins come with me and we clamber over the rocks. Baby mussel cousins are thriving further out in the bay. They have not all gone. But, in the summer of 2019, the adults have gone. We don't know where, but we fear the worst. My aunt tells the story that, decades ago, in our family house in south-west Kerry, there were so many daddy longlegs flittering around the lights every evening. Now, after a ten-day visit in the height of summer, I have not seen even one. The swallows are still here, soaring and diving and perching on the telegraph wires. I determine to love them fiercely and to join a swallow society. I am reminded that my more-than-human cousins are vulnerable to our actions.[66]

One of the central tenets of understanding and living by a different paradigm is appreciating that we are an integral part of Gaia and the Cosmos. We are neither detached nor superior observers. Freya Mathews (2016) argues that simply by having a theory, we separate ourselves from nature. My actions at the seaside are a way to cultivate an appreciation of belonging through experience. My extended ways of knowing led to action. I could not find a swallow society so, on the advice of Sea Synergy, a local NGO, I join Birdwatch Ireland.

A Neighbourhood Festival

One of my neighbours set up a social enterprise, *healthy me healthy communities*.[67] In the wake of austerity and the closure of local authority and public health community development services, it provides community development services in Manchester.

In 2014, our neighbourhood social enterprise applies for and gets funding to hold a festival, to foster community and counter loneliness. The Festival of Rusholme is arranged as a health and well-being festival, featuring films, activities and creativity. The opening night is held at our community centre, a former nineteenth century school. I am invited to show the Journey of the Universe film. We are welcomed by our long-serving local MP. After the film, we sit as neighbours with our local councillors, drinking cups of tea at trestle tables. In front of us are sheets of A4 paper and coloured pens. There is a lot of laughter and joy around the table. We draw our streets and our neighbourhood, then our neighbourhood within our planet and, finally, our neighbourhood within our Cosmos. It seems easy, on this February evening, with laughter, to imagine ourselves as part of the wider Cosmos.

Growing transformative communities

At the business school where I teach, we provide outreach to local communities. Working with the Professor for Sustainability and Innovation and colleagues, we are developing a transformative communities initiative, linking the local community of Rusholme with our Department in the Business School. The focus is bringing students and staff to local projects. My work granted me the funding to attend a conference related to the themes of the initiative.

I'm in Dundee at the 2019 Annual International Community Development Association Conference. The place is buzzing with five hundred delegates crammed into a university building. Noise levels in the atrium rise and fall as sessions stop and start. Each evening, we have Scottish music and dancing and talks on the radical history of Dundee. I present a paper on Earth as Community at the Climate Justice panel. I'm allowed to use no more than eight slides, so I decide to use photographs. I choose my favourites — an image of the North West Community Empowerment Award in 2011 to represent working for social justice. Earthrise, to represent a new holistic story. Our Pale Blue Dot to start to imagine creating a manifesto for Earth as Community. I talk about how we can put nature, communities and community development at the heart of tackling the climate emergency, biodiversity loss and social justice. I am thrilled by the supportive questions from the audience. In the midst of the COVID-19 pandemic, I write my conference paper into an article for Practice Insights Magazine. The editor asks for a headline sentence. I choose: "This is a call to become community development workers and activists not just for our human communities, but for our animal, bird, insect and climate communities as well."[68]

These three stories of the intersection of community with Cosmos, Gaia and self are all second-person learning experiences that include first-person learning. These stories highlight the simultaneous use of a variety of extended ways of knowing, with different emphases according to the setting and they demonstrate the learning that can take place.

The twelve stories in this chapter highlight the value of action research to learning to live in the Cosmos.

Reflections

So far in this chapter, I have presented stories that illustrate how action research can help us to learn to participate in our universe. They combine learning, as individuals, with family, community, work and daily life. A number of themes emerge that illuminate how we can learn to leap within the greater curvatures of space and the planet, and within ourselves and our communities. Extended ways of knowing help us to move beyond our computer screens and consumerism. Time becomes integral to learning and can extend over decades. Learning practices across the generations emerge. These learning experiences highlight the potential of lifelong learning across all aspects of life, in ways that make ideas accessible to all.

 Creative Learning Exercises

In creating your own stories for living in the Cosmos, consider the stories you find in books, articles, films or videos. Can you choose stories from a diverse perspective and which have a theme of equalities in whatever form?

Create your own list of books for children and young people that link together diversity, the individual and community, the Planet and Cosmos. You can draw, paint or create them from collage materials. Share these lists with friends, family, colleagues, local libraries and elsewhere.

○ **Hopeful Companions**

Some diverse children's books to start the journey.

Books
Bryn K. and Bryan J. 2020. *My Mummy is a Firefighter.* London: Butterfly. Explores careers open to everyone regardless of race, gender or background.

Burnell, C. 2020. *I am Not a Label. 34 People with Disabilities.* London: Wild Eyed Editions. A celebration of 34 disabled artists, thinkers, athletes and activists from past and present.

Children's Books Ireland and An Post. 2022. Pride Reading Guide, 100 Great Reads for 0 – 18. Dublin: Children's Books Ireland: https://childrensbooksireland.ie/news-events/100-lgbtqia-reads-discover-our-pride-reading-guide-post

Dean. B. (author) and Prablant, S. (illustrator). 2020. *Me, my Dad and the End of the Rainbow.* London: Simon and Schuster. Exploring LGBTQ+ themes with joy.

Nichols, C. (author) and Dennington, B. (illustrator). 2002. *Harriet Tubman.* London: Scholastic. Exploring Harriet Tubman's life helping over 300 slaves escape via the Underground Railroad.

Emerging first-person inquiry at the intersection of Cosmos, Gaia, community and self

First-person inquiry is a way to use all of our senses to come into the presence of Gaia, to notice what is happening around us, to pay attention to a river, a mountain, the land and the sea shore, to leave behind the computer screen and become immersed in the physical reality of nature. As we notice and pay attention, we get the occasional glimpse that mind and sentience are not simply within ourselves but within the planet (Weber, 2016).

First-person inquiry opens us up to the wonder of the universe. We learn and understand more about the Cosmos, and come to the realisation that we are the reflective and thinking part of the universe (Berry 1999; Swimme & Tucker, 2011; Cox and Cohen, 2011). First-person inquiry allows us to engage differently with scientific knowledge by, for example, hearing and seeing the periodic table as an epic story.

First-person inquiry allows us to take risks and offer ideas, to pay attention to others, to understand the perspectives of the wider community. It asks if we have the courage to help others see the world differently or to move between paradigms. It takes us on a journey of participation, with hearts full of love for the learning journey.

First-person inquiry helps us to search for reflective practices within ourselves and find meaning in the world. It helps us to understand and identify something bigger than ourselves and gives that something a name that is meaningful to each one of us as individuals. First-person inquiry is a journey to live in relationship with life and to make contact with our personal notion of Higher Power. Through meditative practice, it opens the way for an experience common across all spiritual traditions (Fox, 1983; Goff, 2019).

Berry (1999: 162) writes of the need to "re-invent ourselves at a species level" and "within the community of life systems" and argues that we need to understand the Earth as a whole integrated community. These forms of first-person inquiry help us on a journey to do this, to develop understanding in our daily lives and to make possible a journey between the different parts of the universe.

Learning to live within different paradigms: Going up and down the universe

Learning to participate in our planet and universe involves a change in the way we perceive ourselves living in our cosmic homeland, the Milky Way Galaxy. As I reflected on these ideas in relation to working in communities and neighbourhoods, I began to see the different worldviews of the people I worked with as a continuum, and I began to understanding that we are all connected. Rather than opposition between the paradigm I present here and current dominant paradigms, a continuum of ways of working to encompass present paradigms within wider paradigms is possible. From the 2000s to the 2010s, as I sought ways to live in the Cosmos while working in neighbourhood regeneration and community development, I began to notice times when neighbourhood problems were at the street level and, at other times, at the city or national level, and action at different scales was required. Sometimes, neighbourhood regeneration colleagues referred to the need for sub-regional or regional approaches. Indeed, a planet-wide perspective has emerged with the Millennium Development Goals and the UN Sustainable Development Goals 2030.

Primack and Abrams (2006) suggest that we must learn to take action at different spatial levels within the Cosmos. This can be done by developing the practice of considering our lives and experiences from several perspectives from the self through community, Gaia and Cosmos, as demanded by the transition to participative and cosmological paradigms. They also suggest that we recognise that we live on a very special planet at a very special time in the history of the universe.

I started to recognise ways to add extra levels of planet and Cosmos to my daily thinking. I imagined a practice of *going up and down* between the different spatial levels of the universe, putting ideas, issues and challenges to the test at these different levels as part of my reflection on finding solutions to problems or to guide my actions towards a more hopeful future. Over a period of years, I put this idea into practice in my thinking, visualising myself moving up and down the different levels.

Reflecting on setting out on a journey of inquiry
Setting boundaries for the journey to be undertaken

One of the biggest challenges I faced was setting boundaries for my research. There is so much territory to explore. I worked across a wide range of academic disciplines, including ecology, economics and philosophy to explore the extensive issue of the future flourishing of both Gaia and communities. Struggling to keep my journey bounded, I used a number of tactics to stay on track. I concentrated on using first-person research methods. I received regular support from my supervisor and engaged in discussions with fellow students, continually setting targets and deadlines. Other research journeys might use second-person research methods, such as appreciative or co-operative inquiry for specific periods of time, or might be focussed on narrower or more contained research questions.

Creative Learning Exercise

Setting out on the journey, you will face challenges regarding how you will approach the journey and the route you will follow. Through reflection, get to know yourself and seek to be comfortable and relaxed about emergence, about letting the journey unfold, sometimes in unexpected ways. Spend time in nature and seek to pay attention to what you see, helping you experience your journey differently.

How to plan a journey of inquiry – emergent research design and presentation

The development of your inquiry belongs to you and depends on your own research questions, the amount of time you have to undertake the journey, the context within which you live and work and many other factors besides. It is my hope in writing this Handbook that you will be inspired to spend time on your own inquiry journey relevant to your own circumstances and research questions. However, three examples of the development of my inquiry at different levels might prove helpful as you set out.

- I created a fourteen-day Gaia's Graveyards challenge (see Chapter 9), to draw or write something every day for 14 days in response to threats and challenges to social justice and the natural world, which I use with students engaging with reflective practice/first person action research.
- A three-workshop course for Co-operative Learning for Resilient Communities in 2017 led to the community project Planting 47 Trees for Sir Gerald Kaufman, our late Member of Parliament, which was completed on the summer solstice 2021.
- Over a three-year period, colleagues and I explored creativity in sustainability teaching and learning. This involved the practical use of creative materials in the classroom, learning what was possible in the time available and what worked best with the students.

My PhD was a five-year inquiry, but your journey might be longer or shorter than that. I chose to do a PhD to frame my journey and to validate the quality of my ideas. Following the initial development of the research design, the subsequent development was iterative and emergent. As a result, it was not possible to categorise the end results at the beginning, or to understand which elements of the research journey would feature in the final dissertation and which would be in the background. This emergent process was framed within Kolb's (1984) experimental, iterative cycles. As time passed, the main parallel cycles of research became linked with each other horizontally and vertically across time. They also linked back into each other and forward into the future, with echoes of a spiral form. From the beginning, extended ways of knowing were central to the research design.

I encourage you to gather evidence from many sources throughout the journey, including propositional academic literature, and to ground your reflection, learning and actions on the foundations of strong evidence. The balance of reading and other forms of learning are entirely at your discretion. A final consideration is how your inquiry can be recorded and shared. For example, my 14-day challenge was confined to my personal notebook and for my own use, while the community project 47 Trees for Sir Gerald involved the creation of a tree map, yarn bombing and the planting of 47 trees.[69] The Creativity in Learning Project, meanwhile, resulted in changes to the teaching and learning practices of three staff members and co-authored articles that generated fun and happiness in the making (Cobb et al., 2016; Wozniak et al., 2017, Kettleborough et al., 2019). The data generated through cycles of action and reflection during my doctoral research were transformed into text. There are many ways to bring together and share the outcomes of research. In Kassel, Germany, for example, artist Joseph Beuys imagined and implemented an artwork that included the planting of a 7,000-tree oak forest (Korner & Bellin-Harder, 2009).

Creating your own map

I invite you to bring all the ideas in this chapter together and to start to live where the greater curvature of the universe holds the earth, our communities and us.

Invitation to Reflect

In your reflections on this chapter, you have now created a number of drawings. Post them on a wall, on a kitchen cupboard, or the door of a wardrobe, or some other prominent place in your home or place of work.

Add to these drawings with stories of your street, your community, your neighbourhood, your organisation, or any other context that is important to you.

Drawing on your own experience, create a story of when you interacted with Gaia, Cosmos and community in your daily life at home.

Reflect on what it means and any practical ways you can start to live up and down between self, community, Gaia and Cosmos.

Having explored the contribution of first-person action research to enable us to live within new cosmologies and paradigms, I will now explore the contribution of second-person action research to this journey.

Notes

[56] See for example, Stephan Harding's film Animate Earth Science, Intuition and Gaia, the trailer: https://www.youtube.com/watch?v=4eMzGl3omXA and his podcast with Camden Arts Centre: https://www.botanicalmind.online/podcasts/gaia-alchemy-with-dr-stephan-harding

[57] 'Six leaps' and 'Our one and only home'. See book chapter co-written with my daughter Nora (Kettleborough & Kettleborough, 2013).

[58] See: https://www.nasa.gov/mission_pages/cassini/multimedia/pia08324.html

[59] For details of their activities, see: https://www.greenandaway.org/camping/ and for a short history of Green and Away see: https://www.resurgence.org/magazine/article3409-green-and-away.html

[60] See the National Trust campaign to encourage children to actively engage with nature: https://www.nationaltrust.org.uk/50-things-to-do and the work of Forest Schools: https://www.forestschools.com/

[61] For a history of Schumacher collage and its ethos, see: https://campus.dartington.org/schumacher-college/history-ethos. The teacher in this story, Stephan Harding explores many of his ideas in his books, articles and YouTube films. For details of Stephan Harding's writing with Resurgence and Ecologist magazines, see: https://www.resurgence.org/magazine/author137-stephan-harding.html

[61] See Marcin Wozniak et al. for an exploration of this learning within the 'I love learning' project: https://ltiammu.files.wordpress.com/2021/05/12_wozniak_etal_working_together_i_love_learning.pdf

[63] See a description of a Higher Power: https://al-anon.org/blog/higher-power-plan/

[64] See https://c4cp.net/about/

[65] The talk by Father John Maine about the Desert Father John Cassain can be found in 'Short Talks by John Main for use before or after Meditation': https://wccm.org/people/john-main-osb/

[66] Insects are threatened with extinction. See Damian Carrington's Guardian article, 'Plummeting insect numbers threaten collapse of nature', 14th February 2019, https://www.theguardian.com/environment/2019/feb/10/plummeting-insect-numbers-threaten-collapse-of-nature

[67] For details of the work of this social enterprise, see: http://www.healthymehealthycommunities.co.uk/

[68] Issue 16, the May 2020 Edition can be found at: https://www.iacdglobal.org/practice-insights-magazine/

[69] Further details on aims and origins, see https://creativerusholme.c4cp.net/ project/47-trees-for-sir-gerald-kaufmann/

Chapter 7: Nurturing growth through second-person action research

Participatory approaches to learning

"Education, if it means anything, should not take people away from the land, but instil in them even more respect for it, because educated people are in a position to understand what is being lost."

Wangari Maathai (2006: 138)

It started with a tree

It's 2007. I live in a pleasant house in inner city Manchester. There are a lot of problems with rubbish and fly tipping in the area. The area feels uncared for and not all the neighbours know each other. The Council is awarding grants to local groups to improve their neighbourhoods. I apply for a grant to plant trees on our street. We can only plant trees outside houses if the residents agree to have a tree. Following the distribution of leaflets, knocking on doors and knocking on doors again, the neighbours agree and we plant thirteen small trees: rowan, hawthorn, cherry and apple. Phil and I follow this up by organising a big clean up on the lane behind our house, and we fill forty bags with rubbish. Organising together from different households, we create a constituted resident's group, which secures funding for a neighbours' day and over a hundred people turn up. We fundraise in response to the floods in Pakistan and raise £700 for medicines. We gather together to learn about transition, linking our streets to our global neighbours. We have neighbourhood days on the street and plant a community garden, dedicating a white rose to the memory of Jo Cox, MP. A group of residents take up yarn bombing, knitting beautiful installations to decorate the street. With neighbours from the rest of the ward, we plant 47 trees to honour our local late MP – oak, Himalayan birch, Manchurian cherry, whitebeam and edible hawthorn. The trees on our street grow up, slowly becoming taller than the residents, participants in the neighbourhood in their own right.[70]

Introduction

This chapter shifts the focus from individual to group learning on themes of participation, social justice and wider paradigms. Individuals, communities and groups can use powerful first- and second-person action research inquiry to flourish. This chapter draws on my own experiences of initiating, commissioning, managing and delivering action research with and in communities. Some of these initiatives were made possible through central and local government funding, and some were delivered by grass roots volunteers. I examine a range of second-person action research techniques to demonstrate their potential for learning. I explore the effects of austerity on such programmes and suggest the value of integrated programmes and expert facilitators. I draw out the lessons learned from delivering these programmes, including the value of volunteer work. In response to current waves of citizen and community involvement, I suggest ways forward, including initiating a mass planting of action research and participatory learning skills, inspired by Wangari Maathai's Green Belt tree planting movement in Kenya, in order to embed such learning in the wider community.[71]

Second-person action research to improve learning

The primary characteristic of second-person action research is the involvement of groups of people learning together over time. Participants are not separated according to subject and object, researcher and researched. Rather, everyone co-learns together, sometimes with the support of facilitators. Marshall et al. (2011: 32) write,

"Second person inquiry takes place when people work together face to face with others interested in issues of mutual concern, usually in small groups. This can range from the relative informality of mutually inquiring friendship to more formal disciplines of interpersonal dialogue and is most fully expressed in explicit methodologies such as co-operative inquiry. Second person inquiry offers a form within which people can explore important issues together; this can be both challenging and supportive."

This definition of second-person action research allows for the development of a broad forest of methodological approaches. Each approach uses different action research characteristics, such as emergence and extended ways of knowing, to develop its particular style. At its best, second-person action research also includes first-person action research, encouraging each participant to reflect on their own individual journey.

There are four key features to second-person action research that help to develop wider paradigms and approaches to help communities address challenging issues. First, it encourages individuals to explore and become conscious of their own worldviews and paradigms and to learn about and discuss these. Second, it encourages individuals and communities to acquire a sense of scale, to gain an understanding that grows from their own street to their neighbourhood, or from their town or city to their region (or bioregion), nation and beyond. In this sense, gaining a sense of scale all the way to Gaia is less important than developing senses of scale operating at different levels. Third, it encourages communities to dream collectively to create a better world, one that meets their needs. Second-person inquiry is not simply about identifying problems. It is also about creating solutions. We can often feel trapped, or simply not see how the world might be different, because the forces against us are so strong. Fourth, it gives people a sense of agency that, individually and together, they can make a difference, no matter how hard the challenges. Second-person inquiry empowers people and communities. This sense of agency is not simply dreaming about a better future, but taking concrete steps to make that dream a reality. In this chapter, I will explore a wide range of second-person learning tools, the great majority of which I have personally experienced or delivered.

Many of the approaches I present here were delivered through three learning organisations which flowered in the North West of England during the first decade of this century, Neighbourhoods NW (North West), North West Together We Can (NWTWC) and RENEW NW. Each was founded on the premise of opening doors to locally and regionally based learning to improve lives and create sustainable communities.[72]

Neighbourhoods NW, which ran from 2000 to 2013, ran accredited training for the blossoming Town Centre and Neighbourhood Warden services.[73] With financial support from central government, this role expanded to offer extensive training to local authority and other public sector staff working in neighbourhoods and employees of local charities and NGOs. Neighbourhoods NW delivered training and learning on subjects ranging from community safety, neighbourhood working, carbon literacy, sustainable communities, community cohesion and health and safety. Training was also offered to neighbourhood residents involved in community activities. These included long and short-term residents, community activists, faith communities and students. Training was developed and accredited under the National Vocational Qualifications national standards framework, contributing to skills development for staff and management.

NWTWC (2007-2013) was the North West regional arm of the national UK Together We Can Partnership Programme which worked to empower neighbourhood workers and residents and support community development. It also worked alongside specific groups of residents, such as members of Black and Asian communities, women, LGBTQ+ communities and the homeless. NWTWC delivered learning seminars, commissioned research, supported pilot community empowerment projects in local authorities and organised two regional Community Empowerment Awards with Manchester Metropolitan University Youth and Community Department.

RENEW NW (2005-2009), a catalyst regional organisation funded by national government, promoted excellence and learning in the fields of urban regeneration and urban design, and included learning seminars, the dissemination of community-orientated research and the promotion of inter-disciplinary learning within and across organisations through continuing professional development (CPD).

Each of these learning bodies was funded to meet government agreed targets, and they were empowered to develop their own locally appropriate approaches to expanding learning within communities, professions and organisations. In 2010, when the UK was hit with austerity, funding to these projects was cut, the organisations closed over the next few years, workers were made redundant and websites were shut down, removing this wealth of learning from society. At the same time, funding to local authorities was withdrawn, so many could no longer afford initiatives such as learning in the community (see Chanan & Miller, 2013; Toynbee & Walker, 2020). I was eager to share the ideas and value of action research and of participatory paradigms; so, with others, I developed a range of voluntary initiatives. Many were second-person action research activities, delivered on a shoestring, by groups of volunteers working together, including within faith organisations and by taking up opportunities within academic spaces.

An ecosystem of second-person approaches

There are many second-person approaches and one challenge is deciding how to group them together. One way is to imagine how trees, shrubs and plants of different heights and sizes grow together to form a mature garden or woodland. I have grouped these learning approaches into four different categories which, taken as a whole, help to develop learning for positive futures in communities and organisations. The first category seeks to create learning together for discovery, curiosity and empowerment. It includes learning seminars, co-operative inquiry groups and action learning sets. The second category is appreciative practice, a concept and method embedded in communities, allowing them to dream a better place and to empower public sector staff. The third category includes methods that promote participation, such as world cafes, citizens' assemblies and participatory councils. The fourth category focuses specifically on developing wider paradigms, including Gaia and the Cosmos.

It is helpful to not be too rigid when considering the definitions offered for these different learning approaches. Indeed, an essential characteristic of action research is *emergence*, as we cannot know what to expect when we start out. Consider how the Earth is held in space – not too tightly to stop the unfolding of creation, but not so loosely that she flies away into space (Berry, 1988). As Marshall et al. (2011) write, we need to dance lightly with the ideas we hold. You may start with one approach, but then find yourself using elements of other methods too. It is my hope that you can pick from these examples those that are most useful to your own particular learning situation.

○ **Hopeful Companions**

Museums, Libraries and Archives.

Bishopsgate Institute: Special Collections and Archives: stories of individuals and organisations struggling for social justice; includes extensive LGBTQ+ collections and stories of the co-operative movement: https://www.bishopsgate.org.uk/archives

The Disabled People's Archive: https://disabledpeoplesarchive.com/

Feminist Archive: national and international history of feminism, 1960–2000: http://feministarchivesouth.org.uk/ and https://feministarchivenorth.org.uk/

The National Archives contain material on work in local authorities for social justice in communities. The catalogue covers records held by the National Archives and more than 2,500 other archives: https://www.nationalarchives.gov.uk/

Resources provided by archivists responding to Black Lives Matter: https://archivesforblacklives.wordpress.com/resources/

Second-person action research in practice
First category: Learning together for discovery, curiosity and empowerment
Learning seminars

Learning seminars empower local staff and community members to feel a sense of agency and enable the sharing of knowledge and learning through formal and informal discussion. The learning seminars organised by NWTWC were provided for free, and designed with minimal funding and resources. Local officers and practitioners presented and shared information about their current practice and experimental innovations for empowerment. In small groups, attendees discussed how these practices could be adopted in their own settings in other parts of the region. Seminars took place in a wide range of venues, across an area of almost 6,000 square miles from Cumbria to Cheshire and from Liverpool to Manchester, and included local community centres, local government offices, higher education campuses and local hotels. As far as possible, local public transport hubs were utilised. Tea, coffee and water were provided and, sometimes, lunch. From 2007 to 2013, local public sector officers worked in conjunction with NWTWC to identify themes of interest. Workshops were held on topics that included generating employment, participatory budgeting and community engagement and development. Seminars were open to community members, public sector attendees and businesses. The format was simple and proved to be popular. From 2005 to 2009, RENEW NW ran learning seminars on a wide range of topics related to urban regeneration. These included improving the role of women in regeneration, improving urban design, promoting sustainability and sharing learning from regeneration practices. Participants came from diverse backgrounds. One of the important outcomes of these seminars was the collaboration and exchange of ideas on a collegiate and multi-disciplinary, multi-interest working basis. In order to keep such learning going over years, one of the challenges is retaining the freshness of learning seminars and relevance to local contexts. A further challenge is to ensure that there is time and space for everyone to speak, requiring sensitive and firm chairing, to ensure that events remain egalitarian.

Communities of Practice

Communities of practice are based on groups of people learning together and within their own professions, organisations or areas of interest. Individuals can share knowledge, skills and experiences and seek to improve practice or gain confidence in their chosen field. This form of inquiry is based on the ideas of Lave and Wenger (1991) and Wenger (2009). Three communities of practice were initiated under Neighbourhoods NW and NWTWC, on knowledge exchange, neighbourhood regeneration and community development. Participants met in different parts of the North West of England to consider a range of issues relevant to their interests. Communities of practice are a straightforward and relatively inexpensive way of enabling public sector workers and community members to work together on specific issues. At their most simple, they provide a safe space for participants to discuss the challenges and difficulties they face. Such a safe space is important for developing ideas and keeping practice fresh. A particularly striking output was achieved by the NW Community Development Community of Practice between 2008 and 2011. Through a series of workshops, a NW Community Development Vision was created, which was published just as austerity hit in March 2011.[74] Depending on group dynamics, the challenges faced may sometimes dominate discussions, requiring intervention and the encouragement of other voices or the exploration of other approaches, such as appreciative practice. It is helpful to have someone who can oversee the community of practice, who can think about discussion topics, attend each meeting and keep track of the subjects discussed. If attendees are keen on action, it is important to draw discussions together towards action at the end of each meeting.

Co-operative Inquiry

Sometimes colleagues might seek to actively work together on a particular challenge or problem. In this case, the more structured approach of co-operative inquiry is useful. Participants become co-researchers, jointly agreeing on the inquiry question and engaging in cycles of action and reflection (Riley & Reason, 2015). Co-operative inquiry finds its strength in the sharing of each individual journey. The method was successfully used by participants on a residential course at Schumacher College to explore deep ecology (Maughan & Reason, 2001).

At a community college in New York, it was used to explore how students could take agency for their learning (Yorks, 2015), and at Manchester Metropolitan University it was used to explore the use of creative writing in learning (Wozniak et al., 2017). Other examples include inquiring into the role of midwives (Baldwin, 2001), leadership for social justice (Yorks et al., 2008) and evidence-based health care (Waterman et al., 2015). These inquiries have used one or a combination of action research approaches. As a method, co-operative inquiry offers a way for groups to learn together more deeply. The inclusion of one or two facilitators helps to keep the group on track and encourages individuals to carry out the required work between sessions. The value of this method is that the process can be lightly or closely tied to a structure according to the wishes of the participants. Co-operative inquiry, by its nature, lends itself to exploring the more-than-human world and how we as humans might set out to engage with this world. It can also be adapted to online ways of working (Kurio & Reason, 2021).

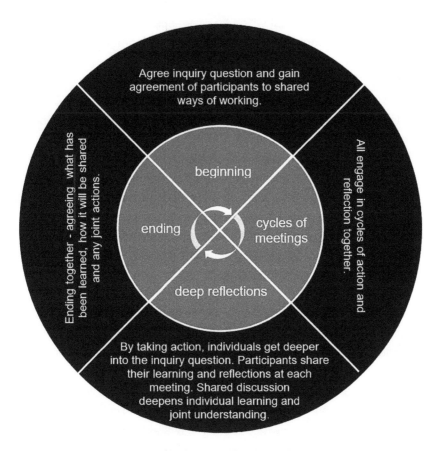

Figure 7.1: Exploring the different elements of the co-operative inquiry cycle, building on the work of Heron & Reason 2001. (Source: Kettleborough, 2023)

Action Learning

Action learning is a reflective approach to learning together about a specific challenge at work or in the community. It was developed by Reg Revans from Manchester University and partly arose out of a critique of traditional business teaching methods. Revans (1971) wrote:

"A man may well learn to talk about taking action simply by talking about taking action (**as in classes in a business school**). But to learn to take action (as something distinct from learning to talk about taking action) then he needs to **take action** (rather than talk about taking action) and to see the effect, not of talking

221

about taking action (at which he may appear competent) but of **taking the action itself** (at which he may fall somewhat short of competent)."[75] (emphasis in original)

Revans developed the idea of action learning groups or sets, in which practitioners discuss their practice and reflect on it for an agreed period of time.

"Action learning couples the development of people in work organisations with action on their difficult problems…[it] makes the task the vehicle for learning and has three main components – *people* who accept the responsibility for action on a particular task or issue; *problems*, or the tasks which are acted on; and the set of six or so colleagues who meet regularly to support and challenge each other to take action and to learn." (Pedler, 1997)

The Liverpool-based interfaith network Faiths4Change established action learning sets to reflect on and learn about community cohesion. The work consisted of a series of learning sets repeated annually over a three-year period to improve reflective and analytical skills.

Action learning sets provide a safe forum for critical reflection on practice at work or in communities. With austerity-related funding cuts, action learning has continued to develop where funding is available. In the NHS, it is now part of Leadership Programmes.[76] Action learning sets expose participants to structured learning and reflection, and offer a way into the future, where ideas, such as sustainability or reducing climate emissions, can be introduced. A challenge is maintaining a sense of the critical without ostracising individual participants. Some organisations do not welcome feedback or innovative ideas, something that participants can explore in their learning set.

 Creative Learning Exercises

Reflect on the tools of second-person action research.

Consider the ways these tools might help your organisation or community.

Think about the questions or issues that can be explored using these tools.

> Think about the different individuals and organisations that could be involved. In your own life, which of these approaches stand out as being most achievable?

Second category: Appreciative practice

Appreciative practice gained some traction in communities in the North West during the 2000s under NWTWC and Neighbourhoods NW. I will return to this method in the next chapter with regard to dreaming a participative universe.

Appreciative practice – empowering and creating new futures

It is all too easy to focus on problems. It can sometimes be very difficult for communities to see solutions to problems, as there are so many. Appreciative practice focuses on "the ability to see and understand what gives life to organisations and to discover ways to sustain and enhance that life-giving potential" (Ludema et al., 2001: 155). Appreciative practice uses a 5D design method and different ways of listening and speaking to imagine new futures.

This 5D inquiry process begins with *defining* and clarifying the question to be explored. This is followed by *discovering* what gives life to the organisation and community. This is often achieved through storytelling. Stories may be written down and shared on walls or tables. *Dreaming* involves all participants imagining what their very best future together might be. Participants are encouraged to dream out from stories of what is already done well. Next comes *designing* together, from the dreams and from what is already good, principles for the future. In the final stage, *destiny*, action planning takes place (Stavos et al, 2018). (See Figure 7.2 overleaf.)

This simple cycle has proven to be transformational and has been successfully used to develop quality in the NHS, on the small community on Rathlin Island in Northern Ireland, in the development of Hull into a Green City and in the creation of a network through the Toxteth BME Community Project to develop collaborative working.[77]

Figure 7.2: Five D Cycle for Appreciative Practice. There are many variants in the literature from which this version is adapted. (Source: Kettleborough, 2023)

○ **Hopeful Companions**

Resources for Action
Imagine Chicago: an initiative to re-imagine the city: https://www.imaginechicago.org/

Imagine Rusholme: https://creativerusholme.c4cp.net/project/imagine-rusholme/ (which includes a link to the late John Popham's video)

For resources on co-operative and participative inquiry see: www.peterreason.net

Appreciative practice uses methods including storytelling, practising deep listening, dreaming a new world and empowering participants to take action (Willoughby & Tosey, 2007). It can be practiced in a variety of settings, including schools and in communities. It is important to choose the most appropriate inquiry question in order to find what gives life to a community or organisation (Grant & Humphries, 2006; Whitney & Trosten-Bloom, 2010).

During the 2000s, NWTWC used appreciative practice in a number of initiatives. The first was a substantial project to empower public sector staff, to understand the challenges they faced at work and to improve their skills in supporting communities. An appreciative practice inquiry was initiated across a number of boroughs that suffered from declining manufacturing and the associated problems of deprivation and poverty. A steering group was established to oversee and modify the programme as it evolved. Frontline staff participants consistently reported that the appreciative practice inquiry made them feel empowered and valued.[78] The inquiries also achieved tangible outcomes. The Broadfield initiative led to a stronger, more active community association, a better understanding of what already existed and of the area's potential. Councillors embraced new forms of community leadership and the approach was integrated into the corporate plan. As a result of the inquiry, new notice boards were set up to disseminate information, a youth group was set up and a Giant Veggie Patch established for the community.

The initiative adopted an innovative approach that filmed participants' responses so that the ideas generated and the techniques used could be shared. The resulting DVD was presented to the Regional Improvement Partnership as an example of good practice and to demonstrate, in an engaging way, how valuable staff had found the process (Mulhern & Emmanuel, 2011).

The appreciative practice of community visioning or dreaming has been successful in cities and in disadvantaged communities around the world. Community dreaming employs the 5D cycle to help people think positively about their locality and devise tangible solutions. Such events require reflective organising and a positive ethos.

Imagine Rusholme!

At the start of Chapter 3, I recounted two large scale appreciative inquiry summits and the energy that this practice generated. The summits took place in an inner-city ward, with a dynamic and diverse population of 14,000 people, centred around the city's famous Curry Mile. The area faces severe challenges associated with littering, fly tipping, fast food waste, transient populations, an over-abundance of student housing and private rental accommodation. The area also has a stable and long-term community that is organised and has developed a number of improvement initiatives. Large-scale community-based appreciative inquiry emerged from a collaboration between local residents and skilled appreciative practice facilitators. The two inquiry events were separated by a number of months and followed a fully formed 5D appreciative inquiry cycle. Intensive efforts were made to get all local stakeholders together, representing a cross section of service providers, residents, politicians and local business owners. Extensive and thoughtful planning was required to run these community inquiry events. The Imagine Rusholme! steering group of five local

Figure 7.3: Running wall visual record of the Imagine Rusholme! Appreciative Inquiry event. (Source: Kate Sibthorpe, 2012).

residents and four facilitators worked together before and during each workshop. Skilled facilitators responded in the moment and worked with the energy and ideas in the room. Such appreciative inquiry events provide steppingstones to the possibility of working with wider paradigms of zero carbon or becoming part of nature and the planet.

The residents adopted a quote from the Trappist monk and social activist Thomas Merton as a slogan for their publicity material:

"Living is more than submission; it is creation.

We can begin now to change this street and this city.

We will begin to discover our power to transform the world."[79]

This appreciative practice created a sense of possibility and of wider horizons, including a broader 'can do' mindset among the residents. Specific immediate outcomes of the inquiry included the creation of seven community work streams with named volunteers and public sector workers tasked with initiating action, several of which took shape and made a difference, and the creation of the book *Stories of a Manchester Street*, which contains interviews with residents from all over the world about living together in a culturally diverse community (Barton & Bishop, 2019).

O Hopeful Companions

Books

Stavos, J. Tores, C., Cooperrider, D. 2018. *Conversations Worth Having: Using Appreciative Inquiry to Fuel Productive and Meaningful Engagement*. London: Berrett-Kohler.

Watkins,J., Mohr B., Kelly, R. 2011. (2nd edn). *Appreciative Inquiry: Change at the Speed of Imagination*. London: Wiley.

Levy, S., Schiller, M., Schiller, S. (authors) and Rudolph, S. (illustrator). 2018. *Stan and the Four Fantastic Powers: The First Ever Appreciative Inquiry For Kids*. Ohio: Tao Institute Publications

Websites
Appreciative Inquiry Commons website for resources: https://appreciativeinquiry.champlain.edu/learn/stories/

Free downloadable material from the Appreciating People Organisation: https://appreciatingpeople.co.uk/downloadable-resources-2/

Third category: Promoting participation

Second-person action research methods can be used to promote participation in a variety of ways.

Participatory research

Bringing learning out of the ivory towers of academia to communities and individual learners is an important method for change. Colombian sociologist Orlando Fals Borda (2001) believed that knowledge should be shared and co-created between academics, workers and farmers. RENEW NW commissioned the dissemination of academic research findings in formats that were accessible to local communities. NWTWC commissioned a series of research projects, including the value of community centres as community anchors, the discrimination faced by women seeking to be councillors, and understanding the disaffection of older men in areas of high unemployment. The findings of these research projects were shared in seminars that linked universities and policy think tanks to communities in real and tangible ways. Time, effort and academic researchers were required to undertake this research, and policy makers had to be prepared to listen to community members and understand their concerns and struggles. The funding needed to expand such research to wide sections of society was cut short by austerity.

World Cafés

One challenge when working face-to-face at conferences or meetings is getting everyone involved. The World Café method enables large numbers of people to work together in the same room and allows for the energy and interests in the room to be captured.[80] At its simplest, participants move between tables, addressing a common question or questions and interacting with the same or different people, and recording reflections and actions in different ways including writing on paper table cloths. World Café techniques can be used in organisational and community gatherings, with trade unions, in community venues and at academic conferences. Depending on the context, the café can be more freely or tightly controlled. It can be run according to a prepared format, or according to the energy of the room on the day. The European Appreciative Practice Network uses the World Café approach in its annual meetings, working with participants from many countries who meet only once a year.[81] The Generation of Peace Project in Brazil used World Café methods to build networks and cultures of peace at high school level, with a commitment to hearing all voices (Steier, 2015). World Cafés are used by many organisations that seek to develop democracy and involvement. Thoughtful preparation of the exact format and type of questions to be used is critical. On the day, facilitators help participants move around, answer their questions and keep the event moving. World Café outcomes are often visual and interconnected, as participants draw and write their own reflections and comment on the drawn and written ideas of others.[82]

Participatory Budgeting

Participatory budgeting aims to involve citizens in the allocation of local or national government funding. The practice emerged in Porto Alegre, Brazil, in 1989, where citizens participate in the annual allocation of budgets. By 1999, the World Bank reported that 40,000 citizens were involved.[83] This innovative and successful example has inspired similar projects around the world. Participatory budgeting can be used to allocate general local government funds or specific pots of funding. In the 2000s, NWTWC delivered participatory budgeting training and encouraged local authorities to adopt the practice. Blackpool Council developed a participatory budgeting programme by identifying funding to be used by its residents. In Scotland, all 32 local authorities are engaged in some form of participatory budgeting. What started as small pots of funding, has now become enshrined in Scottish law with growing amounts being distributed.[84] In England, participatory budgeting struggled under austerity. However, Social Enterprise Shared Futures is now exploring how participatory budgeting can assist councils following the declaration of a local climate emergency.[85] Global research in participatory budgeting shows it can lead to increased participation amongst sections of society and improved engagement in municipal decisions on services (Bartocci et al, 2022).

At a smaller scale, local funding can be allocated to specific areas or wards. An important outcome of local participatory budgeting initiatives is that, when funding is unavailable, communities share and offer each other resources to make initiatives and ideas a reality. Participatory budgeting requires resources from local government and the time and effort of organisations to help organise events. These human and financial resources must be built into the concept. Participatory budgeting is not a panacea and care must be taken that communities do not spend large amounts of their volunteered time on small funding streams.

Participatory Councils

The think tank Compass reports that Preston Council in the North West of England encourages the local in local economic activity through community wealth building and the setting up of co-operatives (Miller, 2019) and Wigan Borough has set up a Community Partnership to support the voluntary and community sector. The London Borough of Barking and Dagenham developed an initiative called Every One Every Day, with neighbourhoods made by everyone, to encourage creativity and innovation amongst all residents.[86] Meanwhile, the Co-operative Councils Innovation Network seeks to improve working with and for local communities.[87] Although these examples represent only a minority of local authorities, they suggest the potential for participatory approaches to engage citizens and help create better neighbourhoods through collaboration between citizens, public sector staff and local businesses. Such initiatives need time and resources and often run counter to the top-down cultures of local authorities.

Citizens' Assemblies

Initiatives to make democracy more participative have emerged in the last few decades. Wakeford et al. (2008) provide a critical overview concentrating on citizens' juries, often involving smaller groups of twenty to thirty people. They explore how planning and delivery must ensure genuine community involvement. Citizens' assemblies rose to prominence in Ireland in the past decade, in advance of referenda on same-sex marriage and the repeal of the Eighth Amendment from the Irish Constitution and in 2022, considering biodiversity loss.[88] Internationally, citizens assemblies are a key demand of Extinction Rebellion activists seeking change in the face of the global climate and biodiversity emergency.[89] Now promoted by the Local Government Association, this type of participation provides larger groups of citizens with opportunities to debate together on complex and often controversial issues and to map ways to move forward, which are broadly agreed on by all assembly participants.[90] Citizen's assemblies are also used to explore themes of health, where participants work together, supported and facilitated by skilled staff, to establish what makes them feel well in their own communities.[91] The Electoral Reform Society has produced a major report calling for the extension of this work in order to deepen participation in democracy in the UK, while the charity Involve explores the use of citizens' juries and assemblies in climate action.[92] The first Citizens Assembly for Climate Change took place in the UK in 2019/2020, and reported to the UK Parliament. A film documentary captured how the Assembly structure enabled participants from very different viewpoints to change and grow in understanding together.[93]

There are many more participatory methods and initiatives in addition to those I have introduced here.

○ **Hopeful Companions**

Articles
Southall Black Sisters Management Committee. 2021. *Activism is the rent we pay to live on this planet. Our Tribute to Pragna Patel*: https://southallblacksisters.org.uk/news/activism-is-the-rent-we-pay-to-live-on-this-planet-our-tribute-to-pragna-patel/

Organisations
Participation of indigenous people and local communities essential for combatting climate change: https://www.un.org/development/desa/indigenouspeoples/climate-change.html

People around the work working together to generate ideas for social change: https://www.participatorymethods.org/task/learn-and-empower

Power Now! 2022. Examples of participation by local people and public services to improve communities: https://www.compassonline.org.uk/power-now/

Public participation to resolve climate change: https://unfccc.int/topics/education-and-outreach/workstreams/public-participation

---

 Creative Learning Exercises

Using coloured paper or different coloured pens, write the names of the participatory techniques on different pieces of paper.

Draw an image or map of your understanding of each method.

Highlight the participatory method(s) you find most interesting and write down why you find them interesting.

Consider ways that you, and your community, can work with these methods.

Consider ways to share these ideas with a colleague or neighbour.

Fourth category: Gaia and the Cosmos

In this section, I will consider learning connected with wider paradigms. The initiatives I describe took place both before and during the period of austerity and were delivered both as funded learning and by groups of committed volunteers. They offer a range of approaches to sharing ideas and demonstrate what can be achieved when individuals, streets and communities work together. The initiatives are loosely grouped according to when they were delivered, thus reflecting the funding available at the time.

Small steps, funded and unfunded

The opportunity to make small changes within organisations presents itself when we think about how to move from our current paradigms to those of Gaia and the Journey of the Universe. The wider paradigms of Gaia and Cosmos are not yet part of mainstream culture and many organisations, despite funding, may not wish to develop these ideas. An initial small step I took was introducing the *Earthrise* photograph into work talks and seminars. Later, I introduced the *Pale Blue Dot* photograph at workshops. These images became a way for me, as a facilitator, to share a sense of both the size of our Cosmos and the extraordinary importance and significance of our planet home, the only place we know to harbour both life and complex life. Participants had to come close to the large whiteboard screen on which *Pale Blue Dot* was projected to find the tiny pale pixel of light that is our home planet, often provoking laughter and discussion.

A further small step was finding opportunities to introduce spiritual qualities into work and community settings. On occasion, I experimented with using stillness and 'sitting like a mountain' to allow space for a different form of learning to emerge. Appreciative practice, through the power of the life-giving positive question, seeks to transform the individual's worldview, even if only for a brief period (Duncan, 2015; Grieten et al., 2018). Spaces of silence and stillness offer glimpses of community action research, allowing inner knowing to emerge for "presencing the future" (Scharmar, 2007). Silence and stillness are ways to gently introduce qualities associated with creating a new world view in conventional public sector and community settings. Increased interest in mindfulness and yoga in recent years to promote mental health and resilience creates spaces for new possibilities and enables the introduction of more holistic qualities into organisational and educational settings (Vu & Burton, 2019).

Funded initiatives

A structured learning programme for learning wider paradigms: Neighbourhoods NW ran a series of interlinked one-day workshops, called *Thinking out of the Box*, in locations across the North West of England to introduce different ways to use action research to improve neighbourhood working and communication (Kettleborough, 2011).

The first workshop taught practitioners the value of complexity theory and provoked interest amongst neighbourhood practitioners trying to simultaneously improve entire geographical areas. The second workshop explored learning to create new futures together by embarking on an intense period of reflection and meditation.

There was also a reflective practice workshop and a workshop that considered appreciative practice around the question "Can organisations which appreciate the best in themselves discover more of what is good?" A workshop on alternative communication in neighbourhoods considered how the role of play and clowning can help residents and officers to develop different means of communicating. The final workshop invited participants to think about creating sustainable futures together through systemic change. Throughout each workshop, conscious thought was given to meaningful participation. Participants were highly satisfied with the workshops and expressed appreciation for having the opportunity to engage in theoretically-based learning.

Neighbourhood Learning: Three Creative Learning for Co-operative Communities workshops taught action research methods and considered how we might live up and down the levels of the universe. These were delivered through a community organisation, with only limited local neighbourhood funding. The sessions took place in a local community college, with access to a shared restaurant facility. The aim was to teach action research in the community, to offer inspiration and explore wider paradigms. Efforts were made to make the sessions as participatory as possible. The half-day sessions included taught input, group discussion, informal discussion and working together on practical ideas. However, residents had to volunteer a lot of their time and it took concerted effort to build up an adequate number of participants for group activities.

The workshops were held three weeks apart and each was structured to introduce a different element of action research. Over the course of the three workshops, the needs and views of local residents were explored, the basics of action research were introduced and new paradigms were explored.

Training courses are often criticised for being no more than talking shops. As a facilitator, I was determined that these workshops would lead to specific outputs. The workshops, therefore, included a tree walk to map out the planting of 47 trees in honour of Rusholme's deceased MP, Sir Gerald Kaufman. The tree planting was completed in 2021.

Volunteer-led learning opportunities

Local Groups: Local voluntary groups, some of which are branches of national organisations, deliver learning across a wide range of topics. GreenSpirit Greater Manchester, for example, active during the 2010s, ran learning events that included an evening talk on the ideas of Thomas Berry and screening the film *Animate Earth*. At another event, participants watched *An Ecology of Mind*, a film about the ideas and perceptions of Gregory Bateson. The North Lancashire and Cumbria GreenSpirit group continues to run a lively programme of events, including learning in and from nature. Such groups nurture human community and being part of the Earth.

Hosting inspirational speakers: Inviting inspirational speakers to contribute to workshops is a voluntary approach that fledgling NGO NLights used to promote ideas about sustainable and ethical communities. This project was hosted in St. Agnes Church, Greater Manchester, through the active support of the local Anglican priest who sought to grow an inclusive community-orientated nature-embracing church.[94] In a two-year period, the Reverend Donald Reeves spoke on reconciliation and forgiveness and the Soul of Europe,[95] Alistair McIntosh spoke about social and environmental justice, including the work of the people of Eigg in Scotland to buy their island back from the landowner, and Satish Kumar spoke about his lifelong work for peace and ecological education and simple living. Such guest speakers provided workshop participants with opportunities to learn in supportive settings.[96]

Volunteers often work with host organisations. The Chaplaincy at St Peters serving the Manchester universities, for example, hosted a one-day conference to consider the teachings of St Francis. The conference was facilitated by four Anglican Franciscan monks, and concluded with a celebration of Mass at the university. At a further workshop, Irish theologian Anne Primavesi talked about Gaia in advance of a day-long workshop. Such inspirational events require the active support of the host organisation. This can be challenging, given the paradigm-challenging nature of the work. Ultimately, holding the space for these ideas belongs to committed voluntary teachers. For example, the Friends of Thomas Berry Group in Manchester grows from the work of NLights, sharing ideas through online means.[97]

One-off workshops: Within the contours of austerity, I have offered a range of one-off workshops, seminars and presentations, to disseminate ideas to academic, community and voluntary sector audiences. These workshops link the participatory paradigm and action research with the Dream of the Earth, biodiversity loss, social justice and hopeful futures.

The focus of each workshop was chosen by the institution or community hosts and included biodiversity loss, the need for a new paradigm for learning and the *Dream of the Earth*. Some workshops focused on helping community groups to renew or find energy and commitment. The concepts and practice of action research, and the paradigm of Dream of the Earth/ Journey of the Universe were incorporated into each of these themes.

In faith communities, the *Pilgrimage for Gaia* workshops use silence and reflection to allow space for grief and loss, but also for appreciation of the natural world to surface. Since 2015, I have organised more than sixteen such workshops.

At university, I taught action research to Master's and PhD students, exploring the emerging participatory paradigm as a methodology that underpins the creation of sustainability and ecological justice. Due to the nature of teaching and learning in disciplinary silos within academia, such as business, the arts, humanities, sciences and engineering, and the narrow and specialist nature of research, PhD students who do not specifically study sustainability or biodiversity loss are less likely to have the space to focus on these issues. Holistic action research workshops offer students the opportunity to engage actively with the planet.

Other one-off workshops are tailored to individual community groups seeking to inspire members using wider cosmological paradigms. One such workshop was with a group of senior citizens who met regularly in a community centre in Manchester. Most were over 80 years old, and one was 100. The use of creative learning in the workshop meant that several participants with dementia could also participate, drawing flowers as I talked about nature. Another group of workshops focused on the ideas of Thomas Berry. Starting with the *Dream of the Earth*, these workshops introduced the concept of action research and the participatory emerging paradigm as a bridge to Berry's hopeful future.

Over a six-year period, several hundred people have participated in these one-off workshops. Workshop attendees have participated through individual writing, working in groups and coming up with potential actions, which they shared with others. The workshops provided me with a way to introduce these concepts within the contours of austerity. The ideas were, in general, well received, with some participants expressing interest in continuing their studies. Such interest was part of the inspiration for writing this book.

Reclaiming participatory learning

The learning methods described in this chapter need to be seen within the context of work for sustainable communities and the UN Sustainable Development Goals (SDGs). Communities, and humanity in general, must reclaim participatory and second-person learning as part of the struggle of communities to improve lives and ensure social justice. In the 2020s, there are global movements for citizen action, from Black Lives Matter to COVID-19 mutual aid groups, to movements to take action against biodiversity loss and the climate emergency. Despite austerity, there is a need to both continue and restart community learning using second-person and participatory approaches. One approach is to follow the green belt movement in Kenya, which, to date, has planted 52 million trees from seeds.[98] At the first UN Conference for Women in 1975, Wangari Maathai listened to women talk about challenges concerning water, fuel and food. She realised the solution was something all communities could do – plant trees. Maathai set out to build an approach in Kenya that enabled women to plant trees. After many challenges and setbacks, a model emerged that encouraged women to grow trees on their own land and to encourage others to plant in different areas, thus creating the self-generating Green Belt movement (Maathai, 2006). A similar approach is needed to plant the seeds of second-person and participatory learning. A strategy to develop millions of learning trees is urgently needed. The value of such an initiative can be demonstrated from the examples in this chapter.

These methods demonstrate the potential for creating alternative paradigms for positive futures together. They are a counterpoint to a consumerist and growth orientated worldview, suggesting that communities can dream and create their own futures (Mulhern & Emmanuel, 2011). In these examples, participants were encouraged, through reflective practice or co-operative inquiry, to develop awareness of their own paradigms or worldviews. Second-person and participatory approaches to learning open doors for communities to envision positive and inclusive futures, and they help participants to think about scale. The Regional Learning seminars in the NW of England, for example, encouraged participants to think from their local street, to the neighbourhood ward, to the city and sub region, and to the region, developing notions of scale as they went along. Participants were encouraged to learn action research methods, to develop their ideas and to share their knowledge. Some of that knowledge was closely allied to ideas of dreaming and the use of the imagination. Workshops offered spaces for knowledge to deepen, for participants to think about values, how they see the world, how they could work together beyond their differences and how they could learn to turn knowledge into practical action. Such learning empowers communities to develop skills to take on the powerful vested interests that oppose them. Participatory budgeting, participatory councils and citizens' assemblies enable communities to critique the growth-orientated, command and control, top-down paradigm that predominates in universities, local governments, public health services, local businesses and multi-national companies, and that militates against communities being actively supported to consider, evaluate and develop their own worldviews (Boden et al., 2015). These learning techniques help communities to become involved in local services, in companies, in their own neighbourhoods, in regional affairs and in the climate emergency, as they grow better futures for themselves and their children (Chanan & Miller, 2013; Ledwith 2020).

This chapter illustrates what engineers refer to as redundancy engineering or building in 'margins of safety' into infrastructure. In nature, animals build up reserves to help them through winters, droughts and other times when there are shortages of food or water. In communities, we also need to build up reserves of both resources and people, rather than driving everything down to the bare minimum. In order to expand learning and development beyond traditional spaces, we need a range of workers and facilitators working within and across communities. Attracting participants requires more than simply advertising. Community members attended NWTWC, RENEW NW and Neighbourhoods NW events because of the dedicated work of community development workers, neighbourhood wardens, neighbourhood workers, Sure Start workers and community learning workers.

DIY Planting Trees of Learning

This chapter has explored the possibilities for individuals and communities to learn together using minimal resources with the help of dedicated volunteers. Learning within structured programmes has a range of strengths, although it is vulnerable to the loss of external funding, while learning that is dependent on individuals is vulnerable to the changing circumstances of those individuals. Individual learning approaches have less capacity for sharing what has been learned more widely and there is a danger of the wheel being continuously reinvented. Without adequate resources, communities and groups face challenges in maintaining on-going long term learning programmes. Finally, the scale of the climate emergency means it cannot be addressed by bottom-up approaches alone.

To expand second-person and participatory learning, the actions described in this chapter need to be practiced in every neighbourhood, with commitments to plant tens, hundreds, thousands and millions of learning trees in the years ahead. Communities need continued or renewed funding. This is happening in some countries, but elsewhere, communities continue to struggle to find funding. Therefore, we need to think more creatively about funding and resources. Shared Futures, a social enterprise in England, for example, is developing ideas around the Green Deal and Citizens' Assemblies, thus "reframing care for our world as part of people led politics".[99]

Many councils are striving to be more participatory, and the Co-operative Councils network, for example, may be open to supporting community learning. Such learning should be intergenerational, and extended and repeated over years, so that learners grow accustomed to this way of experiencing the world. Our institutions must begin to think about communities over generations. I will return to this theme in Cycle Five.

 Invitation to Reflect

Consider the potential of second-person action research and participatory approaches to learning.

In what ways can you develop these approaches in your own community, organisation, faith community or trade union?

In what ways can you, or your community, contribute to planting a million seeds for action research and participatory approaches to learning?

How can you, or your community, make connections with others through and for this learning?

Notes

[70] See https://creativerusholme.c4cp.net/project/stories-of-a-manchester-street/

[71] For a biography of Wangari Maathai and links to her publications and speeches: http://www.greenbeltmovement.org/wangari-maathai

[72] An extensive collection of resources related to these organisations is now deposited as the Living Archive for Community Resilience, Accession 2019/88, Manchester Libraries and Archives. In the future, work will take place to apply for funding to improve accessibility to the collection, including cataloguing and digitisation to make it available both in the search room and online, and for engagement work to ensure the archive is a living collection which inspires learning and activism to as wide a range of people and communities as possible.

[73] Town centre wardens help with queries and advice and play a problem-solving role: https://www.ardsandnorthdown.gov.uk/news/new-wardens-to-help-keep-town-centres-clean. Neighbourhood wardens help local communities in many different ways, for example: https://www.southampton.gov.uk/housing/your-tenancy/neighbourhood-wardens

[74] It is planned that this will be available through the Living Archive for Community Resilience, Manchester Libraries.

[75] Revans, 1971: 54-5 in Pedler and Burgoyne, 2008: 330.

[76] https://www.leadershipacademy.nhs.uk/programmes/als/

[77] Examples are from case studies from the Appreciating People Organisation: https://appreciatingpeople.co.uk/case-studies/

[78] See Mulhern and Emmanuel (2011)

[79] Quoted in Brown (2004: 394)

[80] For simple guidelines for running a World Café: http://www.theworldcafe.com/wp-content/uploads/2015/07/Cafe-To-Go-Revised.pdf

[81] http://aicommunity.net/

[82] https://www.local.gov.uk/topics/devolution/engaging-citizens-devolution/approaches-civic-and-democratic-engagement-0

[83] For an account of participatory budgeting in Puerto Alegre see: http://documents.worldbank.org/curated/en/600841468017069677/Participatory-budgeting-in-Brazil

[84] https://www.gov.scot/policies/community-empowerment/participatory-budgeting/

[85] https://sharedfuturecic.org.uk/report-of-our-money-our-planet-workshops/

[86] https://www.weareeveryone.org/

[87] https://www.councils.coop/

[88] https://www.citizensassembly.ie/en/

[89] https://rebellion.earth/the-truth/demands/

[90] https://www.local.gov.uk/topics/devolution/engaging-citizens-devolution/approaches-civic-and-democratic-engagement/citizens

[91] https://sharedfuturecic.org.uk/central-blackpool-health-wellbeing-inquiry-interviews/

[92] https://www.electoral-reform.org.uk/westminster-beyond-brexit/

[93] https://www.climateassembly.uk/report/. For the BBC programme, see: https://www.bbc.co.uk/programmes/p097sbzc

[94] https://teilharddechardin.org/mm_uploads/TP_Fall_Winter_2014.pdf

[95] Donald Reeves, formerly Rector at St James', Piccadilly, London, was instrumental in supporting the fledging GreenSpirit organisation. For current work see: https://soulofeurope.org.uk/

[96] For a list of speakers, see: https://www.greenspirit.org.uk/gs-magazine/GreenSpiritInTheCommunity.pdf

[97] For an account of the work of the Friends of Thomas Berry Group see Kelvin Ravenscroft, 2021 : https://thomasberry.org/thomas-berry-manchester-newsletters.

[98] https://greenbeltmovement.org/who-we-are

[99] https://sharedfuturecic.org.uk/reframing-care-for-our-world-as-participatory-people-led-politics/

Fourth Cycle: Delving deeper into new paradigms

"What patterns connect the crab to the lobster, the orchid to the primrose and all four of them to us? And me to you?"
Gregory Bateson (quoted in Frijoza Capra, 2010)[100]

"To create a healthy and sustainable world, it is biodiversity that we ought to be cherishing."
David Attenborough (2020: 178)

With hope, awe, wonder and participation, we can now use the tools from the action research toolbox to delve more deeply into new and expansive paradigms. As we travel through our ancient Cosmos to hopeful futures, we need new dreams and visions of what is possible to inspire and drive us forward. Through our participation in the Earth, both individually and with each other, we begin to dream a dream for the whole Earth. We can explore those dreams using our tools of first-person practice, including the creation of new maps. As we identify the qualities of our dreams, we must safeguard against the dreams of exploitation that have driven us in the past.

Driven by awe and wonder, we can now delve deeper into becoming part of a participative universe. This can start with our own individual engagement, through sitting like a mountain. Through this practice we can catch glimpses of ourselves as part of a participative universe. Again, we can use the tools of first-person practice to bear witness in order to deepen our understanding of the tragedy facing the planet and our fellow human beings. I encourage you to start this journey of participation, encountering wonder, as well as grief, in unexpected places. As part of this odyssey, you will glimpse the need for this journey to be deep and intergenerational, as a route to the next cycle.

CHAPTER 8: The Dream of the Earth

"Let us not wallow in the valley of despair, I say to you today, my friends. And so even though we face the difficulties of today and tomorrow, I still have a dream...."
Martin Luther King (1963)

"There is only one way out of this crisis that we ourselves have created. We must *rewild* the world!"
David Attenborough (2020: 121)

At the beginning of the third millennium, during my weeklong residential course at the ecological Schumacher College, discussions with fellow students and teachers encouraged me to dream a future with Gaia. Can we replant 80% of England with natural woodland by 2100 (Harding, 2000)? Can we replant our cities to be within woodland? Can we grow our own food organically using permaculture? Can we create interlinking green corridors to save nature? Can communities lead as governments have not? Such dreams stayed with me as an abiding inspiration. Several years later, I had the privilege of visiting my eldest daughter who was teaching in a primary school in Venezuela. Merry arranged an expedition into the rainforest for us all. Journeying in a dugout canoe up a tributary of the Orinoco River, our guide was an inspirational leader who loved and treasured nature. Arriving at a sandy beach, we clambered up through the rain forest to the top of the magnificent Salto Para waterfall. Above the waterfall, we walked out onto a rocky plateau and, before us, for miles upon miles, was the rainforest, stretching as far as the eye could see. I had found my dream of trees, a humbling and awe-inspiring vision.

Returning home to Manchester, I started to appreciate more the long-established older trees in our neighborhood, which unbeknownst to residents, were highly vulnerable. Local university redevelopment plans and, to a lesser extent, a new cycle path through the University quarter resulted in chainsaws sounding the deaths of over 120 semi-mature trees. As locals, we were powerless, prompting my partner, Phil, to create a year-long art event he called the Oxford Road Murders (see Chapter 9). Yet, despite this local destruction, we chose hope. At a faith retreat centre, I discovered tiny seedlings under yew trees, which might live for hundreds and even thousands of years. We asked the warden for permission to collect them. He gave us his blessing and a trowel. We found over 20 seedlings and carefully transferred them into pots in our garden. Over the next few years, at closing ceremonies to end our Pilgrimage for Gaia workshops, we sang 'The animals went in two-by-two' and gave our hosts a yew seedling. The dream blessing given to all attending the workshops was that the atoms of those of us receiving or planting the yew tree would meet again with the yew tree in 1000 years' time, joining us together across time and space.

Introduction

Thomas Berry's *Dream of the Earth* can be read as a participative concept and an aid to dreaming. My own concept of Gaia's Equation helps us to delve deeper into that dream and into a worldview that, practiced in daily life, searches for the connecting patterns in everything. However, we must be alert to the qualities inherent in our dreams and avoid the dangers of dreams of destruction.

Growing from the destruction of the planet and her people

The story of tree planting and of killing trees in my local community resonates around the world. The world lost the equivalent of thirty football pitches of forest in every single minute of 2019 (Stubley, 2019). More and more trees are dying early as soils dry out due to global heating and render them vulnerable to disease and pests (Le Page, 2021). Forest fires are now igniting around the world, from Brazil and Columbia, to Thailand, Russia and Australia (Tyukavina, 2022). We are no longer in any doubt that icecaps are melting, sea levels are rising and temperatures are increasing. It all seems mad.

Thomas Berry (1988: 205) wrote that "the difficulty of our times is our inability to wake out of this cultural pathology" of consumerism and growth, while Weber referred to a "disenchantment" with nature due to the rise of secularism and capitalism (in Tarnas, 2006). Primack and Abrams (2006) compare humanity to the *Sorcerer's Apprentice* who sees his master magically making the broom do the housework. The apprentice copies the spell and, when his master is not at home, makes the broom do his work. But the apprentice does not know how to stop the broom and trouble ensues. Like the apprentice, we are so caught up in our consumerist vision of progress that we do not know how to stop it (see Skolimowski, 2015). In addition to the physical destruction to our planet, this cultural pathology is harmful to our mental wellbeing. Albrecht et al. (2007) have coined the term *solastalgia* to describe the grief and distress caused by the destruction of well-loved landscapes and species. Around the world, indigenous cultures are threatened or destroyed, resulting in the loss of knowledge of how to live in harmony with nature (IPBES, 2019). Such extreme cultural pathologies can make us feel powerless. Yet, if we delve deeper, we can find a different way to live with and in the world. We can learn to reengage with our planet and cosmos instead of living according to our current deeply ingrained mechanistic paradigm. However, to do so, we must, as Tarnas suggests, imagine that we ourselves are the Universe. He asks, if you were a universe, to whom would you reveal your secrets? Would you reveal them to the person who sees nature as simply a resource to be used, or to the one who sees the universe,

"...at least as intelligent and noble, as worthy a being, as permeated with mind and soul, as imbued with moral aspiration and purpose, as endowed with spiritual depths as he was?" (2006: 39)

For Tarnas, many humans within the western mindset are not only disenchanted with nature but with the entire universe. The emerging participatory paradigm (see Chapter 2) is a story of humans re-engaging through different ways of knowing. However, true understanding that we are part of a living universe is not so easily acquired. Every day, mainstream literature, science, the media and how we organise the world shape our perceptions of a mechanistic universe. The rise of popularism, nationalism and fundamental forms of religion often oppose wider, holistic views of the world. The agents of these paradigms are numerous and powerful, from retail corporations to airlines, from electoral politics to modern medicine, and from the Internet to formal education.

◯ Hopeful Companions

Books
Feldman, C. 1994. *The Quest of the Woman Warrior. A Path of Healing, Empowerment and Transformation*. London: Thornsons.

Films
BBC *Natural World. Earth Pilgrim. A Year on Dartmoor.* 2008. Satish Kumar (Actor) and Andrew Graham-Brown (Director). A physical pilgrimage exploring nature and the Dartmoor landscape and reflections on inner and outer transformations: https://archive.org/details/BBC.Natural.World.2008.Earth.Pilgrim.A.Year.on.Dartmoor.DVB.XviD.MP3.www.mvgroup.org

---

My experience of being 'Gaia'ed' (see Chapter 6) was part of a structured learning environment in a college noted for its social justice and ecological learning. The aim of the course was to bring participants into sustained contact with nature. Through this experience of walking in a wood and seeing the wood from the perspective of the trees; holding a plant with my eyes closed to feel the plant touching me; sitting by a river and attentively listening to the sound of the water; going outside at night to feel the darkness and some sense of fear of the unknown; and sitting in ritual with fellow students I developed a sense of Gaia. Such a deep learning experience enabled me to be more open to a wider sense of participation in the planet.

When I first read *The Dream of the Earth* by Thomas Berry in the 1990s, it left a deep impression on me. It became my practice to read segments of the book, reflect on them, leave them and return to them months or a year later. They became a guide to how we might create a vision of a different future. The text evoked certain feelings and emotions in me and, as I sought to understand Berry's ideas of dreaming, I began to see its clear connections with first-person action research.

Dreaming, imagination and the action research family

Dreaming and imagination have the power to transport individuals and communities to more positive and hopeful ways of thinking. In the last chapter, we explored how dreaming is at the heart of appreciative practice and is the third of the five-part cycle of inquiry. In the Dreaming cycle, individuals are asked to dream and imagine new futures and to share those dreams, in order to create a collective vision. We examined how dreaming can be practiced on scales ranging from the neighbourhood (Imagine Rusholme!) to the community (Rathlin Island) to the city (Hull Green City).[101] Dreaming operates in both spiritual and physical spaces. Douglas Christie (2013) suggests that to become part of the world we must reimagine it as a whole and reimagine paradise, while continuing to live in the world as it is.

Around the world, dreaming has been integral to work for social justice, as exemplified by Martin Luther King's *I have a dream* speech, which clearly sets out both the dream and what the future might look like.

> "I have a dream that one day out in the red hills of Georgia the sons of former slaves and the sons of former slaveowners will be able to sit down together at the table of brotherhood."[102]

Dreaming within appreciative practice is action orientated and seeks to systematically tackle challenges and issues. Dreaming is crucial to the creation of hopeful futures, although it is not a panacea. It requires focus and attention and must be more than a mere superficial exercise. For Berry, the process of dreaming the *Dream of the Earth* deeply connects us to the Earth and the universe. As we dream, we loosen the power that the current paradigm has over our thoughts. Berry proposes a number of ways to understand the *Dream of the Earth*. I explore these ways, below, highlighting participation and the sharing of dreams.

Voyage to the Dream of the Earth

The voyage to dreaming the *Dream of the Earth* does not begin from the human perspective but from the perspective of the Earth herself and her powers to bring forth life. The very words *'Dream of the Earth'* can remain with us, and sit with us. The power of those words alone conjures hope.

Berry urges us to glimpse the awesome qualities of beauty inherent in the Earth, which is both magnificent and amazing in the multitudinous forms of life and the species into which it has evolved.

To better understand Berry, I return to the Gaia's Graveyards newspaper cuttings. Only after spending time with individual cuttings did I begin to appreciate the diversity and magnificence of life on Earth. I spent time with the clipping of the bumblebee facing "a perilous decline" (Jha, 2010), the death of a sperm whale from plastic ingestion (Tremlett, 2013), and Prince William saying that "our children will not see these animals [rhinos]" (Lydall, 2012). At the Pilgrimage for Gaia workshops, I displayed these cutting on the floor, so that participants could appreciate the extraordinary variety and beauty of life on Earth.

○ Hopeful Companions

Books
Tucker M., Grim, J., Angyal, M. 2019. *Thomas Berry: A Biography.* New York Columbia University Press.

Films
BBC *Blue Planet* series: David Attenborough narrates a natural history of the oceans: Blue Planet I (2001): https://www.bbc.co.uk/programmes/b008044n/episodes/guide and Blue Planet II. (2017): https://www.bbc.co.uk/iplayer/episodes/p04tjbtx/blue-planet-ii

David Attenborough. 2011. What a wonderful world. BBC, 7 December. https://www.youtube.com/watch?v=iYXBJmrsxZU

Organisations
International Union for the Conservation of Nature: Nature based solutions: https://www.iucn.org/theme/nature-based-solutions/our-work

The Indigenous Foundation: a 'grassroots youth led organisation of change-makers and activists ...striving to uplift and advocate for and raise awareness about Indigenous Rights': https://www.theindigenousfoundation.org

---

This dream of the whole Earth, with her own qualities and sense of Presence, is a great shift from the human perspective that occupies us now. The *Dream of the Earth* requires a new awareness.

"At such a moment a new revelatory experience is needed, an experience wherein human consciousness wakes to the grandeur and sacred quality of the Earth process." (Berry, 1999: 165)

The *Dream of the Earth* asks us to take a step outward, from our own homes and neighbourhoods, our cities and nations, to gain a far greater perspective of where we are from. We must see the Earth as part of the unfolding history of the universe, of billions of interconnected years, transforming along the straight arrow of time. We must imagine that, in the eons of time before complex life evolved on Earth, the Universe held no blueprints for what was to emerge. We must sit with and be awestruck by the splendours the Earth has created.

"What primordial source could, with no model for guidance, imagine such a fantastic world as that in which we live – the shape of the orchid, the colouring of the fish in the sea, the winds and the rain, the variety of sounds that flow over the earth, the resonant croaking of the bullfrogs, the song of the crickets, and the pure joy of the predawn singing of the mockingbird?" (Berry, 1988: 197).

To truly appreciate the glories of life and the emergence of complex life over the preceding billions of years, we must listen to the Earth in the depths of our being.[103] We need to contemplate the great diversity of life which burst forth on our planet: the plants, trees, insects, mammals, around 8.7 million species, including the human family. Images such as Earthrise or Pale Blue Dot can help us to make real this sense of the Earth as one. Alongside images of the species of the Earth, these images manifest the glory of nature and her creative process.

For Berry, the *Dream of the Earth* is a cosmic creative process, from which we might imagine that the world has been created out of 'imaginative power'. The imagination is most free in dream visions and creativity is often linked with dream experiences. Dreaming, in this sense, is a spiritual process that links into the powers present on the planet. Dreaming is

"…a way of indicating an intuitive, nonrational process that occurs when we awaken to the numinous powers ever present in the phenomenal world about us, powers that possess us in our high creative moments." (Berry, 1988: 211)

The numinous is both an overpowering and inspiring experience and a feeling that includes qualities such as mystery, energy and fascination (Otto, 1923). For Berry, the entire planet is numinous and this quality can speak to us, whether or not we are from a religious or spiritual tradition, if only we pay deep attention.

At certain times of the day, the *Dream of the Earth* can be more easily sensed. At dawn, there is stillness and expectation and, at dusk, the light to the west holds the promise of something larger than ourselves. Each one of us can learn to experience these special moments. Such moments offer us a chance to alter our relationship with the world and, for a brief moment, participate in the Earth, rather than merely observe her from the outside. Berry argues that it is difficult for humans to move from our present addiction to progress and consumerism. He writes, "[the dream of progress] has proved too much for humans to manage in any disciplined way" (1988: 205). However, in these dream moments humanity can find the psychic energy to address the challenges we face and to change course (Reason, 2001a).

As we come to understand the great profusion of life created by the Earth, a dream of participation emerges. Every living being participates with every other being in this magnificent community, extending beyond the great co-operative ecosystems to the long history of the planet during which those ecosystems were created. Indeed, we are all participants in the long history of the universe, the creation of the galaxies and the first stars. From this participative view of the Cosmos, Berry describes all the species and rocks of the Earth as one community and argues that participation is an essential part of the Cosmos. In this sense, the *Dream of the Earth* requires our active participation. We cannot be passive observers. We must become more aware of the Earth and all of her species.

> "We probably have not had such participation in the dream of the Earth since earlier shamanic times, but therein lies our hope for the future for ourselves and for the entire Earth community."
> (Berry, 1999: 165)

Attempts to meet the challenges facing the world demonstrate humanity participating in the *Dream of the Earth*, both as individuals and as diverse groups of people.

Aids to dreaming

We all need help to dream. I offer five aids to dreaming, from my own personal experiences and reflections. I hope they will grow the seeds of imagination, inviting wider reflection on how we might create vibrant creative dreams that attract and entice others to join in this participative process.

Journaling, drawing and healing

Writing as inquiry allows us to dream without being judged by others and without the need to be practical or realistic. Freefall writing gives us permission to dream deeply and broadly. Drawing also allows us to visually explore our dreams. One aid to dreaming is to use freefall writing or illustration to explore each of Berry's ideas.

From the start of my own participatory practice, I related the *Dream of the Earth* to social justice and equality. I engaged in cycles of action and reflection to create a bridge to what, at first, might seem to be two different visions – mine and Berry's. I worked on a regeneration project on a large, disadvantaged overspill estate in Greater Manchester. Over a cycle of several months' reflection, I considered ideas of healing, growing self-esteem and self-confidence, inspired by a variety of self-development writers, the Christian New Testament and my experiences in this particular neighbourhood. I explored healing the self as well as healing communities and the environment. Dreaming such dreams, I began to fill my journals with diagrams and images instead of text. I examined whether, if we can heal ourselves with practices such as prayer, meditation, reflection and improving self-esteem, can we then move on to healing our local neighbourhoods and contribute to healing the wider Earth? In one illustration, I experimented with putting love at the centre of the process to heal ourselves, each other, our communities and our planet in a self-re-enforcing loop.

Two themes emerged from this work to become a significant part of my practice. The first is the appreciative nature of an action research approach that seeks to build on dreams and on the question "what gives life?" The second is an emphasis on love as integral to the process of ecological healing. Between 1987 to 2011, I gained experiential and practical knowledge as I grew into an understanding of the role of healing and love in community and ecological renewal. This translated into an outward manifestation of healing in my professional life in human resource management and staff development. It also included managing a local authority business unit that sought to enhance social inclusion and learning among those who were socially excluded due to a variety of forms of discrimination. I had to adapt words such as 'healing' and 'love' to language appropriate to the local authority context, such as 'well-being', 'personal development', 'targeting and supporting marginalised communities', each of which were used towards the same ends of healing and love. This work contributed to collaborative action undertaken by staff, local residents and councillors that had a profound effect on the neighbourhoods involved. It included hiring neighbourhood rangers to help improve neighbourhood cleanliness, supporting both communities of interest and geographical communities, obtaining European Union funding to create learning champions in disadvantaged areas, supporting the local Credit Union to provide low-cost loans and launching a training scheme for neighbourhood workers in the North West.

Inspired by others – 'Join Up the Pieces'

My dream of the earth has been inspired by others. Inspirational stories can resonate or explain how ideas developed. One such story explained a dream of connecting the Earth's biodiversity. Here I recount a story told by a fellow student, Simon Hicks, who worked at the Gerald Durrell Zoo in Jersey.

In the 1990s, two women from Sao Paulo in Brazil visited the zoo. They wanted to save a threatened species of monkey that lived in their area. The zoo often received such requests. They told Simon that they worked with children in a poor neighbourhood, planting and growing seedlings at the local school. They said that the monkeys survived in only a few isolated patches of habitat. In discussions together, it emerged that, to save the species, the habitat had to be saved and joining up the isolated islands of habitat was the first and most important task. The women left and Simon heard no more from them. He assumed they had given up, as the task was too daunting. However, the following Christmas he received a card from Brazil. It read, "From Join Up the Pieces". Nothing more. The next Christmas, he received a small parcel from Sao Paulo. Inside was a mug with the inscription: "Join Up the Pieces". Another year passed with no further communications. Several years later, the story came back to Simon, as a source of inspiration while we were students at Schumacher College and were discussing Stephan Harding's proposal to return 80% of England to native oak woodland. This would benefit biodiversity, mitigate climate change, preserve the soil and help regenerate communities. The only way to make a sensible start, Stephan said, would be to "join up" existing pieces of woodland and start from there. (see Lovelock, 1988; Wilson, 2016).

The story resonated with me on a number of levels. In 2000, I was a local authority social inclusion project manager and the disjointed nature of the work was challenging, split as it was between many different departments. The story inspired me to write a report, *The Joined-Up Pieces Project: Achieving Social Inclusion in Stockport Metropolitan Borough Council.* Although reviewed favourably by senior management, it did not gain traction to be implemented. However, it contributed to the evolution of my thinking on the importance of integrated work. Later, colleagues and I successfully applied for funding for a knowledge hub to 'join up' regional knowledge related to community empowerment and neighbourhood development. This became part of the work of the Neighbourhoods NW and North West Together We Can initiatives.

The story remained with me as an abiding model for what we need to do and how we might achieve long-term biodiversity and species protection. 'Join up the pieces' resonates with proposals to develop green corridors to enable species displaced by climate change to move to higher latitudes. The Woodland Trust now seeks to join up the pieces to prevent the islandisation of habitat[104] and green infrastructure is now accepted UK Government policy.[105] The ICCA Consortium, a global not for profit organisation, supports indigenous peoples and local communities who are taking care of their homelands and protecting the trees, rainforests and biodiversity from being destroyed or broken up (ICCA, 2021).[106] This story of two women from Sao Paulo gave me a glimpse of the *Dream of the Earth* that I was able to follow in my daily practice.

Learning dreams from reading

Thomas Berry's *The Dream of the Earth* is not the only book that has enabled me to glimpse "…an experience wherein human consciousness wakes to the grandeur and sacred quality of the Earth process" (1999: 106). Myers's (1985; see also Myers & Kent, 2005) *The Gaia Atlas of Planet Management* comprehensively surveys all the world's ecosystems and presents an idea for their protection and care. Milbrath's (1989) *Envisioning a Sustainable Society* suggests how society might be organised with values and learning for an ecological planet. Botkin et al. (1979) have written of the potential of learning to counter humanity's destructive pursuit of growth, while Shiva's (2005) *Earth Democracy* imagines a world that cares for the rights of small producers and farmers and works towards a planetary society. In *The World We Made*, Porritt (2013) imagines an ecologically sustainable world in 2050 and writes, from the perspective of the future, about how we went about achieving it, setting out that imagined journey in a clear and inspiring way. In *How to be an Antiracist,* Kendi (2019) imagines a world where anti-racism is the overriding policy for action, in all parts of society. "*Just imagine: Trees Returning"* writes Attenborough (2020) in his vision for the future. There are many other resources that can help us to glimpse Berry's *Dream of the Earth* and inspire action.

Holding a dream over time – it started with a tree

A final process that inspires me is holding the dream in the heart for many years. Irish writer Arthur O'Shaughnessy's poem *Ode* (1873) includes the following verse:

> "We are the music makers,
> And we are the dreamers of dreams,
> Wandering by lone sea-breakers,
> And sitting by desolate streams; —
> World-losers and world-forsakers,
> On whom the pale moon gleams:
> Yet we are the movers and shakers
> Of the world for ever, it seems."

Other creative methods, such as drawing, collage, photography, lino prints and woodwork, offer different approaches to dreaming. These methods allow us to embody our dreams in physical reality, sensuously engaging with the world. Gawain (1978) suggests using creative visualisation to make a treasure map to where you want to go. Such a map could be digital, made from cut-up newspapers or using a variety of forms of printing. It could be a guide for a year or for many years into the future. One of my long-term dreams is for my university department to adopt the *Dream of the Earth* as part of transforming communities – harking back to my long-ago dream of an England with 80% tree cover through to my current project to plant 470 trees in Rusholme.

 Creative Learning Exercises

Write or use craft materials, coloured pens, blank paper, drawing pencils or a laptop to engage with the following:

Make a drawing of what the Dream of the Earth invokes in you.

For you, what other thinkers and ideas connect with the Dream of the Earth?

Which of the aids to dreaming the Dream of the Earth do you find most useful?

Are there other aids to dreaming that you can add to the list?

Think of other stories or case studies that illustrate approaches to dreaming and inspiration in a participative universe.

Achieving the *Dream of the Earth* requires a paradigm shift, from seeing the world as a resource for humans to living nature. While such a concept is intellectually achievable, it is more difficult to enact in our daily lives of family, work and other commitments, as we worry about social justice and poverty in the face of a powerful and seemingly inexorable business-as-usual model. Poetry can help us to understand the importance of such a transition. In 1818, John Keats wrote, "Axioms in philosophy are not axioms until they are proved upon our pulses" (in Forman, 142). Inspired by these aids to dreaming, in the next section I chart how we might birth a new world view out of our daily lives.

My journey into a new worldview

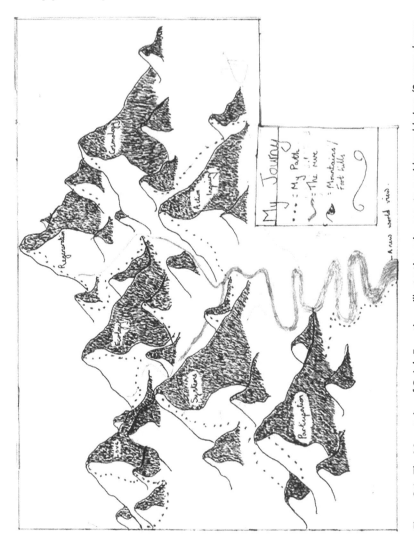

Figure 8.1: The Mountains of Gaia's Equations, illustrating a journey to a wider world view. (Source: drawn by my daughter Ita Kettleborough, aged 13, in 2003, cited in Kettleborough 2014: 158)

The Mountains of Love

When I started my journey over two decades ago, I didn't realise I was going on a 'quest' and that there would be mountains ahead. I simply started to write one day in a brand-new journal. I started to journal because I wanted to improve my life. When I came across a book that a friend recommended, I transcribed parts of the book into the journal and studied them. I transcribed affirmations and wrote my own. I spent many years on what became known to me as the *Mountain of Love*.

I studied the work of Louise Hay (1984), who argues that we can heal and learn to love ourselves. I read Robin Norwood's (1986) *Women Who Love Too Much,* drawing on the Al-Anon spiritual programme. I went to Al-Anon meetings to understand my own history, learning forgiveness for actions and compassion and understanding for others at rock bottom. I studied the Al-Anon spiritual programme of review of actions, self-responsibility and giving to others. I read the works of authors who explored spiritual practice, including feminist explorations and the perspectives of other traditions, including the Tao Te Ching, the writings of Thich Nhat Hanh and Black Elk's visionary experiences.

I spent years on what I came to see as the *foothills* of the Mountains of Love, experiencing love as the values with which it is associated, including the healing and nourishing love of self, the love of children and family, the love of volunteers for each other, their children and their marginalised communities, and the striving for justice in the world.

The Meadow across the Creek

I next travelled into the *Mountain of Ecology.* Berry describes his "meadow across the creek", the formative place where his ecological thinking took hold. The meadow of Berry's childhood taught him an abiding sense of the rightness of place. My own formative place is a beautiful rocky beach, in Co. Kerry, Ireland, where my family live and where I spent my childhood summers. The shoreline is home to mussels, barnacles, limpets and periwinkles and, at night, the unending call of the waves can be heard crashing on the shore. In the early 1990s, when my children were small, we joined our neighbours to annually clean up our local brook and to plant tree seeds. I set up a green group with friends, and I was active in a women's environmental group, promoting the use of reusable nappies. My ecological mountain was a mountain of practice.

Rebirthing life

The next mountain I to travelled was the *Mountain of Regeneration.* My professional work sought to improve neighbourhoods, involve people and create connections between services, communities and councillors. I read central and local government reports. I read about practitioners linking spirit and work for justice in Brazil, North America and South Africa. From spiritual readings, I rediscovered the concept of regeneration linked to the spring and the rebirth of life after winter, related to the Goddess and the divine feminine. For most of us, our life patterns and experiences are no longer linked to the great cycles of the Earth. But, through neighbourhood regeneration work, centred on streets, parks, district centres and the local, I came to understand that we have a route back to the cycles of the earth.

Engaging with the Universe

The final mountain, for the time being, was the *Mountain of Cosmology*. In my mind's eye, this mountain looms large and mysterious behind the others, huge, craggy and reaching into the clouds. I became acquainted with cosmology through my participation in the work of GreenSpirit, through which I started to avidly read the works of Matthew Fox, Satish Kumar and Thomas Berry. I participated in creative workshops, sang to the Leader of Leicester City Council with June Boyce-Tillman conducting, listened to David Abram recall an encounter with seals, and heard Brian Swimme speak of the wonders of the Cosmos. As I walked the mountain of cosmology, I began to engage again with the universe, and to feel in my bones that we live in a universe that is 13.8 billion years old.

We live in communion

Although I have separately described my journey to each of these mountains, they were, in fact, intertwined. This is a key message that living in a wider universe has taught me: in a very practical sense, everything is connected to everything else. We are connected from the very beginning of the Universe to the very end. We are made of stardust. I did not leave love behind at the first mountain. It was with me every step of the way. Did I see where I was going on this journey? Certainly, by the early 2000s, I had some sense of being on a journey. Looking back, I like to think that this was a journey given to me and drawn by the Earth. I could not see through the mists, but I sensed I was being drawn on. Berry (1988:215) writes,

"Only now have we begun to listen with some attention and with a willingness to respond to the earth's demands...that we renew our human participation in the grand liturgy of the universe."

New Mountains

I was drawn further in. I saw an advertisement for a Master's Degree in Responsibility in Business Practice. As I began my degree programme in 2000, my journey resumed. The next mountain I climbed was the *Mountain of Action Research*, which taught a spiritual approach in a language appropriate to the workplace. I learned to talk about cycles of action and reflection, storytelling and first-person truth telling. In that degree programme we sought to visualise an economic system which was just for all members of the human family, without destroying the Earth or human beings or communities. We debated creating diverse and inclusive global communities. In the classroom and on the banks of the River Dart, Stephan Harding taught about Gaia. Sitting in silence, listening to the river, learning to hear her talking to me, I was Gaia'ed. Later, I talked with my fellow students, as we sought to articulate the experience of deep ecology and our affinity for the Earth. I began to feel that my journey was connected to Gaia.

Systems thinking is integral to action research. This led me to the *Mountain of Systems*, an approach in which everything is connected, from the lobster to the crab, from the rose to the human, from Earth to space (see Senge, 1990). Finally, I climbed the *Mountain of Participation*, something I had been doing in my work over many years starting with youth work with young women and girls on a disadvantaged estate. I called it community development and recognised its connections with the roots of action research. It became part of my desire to share my ideas with others.

I had found that my path led through the mountains.

My story demonstrates how a journey into wider paradigms can start from personal exploration of healing and spiritual practice. It illustrates how, through the practical embodied nature of lived practice in self, family, local community and employment, a journey into a wider worldview can take place. It demonstrates how openness to emergence and many ways of knowing deepens and strengthens one's learning and practice. This journey drew me towards more hopeful futures for myself, my family, deprived communities and the more-than-human world.[107]

The Mountains of Gaia's Equation: a visual image of the journey to a wider worldview

My journey into a wider worldview was one of going up and down mountains, crossing rivers and, along the way, marking out a route for the road travelled. This gives an alternative understanding of the concept of a worldview. The journey to a new worldview became a physical and intellectual journey, taken step-by-step and involving challenges and difficulties and an emerging sense of the route ahead. The journey was slow, returning to the values of indigenous peoples and learning to experience the world as a "place of Presence and of presences" (O'Donoghue, 1993) that we share with each other and all the beings of the planet.

Visual images can help us to picture how we live in the universe and the breadth of the changes in thinking that a Gaian worldview demands. They also help us to see the journey into a wider worldview as a holistic adventure, with the many different aspects of our lives interconnected through the different mountains travelled.

Seeking emergent patterns: Writing into Gaia and a new worldview

I sought those connective patterns, through a process of study, reflection and journaling, I identified a series of patterns in several of my earlier journals spanning the 1990s and early 2000s. I explored how I might put these patterns together. At first, I identified four patterns:

love + ecology + regeneration + cosmology

Then a further three:

+ action research + systems + participation

These patterns seemed to be connected. One day, on the train from Bath Spa to Birmingham New Street, I read a series of articles and began to find the words to articulate that the patterns I had discovered in my journals could be described as a journey to a *new worldview*. The articles started from personal experience (Reason & Torbert, 2001b), moved through participation as part of the living world and Planet (Laszlo, 2001), shared stories of participation in professional lives (Quincey et al, 2001) and concluded with reflections on this emerging worldview (Reason, 2001b). While the authors referred to an emerging participatory worldview, I felt more grounded within Gaia from the personal journey I had taken and tracked through my journaling. I named the equation of this new world view 'Gaia's Equation' and completed it thus:

love + ecology + regeneration + cosmology + action research + systems + participation = a new worldview

Defining the story through an analysis of the written accounts of my daily life and identifying patterns offered me a way to perceive and then understand what a journey to a wider worldview (or Gaian-view) might look like. Each one of us can embark on this journey.

Gaia's Equation became the foundation of my practice at work and at home. It was no longer possible for me to work on only love or regeneration, or ecology and cosmology, or action research and participation. Gaia's Equation cemented action research into my worldview, and I sought to share second-person action methods as a way forward. As far as possible, in everything I did, I tried to incorporate as many of the elements of this worldview into my work. If my work team was thinking about regeneration, could we think about green regeneration? If we were thinking about learning, could we incorporate elements of action research? If we were undertaking a participatory exercise, could we include diversity and inclusion? I worked with others to grow enthusiasm and consensus for such an approach. Sometimes, my line manager told me to focus. I tried to be creative with such advice, seeing the pull of Gaia's Equation as long-lasting and regenerative. In the local authority Social Inclusion Unit, staff members set up a working group on the environment and community development. We invited speakers from Ashton Hayes, a village in Cheshire, that was attempting to become zero-carbon, and Incredible Edible, a town project in Yorkshire growing vegetables and fruit on public land.[108] With members of the local Asian, African and Caribbean communities, the community development staff teams organised the annual Black History Month celebrations in the Borough and established the first Civic Asian Mela in the Town Hall.[109] We worked with the Youth and Community Department at Manchester Metropolitan University and NWTWC to explore the principles of community empowerment, which led to creative connections – networking to raise our sights across the region. Trade unions were also interested in becoming involved with environmental issues. As staff members observed, the cross council working group, which included health service workers, made us aware of the possibilities and constraints we were working within. Awareness of interconnectedness was not easy to put into practice within a local authority with narrower specific priorities, but we kept the holistic community development vision in sight.

One of the downsides to this interconnected approach to social justice is that I have often tried to do too much, trying to keep too many plates spinning at once. Any manager is prone to human failings, but a target driven local authority environment can make any mistake into a punishing experience when line managers are unsparing. One such failing, when I offended a senior politician's sense of position – resulted in me being severely verbally castigated. This affected me mentally and physically and led to my search to find a management practice for Gaia, including loving and spiritual qualities. Ultimately, this led to my work to create the tools that can help us all to travel safely to hopeful futures.

 Creative Learning Exercises

Create your own map of your journey towards a new worldview. You can do this by reflecting, drawing, writing or creating responses to the following questions:

When have you felt close to and even a part of the natural world? Write or draw an account of being 'gaia'ed'.

Draw a timeline of your life to date. Underneath your timeline, set out the things that were important to you at different times in your life. Above the line, add your widening understand of what is happening to the planet.

Create your own 'Gaia's Equation', using the key words or concepts that encapsulate your widening worldview. Reflect on how these words connect with one another and with your experience. How might you share them with others?

Imagine how you might start living your daily life into such a worldview.

Sharing the dreams...

Up to now, I have focused on my individual participation with Gaia. But the *Dream of the Earth* belongs to us as groups and communities. One important practice, therefore, is more widely sharing insights into that worldview. Such sharing often provides me with new insights, stories and inspiration, as the process strengthens my own cycles of action and reflection and gives me succour on my journey. Such sharing was achieved through finding and working participatively with others seeking to explore dreams for better futures.

In building a hopeful and inclusive Anglican community at St. Agnes, the priest, Clive Larsen, invited spiritual scholars Matthew Fox and Sister Ilia Delio to speak.[110] Working in partnership, I invited Mary Evelyn Tucker and John Grim, both Thomas Berry scholars, to lead a workshop. An evening screening of the *Journey of the Universe* film preceded a day-long workshop on the philosophy of Thomas Berry. Mary Evelyn and John also spoke at Gorton Monastery in inner east Manchester.[111] I presented at a spiritual discussion group and open meeting, hosted at the inclusive St Brides Church, Liverpool. The same church hosted the Gaia's Graveyard Timeline 2000–2015 and the Cabinet art installations, and was the venue for an exploration of the *Dream of the Earth*.

I gave talks in educational settings and at the Well-being Beyond GDP symposium at the 2015 Manchester Science Festival, inviting participants to draw their own dreams of the Earth. In 2017, I presented the *Dream of the Earth* at the Learning Landscapes Community Learning Festival in Co. Kerry, as part of a panel linking the marine environment with the local community. The ideas of Thomas Berry resonated in a community with deep Celtic spiritual roots.[112] In my presentation, I referred to the Irish monks who left Ireland in the Middle Ages to take their love of nature, the gospels, Greek and Latin to Britain and mainland Europe.[113] At the end of the talk, the participants had generated 138 ideas for taking care of the local ecology. A favoured suggestion was to create a Marine Protected Area around the rocky island of Skellig Michael, a medieval monastic settlement.

At each of these sessions, I sought to tailor the ideas to the specific interests and context of the participants. The sessions raised questions that required further exploration. Participants took home the understanding that some dreams can be destructive, such as our dreams of unlimited growth, consumerism, populism and nationalism, and that quality guidelines are needed as starting points.

Qualities of dreaming the Dream of the Earth

We know that dreams of unending growth and progress and dreams of nature as dead and inert are not helpful. Therefore, we must be guided by particular qualities in our understanding and sharing of the *Dream of the Earth*.

Avoiding nightmares

To move towards an Earth-centred, participatory paradigm, we need to dream for ourselves, our communities, our planet and our Cosmos. Our practice, therefore, must be rooted in action research or a similar methodology to ensure that our dreaming is ethics- and values-based. If the dream is only for humans, or only for more privileged humans, then that is not a *Dream of the Earth*. In our dreaming practice, therefore, we must continually review the dream and the process of dreaming so that it does not become a dream of power over others or of imposing a dream on others. Is it a dream that dismantles inequalities of race, class, disability, gender and sexuality? Action research practices are one way to ensure the continued quality of the process. As I explained in Chapter 4, such a process asks us to continuously reflect on what we are doing, to consider issues of power and to consider the end points of our actions. Do our dreams seek the flourishing of all diverse human communities and of nature?

Knowledge in action and action in knowledge

One way to ensure quality of practice is to draw on and regularly refer to those thinkers who have gone before. In that way, we can be assured that our process is true to the qualities of those who devote their lives to thinking deeply on these subjects. I responded to Berry's (1999: 159) invitation to explore the *Dream of the Earth* – not humanity's dream, but the dream of the Earth herself which would "re-invent the human though story and shared dream experience". I also responded to Swimme's questions regarding living into a new way of being in the universe through our daily lives. I returned to Harding's concept of "being Gaia'd". In contemplating action, do I, as Sathnam Sanghera (2021) suggests, consider the legacy of colonialism and empire and seek to take action to challenge this legacy within my own sphere of influence? I regularly tested my inquiry against Reason and Bradbury's (2001: 2) principles of action research:

> "A primary purpose of action research is to produce practical knowledge that is useful to people in the everyday conduct of their lives. A wider purpose of action research is to contribute through this practical knowledge to the increased wellbeing – economic, political, psychological, spiritual – of human persons and communities and to a more equitable and sustainable relationship with the wider ecology of the planet of which we are an intrinsic part."

As the inquiry progressed, it became evident that I should draw on the widest set of ideas available, sharing and developing knowledge within communities of practice. I approached this by accessing the community book service, GreenSpirit Books, visiting university libraries and engaging in structured learning through higher education. I am fortunate to have enjoyed these opportunities and it is one of the purposes of this book to contribute to widening access to these ideas. The Covid-19 pandemic saw an explosion of knowledge-sharing through the internet, online meetings, training events and the expansion of MOOCs (massive open online courses). While this is greatly to be welcomed, support and signposting through this mass of resources is needed, together with opportunities to reflect with others on the material. The 'curating' of this knowledge can make it accessible through public libraries, newspapers, reports and papers available on-line and the acquisition of a few key textbooks. When the GreenSpirit Book Service folded, for it could not compete with Amazon, the charity developed the idea of 'books in a suitcase', a small collection of key texts for conferences, meetings and workshops, and provided seed funding for the purchase of books. For a number of years, I followed this idea, taking a selection with me to the workshops I delivered. The intention was not so much to sell books as to make the ideas in those books accessible, by giving participants the opportunity to browse through them, as was Alan Shephard's aim with the GreenSpirit book service. With imagination and creativity, specific knowledge for hopeful futures can be made more widely accessible at the community level, linked into small collections of books in streets and workplaces, within university and public libraries and offering opportunities to share knowledge with individuals and groups.

The best of what is: listening with the heart

A central question regarding the validity of research is why particular data and criteria were chosen. Appreciative inquiry helps in this respect, as it guides the selection through asking the question "What gives life?" and encourages a search for "the best of what is" in situations and actions. Throughout my journey, I explored possibilities and the positive images that can be created while seeking to avoid misrepresenting or distorting the source material (see Zandee & Cooperrider, 2008).

When undertaking writing as inquiry, "What gives life?" can be referred to as "data of the heart". De Vaal (1997) describes how St Benedict encouraged those who followed him to "...listen with the ear of the heart." I use the phrase "knowing of the heart" to discover the best of what is. A challenge to curating the research material is appropriately transposing it into a rational and ordered frame. I sought to capture the energy needed to create change for justice and considered this type of knowledge important for working towards wider paradigms. As McIntosh (2001) writes, "There also had to be magic: a constellating force that provided vision."

Planting seeds and trusting emergence

An important quality of the participatory paradigm and of action research is what Reason and Bradbury (2001) call "enduring consequence" or the long-term consequences for practice. I have used journaling to record this by tracing how ideas expressed in a journal inspired action years or even decades later. There is the sense of planting seeds of knowledge or practice and not knowing when or if they will grow. But they must be first planted and trusted to emerge with enduring consequences. Vandana Shiva (quoted in Korten, 2006: 357) reflects:

> "I've learned from the Bhagavad Gita and other teachings of our culture to detach myself from the results of what I do, because

they are not in my hands. The context is not in your control, but your commitment is yours to make."

Activism, even when the forces pushing against ecological and social justice seem very strong, suggests that we can all make a difference. As Satish Kumar (2017) reflected at an NLights workshop,

> "Every human being is given imagination, can be an artist. You don't have to go to the supermarket to buy imagination. So, if we want Manchester to be sustainable, Manchester has to become a city of artists, of makers, not consumers, of poets who use our imagination."

Waking up to acting in deep time

A further quality is seeing your dreams across a longer timescale than your own personal development and lifespan. A number of writers ask humanity to place itself within a cosmic timescale. Futurist Hazel Henderson (1996) asks how we can continue the evolutionary journey of billions of years. Buddhist Joanna Macy (2013) calls on us to act our 13.8 billion-year age. Stager (2011) asks us to think in longer time scales in order to understand the damage of climate change. We know that changes to the climate that are already occurring will take tens of thousands of years to be reversed even if we were to stop putting carbon into the atmosphere today (IPCC, 2021). To achieve such thinking at a community level, the Haudenosaunee Confederacy teach us to change our values and to incorporate thinking seven generations into the future, so that the generations as yet unborn are part of our planning.[114] It is important to practice thinking in the very long-term. The work for the *Dream of the Earth* is needed over many years. Indeed, if we can begin to think to the seventh generation, we will have extended our time span a little.

The long-term nature of the work to build new paradigms

As we seek to call forth a new paradigm, we must acknowledge that the work to change paradigms and transform worldviews is long-term. A paradigm not only refers to how we see the world. George Lakoff (2010) recalls his instant sense of alarm when he first heard that the world was going to warm up by at least 1.5°C. He argues that scientific facts about what is happening to the environment need to fit into people's pre-existing frames. But such frames can take a long time to change. Work is needed to build longer-term ecological and social justice frames that incorporate and depend on immediate action.

In dreaming the *Dream of the Earth*, we are offered the opportunity to see the earth holistically, to see that all the challenges humanity faces are interrelated and must be tackled systematically. A number of design steps are needed. We must grow our thinking over time, building on pre-existing knowledge. If we don't, then initiatives will fail. As the WWF (2021) puts it, "work with nature...with age old wisdom....to create nature-based solutions" to tackle poverty, hunger and inequality. Whilst COICA, the coordinator of the indigenous organisations of the Amazon Basin, call for the protection of indigenous peoples whose existence is "framed in the defense of life and of the Amazon to continue as a seed on earth and conserve mother nature" (2022)[115]

Creative Learning Exercises

Rather than talking only of the challenges and difficulties facing the world, we can talk about our dreams for a better world. Rather than the supreme pathology of unlimited growth on a finite planet and extreme inequality, we can become the dreamers who call forth the Dream of the Earth. Dreamers operate at all levels of society and all over the world. There are individual dreamers who inspire, in every country:

From Martin Luther King (1963):
"I have a dream that my four little children will one day live in a nation where they will not be judged by the colour of their skin but by the content of their character."

To Vandana Shiva (2005):
"We are all members of the Earth community. We all have the duty to protect the rights and the welfare of all species and all people."

To Satish Kumar (2017):
"Let every citizen [...] proclaim, 'We are not consumers; we are makers.' Makers of food, of energy, of gardens, clothes and furniture, of compost; bakers, cooks, artists."

Start a practice of dreaming. Imagine your own Dreams of the Earth. What do you see?

Test those dreams against what you imagine the Earth herself might be dreaming. How do your dreams measure up?

Set aside time for your own regular practice of dreaming. Regularly reflect on your dreaming using the tools and values of action inquiry.

Keep a folder of your Dreams of the Earth, on paper or on your laptop or mobile phone.

Notes

[100] Capra, F. 2010. Homage to Gregory Bateson, for the film An Ecology of Mind – A Daughter's Portrait of Gregory Bateson: http://anecologyofmind.com/gregorybateson.html

[101] https://appreciatingpeople.co.uk/case-studies/

[102] For an animated version of Martin Luther King's speech, see http://freedomsring.stanford.edu/?view=Speech

[103] See Michael Marshall, 'The full story of life on earth can finally be told', New Scientist, 12th January 2019, Issue 3212. And 'How did complex life evolve?' New Scientist Definition: https://www.newscientist.com/definition/complex-life-evolve/

[104] Woodland Trust: https://www.woodlandtrust.org.uk/about-us/woodland-creation/

[105] For UK Government guidance on green infrastructure, see https://www.gov.uk/guidance/natural-environment#green-infrastructure

[106] ICCA Consortium is an organisation that supports the conservation of territories and areas by indigenous peoples and local communities. See https://www.iccaconsortium.org/index.php/discover/. See the UN EP (2021) on the importance of indigenous communities to saving nature: https://www.unep.org/news-and-stories/story/how-indigenous-knowledge-can-help-prevent-environmental-crises

[107] See the Ministry of Housing, Communities and Local Government, English Indices of Deprivation, 2019. These include 39 indicators cover such financial, health, education, living environment and barriers to housing factors: https://assets.publishing.service.gov.uk/government/uploads/system/uploads/attachment_data/file/835115/IoD2019_Statistical_Release.pdf

[108] For the carbon neutral initiative, see http://www.goingcarbonneutral.co.uk/. See Incredible Edible in Todmorden https://www.incredible-edible-todmorden.co.uk/

[109] See Black History Stockport: Uncovering Stockport's African and Caribbean Heritage: https://blackhistoryinstockport.com/

[110] Matthew Fox pioneered the ideas of creation spirituality. See https://www.matthewfox.org/ which helped initiate GreenSpirit in the UK. Sister Ilia Delio is a Franciscan sister and noted scholar on the works of Teilhard de Chardin who developed his spirituality within the universe: http://idelio.clasit.org/

[111] For an account of their visit, see Coming Home to Community, by the Rev Clive Larsen: https://teilharddechardin.org/mm_uploads/TP_Fall_Winter_2014.pdf

[112] For an exploration of Celtic spirituality and its deep relevance for the ecological crisis facing the planet, see Noel O'Donoghue, (1993) *The Mountain behind the Mountain*. Edinburgh: T&T Clark.

[113] See Helen Waddell (1927/1989) *Wandering Scholars*, USA: University of Michigan Press; Ludwig Bieler (1965) *Ireland: Harbinger of the Middle Ages*, Oxford: Oxford University Press; and Thomas Cahill (1995) *How the Irish Saved Civilisation*, London Doubleday.

[114] See the Haudenosaunee Confederacy: https://www. haudenosauneeconfederacy.com/values/

[115] COICA, Coordinator of the Indigenous Organisations of the Amazon Basin. 2021. https://coicamazonia.org/somos/

CHAPTER 9: Delving deeper still
Dreaming a Participative Universe

"We can make a magical transition from one kind of place to a completely different kind of place and do it, if not quite simultaneously, then certainly within astonishingly few minutes."
Simon Barnes (2018: 22)

"Our human scale…is midway between the largest and the smallest sizes [found in the universe]"
Joel Primack and Nancy Abrams (2006: 161)

"I know that we all come from the stars. That we and the stars are one. That the whole cosmos is one essential unity of extraordinary complexity and simplicity at the same time. I know that it is a strange idea that I can talk to a star."
Henryk Skolimowski (2015: 2)

It's late August and I am sitting on the rocks by the shoreline, warmed by the sun. I am next to a rock pool, crystal clear with a cream lichen base. As I idly watch, I notice a tiny fish dart by. Intrigued, I stare a little harder. At the bottom of the pool, I can see miniscule red creatures skittering along. The sea anemones are waving their tentacles in the water, slowly moving back and forth with the slight breeze on the surface of the pool. Another tiny fish darts by, and then another. Lazily, I bend closer and take up a periwinkle, turning it upwards so that I can see the little creature inside closing its shell as it is lifted from the rocks. The limpets are harder and, though I tug at them and they shift imperceptibly, they do not loosen their hold. I know the only way to dislodge them is to tap their sides with a stone, and I do not want to. I run my fingers over the barnacles, the tiny baby barnacles, and the larger older ones. Some of the shells are empty. I am content to sit by this pool. I raise my eyes, listening to the swish of the waves coming in over the sand beside me. In the distance, across the sea, the mountains of the Dingle Peninsula, hazy in mist, a grey blue smudge on the horizon. Sitting there peacefully with the tiny world of the rock pool, between the mountains and the sea, I realise I am happy.

When I return to my inner-city home, I periodically remember that sensation and attune myself to the nature around me. It is a gradual process of remembering and forgetting, but all the time going back to being quiet and still. Walking beside a brick wall of the university, I notice how the moss and lichen have quietly taken up residence on this city street, softly covering the top with green. In the spring, I develop a relationship with the frogs who live in our pond, appreciating when they are basking in the sunshine, motionless, heads above water.

Introduction

Using the tools of action research, we can delve deeper into our *Dream of the Earth* towards a participative universe that inspires awe and wonder. I offer you seven waymarks for the journey – methods to familiarise yourself with a participative universe. Such explorations offer a wider understanding of being in communion and empathy with each other, and with the living and other elements with which we share our planet and all that exists beyond our planet in the wider Cosmos. We need time to undertake this journey. I invite you to stop at each of the waymarks, consider how or if they call to you and undertake your own exploration.

I start this deeper journey by revisiting Base Camp, where we sought to understand what humanity is doing to the planet, and where we saw the Earth in her wholeness from the perspective of the moon. Rockström et al. (2009) identified nine planetary boundaries that humanity should not breach, four of which we have already breached. Exceeding the remaining boundaries will have disastrous consequences for life on Earth. The 2021 IPCC report has issued a dire warning on the impact of rising global mean temperatures on desertification, environmental degradation and food insecurity. The UN

Refugee Agency reports that over 84 million people have been forced to move from their homes, their situation, in many cases, exacerbated by climate change.[116] In its inaugural year, 1970, Earth Overshoot Day, the day when humanity exceeds the Earth's carrying capacity, was 29 December. In 2020, it was 22 August and, in 2021, it was 29 July.[117] We need to find an urgent means of limiting our actions, otherwise the planet will impose its own limits with devastating consequences for all her inhabitants. As Rockström argues (see Watts, 2020), activists *and* bankers need to come on board. In Chapter 2, I explored the paradigms that can help us to transition to a wider, participative worldview that places us at the heart of the Cosmos and not separate from it. If we are to develop a desire for healthy ecosystems, we must first value them, not simply for their monetary value (natural capital) (Porritt, 2005) but for their intrinsic value, just as we value our children for who they are rather than against the financial cost of bringing them into the world and raising them. We can learn to change how we see the world by moving from the perspective of observers to that of participants.

Glimpsing, living into and sharing our new insights

This chapter delves deeper into that participative universe. I offer you a journey of glimpsing, living into and sharing the participatory universe through seven waymarks. The idea of *glimpsing* is very important. Our understanding of this participative universe might be fleeting, understood once and then not again for several months or years, or it might remain a puzzle to be teased out until, one day, it is illuminated. In his final months, broadcaster and writer Clive James wrote,

> "Looking back, you realise that glimpses are all you ever get. There is so little time."[118]

The idea of a participative universe is so overwhelming and hard to imagine that glimpses are all we can hope for. We will all make the journey in different ways and in different directions. Some waymarks may appear too strange or incomprehensible. If so, then simply let them go. After glimpsing a participatory universe, we need to seek *to live into* these glimpses in our daily lives and *share* our understanding of this participative universe with others so that they too can embark on the journey.

Creative Learning Exercises

As we seek to delve deeper into a participatory universe, immerse yourself in nature and in the universe herself.

Set aside a small amount of time each day to become part of the participatory universe. Can you explore each of the waymarks and see how they are meaningful?

Do you feel there are other waymarks which need to be included to participate in our universe? Can you draw and describe them?

There are Hopeful Companions alongside the waymarks. Identify a book or a film to explore in greater depth or set out to research further and find your own learning friends.

Gather together those resources that have the most meaning for you and keep them with any drawings or reflections from this chapter.

Commit to recording your thoughts and observations on the issues raised as you examine and study this literature.

Waymarks for glimpsing a participative universe
Engaging

Presentational knowing, through such creative acts as art, music, free fall writing, journaling, story, gardening, woodwork, photography, knitting, cooking and craft making, is an important way to engage with the universe. These processes help to get to know the close, sensuous detail of the world. By knowing and concentrating, we lose the sense of being outside observers. One way to express such a sensuous way of knowing is to capture the rich experience of being embodied in the moment. A series of residential workshops on action research taught me how to capture simply being in a participative universe. We used free fall writing to write in the moment and were encouraged to write as exuberantly and abundantly as we could. We were also encouraged to take up the practice of writing first thing in the morning and late at night (see Seeley & Reason, 2008). While my tutors chose writing as the means of expression, they could equally have encouraged us to use singing, clay or food to express ourselves. We also learned and practiced meditation and silence to develop deeper engagement.

Seeley and Reason (2008) suggest four ways to understand the world and nature. *Sensuous encountering* includes appreciating, listening and being with nature. *Suspending* the immediate response of the rational mind allows us to engage in sensuous knowing. For instance, the rational mind may tell us that it is not possible to engage in dialogue with the stars. By suspending rationality, we can do so. *Bodying-forth* is the expression of sensuous knowledge through the body, in dance, clowning or through artistic expression, such as drawing, painting, craft making or singing and music making. *Being informed* ensures that this sensuous knowledge remains with us and informs our thinking and actions.

In *The Spell of the Sensuous*, Abrams (1996) explores the evocative process of writing by crafting the words back into the land, back into the leaves and the soil. In *Earth Cosmology* (2010), he describes listening to the Earth and her beings, seeking to understand their discourse and capturing this in journal writing. He describes entering into a relationship with house beams to say goodbye to them as he leaves his home and listening to the discourse of birds as he learns their songs.

Photography also allows us to capture the sensuous detail of the participative universe, from photographs of the Cosmos captured by the Hubble and James Webb telescopes to photographs of wildlife and nature in our own back gardens. We can share these images on social media, thus rendering them more participative. Other forms of art allow us to participate in our universe through our senses, learning to listen and experience the many presences around us.

⭕ Hopeful Companions

Books
Miller, J. (author) and Quartey, A. (Illustrator) 2022. *Leland Melvin, Leaders like Us*. USA: Rourke Educational Materials.

Creativity
Sonia Boyce: Feeling Her Way. 2022. https://www.youtube.com/ watch?v=Aw_-36NXOV8 and Meet the Artist and Curator 2022: https://www.youtube.com/watch?v=7jJm6Q8WiYU British Pavilion Venice Biennale. British Arts Council films

Resources for Action
Nous Les Arbres (We the Trees). 2019. Exhibition, Paris, celebrating trees: https://www.fondationcartier.com/en/exhibitions/nous-les-arbres?locale=en.

> The Botanical Mind: Art, Mysticism and the Cosmic Tree Exhibition, London: https://www.botanicalmind.online/

Understanding

Scientific or propositional knowledge made accessible through scientific writing offers ways to understand the participative universe. The following journal extract captures how I grappled with understanding how to live in a participative universe. It was written nearly a decade on from sitting by the rock pool in Co. Kerry. It started off as a piece of free fall writing, which I have since reworked to share with others.

Thomas Berry writes about how we glimpse the Dream of the Earth through the mist. One way to dwell in the Cosmos is to read the works of different authors.

I go down to London for some meetings. The first meeting is cancelled. I walk past University College London and into Waterstones bookshop. On the way to the café, I pass the Cosmology section and pick up The Goldilocks Enigma by Paul Davies, about how the universe is just right for life. On page 281 he writes, "Conventional science assumes a linear logical sequence, cosmos to life to mind. [But] Wheeler suggested closing this chain into a loop: cosmos to life to mind to cosmos." Davies continues, quoting Wheeler, "'Physics gives rise to observer-participancy; observer-participancy gives rise to information, information gives rise to physics.'" In a footnote, Davies writes, "The concept of a self-explanatory loop is reflected in the ancient mystical symbol of the Uroboros, represented as a snake eating its own tail" (Davies, 2006: 281). He rejects the idea of the universe as a machine subject to fixed a priori laws and replaces it with the idea of a self-synthesising world that he calls "the participatory universe."

Primack and Abrams (2006: 161) explore the mythical concept of the serpent swallowing its own tail. Their Cosmic Uroboros represents the smallest possible scale — 10^{-25} cm — to the largest — 10^{30} cm. If this scale were the face of a clock, humans would measure between 5 and 6.30 pm, in what Primack and Abrams call Midgard, meaning our human scale homeland in the modern *universe – "midway between the largest and the smallest" things (See Figure 11.3)*

This was an important moment in the development of my understanding of the emerging participatory paradigm. What I had already embraced from a community development perspective now had a theoretical basis in physics. The participatory principle that works so creatively for communities is reflected in the workings of the universe. This helped me to develop greater empathy towards my fellow human beings, and understand that we are part of a shared universe, each of us expressing the workings of the universe in our own lives and communities. These ideas were not easy to grasp, but I continued reading and deepening my understanding. Such a participatory view is contrary to the current dominant paradigm of a universe devoid of meaning, on a planet where living nature is only of economic value, to be torn up and concreted over or covered with monoculture at will. Mathematician and teacher Chris Clarke's (2002)[119] account of making sense of a participatory world view helped me to understand that I was grappling not simply with reading about a participatory worldview but with living it in my daily life. I began to sense intuitively that the participatory nature of the universe is crucial to our future. As Berry (1988: 91) wrote, "The universe is a communion and a community".

Being the mid-point in the size of the universe means that we are not dwarfed into insignificance. We live our lives not only in our streets, our towns and cities and our nation states, but in our universe. The everyday act of being alive is, in itself, totally extraordinary, because it took the universe 13.8 billion years to create us. Such lived understanding of how we are active inheritors of an ancient living planet, located in the habitable part of our galaxy, orbiting around a star that, unusually, produces a consistent amount of energy and positioned in the continuously habitable (or 'Goldilocks' zone) of the solar system – neither too hot nor too cold – evokes feelings of compassion for our fellow humans and other species, at the one in a trillion chance of our being here (Gribben, 2011).

○ **Hopeful Companions**

<u>Books</u>
Abrams, N. 2015. *A God that Could be Real: Spirituality, Science and the Future of Our Planet*. Boston: Beacon Press.

Davies, P. 2007. *The Goldilocks Enigma*, London: Penguin.

<u>Films</u>
Abrams, N., Primack, P. 2011. 'Changing the world through a shared cosmology, TED talk': https://www.youtube.com/watch?v=e2qoKR78a6s

<u>Websites</u>
Astronomy without Borders: We all share the same sky and AWB brings the world together to share our passion of astronomy and to share the wonder of the Universe: https://my.astronomerswithoutborders.org/about/vision-mission-and-goals

Living into

Simply being or living into the participatory universe is a way of learning. Reviewing my journals and field notes, I sought glimpses of living into a participatory world through my senses. I found instances of engaging directly with the Earth both at home and elsewhere. These were not experiences meditated through a digital screen or through the written word but experienced directly through my animal body, as I saw the maple and the ash trees in my garden or listened to the song of a blackbird in the early morning. Sensing the stillness or hearing the birdsong, my feet touched the cold earth as I opened the back door. Such an experience is captured through the following extract from 25 September 2011:

Suddenly, the back garden is like Piccadilly Circus. It is only one day since the bird feeder went up. Three days ago, the blue tits and the blackbird came looking and, within a day, I gave in and put the feeder up. Today, the green finches are back and there is a robin standing on the garden chair. Ollie the cat is now in — it's the safest thing I can do, because blackbirds and robins are ground feeders. The garden is full of life, the birds soaring and diving, blue tits swooping from branch to twig to feeder.

Watching and observing with intent can help us to pass through the veil between us and nature that persists in our consumerist culture. We can be like Lucy, awestruck as she steps through the back of the wardrobe in CS Lewis's *The Lion, the Witch and the Wardrobe* to find a world of snow, beavers and fauns. Reflecting on such a journey of transformation, conservationist Simon Barnes (2018) writes that we can create magic spells to take us from our present human-centred world into the world of nature. Rather like the garden birdfeeder, he suggests planting a buddleia to attract butterflies and, by taking the time and effort to learn the names of the common butterflies, we can start to see those that are around us. Or we can cast a spell and enter the world of the sea. The cry of seagulls heralds this spell and a boat trip from a seaside resort is the easiest and cheapest way to travel. Once on board, you are in a new place, the magical domain of the sea, a place apart from the land. Or you might acquire magic trousers. These turn out to be waterproof, enabling you to be out in the rain. These simple actions help us to get closer to the nature around us. In this state of being, we can begin to develop the sense of altruism and generosity of mind to take wise action for nature. Many of Barnes's spells encourage stillness and quiet, helping us to enter a different world. This leads to our next waymark, sitting like a mountain.

Sitting like a mountain

I call the experience of being close to nature 'sitting like a mountain'. Inspired by Aldo Leopold's encounter with the mother wolf, it is a practice that has taken on a deeper sense over the years.

Leopold saw that humanity needed to become part of the community of the whole Earth, to see our relationship with the natural world from the perspective of mountains that are millions and millions of years old, rather than from the human perspective of three score and ten years. This remains an abiding inspiration for me. I used Leopold's story as a point of reflection as I set out to practice sitting like a mountain. I took the time to get close to tiny parts of nature, noticing, for example, the teeming life in the world of a rock pool.

My practice of sitting like a mountain developed over time to take on the specific quality of developing a relationship with wherever I was in nature. It also took me back into time, to the ancient nature of our planet. The practice of presence with the more-than-human world helped me to value nature and to see humans as part of this wider world, in communion with all things (see Berry, 1999).

The practice of 'sitting like a mountain' appears repeatedly in literature in different ways. The seventeenth century Carmelite Brother Lawrence wrote that the presence of God was something he practiced every day. Working in the kitchens and sometimes carrying out difficult tasks, such as taking flagons to another monastery, the practice brought him great joy and became second nature (Brother Lawrence, 1923). Richard Louv (2011) describes exploring woods near his home as a child, climbing the trees and feeling the wind; experiences which restored and calmed him, stayed with him throughout his life and taught him the value of nature. In walking 8000 miles for peace, with no money and trusting the world for food, shelter and travel, Satish Kumar developed walking as a practice of 'sitting like a mountain' (2009).

Closely aligned to practices of mindfulness and meditation, 'sitting like a mountain' is a search for presence and awareness in the moment. It requires only the practice of attention and an appreciation of nature. Having practiced for many years, I can now sometimes sit like a mountain unbidden, seeing leaves in relief against a numinous evening sky, or delicate flowering moss and lichen patterns, or sensing the stillness of our garden in the early morning. Such a practice cannot be willed, but it can be learned. Even in its naming and description, the practice can be widened. Reflecting on living beside Walden Pond, Thoreau (1854: 80) wrote,

"I went to the woods because I wished to live deliberately, to front only the essential facts of life, and see if I could not learn what it had to teach, and not when I came to die, to discover that I had not lived."

◯ Hopeful Companions

Books
Brother Lawrence. 1923. *The Practice of the Presence of God.* London: Mowbray and Co.

Reason, P., Gillespie, S. 2019. *On Presence: Essays/Drawing.* The Letter Press.

Reason, P., Gillespie, S. 2021. *On Sentience: Essays/Drawings.* The Letter Press.

Films
Reflections on Henry David Thoreau's Vision of Walden Pond, on the 200th anniversary of his birth, July 12, 2017, New York Times Daily 360: https://www.youtube.com/watch?v=7jJm6Q8WiYU

Sitting like a mountain can start with an appreciation of our gardens or parks, and of the wild things that COVID-19 brought into our lives. A walk in deep time back through the history of our planet can add the learning of the mountains to our practice. Such learning can take place in groups to broaden experiences and ways of thinking, such as the second person practices described in Chapter 7. These examples of experiencing sitting like a mountain take place within our own home planet, but can offer us a further glimpse of our participative universe, out there, amongst the planets and the stars.

Looking up and conversing with the universe

Since ancient times, the planets in our solar system have caught our attention as wandering stars. The larger planets were critical to Earth's formation, protecting her from bombardment. They are Earth's siblings, protecting her so that life could take hold. But how can we participate with these other objects in the universe? One way is to pay attention to them, notice they are part of our lives, as we do at home from our street in Manchester. Occasionally, the clouds part and we can see Mars high in the night sky overhead, a distinct red twinkling dot. Or maybe it is Jupiter, a brilliantly bright light in the sky, moving over the rooftops as the evening progresses. I remember one particular winter's evening when we saw Mars, Jupiter and Venus – close to the moon, ethereal and stunning – all lined up.

I took to sharing these awe-inspiring experiences with neighbours and, in so doing, we started to glimpse the participatory nature of the universe. Gazing towards the heavens is an ancient practice, but now, in the twenty-first century, with the night sky dimmed by light pollution in our ever-expanding cities, the stars are no longer part of our lives.[120] It is with increasing effort that we look up and see the heavens. Yet, the idea of a participatory universe of which we are a part has long been understood by our mystics and spiritual thinkers. St Francis suggested that we could learn to see nature, and the sun and moon as our sisters and brothers. In *Canticle of the Creatures*, he writes,

"Be praised my lord, for all your creatures,
But especially with Brother Sun,
Because you show us light and day through him
And he is lovely glowing with great shine
From you my lord his definition

Be praised my lord, for Sister Water
Because she shows great use and humbleness in hers and
Preciousness
And depth

Be praised my lord because our sister
Mother Earth sustains and rules
Us and because she raises
food to feed us , coloured flowers
grass..." [121]

The concept of the planets and the sun being our brothers and sisters resonates with philosopher and poet Henryk Skolimowski's (1994) concept of a participative universe. Skolimowski (2015: 74) wrote,

"We must be truly open to the magic of the cosmos, and of the stars, to be able to truly appreciate who we are and what it is all about."

Being open to the stars can begin by simply noticing them within the context of your own neighbourhood, even if only a handful of stars are visible above the city lights. In Byron and Adeola's (2019) children's story *Look Up*, the heroine, Rocket, berates her brother for always being on his mobile phone and asks him to look up at the sky. Eventually, their entire neighbourhood is looking up at the Phoenix Meteor Shower. For people living in light polluted areas, Dark Sky Reserves offer an opportunity to see the stars. Or, we can find inspiration in the beautiful images from the Hubble and James Webb Telescopes and we can mentally take the six leaps around the Cosmos that I introduced in Chapter 6. These small steps help us to grow a sense of connection and start a dialogue with the stars and enter into relationship with the dynamic powers of the universe.

◯ Hopeful Companions

Resources for Action
International Dark Sky reserves: https://www.darksky.org/our-work/conservation/idsp/reserves/

BBC2 Stargazing: Guides and Downloads – free resources to get you started on your journey to the universe: https://www.bbc.co.uk/programmes/articles/2pZFdnsPGl1DDwH6pZbJKkh/guides-downloads

BBC: Sky at Night – resources for watching the night skies through the year: https://www.bbc.co.uk/programmes/b006mk7h

Websites
NASA Image of the Day: https://www.nasa.gov/multimedia/imagegallery/iotd.html

---

The powers of the universe

In *The Great Work* (1999), Thomas Berry argues that humanity does not face its challenges and problems alone. The powers that created the universe are on our side. However, we cannot command those powers, we can only invoke them. Swimme (1984) suggests that we can learn about the dynamics of the universe and evoke them to help us on our journey. He argues that, unlike human power which is often weighted towards discrimination and social injustice, the powers of the universe are open to all. These powers are all around us and we must learn to be among them.

Swimme (1984) explores those powers that are most open to us. Gravity holds the universe together, which we might appreciate as love. Fire is the emergent quality of being in the universe, where the sum is more than the individual parts. Wind carries generosity and signals the interconnected nature of the universe. Life in all her glory carries exuberance, play and learning. The mountains and land carry the cosmic memory of the eons of time it took to create our living planet. How can we learn about and appreciate these powers? The practice of sensuous appreciation that I explored earlier is a way to sense the warmth of the sun, listen to the wind in the trees, remember the immeasurably old cosmic origins of the mountains we see or feel the soil beneath our feet. When we see life, in any of its forms – a leaf, a butterfly, a human child – we should be grateful for what we see and appreciate their joy and beauty. This relearning leads us back to seeing ourselves within a participative universe, and as part of these awesome powers. Swimme (ibid: 87) writes,

> "To become fully mature as human persons, we must bring to life within ourselves the dynamics that fashioned the cosmos."

As we bring this participative universe into our lives, the energy and power of these dynamics open up to us. We begin to experience how we can get help from the universe herself to provide the energy and vision to change our lives and our societies from their present trajectory to become ecologically and socially sustainable.

Bearing witness

One of the manifestations of the universe on Earth is the presence of life. In becoming part of the universe, Swimme urges us to learn about and offer immense gratitude for this. Yet we know that biodiversity is threatened as never before. If the practice of learning about the powers of the universe changes our relationships with nature and the planet, the practice of bearing witness instils in us empathy for both humans and for nature. The practice of bearing witness is found in many faith traditions. Quakerism, which links bearing witness to work for social justice, calls us to "Bear witness to the humanity of all people, including those who break society's conventions or its laws…. Seek to understand the causes…." (Yearly Meeting, 1995).

Many other faith traditions bear witness to what is happening to the Earth. The 1985 Assisi Declarations, *Messages on Humanity and Nature from Buddhism, Christianity, Hinduism, Islam & Judaism,* reflected on what humanity is doing to nature and how faith communities can contribute to healing the Earth[122]. Recent faith work on bearing witness is found in the United Nations Environment Programme's *Faith for Earth Initiative*, which seeks to mobilise all religions to achieve the UN SDGs and to address biodiversity loss.[123] Pope Francis's environmental encyclical *Laudato Si*[124] and the *Islamic Declaration on Global Climate Change*[125] are examples of specific faith communities addressing the environmental crisis.

As I write, people around the world are bearing witness to police brutality against Black communities in America and around the world. Allissa Richardson (2020) has examined how Americans, using their bodies and their mobile phones, bear witness to everyday violence. Video footage of the death of George Floyd at the hands of the police circulated on social media in 2020, contributing to the resurgence of the Black Lives Matter movement.

Richardson has traced the role of Black witnessing in changing the national narrative on police brutality. In the UK, Maron Osieyo, writer and advocate for the UN SDGs, has reflected on the effects of the Grenfell Tower fire (2017), arguing that we must learn to sit with pain and suffering to uncover the systemic causes of injustices.

Finding your way to bear witness

There are many ways to bear witness to the devastation of our planet and to issues of social injustice. My chosen method started with collecting newspaper cuttings with my daughters at the Millennium. It is a practice which continues to this day. Together with cuttings of despair, I collect those of hopeful solutions and stories of awe and wonder at the magnificence of our universe. Taken on their own, the cuttings of despair become too sad to contemplate; taken within the history of the universe, I feel a sense of love and empathy for our planet and her creatures.

Your own practice of bearing witness may be through working with your children, through art or through music. My partner, Phil, bore witness to the cutting down of 120 semi-mature trees in our community through his *Oxford Road Murders* art installation.[126] The Reverend June Boyce-Tillman has composed a choral work, *The Great Turning*, which bears witness to people taking action for the planet within the story of the universe. This choral work has been performed by adult and children's choirs and an online performance has been created to share the work more widely.[127]

There are several practical issues to consider when choosing your practice of bearing witness. Bearing witness is a physical act. For example, in the act of cutting out and contemplating news stories, I came to recognise the value of physically holding the newspapers. I was choosing to engage with biodiversity loss, not simply through my mind, but through my body, through holding the newspapers, finding and picking up the scissors and cutting the stories out, contemplating the pieces of paper, scrawling on the date, and adding to an ever-growing pile.

Bearing witness is often a visual practice. For example, Black Lives Matter activists record images and film of police brutality. Richardson (2020) writes that the movement:

> "...is sustained by a fresh crop of black witnesses who risk their lives to document police brutality with little more than a smart phone, Twitter and a speedy internet connection."

These images have had a profound effect on communities of colour and protest movements around the world, triggering hope for real change.

When I make cuttings of biodiversity loss, it is often the illustrations that remain with me the longest. After a decade of collecting, I reflected:

The cuttings call through their visual images, which evoke a different response than the words alone. It is not simply gorillas that are threatened; it is the gorilla in the picture who stares me in the eye and keeps staring over the years. It is not simply frogs, but the blue and black tiny creature perched with its front and back feet on a branch. A handful of cuttings, which particularly called me, became part of a collection on my desk and in my notebooks. These are species that call and haunt me to do something. I feel the stories tugging at my heart strings.[128]

The knowledge I have gained from bearing witness is the knowledge of the heart. It is the learning of emotions and not simply facts. To appreciate and take care, we must love. Therefore, some of our learning must be affective learning – learning through our feelings and emotions. According to Illeris (2017), there are three dimensions to learning to have power – content, the mental energy to mobilise, and interaction with others and with the environment. As we bear witness and pay deep attention, the struggles of species and nature become our struggle, the melting of the glaciers is the melting of us, the attacks and murders of rangers defending wildlife are attacks on all of us. We start to care deeply at a number of different levels, illustrated in Figure 9.2 (overleaf).

The Guardian | Friday July 7 2006

Science

guardian.co.uk/commenti
Parental challenges to city ac
could derail the project, says

Disease, habitat loss and climate change threatens amphibians

Third of species at risk, say scientists

Rescue breeding urged to counter extinctions

Ian Sample
Science correspondent

Fifty of the world's leading conservation experts are calling for an urgent rescue mission to save frogs, newts and other amphibians from extinction. They believe fast action is needed to save the planet's 5,743 amphibian species after research showing that 32.5% are threatened.

Up to 122 amphibian species have become extinct since 1980. Since the 1960s these vertebrates have gone into sharp decline as humans have encroached on their habitat. Climate change and infectious diseases have also taken their toll.

Writing today in the US journal Science, the conservationists propose a $400m (£217m) initiative, the Amphibian Survival Alliance, to dispatch "rapid response" teams to collect endangered amphibians for captive breeding. The alliance is also to investigate lethal amphibian diseases and environmental changes.

The alliance is expected to become part of the World Conservation Union, which monitors endangered species and which has developed international treaties to urge governments to fund conservation.

Amphibians are considered delicate sentinels of environmental change. Sudden collapses in their populations in the 1980s and 1990s sparked research. Some scientists believe the fungal disease chytridiomycosis, which has spread round the globe, may be to blame in many cases.

Last year, English Nature said the disease was found in Britain for the first time, after infected bullfrogs, imported from North America, had escaped. The organisation destroyed 11,000 infected frogs and is investigating to see if the disease is established here. Predictions suggest that the fungus – which can wipe out 50%-80% of amphibians within four to six months of its appearance – emerged from South African toads but is spreading steadily, by about 17 miles a year.

The alliance will boost existing conservation efforts to protect species such as the dyeing poison frog, the splash-backed

Leap of faith
Environmentalists are calling for action to save endangered frogs such as (clockwise from top) the poison arrow frog, the tree frog, the dyeing poison frog, and the splash-backed poison frog
Photographs: Ron D Holt/PA

Figure 9.1: Disease, habitat loss and climate change threatens amphibians.
(Source: Ian Sample, The Guardian, 7 July, 2006,
Photographer: Ron D Holt/PA)

Bearing witness must also occur over time. Richardson (2020) writes of the 200-year history of witnessing violence and brutality against Black communities in the US. Over my years of bearing witness, increasing evidence emerges that we are now in the midst of the sixth great extinction in our planet's 4,500,000,000-year history. The latest research suggests that more than a million species are at risk of extinction (IPBES, 2019). This is too many to contemplate. I continue to collect these cuttings as part of my practice of bearing witness.

In all our organisations & institutions, bearing witness every day to what is happening to social justice and the planet to inform our policies, our strategies and our financial & economic commitments.

Starting from where we are, bearing witness with others, learning together what is to be done, everyone participating, creating stories to inspire and motivate us, taking wise action.

Planet

Community

Cosmos

Self

Awe & wonder: understanding our planet's amazing variety of living beings and as an integrated being, Gaia, special in galactic history and a unique cosmic jewel to be treasured with her children - human and more-than-human.

Taking time out of our busy schedules to relate to and connect with social justice, species, stars, climate and ourselves.

Figure 9.2: Bearing Witness within Self, Community, Planet and Cosmos. (Source: Kettleborough, 2023)

○ **Hopeful Companions**

Towards inclusivity...

Articles
Aarnio, A., Murphy, N., Knierman, K., Diez Merced, W. et al. 2019. *Accessible Astronomy: Policies, Practices and Strategies to Increase Participation of Astronomers with Disabilities*. ArXiv Astro-ph. https://arxiv.org/ftp/arxiv/papers/1907/1907.04943.pdf

Films
Hidden Figures. 2016. Recounts the role of African-American women mathematicians in NASA's early space programme, including Katherine Johnson.

Resources for Action

Corbyn. Z. 2020. Q & A Allissa Richardson: The academic and author talks to Zoë Corbyn about why smartphones are a game changer in the African American struggle against the police brutality and the ethics of sharing violent images. The Observer, 16 August: https://www.theguardian.com/world/2020/aug/16/allissa-richardson-its-telling-that-were-ok-with-showing-black-people-dying

The American Astronomical Society (the organisation for professional astronomers in the USA) endorses moves for more inclusive and diverse astronomy and cosmology. See the Nashville Recommendations: https://tiki.aas.org/tiki-index.php?page=Inclusive_Astronomy_The_Nashville_Recommendations

Bearing witness through first-person action research

There are many ways to begin to bear witness and confront what Lovelock (2009) calls "the vanishing face of Gaia" and social injustice in all its pain and being open to participating in change:

- **Faithfulness** in collecting data and deepening our knowledge about threats to species, glaciers, rivers, human inequalities and violence. An emerging characteristic of faithfulness is that the act of bearing witness over years and decades becomes interwoven with other research into the creation of patterns and connections. In such faithfulness lies hope, that as we continue the tradition of bearing witness across the generations, the world will change in as yet unknowable ways (Richardson, 2020).

- **Deep listening** to the stories of animals, nature and people is an act of bearing witness. One important element of action research is attentive listening (Fisher et al., 2002; Pyrch, 2015). When we listen attentively, we can hear the "sound of the earth crying" (Thich Nhat Hanh, quoted in Macy & Brown, 1998: 91) and, when we deeply attend to the data, we do not judge, excuse or ignore, but simply receive. Deep listening pays attention to the spiritual qualities of contemplation in the world, while at the same time stimulating action (de Vaal, 1997).

- **Seeking patterns**. When we bear witness, we seek to find the "pattern that connects" (Bateson, quoted in Capra, 2010). As information and stories start to relate and connect, it becomes easier to see the world holistically and to apply practical knowledge to propositional data. We can all learn to see the world as interconnected, by sitting like mountains and engaging with the news of the planet.

- **Make time,** stop being busy and ignore the tempting (and often convenient) distractions of our technological wonder world (Honore, 2004; Louv, 2011, Saad 2020). Each of us must make an individual journey to personal understanding of biodiversity loss, climate change and social injustice, to pass through the shadow of death and to emerge determined to contribute to a hopeful future.

- **Critical reflection** within the planet and the cosmos on how humanity is causing injustice and biodiversity loss is important. However, it must be set within a wider context beyond humanity to understand the systemic interconnections of the whole Earth. We can reflect within community, within a Gaian context and within deep cosmological time (Boff, 1997; Stager, 2011).

- **Joy** is that important quality of appreciation for all children – human and other-than-human – for the wonders of nature and for the wonder of the universe and how good this makes us feel.

- **Love** for the human and for the other-than-human inhabitants of our planet and universe. Michael McCarthy (2015) describes the "fierce love" we can feel for the swallow, the mackerel and the crane fly because we know that, next year, they may not be here.

- **Participation with others**, including with other beings and the wider Cosmos, is central to engaging people, encouraging participation, co-creating a new paradigm and taking wise action for a flourishing humanity and a flourishing Gaia.

As you develop these qualities and take them into your own life, you will develop your practice of bearing witness. In a participatory universe, such a practice includes developing an ethics for the Ecozoic, something I will return to in the next cycle. As we faithfully undertake the practical experience of bearing witness, over time this becomes embedded in an emerging and wonderful universal paradigm, and part of a long transformative history. As such, the daily practice of bearing witness contributes to an embodied understanding that the universe is participatory, that humans participate with each other, that life and the planet have participated together over eons to maintain the conditions for life. Our planet participates daily with her brothers and sisters in the solar system, and the sun and her children participate in our journey around the Milky Way Galaxy which, in turn, participates in the cosmic superstructure of Immeasurable Heaven. Out of such understandings of participation, we can create hope for our fellow humans threatened by poverty and violence, for our endangered species and for Gaia herself.

 Invitation to Reflect

Bearing Witness.

Reflect on the practice of bearing witness. Seek to identify your own witness bearing practice.

Consider how you might bear witness to what is happening? What methods might you use? Where would you start?

How might you carve an amount of time each day to bear witness?

Draw, write, or otherwise create your own version of the qualities of bearing witness.

How can you bring this practice of bearing witness into your life at home, at work, in your faith community or in your leisure time?

 Invitation to Reflect

Our Participative Universe.

Consider ways to capture and express your experiences of living in a participative universe.

Reflect on what a participative universe means to you.

How do you imagine yourself as part of that universe?

Which of the seven waymarks are meaningful to you? Consider starting your journey towards a participative universe from those.

In what ways can you capture this journey? This might be through writing, photography, music, clay, gardening, sitting in silence and sharing with others.

Notes

[116] See UNHCR report for mid-2021 figures: https://www.unhcr.org/mid-year-trends

[117] Every year Global Footprint Network calculates Earth Overshoot Day marking the date when humanity has used all the biological resources that Earth regenerates during the entire year: https://www.overshootday.org/about-earth-overshoot-day/

[118] https://www.theguardian.com/lifeandstyle/2015/oct/24/clive-james-spring-poetry-methinks

[119] Chris Clarke's website is now a memorial to his writing and thinking on science and spirituality: https://www.scispirit.com/

[120] The International Dark Sky Association explains the different forms of light pollution and offers ways to take action: https://www.darksky.org/light-pollution/

[121] From Roberts and Amidon in Earth Prayers (1991) pp. 226-227

[122] For the full Declarations, see: http://www.arcworld.org/downloads/THE%20ASSISI%20DECLARATIONS.pdf

[123] https://www.unep.org/about-un-environment/faith-earth-initiative

[124] https://www.vaticannews.va/en/pope/news/2020-05/laudato-si-encyclical-pope-francis-summary-5th-anniversary.html and https://www.ifees.org.uk/projects/

[125] International Islamic Climate Change Symposium: https://unfccc.int/news/islamic-declaration-on-climate-change

[126] For an overview of the installation, see: https://philbartonartist.c4cp.net/project/the-oxford-road-murders/

[127] See the Music, Spirituality and Wellbeing International Network for events, activities, publications and the online version of The Great Turning: http://mswinternational.org/

[128] Kettleborough, H. 2019. page 299.

Fifth cycle: Love and a Sacred Universe

"The New Story of the Universe is a biospiritual story as well as a galactic story and an Earth story."
Thomas Berry, edited by Mary Evelyn Tucker (2006: 57)

It is time to journey into our ancient cosmos, to sense the sacred nature of the universe and explore the practical consequences of that sacredness for our lives and our planet. We will inquire into loving and spiritual qualities inspired by the Dream of the Earth and the participative universe. This journey to hopeful futures needs to be deep and intergenerational. This is a personal spiritual journey of curiosity, practice and understanding, starting from where we are and growing into wider paradigms, as we follow a Cosmic Road Map that takes us on an exploration of loving and spiritual qualities, inspired by the Twelve Steps of the Al-Anon programme. It is also a personal and community journey to discovering, encountering and embedding the sacred cosmos and the living planet in our lives, and sharing these qualities and practices more widely. Both journeys need to be undertaken faithfully as part of daily life and taken out into the community, to workplaces, organisations and businesses. This cycle hones in on the spiritual journey at the heart of this book.

Chapter 10: Adding loving and spiritual qualities to the hopeful futures tool kit

"Our experience... has affirmed that [the] five tools [of visioning, networking, truth telling, learning and loving] are not optional, they are essential characteristics of any society that hopes to survive over the long term."
(Meadows et al., 2004: 271)

"The Tao that can be talked about is not the true Tao. The name that can be named is not the eternal Name."
Tao Te Ching (Kwok et al, 1993: Chapter 1)

Education and learning were important to my parents and I grew up loving books. Whenever I faced a challenge, I turned to books for inspiration. Two decades ago, I found myself searching the bookshops of Manchester for material on self-development and healing. Back then, Manchester city centre was still home to a collection of radical, independent and faith bookshops. My journey started with a spiritual book which took an ecological approach to prayer. Thus began my exploration of a spirituality that connected with the Dream of the Earth and a participative universe. That book led me to Alan Shepard's GreenSpirit book service. The book service had books for all ages, linking spirituality to ecology, revealing the sacredness of the planet and cosmos, calling for spirit-based activism and social justice, and offering daily practices to celebrate the seasons. The books represented many faith traditions. I had started the journey home. Alan believed in the power of books and ideas to bring about change and was inspired by Thomas Berry's poem, To the Children, on the front sheet of The Great Work (1999), which he loved to read out loud at events:

"To the children
To all the children
To the children who swim beneath
The waves of the sea, to those who live in
The soils of the earth, to the children of the flowers
In the meadows and the trees in the forest, to
All those children who roam over the land
And the winged ones who fly with the winds,
To the human children too, that all the children
May go together into the future in the full
Diversity of their regional communities."

Introduction

This chapter is the first of a two-pronged spiritual journey of curiosity, practice and understanding. It offers a starting point for your own personal quest. Action research offers a reflective way to undertake this journey, to acknowledge and address some of the critiques of religion and to offer definitions of spirit that will help your inquiry as you make the journey. I explore the evolution from human-centred spiritual practices to wider practices in a participative universe. I also explore qualities essential for hopeful futures and consider how spirituality can flourish even in the bleakest times.

Healing, self-development, spirituality and the sacred in our world today

COVID-19 abruptly changed our world. It led to a greater interest in wellbeing and mental resilience, and it increased encounters with our mortality and with challenges to our free will. Despite growing secularism, most people around the world report belonging to some religious faith.[129] There is an increasing trend towards ecumenical religious practice, honouring and respecting other faiths and traditions. Faith traditions work extensively for humanitarian causes, social justice and, increasingly, the environmental crisis, evidenced through the Assisi Declarations on Humanity and Nature from Buddhism, Christianity, Hinduism, Islam and Judaism in 1986,[130] to the ongoing work of the the World Parliament of Religions for a just, peaceful and sustainable world.[131] The twentieth century has also seen a growth in the number of people who are non-religious, humanist, atheist and agnostic. Many people, both religious and non-religious, no longer live in a meaningful physical world. Consumerism, the throw away culture and overuse of resources in pursuit of progress, has become a pathology that is too strong for humanity to resist.

Through first- and second-person action research, we can begin a journey into healing and love on a living planet and an awesome and wondrous Cosmos. Without these hopeful journeys, we cannot live in peace with each other or with the planet. A first step is to reflect on religion which, for many, is conflated with spirituality. It will also be helpful to develop definitions to guide us through the journey. I have been inspired to undertake this work through my experience of living for over thirty years on a Manchester street, where people from many different cultures and religions live together in harmony and peace (see Barton & Bishop, 2019).

Religion has been criticised as being part of the justification for the destruction of indigenous peoples and cultures in the Americas, Africa, Australia, and elsewhere (Neihardt & Black Elk, 1932; Boff, 1995; Primavesi, 2013). Within the Judeo-Christian tradition, the creation story describes a world given to humans, to "have dominion over...every living thing" (Genesis, 1, verses 26-30). This cosmology continues to shape the modern Western worldview that the world can be treated as a resource solely for human use. The separation of spirit from other species and matter in this worldview has also contributed to the destruction of the natural world. Today, faith traditions can still be criticised for not speaking out strongly enough against ecological destruction (see Boff, 1997; O'Murchu, 2000; Cobb, 2001). Some religions and faith communities are also criticised for their rejection of full gender equality, for actively working against women's reproductive and human rights, for rejecting LQBTQ+ rights to live without persecution and for the rights of children to live free from abuse (McIntosh & Carmichael, 2016).

These criticisms of organised religion can lead to an outright rejection of their spiritual qualities. However, it is important to remember that, as an organisational entity, the institution of religion is not always synonymous with the values expressed by the faithful. Those from a spiritual tradition can adopt self-reflection as an essential part of individual religious practice. This can mitigate against adopting harmful practices towards others or assuming the supremacy of one's own faith tradition. A daily practice of reflection and questioning one's beliefs can lead to humility when considering the ideas and beliefs of others (MacDonald, 1984; de Mello, 1990; Hanh, 2010). Such a practice can be optimistic, as it nurtures critical reflection that furthers the spiritual qualities of one's faith rather than pursuing dogmatic religious beliefs that oppress the beliefs of others.

An analysis of my own spiritual journey has revealed the extent to which my work on action research and spiritual approaches is centred on Western Christian traditions. This recognition has allowed for greater critical reflection of my practice and my sources, and acknowledgement of the limits of my knowledge.

The world is facing multiple environmental and social tipping points. It could be argued that it is too late for spirituality and love as an approach. Instead, technological and geoengineering solutions are the answer within the timescales left to make a difference. However, historians have discovered that a key period in the development of spiritual thinking was during the Axial Age, 900-200 BC. Karl Jaspers (1953) has identified this as a period when qualities such as compassion, wisdom and love for our neighbours were named, practiced and shared. But this was not an era of kindness and peace, but rather a bleak and violent time (Armstrong, 2006). The sombre times in which we live can also be a time when a transformation of qualities, ethics and values is exactly what is needed to provide the personal energy and faithful determination to address the severity of the challenges we face. Spirituality enables dynamic learning, which can change to embrace different values and traditions and lead to repentance and humility concerning past behaviours. Such learning can be seen in the eco-theology movement which, in embracing the need to heal the Earth, contains a cosmological perspective (Deane-Drummond, 2017; Pihkala, 2017). Such dynamic learning has led to the appointment of women priests and bishops in the Anglican Church and faith community support for the Black Lives Matter movement in the US and the UK in 2020.[132] It also leads to the birth of an *ecotheology* movement, growing from Islamic, Buddhist and Christian traditions (Tomren, 2021),

This is a journey we all must take, irrespective of our faith or religious beliefs, our humanist or non-religious beliefs. The first set of tools we can add to our action research tool kit relate to the concept of the sacred.

◯ **Hopeful Companions**

Books
Andrianos. L. and Tomren, T. (eds) 2021.*Contemporary ecotheology. climate justice and environmental stewardship in world religions.* Crete:Embla Akademisk (Orthodox Academy of Crete) and the Book Launch Webinar: https://www.youtube.com/watch?v=gotq6C1Q6S0

Dunn, J., Joziasse, H., Patta, R. and Duggan, J. (editors) (2019. *Multiple Faiths in Post Colonial Cities: Living Together after Empire.* London: Palgrave Macmillian: https://link.springer.com/book/10.1007/978-3-030-17144-5

Postcolonialism and Religions: Bridges secular and sacred and features global indigenous authors: Series Editors: Joseph Dunn and Jayakira Sebastian: https://link.springer.com/series/14535

Resources for action
See the *Faith for Change Initiative* from the UNEP: 'To encourage, empower and engage with faith-based organizations as partners, at all levels, toward achieving the Sustainable Development Goals and fulfilling the 2030 Agenda': https://www.unep.org/about-un-environment/faith-earth-initiative

---

Reflecting on the sacred

Definitions of spirit help us to establish a basis for how spirit can guide us on our journey. John McQuiston II's (2006: 29) interpretation of the Rule of St. Benedict, a set of sixth century guidelines for living together in a spiritual community, takes a modern turn:

> "We all have our own perception of and relationship to some God. We may not use the name 'God'. We may think in terms of Reality, Nature, the First Cause, the Behaviour of the World, the Other, the All, the Ground of Being, the Force of Evolution, the Life Spirit, or Things as They Really Are. Each of us creates an image of the supreme mystery in which we find ourselves, and we are always in a relationship with it."

However, such a definition lacks meaning for those who reject the idea of God, however named. In the Al-Anon programme, the concept of 'God' is defined in terms of each participant's personal understanding and can be referred to as a 'Higher Power'. The term 'Higher Power' acknowledges the humility of the participant, and the acceptance that we do not know all the answers and that 'our will' will not always be done. Those who do not believe in 'God' or a 'Higher Power' are encouraged to find a sense of a bigger self or a sense of a power outside their individual self within their Al-Anon group.

McQuiston II's phrase 'supreme mystery' can be placed within the cosmological context of a 13,800,000,000-year-old universe that is home to billions of galaxies. The awe and humility we experience in the face of such antiquity and vastness could be understood to be spiritual. Neil Armstrong looked up at the Earth from the Moon and blotted her out with his thumb. When asked if this made him feel big, he said, no, it made him feel very small. This brings us back to earlier explorations of Rudolf Otto's (1923) definition of numinous as "an experience of a mysterious terror and awe (*mysterium tremendum et fascinans*)", which contains majesty (*majestas*) and an "entirely other gaze" (*das Ganz Andere*). Awe and wonder lead us to a sense of the sacred. In Otto's definition of the numinous there are feelings of awe, of the smallness of the human in the face of the divine, and feelings of fascination and beatitude. The concept of the numinous might be more useful on our journeys to hopeful futures, given its less direct connections with organised religion and belief in God.

The paradigms within which humans might understand our place in the world raise the question of whether 'God' is transcendent, that is, outside of the physical world, or whether spirit is 'immanent', that is, in the whole world and Cosmos (see Skrbina, 2007; Matthews, 2016; Weber 2016). Our answers to such a question in relation to the Cosmos, might, understandably, be somewhat fuzzy. Thomas Berry (1999) refers to 'subjectivity', a way of seeing the universe as a communion of subjects rather than a collection of objects. Rather than seeking definitive answers, we might simply appreciate the value of spiritual teachings. Primack and Abrams (2006) suggest that we can learn to understand the universe and find our way to live meaningful lives through metaphor.

As we make this journey, I suggest moving up and down different levels of spirituality related to the self, community, planet and Cosmos. At the level of the Cosmos, Swimme (1984) suggests learning from and examining the dynamics of the universe. Berry (1999) sees the universe as a spiritual and sacred place, while spiritual teacher William Bloom proposes that spirituality is everyone's natural "connection with the wonder and energy of life" (2011: 39). Bloom (ibid.: 245) examines spiritual health according to three questions: Am I connected to the wonder and energy of life? Do I have peace of mind? Am I caring and connected to others?

I define spirit and the spiritual as individual recognition of a transformative or higher power within and outside of the self that works with others for change. Gaia is our living planet and Life plays a central role in our planet. After many years of journeying, I see the planet and Cosmos as sacred. I use the words awe, wonder and sacred to describe the Cosmos, in order to maintain an open-ended journey accessible to everyone, irrespective of faith. Through my research practice, I have arrived at the phrase 'loving and spiritual qualities' which I use as part of the journey to hopeful futures.

 Creative Learning Exercises

Find a quiet place to be with your journal or pens and colours. This might be a park, café or library, somewhere where you can be with others while remaining apart.

Use this time to consider how you think about qualities of love, reflection and spirituality.

What did you learn about these qualities from your parents and other family members? Which, if any, aspects of what you learned remain valuable to you today?

How are you supported when life is difficult and challenging or when you are facing or pondering death?

In what ways do you relate to undertaking a journey into loving and spiritual qualities in order to create hopeful futures? What are your views on such a journey?

If you were brought up in a faith tradition, how does it encourage you to see "awe, wonder and the sacred" in Gaia and the Cosmos? How does it respect a "transformative or higher power" both for you and those from other faith traditions?

First-person practice – exploring loving and spiritual qualities on the journey to hopeful futures

As I wrestled to find a form for this chapter that was most helpful, I was reminded of how hard it is to discuss or reflect on spirit and religion in a society overwhelmingly focused on consumerism and instant gratification. I was reminded of Sparkes' (2020) reflections into the self-indulgence of focusing on personal experience. The spiritual dimension of inquiry might also appear in this light when there are so many pressing issues to be tackled in the world. I explored how other people had written about spirit and concluded that action research offered the best way to undertake this journey.

Heron's (1996) extended ways of knowing helped to draw out multiple aspects of the spiritual journey, starting with the experiential knowing of daily life. Presentational knowing of metaphor, art and prayer helped in understanding the unnameable. Propositional knowing gave me an insight into what humanity is doing at present and how to attain a sustainable society. Building on these ways of knowing helped me to consider how to spiritually and practically respond to current challenges. The quality of emergence helped me to explore the spiritual journey, even though the endpoints were not visible at the start. I pondered the question of which aspects of an inner journey are appropriate to share. Gordon MacDonald (1984) suggests that parts of the spiritual journey are private to the individual and God. First-person action research helped me to understand the nature of my spiritual journey.

I organised the data from my journals, notes and research, paying attention to quality, and concerned myself with critical reflection and awareness of beauty and power. Over the years, these documents tracked the development of my spiritual journey. My inquiry, through emergence, intuition, cycles of action, reflection and extended ways of knowing, demonstrated how my personal spiritual practices grew imperceptibly to embrace wider paradigms and ways of being. My analysis of the journey revealed several cycles of action and reflection involving intense periods of exploration. Each of these had validity at the time, but shifted as the journey progressed. Spiritual practices became embedded in my daily life over several decades and grew into being part of the Earth and Cosmos. I tracked this process through first-person inquiry methods of living life as inquiry and writing as inquiry. The emerging practice of spirituality within a wider context is a long-term process and the practice of writing as inquiry enables reflection.

My emerging journey had a number of strands:

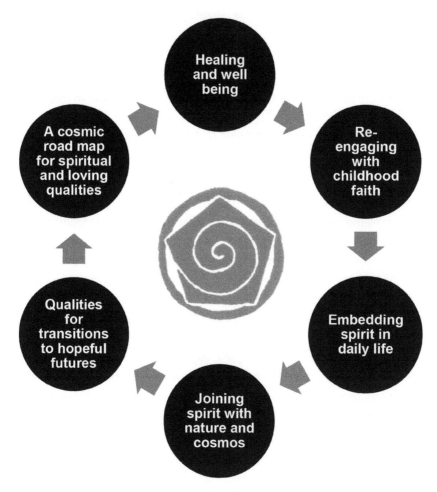

Figure 10.1: A first-person inquiry into loving and spiritual qualities.
You can join the inquiry at any point in the cycle. (Source: Kettleborough, 2023)

I could have joined this spiritual journey at any stage, depending on where I was in my life. If I faced great challenges, I would start again with healing and prayer. For example, when the Covid-19 pandemic began in March 2020, I returned to prayer, meditation and care for my mental health.

Creative Learning Exercises

As you follow this personal spiritual journey, use different colours to record your responses.

Take note of insights for your own journey.

Take note of books, articles, films, etc., that you would like to follow up on from your own journey.

Draw Figure 10.1. Create your own text for each circle.

Starting out – a journey of healing and well being

Critical elements of my personal exploration of self-development and healing included taking responsibility for what was going on, and putting a higher power at the centre of my life. I read and used journaling to reflect on new ideas, put those ideas into action, reflect again and either re-enforce or reject what I had learned through further literature research. Spiritual writers, such as M Scott Peck (1978) and Richard Carter (2019), emphasise the importance of reading inspirational text on a daily basis. I engaged in Louise Hay's (1984) healing exercises, exploring the qualities of learning to love myself, and created healing prayers for reflection and learning. Susan Jeffers's writing offered spiritual perspectives based on seeing life within the parameters of nine boxes with a higher power at the centre (see Chapter 6). Robin Norwood's (1986) exercises offered a feminist perspective on the importance of attaining self-worth, drawing on the spiritual path of Al-Anon and the Twelve Steps. I read collections of spiritual writings, such as those collected by Ducrocq (2011) to re-enchant daily life and as a focus for reflection and prayer. I studied chapters from the Tao Te Ching and the ecumenical meditations of Thich Nat Hanh. I engaged with approaches that do not involve God, such as Alain De Botton (2012), who seeks to take what is valuable from religion while leaving out God. William Bloom's holistic spirituality is not based on a particular faith tradition, but on our connections to all other human beings, nature and the planet. This sense of connection can be accessed through reflection and spiritual practices and through being of service to others and the planet with the aim to 'do good' as the expression of that connection. He argues that we need to see the best in others and bring out the best in ourselves (Bloom, 2011).

The journey of healing led me to the ecumenical teachings of Al-Anon, using the spiritual principles of the Twelve Steps.[133] It suggests a daily regime of prayer, reading, reflection and participation in community. It posits that "we all have the power to turn on the light", we must be humble, and we must accept that we cannot make changes on our own but need the help of a "power greater than ourselves", which each member is free to define in their own way. Such journeys led me back to the beginning of my spiritual practices.

Re-engaging with childhood faith traditions

I explored my childhood spirituality, re-examining and re-evaluating the practices I learned from my family. This included Irish Catholic spiritual practices of prayer, sacred spaces, community and the sacraments. I read scripture and other works of inspiration from earlier times, and reflected on, and tried to practice, the Christian New Testament admonition to forgive others, not once, not seven times, but seven times seven. Prayer became important for me, as I followed prayer books and created personal prayers that adapted and evolved with the passing years. These were prayers of intercession for myself and others, for loved ones and family members, for neighbours, and for humanity. I prayed to honour ancestors who had gone before, lit candles of intercession to celebrate happy occasions and to light up sacred spaces; I sang, listened to or made sacred music and burned incense in sacred spaces. Prayer involved blessings for the living and the dead, for world leaders and community members, for the sick and the dying. The prayers and structure of the community services for worship, Mass, involved an appreciation of the Divine Feminine within this tradition (see Spretnek, 2004). Expressions of my childhood spirituality involved community services of shared spiritual devotion, and understanding the process of the sacraments that mark rites of passage through life. The spiritual processes associated with death were important, and included prayers before and after death, honouring the dead through attending community services for worship a month and a year after the death and on the anniversary of the death every year after that.

On reflection, I found this tradition of spiritual rules to live by helpful. The twenty-first century ecumenical version of The Rule of St Benedict examines spiritual practices for self and for living in the community, concluding with observations for meditation (McQuiston II, 1996: 11). The practice of daily prayers and readings provided an anchor for my spiritual practice. The Rule recommends stopping seven times a day to say a prayer of thanks (ibid: 85):[134]

> "Consider how it would be impossible to do this every day for a lifetime and to be miserable. Every day we must repel our thoughts of apprehension, melancholy and selfishness. By repetition of our meditations, and training ourselves daily to express hope and joy and thanksgiving, we will come to have the peace and stability we require."

A further expression of gratitude was saying grace. In 1994, my four-year-old daughter gave me *A Grateful Heart*, a book of graces, containing verses from all faith traditions and none, exploring ideas of gratitude. It has since become a family tradition that on Sundays or special occasions a family member or visitor reads a grace. The reader allows the book to fall open at random and then reads the shortest verse. There are many family favourites, including from the Tao Te Ching:

> "Do you have the patience to wait/ till your mud settles and the water is clear?/ Can you remain unmoving/ till the right action arises by itself?" (in Ryan, 1994)

Pausing to say grace and expressing gratitude started the process of exploring these childhood practices again. The sacraments came back to me as special moments in my life. In a two-decade long process, I came to internalise them and to understand that they were easier to follow because they resonated with my childhood.

Embedding spiritual practices in my daily life and discovering reflection in action research

The third stage of my journey arose out of these explorations, as I sought to embed spiritual practices in my daily life. How could I practice spirituality day-to-day? How could I share it with wider than faith communities? Could action research help?

In faith traditions, spirituality is practiced communally and individually.

Many faith traditions have led to the creation of physically beautiful sacred spaces and many sacred places are joined through pilgrimage.

But how can we know the fruits of the spirit? Through the principle of service, we can find many means of expression. The strong principle of social justice is connected to service within many faith traditions. Many of the community volunteers I encountered during my work in urban regeneration were from faith communities (McIntosh & Carmichael, 2016). In recent years, faith communities have played an active role in creating and supporting food banks, cooking food and taking food to the homeless. In recognition of the urban lives that most people now live, often with no escape, lay brother Richard Carter has located his spirituality within the city. In *The City is my Monastery*, he finds spiritual practice within the Church of St Martin in the Fields, in the City of London, a church known for its work with refugees and the homeless. Following such a tradition, I undertook community development work, delivering workshops aimed at healing communities and building community resilience, and working in my home community to organise clean ups of the local brook and regular litter picking in our local street.

I became interested in the links between spirituality and action research as ways to capture and grow a spiritual journey. During a silent retreat in mid-Wales, I explored the practice of mindfulness, and I read and meditated on the Buddhist concept of compassion. In my work, I began to explore developing action research as a research methodology and a means of encouraging spirit, and I sought to understand how spirituality could be translated into the language of work.

My journal became a spiritual place to hold myself to account. The Fourth Step in Al-Anon is to "take a total and fearless self-inventory", to make restitution and to "continue to hold oneself to account" thereafter. My journals operated as a place where I could hold my conduct to account. And, continuing to record in my journals encouraged an orientation towards the best. This record of my daily life created a space to acknowledge the need for ongoing inquiry.

Joining spirit with nature, planet and Cosmos

In another turn in my spiritual journey, I read a book that linked spirit to ecology. Now, the spiritual practices I had developed through healing and exploring my childhood faith tradition expanded into a wider ecological perspective. In my activism and journey to hopeful futures, this discovery of spirit and ecology gave me an understanding of the interconnected nature of everything. Douglas Christie (2013: 5) refers to the creation of a "contemplative ecology":

> "This double insight – that spiritual thought and practice is immeasurably enriched through being situated within the natural world, and that ecological understanding is given added depth and meaning by extending the ecological field to include the traditions of spiritual thought and practice – comprises the heart of the emerging spiritual ecology."

From familiar human-centred spiritual practices, I began to explore a spirituality that extended outwards. Matthew Fox's creation spirituality was an early inspiration for the GreenSpirit movement, urging that in the beginning was Blessing not Sin and that the Christian tradition must return to the element of creation. Fox describes four paths to spiritual enlightenment – the positive, the negative, the creative and the transformative (1983). His teaching offers a positive spiritual message that focuses on the central role of creativity. I explored Thomas Berry's (1988) *Dream of the Earth* and the participative universe. The more I read, the more my earlier spiritual practices evolved into wider practices that embraced the planet and the Cosmos. It was a simple step to take the spiritual practice of prayer and extend it into nature and the Cosmos. David Abram (2010) reflects on the offering of prayer within nature and within faith traditions, as both offer concentrated intent and good for others.

Roberts and Amidon (1991) have described their desire to find prayers for the Earth from a range of traditions around the world. Their book, *Earth Prayers*, includes blessings for animals, prayers for finding one's ecological self, blessings and invocations, prayers for the passion of the Earth, for the cycles of life and for the daily round. They note that when we pray, we acknowledge the forces and energies within the Earth and Cosmos and join with them. This prayer from John Wright within the collection speaks to the challenges of today:

> "Let the trees be consulted
> Before you take any action

Every time you breathe in
Thank a tree
Let tree roots crack parking lots
At world bank headquarters
Let loggers be druids
Specially trained and rewarded
To sacrifice trees at auspicious times
Let carpenters be master artisans
Let lumber be treasured like gold...."
(in Roberts and Amidon, 1991: 105)

 Creative Learning Exercises

As you contemplate these stages, find a quiet place to explore your own journey into loving and spiritual qualities. The following questions will help you to reflect:

What areas of healing and self-development do you need to explore? How will you undertake such an exploration?

What, if any, elements of your childhood faith, or spiritual qualities you learned in childhood, continue to be meaningful to you?

In what ways can you or do you express your loving spiritual qualities in connection with nature?

Consider the connections between reflection, spirituality and action research. How can these connections be further developed?

Explore the global response from faith communities concerning the current crisis, noting what inspires you. One starting point is the United Nations Environment Programme Faith for Earth Initiative: https://www.unep.org/resources/publication/faith-earth-call-action

Read Pope Francis' (2012) call to action, *Laudato Si' On Care for Our Common Home*, and his call for all citizens of Planet Earth to take action: https://www.vatican.va/content/francesco/en/encyclicals/documents/papa-francesco_20150524_enciclica-laudato-si.html

---

At the same time as encountering a spirituality based in the planet and the Cosmos, I enrolled in higher education and started to explore academic literature regarding the qualities needed to make these transitions. I had now moved on to another stage of my journey.

Qualities for transitions to hopeful futures

In the fifth stage of my journey, I explored the work of philosophers, scientists and other experts to identify the qualities they suggest are needed to successfully transition to hopeful futures.

Thomas Berry (1999:159) suggested that the task before us is to "re-invent the human". We need to do so both within the journey of the universe and with the community of all life on Earth, using the qualities of story and shared dream experience. Such a journey is not easy to imagine. Shared dream experience can awaken in humanity awe and wonder at the universe and at the potential for the future. But how do we find the energy for such a total re-think of society? Rather than the qualities of the teacher or the businessperson, Berry suggests that we need the qualities of the shaman, with the ability to go back to the universe to acquire the energies needed for the tasks ahead (1988). It is not simply a matter of seeing ourselves as sacred, but of seeing the universe as sacred as well. He argues (1999: 115) that we need to see the community of the Earth:

> "...as a spiritual fulfilment as well as a mutual support. It is a commitment, not merely a way of survival. Anything less, to my mind, will not work. The difficulty we confront is too great."

Qualities such as sacredness and faithfulness are important for the journey ahead. Paleo-climatologist Curt Stager (2011) argues that our present release of carbon dioxide waste into the atmosphere will have long term cosmological effects into the future. He suggests that respect for each other is a key quality to overcome this. If we can respectfully listen to other people, we can learn about their hopes and dreams and we will be better able to work together. Paying attention to other views is an essential quality for the future. Stager (ibid: 233) writes, "the smartest and most ethically sound solution is to pause, listen to one another carefully and respectfully and then try to move ahead as a single species on our singular planet."

Respectful listening is closely aligned to the participatory learning practice of active listening – but social media does not make this easy.

Stephan Harding (2006) argues that we must make inner changes in addition to concentrating on outer action in order to live in harmony with Gaia. He refers to the potential of technology to help humanity but argues that we need wisdom to ensure we use such technology with care. Harding also argues for the quality of accountability, not only to ourselves and other humans, or the bottom line of a spreadsheet, but to Gaia herself. We must "develop ecological wisdom" that puts the planet at the heart of decision making, and we must learn to see Gaia not as an object, but as a person. Harding believes that learning more about our planet can help us to develop these qualities. Echoing the idea of a participative universe, he suggests (2006: 244),

> "Right action requires us to live into the body of the earth so that we care equally for the other species and elements as we do for the bricks and mortar we have made."

In this way, we can change how we view our lives and our planet and develop the ability to think about our actions from the perspective of the planet. It is within this context that Harding calls for the quality of respect. As we develop our understanding of how Gaia works, we start to think about respectful actions towards her. Harding argues that we need a moral commitment to our planet, to dedicate ourselves to her service to restore her ecology and nature and protect her species, within the context of social justice. He writes (2006: 244), "Every pledge we make is a pledge of service and allegiance to the greater personhood of our planet."

Theologian Anne Primavesi (2013) explores how we have systematically and destructively abused the planet over the centuries while simultaneously abusing and oppressing each other. Western societies have treated the planet and indigenous communities in the same way, colonising both and perceiving them merely as resources to be used. Human beings and nature have been monetised, marketised and discarded when no longer of economic value.[135] Primavesi (2003) argues that the planet treats humans very differently, giving freely of her gifts of air, water and life. She urges humanity to adopt these same qualities, to learn from Gaia's generosity in our dealings with each other, and to offer our gifts freely without monetising, exploiting or abusing either other humans or nature.

Theologian Leonardo Boff (1997) argues that work to free the poor from oppression must be combined with work to end the destruction of ecology. Such an endeavour will simultaneously restore the dignity of the Earth and her people. The roots of our current crisis can be traced to the profound loss of connection between people, between people and nature and between people and the Cosmos. He explores how mega development projects are destroying both the ecology and indigenous cultures of the Amazon and reflects, "Without a spiritual revolution it will be impossible to launch a new paradigm of connectedness" (ibid.: 139). Boff argues that we must develop an ecologically sustainable spirituality which sees humanity as part of the Cosmos, appreciative of being alive and of the glory of creation. We need "unlimited compassion and shared responsibility" to achieve this form of spirituality (ibid.: 135). In our material lives, we must nurture the qualities of living simply and in co-operation with all beings. Boff suggests St Francis of Assisi as a role model who combined simplicity, poverty and love for all creatures. In a similar vein, it was seeing the plight of local farmers in India that helped environmental activist Vandana Shiva to understand that big corporations want to privatise and monopolise our planet's biodiversity, leading her to campaign against corporations, such as Monsanto, from owning seeds which farmers are then forced to buy. Shiva's reflections on these and other global campaigns against corporations and the privatisation of resources led to the concept of Earth Democracy, which seeks to ensure that the rights of all peoples, cultures and nature are enshrined in Ten Principles of Justice, Sustainability and Peace. Such a movement prioritises the safeguarding of nature, community decision making and advocates a living economy tied to a living Earth. Earth Democracy seeks to unite people through "circles of care, cooperation and compassion... [and] globalizes compassion, justice and sustainability" (Shiva, 2005: 11).

A thirty-year longitudinal study by Meadows et al. (1972; 1992; 2004) explored human use of resources, and led to recommendations about living within the limits of the planet. In 1972, they described a number of tools to help make the transition to living within the planet's limits. These included "visioning, networking, truth telling, learning and loving" (2004: 271). In 2004, they concluded that these tools were no longer optional but critical to the long-term survival of civilisation. While these are not the only approaches, they explained their importance thus (ibid.: 281):

> "It seems like a feeble list, given the enormity of the changes required. But each of these exists within a web of positive loops. Thus, their persistent and consistent application initially by a relatively small group of people would have the potential to produce enormous change – even to challenge the present system, perhaps helping to produce a revolution."

Meadows et al. argue that we need to develop the best, rather than the worst, in human qualities, and raise the possibility of creating a society that can operate for the common good rather than one dominated by individual needs and the inability to see beyond the immediate. They acknowledge the difficulty of acting from a different set of values (ibid.: 282):

> "It is not easy to practice love, friendship, generosity, understanding or solidarity within a system whose rules, goals and information streams are geared for lesser human qualities. But we try, and we urge you to try."

Meanwhile, environmentalist Jonathon Porritt considers the business qualities needed to value the Earth. His research into capitalism found evidence that increased wealth has not necessarily led to increased happiness (2007; see also Piketty, 2014). Re-considering how capitalism might look if we truly valued the earth, Porritt suggests we embrace a wider set of capitals, including natural, human and social capital. We need new qualities to develop this version of capitalism, with values that include understanding and knowledge of our interdependence with each other and the planet. He argues that sustainable development and related core values are two ways that humanity might move forward. He identifies these core values as "interdependence, empathy, equity, personal responsibility and intergenerational justice" (2007: 324). Porritt continues to see values as important in addressing the unfolding climate crisis calling for justice between the generations and committed action from individuals (2020: 340).

This emphasis on qualities for the whole Earth community are also found in scientific and policy research. The Millennium Eco-Assessment

(MEA) (2005) states that social and behavioural responses "can be instrumental in responding to the problems of ecosystem degradation". Qualities recommended by the MEA include the empowerment of groups dependent on ecosystem services, indigenous people, women and young people, and education and communication of the issues around ecosystem loss. The 2012 Blue Planet Laureates stated that there is enough for the more-than-human world if humans are less greedy and empower women and local communities.[136] Cebellos and Ehrich's (2017) study of "biological annihilation" concluded that it is "irresponsible and unethical" not to act on the sixth mass extinction. In 2019, the International Science-Policy Panel on Biodiversity and Ecosystem services considered the transformative changes needed to save biodiversity, restore the climate and achieve the UN SDGs. The study concluded that technological solutions alone are not enough. Instead, they must be combined with science, society, governance, knowledge sharing, indigenous knowledge, communities, learning and values. As ways into transformative futures, their Global Assessment Report recommends "unleashing values and actions, embracing diverse visions of a good life and promotion of education and knowledge generation and sharing" (IPBES, 2019: 41 and Figure 3.1).

Qualities associated with spirit and love are essential elements of the transition to hopeful futures. Despite their differences in emphasis, these scholars and activists agree on the value of a range of qualities that are broadly similar across disciplines and perspectives. As such, they help to build the case for the necessity of loving and spiritual journeys for the road ahead. The COVID-19 pandemic briefly brought many of these qualities and values to the forefront of society, with an increased understanding within the field of policy of the importance of healing, mental resilience and well-being, alongside supportive spiritual qualities in the face of death and grief.[137] Such ideas lead back to all parts of this cycle and to each individual's personal journey of exploration.

I realised that this personal journey to spirit, which had joined a wider sense of the Cosmos and planet, was integral to creating socially and ecologically just futures. My journey became multi-faceted. How might I capture and share this action research journey of ideas, practice and reflection and how could I take my work out into the community and into my work within education while continuing to live the journey? How might I explore loving spiritual qualities with others?

Creative Learning Exercises

Make a list of the qualities suggested in this chapter for transition to ecologically sustainable and socially just futures:

What other authors, thinkers and artists would you like to add? Do they bring any further qualities?

Are there any qualities you think are missing? Can you add?

Taking all these qualities together, identify the ones you think are the most important in transitions to hopeful futures:

Draw a picture of how these qualities fit together.

Think about ways that we can grow these qualities.

A Cosmic Road Map for exploring Loving and Spiritual qualities within the planet and Cosmos

The challenge is to find a language which allows people to explore loving and spiritual qualities on their own terms, in a world with a dominant mechanistic and consumerist paradigm. How can we explore such qualities as part of our journey to hopeful futures? There is no blueprint for how to undertake such an inquiry and we each must work out our own route map. However, from my many years of reflective travelling inspired by the Al-Anon Twelve Steps programme, I offer the following tools to help you undertake this wider journey into loving and spiritual qualities.

Step 1: Engage in a daily practice of bearing witness. Come to understand that we have reached rock bottom as individuals and a society, threatening every species, the viability of our climate for life, the boundaries of our finite planet, and failing to treat all members of the human family with respect, dignity and equality.

Step 2: Call on our understanding of our spiritual sense, our sense of a higher power or our sense of a deeper purpose from those we love. Use this understanding to heal ourselves, each other, our communities, our planet and our shared cosmological future.

Step 3: Make an inventory of those we have harmed – the human and the more-than-human – acknowledge our mistakes and ask forgiveness. Seek to put right these wrongs in whatever way we can. Share with a trusted individual or community.

Step 4: Commit to loving and spiritual qualities in our lives, grow qualities of respect, compassion, kindness, mercy, courage, forgiveness and love as part of thought and action.

Step 5: Develop a sense of awe and wonder as part of loving and spiritual qualities. Embed in our lives spiritual practices that grow into our living planet and our sense of wonder for our Cosmos. Through learning and reflecting, come to understand ourselves as part of the greater whole, in our living Earth and participative universe.

Step 6: Strive for justice as part of spirit. Take urgent and wise action for the flourishing of human and ecological communities working to create systemic conditions for a better world. Commit to long term faithfulness and fierce love for our fellow human and more-than-human citizens.

Step 7: Take thoughtful action based on loving and spiritual qualities. Take care of our physical and mental health and offer deeds of kindness, help and care for others, for humans and the more-than-human, nature and our climate, locally and globally. As we heal ourselves, we heal the planet, for we are part of Gaia.

Step 8: Maintain a practice of daily reflection and review of conduct in our lives and continue to make amends as needed to other human beings, the climate and to the species of the planet.

Step 9: Become a creator and a maker, not a consumer. Create stories for our Earth, cook, play music, walk, read, recite poetry, plant trees, knit, paint, sing our way into a better future. Become artists in our own lives, in whatever ways speak to us. Dream and grow the Dream of the Earth.

Step 10: Develop values out of loving and spiritual qualities, be guided by values and ethics that belong to our planet and Cosmos, our communities and ourselves. Such ethics include and extend beyond tribe or nation, are respectful and listen to others.

Step 11: Strengthen wider loving and spiritual qualities within our lives. Make time daily to pause and reconnect with our inner spiritual core and become present to our living Earth and cultivate wonder for our ancient and awe-inspiring Cosmos.

Step 12: Share loving and spiritual journeys with others within our planet and our Cosmos, taking our skills, knowledge and awakening out into the world. Have conversations about the need for loving and spiritual journeys of discovery and the need for urgent and wise action.

This is not a proscriptive route map and it can be altered to reflect different perspectives. It offers a broad road to travel. The journey undertaken suggests that loving spiritual qualities are essential and, in practicing them, we extend them from the human to the planet and Cosmos beyond.

These loving and spiritual qualities can be practiced by individuals, but their value lies in being practiced together. I offer them as a response to the range of challenges facing society and our planet, and to the barriers to tackling ecological and social justice.

 Invitation to Reflect

Take some quiet time outside in nature and explore the following questions, through any medium.

Draw the journey offered in this chapter. Reflect on the stages of your own reflective or spiritual journey. What similarities, if any, do you find between your journey and mine? Where do our journeys diverge?

Reflect on the 12 points of the Cosmic Road Map for loving/spiritual qualities. In what ways can you incorporate these into your life?

Are there other Road Maps that you might follow?

Have a go at creating your own Cosmic Road Map of loving and spiritual qualities for your journey to hopeful futures.

Notes

[129] For information about religions of the world and numbers of adherents, see https://www.religioustolerance.org/positive.htm

[130] http://www.arcworld.org/downloads/THE%20ASSISI%20DECLARATIONS.pdf

[131] https://parliamentofreligions.org/our-work/mission/

[132] For examples of Christian faith responses to Black Lives Matter, see Lauren Brownlee on the Quakers https://www.afsc.org/blogs/acting-in-faith/honoring-light-black-lives and Franchesca Merlo on Catholic protesters https://www.vaticannews.va/en/world/news/2020-06/peaceful-protests-around-the-world-for-justice-for-george-floyd.html

[133] https://www.al-anonuk.org.uk/

[134] Stopping for prayer throughout the day is practiced in many faith traditions. For example, Muslims offer prayers five times a day. See Raz Shah-Kazemi (2011) *Spiritual Quest, Reflections on Quranic Prayer, According to the Teachings of Iman Ali.*

[135] See David Attenborough's *Extinction: The Facts* for a visual expression of the monetarisation and over-exploitation of the Earth's resources: https://www.bbc.co.uk/news/science-environment-54118769

[136] The Blue Planet award is granted annually by the Ashti Glass Foundation for outstanding contributions to the environment. In 2012, Blue Planet Award laureates came together to issue a report on the need for action: http://saveourwoods.co.uk/wp-content/uploads/2012/02/Blue-Planet-synthesis-paper.pdf

[137] See Roman et al. on spirituality: https://www.ncbi.nlm.nih.gov/pmc/articles/PMC7343955/; see Cooper and Kramers-Olen on inequality: https://journals.sagepub.com/doi/10.1177/00812463211015517 and Ferrell et al. on palliative care: https://pubmed.ncbi.nlm.nih.gov/32629084/

Chapter 11: Engaging with a living planet and an awesome wondrous Cosmos

"Spirituality means waking up. Most people, even though they don't know it, are asleep… They never understand the loveliness and the beauty of this thing we call human existence. You know, all mystics…are unanimous on one thing: that all is well, all is well."
Anthony de Mello, 1997: 5)

"Each of us is as old as the universe and experiences our greater self in the larger story of the universe. So, we are as old as the universe and as big as the universe. This is our great self. We survive in our great self."
Thomas Berry (in Tucker et al., 2019: 155)

December 2013, we stand together, a small group of neighbours gathered to honour the life and death of Nelson Mandela. At the centre are the tea lights from our daughter's wedding in decorative glass jars. One by one, we light the candles, which flicker, safe from the wind in their miniature shelters. The children hold candleholders from which tiny flames glow. First, there is silence, and then one, two, three, four voices speak of our gratitude for what Nelson Mandela has done. We speak from diverse global origins, from China and Pakistan, the United States and Britain, sharing our admiration of Nelson Mandela's contribution to peace and justice. Finally, we stand in silence, united together on our small street many miles from South Africa. Three weeks later, we gather as a resident's group to dress our street trees for the festive season. Children, adults and grandparents come together, sharing chocolates as a celebration. We have a small three-step ladder for the children and a decorating ladder for the adults, who hold on to each other as we take turns mounting the steps and attaching shiny baubles to the trees. Around the trunks of the trees, the children twist strands of glittering tinsel, which shimmer in the mid-winter afternoon. We assemble in the community garden, the ground dug out, the earth bare, to decorate our living Christmas tree. We survey our work, satisfied. Happy festive season! Happy Christmas! we tell each other. Later in the day, the baubles on the trees spin and glitter as the winter light dims. For all who see them, they are symbols of love and hope. And so, they remain, until the 12th Day of Christmas, when they are carefully washed and stored in the attic for another year. The years pass. The yarn bombers knit woolly baubles and tree decorations and scarves for each tree. Now, this annual tradition has travelled to other sets of trees which shine and gleam many miles away, decorated by the children and grandchildren of this street.

Introduction

The Cosmic Road Map has set us on a journey of curiosity and discovery, an exploration of our awe and wonder at the universe, as we seek inspiration for how to live our lives. In Chapter 2, I explored the family of paradigms that enable us to see the Cosmos and planet as ancient, interconnected, living, sacred and participatory. Throughout, I have explored aspects of these paradigms in our lives and, in the last chapter, I explored my own journey of healing. Here, I explore how first- and second-person action research methods can guide us on a journey of outward discovery of our living planet and our awe-inspiring Cosmos. I will explore a series of practices of gratitude, grief, hope and love that can be undertaken individually or collectively, making way for the emergence of a sense of the Cosmos as sacred. Figure 11.1 is a road map for this journey, and the journey can begin at any point on the map.

Figure 11.1: A journey to discover our living planet and awe-inspiring cosmos.
(Source: Kettleborough, 2023)

Tools for journeys of awe and wonder

According to Judi Marshall (1999; see also Gearty & Marshall, 2021), one quality of first-person inquiry is ongoing questioning and never seeing things as complete or finished. This journey into a wondrous Cosmos and living planet is an ongoing process that will never feel complete. Second-person and participatory inquiry methods can help us to discover, in the presence of others, a living Gaia and an awesome Cosmos. The action research skills that can guide us on this journey include presentational knowing of music, ritual, silence and meditating on text. Over many years, the cyclical nature of this process has enabled me to continue probing and deepening my knowledge and understanding. As TS Eliot (1963) wrote in 1943,

"We shall not cease from exploration
And the end of all our exploring
Will be to arrive where we started
And know the place for the first time."

Exploring the concept of power is a key part of the journey. This includes the power of humans over each other and over nature and how loving and spiritual qualities and practices can be used to tackle systemic structures and root behaviours. Action research offers a methodology to critically reflect on the qualities of awe and wonder. The language of action research enables a journey of reflection to expand into wider paradigms. Extended ways of knowing help us to sense and learn about the dynamic powers and qualities of the universe and, potentially, to learn how to operate from them. Such explorations enable us to be in awe and wonder at the nature of the Cosmos in the daily circle of life. This chapter draws on the meditative processes of extended ways of knowing, through propositional knowledge and presentational knowledge, reflection, drawing, repeated engagement and note taking, allowing new knowledge to seep into consciousness. Rudolf Otto (1923: 7) suggested that knowledge "of the spirit" cannot "strictly speaking be taught, it can only be evoked, awakened in the mind." This chapter seeks to combine the propositional knowledge of our scientific story with a re-awakening of awe, wonder and spirit.

Practices and rituals for nurturing awe and wonder

Through relationship we can enter into an understanding of the Cosmos by practicing the ancient art of cosmology in our daily lives (Swimme, 1996). Here, I suggest practices which ask us to enter into a different relationship with our universe. In undertaking these practices with faithfulness, we are filled with awe and wonder at our universe and we understand that every part of our planet is precious. Such practices bring us to an understanding that we belong to this meaningful universe. We might come to understand our universe as sacred. Such appreciation may occur suddenly, or may take years or decades.

Meditating on the gifts of the sun

A humbling and inspiring meditation is reflecting on the 'free lunch' that is the sun (Swimme, 1996). The sun offers all of planet Earth unlimited light, energy and gravity, free of charge, to hold, power and sustain our amazing, complex existence. Our planet is in a relationship with the sun. One wonderful characteristic of Gaia, that I explored in Chapter 2, is that as the sun grew hotter, the Earth retained the optimal temperature for life (Lovelock, 2006). Our planet and all who live here are embedded in 4,500,000,000 years of universal generosity. This quality of faithfulness makes an important contribution to our understanding of the qualities of our Cosmos. How can we emulate these qualities of universal abundance and generosity in our communities and our economies? Although our life spans are infinitesimally small in comparison, how might we appreciate the length of such faithfulness and learn to see it as a guiding star in our lives? The mediaeval cathedral builders knew they would not live to see their creations completed but steadfastly built them nonetheless. Can we be faithful to the Earth in the same way that the sun is faithful to us? How might we use this idea to make the paradigm shifts needed to reorganise our own societies?

Looking down into the Cosmos

From our planetary perspective, it is difficult to get a physical sense of the immensity of space within which planet Earth sails with the sun and her sister planets around the Milky Way. From such immensity arises a sense of awe and wonder. To get some sense of this, Brian Swimme (1996) proposes lying on our backs under the Milky Way and imagining that, instead of looking up, we are looking down. Rather than feeling the comfort of the planet below our feet and the sky above us, we can look down into the infinity of space. There is no end to our fall from our planet downwards through those depths. This is an exercise I have practiced with my family over the years, amidst laughter and glimpses of how difficult it is to change our perspectives. With practice, I have sometimes felt a sense of being held by gravity, which holds the entire universe together and stops everything from flying apart. As humans, we might understand gravity as allurement or love and an essential part of our Cosmos (Swimme, 1984). Another way to learn to appreciate such power when looking up at the night sky is to search out the stars and the constellations. You may need to be persistent in undertaking these practices, given the light pollution in urban areas. But, the unpretentious practice of stargazing gives a sense of awe and wonder and can help us to understand the cosmic qualities of gravity and love; qualities that can help us through the challenges of transitioning to an ecologically sustainable society (Swimme & Tucker, 2011). When we look to the stars we are looking back in time.

The Cosmic Walk

In a pamphlet for GreenSpirit, Erna and Michael Colebrook (2000) created guidelines for undertaking a Universe Walk. This two-hour, 1.4km walk involves a group of people walking the history of our 13.8-billion-year-old universe, stopping at key points to reflect and ponder, with each metre of the walk representing 10 million years. It consists of 31 stages and 2,800 steps. Each step includes a short explanation about what is happening to the universe at that moment in its history, in line with our best scientific knowledge. In this representation of the universe, planet Earth only emerges at step 1,920, life on Earth emerges at step 2,030, which is 3,900 to 3,850 million years ago. The final half step covers the last 5 million years. "The last 5mm brings us to the present. The last thousandth of this last step, the last half a millimetre, represents the span of recorded human history" (ibid.: 40). Through the act of walking, we physically enter into respect for the great age of the universe. Walking across billions of years teaches us about the dynamic of the arrow of time as it moves forward in a series of irreversible steps (Primack & Abrams, 2006). As we listen to the narrative of key points in the journey, we appreciate in our bodies and hearts the complexity and mystery of the universe and all that happened to birth humanity.

Walking the Sacred Story embodies our place in the Cosmos and allows us to physically understand our relationship to everything in the universe. The Colebrooks (2000) argue that the walk allows us to feel a different relationship to the Divine or sacred – not as something 'out there' but something that is part of everything we see and feel. They conclude that we might begin to feel nourished by this journey and understand that the work we must do to bring us back into harmony with nature is rooted in the transformational journey of the Earth and the Cosmos. This walk can be undertaken in any setting. It requires a volunteer to research, count out and mark the steps, and recount the story. At a Universe Walk in our local

The Long Walk

1.37Km

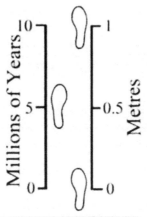

Distance	Years
1m	10,000,000
0.5m	5,000,000
10cm	1,000,000
1cm	100,000
1mm	10,000

It is important to make sure that participants have a clear idea of the time scale of the walk. It might be an idea to give each participant a grass stem or twig just 10cm long and representing 1 million years. The thickness of one of the pages of this book represents about a thousand years.

Figure 11.2: The Scale for 'The Long Walk' illustrating the scale used to allow one to 'walk' the universe story. (Source: Erna and Michael Colebrook, 2000. Walking the Sacred Story: A New Ritual for Celebrating the Universe. Greenspirit Pamphlet No. 3, London: Bookforce)

inner-city park, the oldest and youngest walkers started the walk by bursting balloons to create the Big Bang! There is a permanent Universe Walk on the campus of Winchester University, with art by Megan Clay highlighting the universe story and marking places for mediation and reflection. From this great age we can speak with authority on behalf of endangered species, our skies and justice for humans and the more-than-human (Macy, 2013).

◯ Helpful Companions

Books
Colebrook, E. and Colebrook, M. 2000. *Walking the Sacred Story, A new Ritual for Celebrating the Universe*, GreenSpirit Pamphlet No. 5, Crediton: Association for Creation Spirituality.

Johnson, K. 2019. *Reaching for the Moon: the Autobiography of NASA Mathematician Katherine Johnson* New York: Atheneum Books.

Films
The Journey of the Universe. 2011. Narrated by Brian Swimme, based on the New Universe story. https://www.journeyoftheuniverse.org/film

Resources for Action
The universe walk Deep Time App is free from: https://www.deeptimewalk.org/ as are 58 Deep Time cards, each covering 100 million years of history, which can be purchased. You can also join the Network at: https://dtnetwork.org

---

Cosmic powers – learning by heart

In Chapter 9, I explored how we might glimpse the participative universe in our daily lives. By learning the characteristics of the universe, we can make them part of our lives. We can all learn from the universe simply by stepping outside of our homes. Such learning can be undertaken as an individual journey of physical encounter with the universe and engagement with science, and together as mutual journeys of discovery. What we can understand as individuals arises at its own pace and cannot be 'willed', as demonstrated through the many stories throughout this book of encountering a living Gaia. We can engage with science at any time and we can learn to appreciate the dynamics of the universe from its manifestations here on Earth.

Swimme (1996) tells us that the sun offers us the dynamics of gift and faithfulness and, peering down into the depths of the Milky Way, we can feel that we are held by gravity, or what humans might refer to as love. The mountains, the land and the soil, which we can find wherever we are on planet Earth, teach us of the eons of time it has taken to create our world. An appreciation of the depth of such timescales teaches us to respect and value that which the planet and the Cosmos has struggled so long and hard to create (Swimme, 1984). The wind, created by the movement of air, sometimes loud, sometimes quiet, speaks to us when we pay attention. The whoosh of the wind in the leaves and branches of the trees teaches us the quality of generosity. We would not exist without the air moving ceaselessly around our planet.

A further quality is life itself, with its play, exuberance, beauty, difference and interconnectedness (ibid.: 122). Whenever we see life in any form, we are reminded of its incredible versatility and, in recent decades, of its vulnerability. In understanding life, we also understand death. Death is part of life, or 'Sister Death' as St. Francis called it in the Canticle of the Creatures. Thomas Berry (in Tucker et al., 2019: 11) argues that death is not to be feared, as it is a returning to the universe from where we have come. Death teaches us to value our lives and to live deeply, to not waste time on consumerism or hate. Swimme (1984) describes fire as demonstrating that quality of the universe in which the whole is more than the sum of the individual parts and, indeed, the whole is not evident in the individual parts. Our individual organs do not reveal the human but, taken together, our body parts create a living, breathing, thinking, feeling human. How might we learn to appreciate different elements of life as self-organising and, therefore, respect and honour them?

A final quality to be learned from the universe is the immensity of time. Chief Lyons, faith keeper of the Turtle Clan of the Onondaga Nation, expresses the views of his ancestors, which is to think seven generations into the future. The timescales we live by in contemporary Western civilisation are very short. However, technology such as the European Space Agency's Gaia telescope can help us to think forward into the future. The constellation Orion was central to the spirituality of the Ancient Egyptians. The ESA Gaia mission has revealed that Orion will only look like Orion for another 50,000 years, at which point, and for the next 450,000 years, the stars will move out of alignment from the perspective of Earth. The Gaia mission also reveals that a rogue star, Gliese, will come close to our solar system 1.2 million years from now, transforming the outer edges of the solar system. Can we learn to think forward, seven generations into the future, or more, and find value in long-term, rather than short-term, thinking?

○ **Helpful Companion**

Resources for Action
Chief Orien Lyons' address to the 24th Annual EF Schumacher Lectures of the US based Schumacher Centre for a new economics, 24 October 2004. *The Ice is Melting*: https://centerforneweconomics.org/publications/the-ice-is-melting/

Slade S. (author) and Jamison, V. (illustrator). 2019. *A Computer called Katherine*. London: Hachette. A children's book on the life of Katherine Johnson.

 Creative Learning Exercises

As you undertake this learning, seek to develop ways of thinking that intuitively mirror the dynamics and powers of the universe. The following questions will help you to think creatively about this:

Think about the stories and practices that allow you to appreciate our living Gaia. Which of these can you undertake regularly and share with others?

Draw around both your hands on a piece of paper and colour in the shape.

Now consider your hands. From the perspective of the Journey of the Universe, write how old your hands are. Add Joanna Macy's words "Act your age".

Draw or illustrate the practices I have suggested for nurturing a sense of awe and wonder at our Cosmos. Which of these practices stand out for you as a way to get into the heart of the Cosmos?

List or draw the dynamic powers of the universe that you can meet outside your back door. In what ways can these dynamic powers inform how you live your life?

Qualities for awe and wonder
Cosmic Gratitude

Gratitude for one's life is an essential loving and spiritual quality. But gratitude goes beyond gratitude for our own lives and families or even for the trees and the birds and the blue sky above. It extends to the moon in her quarters, the planets in their sweeps around the sky, our sun, our galaxy out of which our solar system was born, and Immeasurable Heaven, our own part of the universe within which we are kept safe. In such gratitude, we can see how, on planet Earth, every part is connected to the whole and every part has something to contribute. Through gratitude, we can understand the interconnected nature of our planet. Being grateful for being alive in a numinous and wonderful universe opens us up to a new order of gratitude.

How can one be grateful in a world where so much is amiss? Primack and Abrams (2006: 157) argue that we need to have a "sense of size scale within the universe". We can be grateful for being alive in our Cosmos while also being conscious of and addressing the challenges facing the planet. We can be grateful and practice loving and spiritual qualities in our own individual journeys. The Cosmic Uroboros (Figure 11.3, overleaf), the serpent eating its tail, is a helpful way to think about this practice. In this version, the scale of a human being is at six o'clock, in the very middle of the scales of the universe. All of these sizes are connected by orders of magnitude. Such a view of where we fit within the scale of the universe allows us to understand our place within it.

It is evident that the vastness and the minuteness of the universe are linked. From the very largest objects we can see at the cosmic horizon, to a supercluster of galaxies, to our own galaxy, to the distance from Earth to the Orion Nebula, to our solar system, the sun, the Earth and a mountain. At our own scale within the universe we are merely in the middle and the scale gets smaller still, from multi-cellular animals to single-celled life forms, a strand of DNA, an atom, a nucleus, the scale of the weak interactions (carried by W and Z particles), dark matter (DM) particles and, at the smallest known scale, the Grand Unified Theory (GUT), which brings us again to the largest scale (Primack & Abrams, 2006: 160). Such an appreciation of our place in the Cosmos helps us to feel gratitude. However, such gratitude can be hampered by our more human failings.

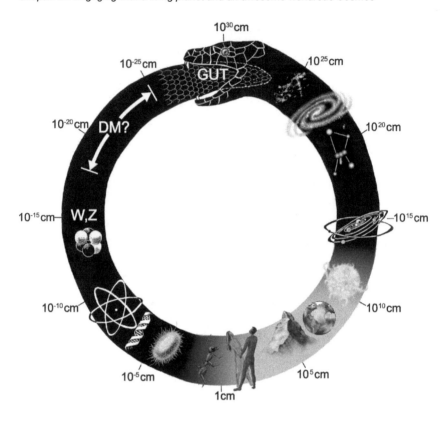

Figure 11.3: The position of humanity in the scale of the Cosmos, illustrated through the Cosmic Uroboros: the serpent eating its tail.
(Source: Joel Primack & Nancy Abrams, 2006: 160, copyright)

Cosmic Forgiveness

Loving and spiritual qualities can help us face the challenges to the planet and to human societies. Many wisdom traditions encourage the acknowledgement of one's faults and sins and always striving to do better. The other side of acknowledging one's faults and sins is forgiveness – learning to forgive yourself and those who have harmed you (Primavesi, 2003). Tarnas (2000: 11) suggests that the practice of forgiveness could be applied to what humanity is doing to the natural world: "I think it will take a fundamental moment of remorse...a sustained grief."

Such an examination of conscience extends to how all sections of humanity have treated each other and the planet. Truth and Reconciliation Commissions in post-Apartheid South Africa and elsewhere are living examples of how this can be done.[138] Elgin (2009) argues that we need many different types of reconciliation, from the ecological to the generational. Showing remorse and seeking forgiveness also requires taking action. One example of such action is the organisational remorse shown by the University of Glasgow following a report on that institution's links to slavery. The University has taken action, including funding reparative justice projects and creating a partnership with the University of the West Indies.[139] Sathnam Sanghera offers examples of actions that are being undertaken by individuals, institutions, educational establishments, museums, businesses and government to address institutional racism and the legacy of Empire (2021: 207).

Layla Saad (2020) suggests that individual remorse for the structural racial injustice facing Black, Indigenous and People of Colour includes deeply engaging with the meaning of racism and white privilege, at the same time as also taking action to end racism in society.

Cosmic Grief and Hope

How do we cope with what we are doing to the planet and to each other? How can we express our grief, sadness, anger, despair and desperation? Increasingly, as the climate emergency and the biodiversity crisis worsen, we lose species, such as the last male northern white rhino and the sphinx macaw, both now extinct in the wild, or the many species critically threatened by fires in the Amazon. The role of bearing witness is to be present and stand with these species. This can be a daily practice of following what is happening, saying sorry, joining up the stories and watching out for the good news. Stephan Harding (2006) suggests we go out into Gaia, beyond our own skins, and experience what is happening to "desperate earth". Thich Nhat Hanh (in Ryan, 1994) says we can become one with all the suffering on the planet, from the suffering of a child born into poverty, to the suffering of the trees and the planet herself. Fellow Buddhist Joanna Macy (in Power, 2013: 87) suggests, "if we feel a great ache in our chest as if our hearts could break....it is said that the heart that breaks open can contain the whole universe". Macy and Johnson suggest putting these qualities together as "grief and hope, hope and grief" (2012). One way to do this is recounted by Clare Power through the creation of a truth mandala. In this ritual, participants are invited to express their grief and sadness and be heard and held by other participants in order to explore their feelings and move beyond them (2013). Hope, such as this one from the Christian tradition, is needed for the journey ahead:

"We humbly acknowledge that/Despite the magnitude of our faults
And the number of our failings, /The inexplicable drive of creation,
The sacred spirit manifest in all there is, /Continuously sustains us
And allows us to begin again at any time
Infused with the might/From which we can never be separated."

(McQuiston II, 1996: 81)

In *Work that Reconnects,* described as a "form of group work designed to foster the desire and ability to take part in the healing of our world", Macy and Johnstone combine grief and hope in a spiral ritual that starts with gratitude and works through grief and pain to seeing with new eyes and emerging into hope. Through this, increasing attention is being paid to decolonising rituals and practices and being aware of the intersectionality of participants coming from different backgrounds as they deal with grief and pain. Sarah Nahar (2017) writes of the need to specifically address the different relationships of communities to grief, including the killing of indigenous peoples, the enslavement of Africans and the effects of migration policies and border controls on communities. Nahar suggests practices that facilitators can follow to make the interconnections between anti-racism, decolonisation and environmental advocacy. The Work that Reconnects is now a global network of people working from Joanna Macy's principles towards mutual learning.

In the tradition of contemplative ecology, the role of hope is in the spiritual work of learning to let go of the ego and live with simplicity and purity of heart, while entering into the pain of what humanity is doing to the world (Christie, 2013: 147). Christie explores the contemplative practice of living with the pain and "practicing Paradise". One GreenSpirit meeting explored the concept of 'milling' – independently moving around the room and engaging with others as a way to encounter our shared humanity, challenges and strengths. Another activity involves working individually or in pairs, to bring into our conscious minds the billions of years it has taken to create each human hand, in order to achieve a sense of hope from such creativity. Other rituals which can address both grief and hope include the Council of All Beings, where participants choose a species and become its voice. The Council is a grief ritual, where the different species mourn what is happening to them. The Council of All Beings suggests a way to include people in giving voice to the destruction of nature through identifying with a particular species. Participants are invited to go outside and allow a species to choose them, and then use their voices to suggest what action needs to be undertaken to protect that species.

O **Hopeful Companions**

Books
Roberts, E., and Amidon, E. 1991. *Earth Prayers from Around the world: 365 Prayers, Poems, and Innovations for Honouring the Earth.* California: Harper San Francisco.

Resources for Actions
To find instructions for milling and links to other rituals: https:// workthatreconnects.org/resource/the-milling/

For the history and an account of a Council of All Beings see: http:// www.rainforestinfo.org.au/deep-eco/Joanna%20Macy.htm.

Nahar, S. 2017. 'The intersectionalisation of the work that reconnects. *While we're all in this together in the Great Turning, we're all in it together differently*: https://journal.workthatreconnects. org/2017/08/29/intersectionalization-of-the-work-that-reconnects/

For resources, a Deep Time Journal and a network for the *Work that Reconnects* see: https://workthatreconnects.org/.

Cosmic sacred space, liturgy and ritual

The Universe Walk encourages us to remember that, before there were temples, mosques or churches, our sacred spaces were in nature herself. Thomas Berry (quoted in Tucker et al., 2019: 259) recalls an ecumenical meeting he attended at St. John the Divine Cathedral in New York in 1975. Among the speakers was Lame Deer of the Sioux Nation, who suggested how strange it was to celebrate the planet inside a building rather than outside:

"with the open sky, with the mountains in the distance and the wind blowing through the trees and the earth under their feet and surrounded by the living sound of birds and insects."

Our search for loving spiritual qualities can be linked to our search for awe and wonder and a sacred Cosmos. Moving from the meditative practices described in Chapters 6 and 10, we can begin to engage in contemplative ecology, widening our meditative practices so they become part of the Cosmos. Similarly, sacred singing and music can incorporate the planet and Cosmos. Existing prayer practices can be expanded into prayers for Earth and Cosmos. New sacred spaces can be created, such as within the recently restored Pugin Monastery in East Manchester, which is an ecumenical centre for tolerance, peace and love for all life, locally and globally, founded on sacred geometry.[140]

Part of this stage of my journey was exploring the contribution of wisdom traditions to taking care of the planet. Although religious traditions can be critiqued for not doing enough, there is a strong strand within all such traditions of caring for the environment and expressing reverence and respect for the planet. Acknowledging and appreciating the contribution of wisdom traditions and their relationship to the planet and Cosmos is an important step towards creating wider understanding and taking action. As part of the community Pilgrimage for Gaia workshops, short extracts from different faith traditions were circulated around the room and participants were asked to volunteer to read these aloud. The World Parliament of Religions has issued a call to all faith communities to take the lead in the third decade of the twenty-first century and implement the Faith for Earth Call to Action, which demonstrates how all faith traditions include reverence for creation and draws out the restoration needed for ecosystems and human inequalities.

Creativity

Creativity helps us to encounter a living planet and a meaningful universe. Philosopher Satish Kumar (2017: 7) has called for the artist in each one of us to come to the fore:

"Nobody is special, but everyone is important. Every person is a special kind of artist, a special kind of leader. We are all leaders.

You can be whatever you want to be; it is within your potential. We all have potential capacity to use our imagination, to re-create it, to serve the world. Whether you are famous or not doesn't matter. Potentially what you do – creatively, imaginatively – that's all that matters."

In Chapter 7, I discussed workshops that use creativity to help participants learn about a meaningful universe and living Earth. In one community workshop, participants drew maps of where they live. In the first exercise, participants were asked to draw their immediate surroundings. One participant put a local green cycleway through the centre of their map, referring to it as "my motorway"; others sketched their streets, including trees and gardens. Next, participants were given extracts from local street maps and asked to locate their neighbourhood on those maps. Then, they were asked to draw the place of their home on our planet and, finally, stepping up the levels of the Universe, their place in the Cosmos. Such resources are accessible and cost very little. Nerantzi (2018; 2019; 2020) explores the role of creativity in learning in higher education. One workshop used food to understand paradigms and worldviews. Participants were asked to arrange a plate of fruit and vegetables to illustrate what a paradigm might look like. This practice had elements of working with the world in an embodied manner and of thinking of food as sacred. Boyce-Tillman (2019) uses music to enable us to be open to a living planet and sacred cosmos. In her choral work, *The Great Turning*, she invites the audience on a journey into the Cosmos, into grief, into mourning and out into action to heal our planet.

○ **Hopeful Companions**

Creativity
Einojuhani Rautavaara. *Concerto for Birds and Orchestra.* Cantus Articus, Op.61: https://www.youtube.com/watch?v=HLjXgV-Mhp0&list=RDHLjXgV-Mhp0&start_radio=1

Abel Selaocoe and the Manchester Collective. 2022. *The Oracle*: Recorded live at the Queen Elizabeth Hall, the South Bank Centre, 1 May. https://www.youtube.com/watch?v=iYsDiOvSpZQ

Films
The Great Turning performance: https://www.youtube.com/watch?v=r0QBo43g_aA

Organisations
International Network for Spirituality and Wellbeing: http://mswinternational.org/_

 Creative Learning Exercises

Consider growing cosmic qualities in your daily life.

Choose and start with one cosmic quality. Practice living your daily life through the lens of cosmic gratitude – for your life, family, community, Gaia and Cosmos. Regularly reflect and review.

Consider developing practices for grief and hope in relation to our planet and Cosmos. In what ways might you develop these within your community?

Think about ways that you can celebrate the wisdom traditions and their reverence for the planet.

Consider how humanity can uphold the Cosmos through creating societies which are anti-racist, where colonialism no longer influences society, where women are equal, where disabled people flourish, where LGBTQ+ people feel welcomed, where poverty and disadvantage are ended and where humanity seriously tackles the climate emergency which all puts humanity on a path to be part of our great Cosmic history. What small steps can you take in your daily life to contribute to these changes?

Love: finding a connection and our way into the future

Teilhard de Chardin (1936) wrote,

> "The day will come when, after harnessing space, the winds, the tides, and gravitation, we shall harness for God the energies of love. And on that day, for the second time in the history of the world, we shall have discovered fire."

The element of love is a connecting thread to all the cosmic practices and qualities I have described. My daughter Nora wrote "in the end, it was all about love" when describing the influences on her upbringing. All spiritual traditions are built on a central tenet of love and compassion. The eighth to third century BCE Tao Te Ching values "the importance of love and nurturing". Thich Nhat Hanh (1995) has explored the importance of compassion in Buddhism. The Christian Gospel of St. John includes the words of Jesus, "A new commandment I give to you: That ye love one another". Mercy and compassion are also at the heart of the Qur'an (Shah-Kazemi, 2007).

Cosmologist Carl Sagan (1985) writes of the protagonist in his novel *Contact*, "She had studied the universe all her life but had overlooked its clearest message. For small creatures such as we, the vastness is bearable only through love." In the previous chapter, I traced research and policy literature that identifies the importance of loving and spiritual qualities for the transition to hopeful futures. Developments such as the UN Millennium Development Goals (2000–2015) and the UN Sustainable Development Goals (2015–2030) express a desire for more harmonious societies, while movements such as BLM, #MeToo, and movements in defence of nature and the climate can be traced to impulses for a kinder and more compassionate world. However, increases in inequality and accelerating climate change highlight the importance of a greener and more just recovery. We know that love is essential for a child's neurological development (Gerhardt, 2004). The Centre for Compassion and Altruism Research and Education was founded at Stanford University to investigate the impact of compassionate behaviour on individual wellbeing and on the wider world (Svoboda, 2013). Meanwhile, the Dalai Lama Centre for Peace and Education in Vancouver recognises that "a deep engagement between science...and Buddhism and other contemplative traditions could make a significant contribution to a deep understanding of the human mind and emotion." The Centre works from the belief that for children to be happy and secure, they must learn about compassion and kindness, thus enabling them to counter hatred and destructive emotions.

Creating a love for the twenty-first century

We need to expand our notions of love to incorporate the planet and the Cosmos. James Lovelock (2006: 8) writes that love for our planet is a way forward:

> "We need most of all to renew that love and empathy for nature that we lost when we began our love affair with city life."

Instead of simply loving ourselves or our human companions, we must love beyond ourselves, and fall in love "outwards" (Abram, 1996). Thomas Berry argues that the natural world is an essential part of the human psyche. Humanity emerged out of the Cenozoic, the geological period covering the last sixty-five million years, which saw the flourishing of life on Earth (Berry, 1999). If we allow so much of the natural world to go extinct, we negate part of ourselves. We must become part of this living world. Michael McCarthy (2015: 246) argues that without nature we lose something fundamental to our wellbeing. He proposes a new kind of love:

> "It will be a love which is informed, but it will also be a love which recognising the scale of the threat, is engaged, a love which, in delighting in a flower or a bird, or a meadow or a marsh, or a lake, or a forest, or a range of grasslands, realises it may not be there next year and will do whatever it can to protect or save it; a love which can be fierce."

This love can be expressed through the language of spirit, of action research or science or through our own creative expression. The most important aspect is that our love for nature is an active, potentially fierce, love. Echoes of such a fierce love can be found in the contemplative ecology of Douglas Christie (2013), wherein practicing a contemplative life we might also need to fight to protect the ecology of the area in which we are meditating. The fierce love we need to feel for nature can be joined with love for social justice, for marginalised and indigenous peoples and for undoing structural injustices.

○ Hopeful Companions

Creativity
Ongoing work is taking place to establish a UK Practice Centre for Mindful living and healing in challenging times: https://plumvillage. uk/beingpeace/

Organisations
Dalai Lama Centre at Stanford University, see: http://dalailamacenter. org/about/history

Resources for Action
Nurse, A. 2022 *Reparations and Anti-Black Racism*. Bristol: Bristol University Press. Establishes the case for reparations as a response to institutionalised anti-Black racism.

Sangherea, S. 2021. *Empireland: How Imperialism Has Shaped Modern Britain*. London: Viking.

Growing into the sacred planet and Cosmos

Glimpses of loving and spiritual qualities can be found in a sense of relation with our fellow inhabitants of the planet and a sense of the interconnectedness of the whole across time and space. How might we describe this sense of a meaningful Cosmos? In Native American traditions, sacredness exists throughout our world, even in the rocks and the moon, which are our brothers and sisters. Black Elk of the Oglala Lakota Nation received a vision as a child, which is evocative of our precious universe (Neihardt & Black Elk, 1932: 33):

> "Then I was standing on the highest mountain of them all, and round about me was the whole hoop of the world. And while I stood there, I saw more than I can tell and I understood more than I saw: for I was seeing in a sacred manner the shapes of all things in the spirit, and the shape of all shapes as they must live together like one being. And I saw the sacred hoop of my people

was one of many hoops that made one circle, wide as daylight and as starlight and in the centre grew one mighty flowering tree to shelter all the children of one mother and one father. And I saw that it was holy."

Indigenous traditions are often closer to a living Earth, making such leaps of affinity easier, as humans are understood to be part of the whole. We can learn from these, and many other wisdom traditions of our planet. In seeing the world as holy, we can come to appreciate every human being as part of this whole.

Seeing the universe as sacred is perhaps the biggest spiritual leap we can take. Modern science can help to expand our thinking. Earlier in chapter 2, we considered Brian Swimme's short history of the universe. Swimme (in Bridle, 2001) suggested that, given that humans emerged from hydrogen gas and developed a knowledge of the sacred, then the universe must have that knowledge too, right from the beginning:

"Hydrogen gas is odourless and colourless, and in the prejudice of our Western civilization, we see it as just material stuff. There is not much there. You just take hydrogen, leave it alone, and it turns into a human; that's a pretty interesting bit of information. The point is that if humans are spiritual, then hydrogen is spiritual. It's an incredible opportunity to escape the traditional dualism you know; spirit is up there; matter is down here. It's different. You have the matter all the way through, and so you have the spirit all the way through."

The sacred cosmos can also be understood through mystical experience. Philip Goff (2019) notes that there is agreement across faith traditions regarding the mystical experience of sensing the world as whole and all of us as one (see Fox, 1984; Elgin, 2009). St. Francis's Canticle of the Creatures is a song of gratitude for all of creation, while thirteenth century Sufi mystic Jalalu'ddin Rumi described humanity as one and part of nature (quoted in Otto, 1932: 74):

"I am the chain of being, the circle of the spheres,
The scale of creation, the rise and the fall.

I am what is and what is not."

In understanding the universe as sacred, the mystics open a doorway for the rest of us to enter. Whether or not we see the Cosmos as sacred or simply something that fills us with awe and wonder, such explorations teach the special nature of our planet in the Cosmos.

Understanding the cosmic exceptionalism of life on Earth and our role as humans

It is important that we recognise just how special life is. In 1961, a group of scientists met to consider why we had not yet found extra-terrestrial life. Frank Drake presented an equation to determine the number of potential extra-terrestrial civilisations in the Milky Way.[141] He calculated that civilisations such as ours might not last long, as technologically advanced societies are more likely to self-implode. One of the implications of Drake's Equation is that Earth may be the only place in the universe to harbour complex life, making it a unique and wonderful place. From this, cosmologist Carl Sagan concluded that humans, therefore, have a moral responsibility to look after life on our planet. A generation later, physicist Brian Cox (2015) argued that life on our planet is wondrous, as is the human ability to explore the universe, both qualities that we must take great care of. It is not simply a matter of not yet having found intelligent extra-terrestrial life. Abrams and Primack (2011) argue that it is essential for humanity's future to understand the uniqueness of Earth's carbon-based life.

Creation stories teach humans our role and purpose in society and in the Cosmos. Is our role one of consumption and destruction of the planet and the killing of those we believe we hate? Berry (1999) argues that humans bring gifts to the universe. With our consciousness and ability to reflect, we become the universe reflecting on herself. We are the universe celebrating her beauty and grandeur, understanding herself. In the human, the universe has birthed a reflective part of herself that can know her own wonders. Maybe this seems too full of hubris. But we have the gifts of knowledge and science to explore the universe. Swimme (1984) writes that when we learn about the dynamic powers of the universe, the planet is self-educating. We are the planet learning about herself. The powers of the universe are here for us and free for all, irrespective of class, gender, ethnicity, sexuality, disability, nationality or creed. They represent characteristics of the universe and understanding and learning about them allows us to structure our lives and our societies differently. They are gifts offered to us to find solutions to our contemporary challenges.

Reflections: Waking up

Yet it is still possible to live one's whole life without knowing the wonder of the Cosmos, or the value of ethics and love. Anthony de Mello (1996) urges us to wake up in our daily lives to appreciate being alive. Berners-Lee and Clarke (2013) and Stager (2011) suggests that humanity must 'wake up' to climate change and to the effects of our actions. Ibram X. Kendi (2019), meanwhile, urges us to wake up to the violence being done to members of Black communities and to the urgent need to build global societies founded on anti-racist principles, policies and interventions.[142] How might we wake up? And how will we know when we are awake? Throughout this book, I have offered a wide variety of ways to wake up to living in our ancient and beautiful universe. The Cosmic Road Map offers signposts to waking up individually to the inclusion of loving and spiritual qualities in our lives. The cosmic practices and qualities in this chapter enable us to wake up to our living planet and our awe-inspiring and wondrous cosmos.

The living Earth and the sacred Cosmos are a long way from our growth orientated and consumerist paradigms. Mary Catherine Bateson, working with her late father's manuscript, considered ways to explore spiritual qualities in society. In faith traditions, such qualities can be explored from within and faith offers us a different way of seeing the world. This is more difficult outside of faith communities, yet these spiritual qualities are needed in many parts of society – in community groups, small and large businesses and institutions of all sizes. Without the use of such spiritual qualities, which allow us to correct our thinking, Bateson reflected that, "It seems that we have the capacity to be wrong in rather creative ways – so wrong that this world we cannot understand may become one in which we cannot live" (2005: 200).

How can we bring together the different reflective and spiritual paths considered over the last two chapters in order that we might share with others? As Paul Hawken (2007) describes, there are many people all over the world working for a more compassionate, socially just and ecological world. One method is to use the model in Chapter 6, and Thomas Berry's suggestion that our way forward is in the place where self, community, planet and Cosmos meet. This approach is illustrated in Figure 11.4 (overleaf). The practices and qualities presented in this cycle can be grouped as relating to a spiritual life within self, within community, our planet and Cosmos.

The power of these practices and qualities lies in working on them all together, rather than singling them out. Figure 11.4 helps us to see ways to develop aspects of such practices and qualities in our own lives. They can be identified as first- and second-person practices to undertake alone or with others. Reflective practice and action research can be used as bridges to help explore these qualities in a wide range of settings, such as organisations, local and faith communities, trade unions and businesses. They can be explored in all levels of learning and education, from schools and universities, to learning and development and continuous professional development within organisations. Universities, in particular, can highlight the role of these practices and qualities on the journey towards sustainable societies.[143] This may require adapting the language used within academic circles to discuss love and spiritual qualities. Goodwin (1999) uses the word 'quality' as code for love, while McNiff and Whitehead (2011) observe that love is not talked about much in research, but it is acceptable in action research. Lincoln et al. (2011: 125) express optimism:

> "We may also be entering an age of greater spirituality within research efforts…[which] may yet reintegrate the sacred with the secular in ways that promote freedom and self-determination."

Noel Charlton (2008) suggests that these qualities can be explored in Meetings for Earth, where people can reflect on what is happening, be energised for the task ahead and appreciate the spirituality of the Earth and the Universe. I reproduce them here because I believe that, in combination with a daily practice of bearing witness (Chapter 9), they offer a way forward for educational institutions, concerned organisations and community groups to explore loving and spiritual qualities and practices towards the Cosmos as a basis for journeys to the future.

Moving up and down from ourselves to cosmos and back again			
...ourselves	...our planet	...our cosmos	...our communities
Learning the knowledge of indigenous peoples, faith communities & science to comprehend our place in the cosmos	Prayers of reverence & respect for ourselves, each other, our planet & our cosmos	Take part in a Deep Time walk to understand our place in the Milky Way & within the cosmos	Planet Earth – a unique jewel in the cosmos - to be upheld as the basis for morals, values & ethics
Adding the planet to meditation and contemplation; Exploring 'rock bottom' in our careless treatment of our planet	Practicing fierce love both for nature which may not be here next year & social justice, leaving no one behind	Take part in a Council of All Beings; Grieve but also hope for nature and social justice	Taking urgent, loving action to live within planetary boundaries, providing enough for all & an end to systematic discrimination & injustice
Review of conduct: repentance and forgiveness for what we have done; Making amends	Living simply and giving to others; Reducing our footprint on the planet	Finding the sacred in nature; Developing liturgy, prayer or reflection outside in nature	Working with others towards kindness, compassion & justice to our human & more-than-human neighbours both locally and globally
Daily reflective healing & spiritual practices	Bearing witness to injustice & what is happening to the planet and to human society	Undertaking practices for life on a living planet & in a sacred cosmos; Meditating on the gifts of the cosmos	Adding compassion, kindness, respect & tolerance to our treatment of ourselves, others, more-than-humans & the planet

The left axis is labelled **Examples of activities and approaches developing a reflective and spiritual life**, with rows labelled (top to bottom): ...our cosmos, ...our planet, ...our communities, ...ourselves.

Figure 11.4: Examples of sharing loving and spiritual qualities and practices between Cosmos, Planet, Community and Self.
(Source: Kettleborough, 2023).

Invitation to Reflect

Meetings for Earth —
"To provide mutual support to each other in all appropriate and necessary ways.

To learn together about the ecological, political, social and psychological aspects of our present world problems.

To share in reflective, creative, and aesthetic group activity focused on the sacred nature of the total web of integrated systems that is Universe and Earth.

To undertake whatever individual and group activity is practicable to (directly or indirectly) ameliorate ecological hazards and enhance awareness of the integrated, sacred nature of the world."

(as visualised by Noel Charlton, 2008, p. 219)

Charlton would like to see the exponential growth of such groups, where people set them up in pairs and take them out from the original group. However, experience suggests that exponentially growing such spiritual groups is challenging.[144] A further way forward is for such learning to become part of many different meetings, workshops and training sessions in society. They can play a role within educational institutions. Teachers and lecturers could adapt their classes, seminars and tutorials in all areas of scholarship to work with the processes of Meetings for Earth. The concept could be extended out from education, so that business and trade union meetings, neighbourhood workshops, and faith community meetings are underpinned by the principles of Meetings for Earth.

Healing, loving and spiritual qualities: love as a motivation for action

The journey in this chapter brings me back to the healing I described at the beginning of the spiritual journey in Chapter 10. To establish Base Camp in Chapter 1, I spent time with the terrible and growing plight of planet Earth. At the same time, I learnt that one million species are currently threatened with extinction, spontaneous fires at high latitudes are releasing even more CO_2 into the atmosphere, and the melting of permafrost and warming oceans are releasing vast quantities of methane, a shorter-lived but more potent greenhouse gas, into the atmosphere. COVID-19 also had a dramatic impact on social justice, setting back work to achieve the UN SDGs, including work to reduce poverty and hunger and action for women's equality.[145] Rates of unemployment and mental ill-health are becoming more obvious with each passing day. Fault lines have also revealed the need to end systemic racism and racial and ethnic discrimination which results in disadvantage and marginalisation on a global scale.[146]

A key element of the work ahead is healing. In this fifth cycle, I outline two spiritual journeys and brought together two emerging ways of perceiving a spiritual journey into the Cosmos. Both journeys highlight the importance of healing ourselves and our communities, of healing nature, the oceans and the climate, of healing the cosmological effects of our carbon emissions on the planet, of healing the structural racism facing Black, Asian and Global Majority communities. These journeys into healing, loving and spiritual qualities that encompass a sacred Cosmos highlight the interconnectedness of social, racial and ecological justice.

 Creative Learning Exercise

We each have our own vision of the healing that needs to be undertaken.

Reflect on creating your own dreams of healing within the planet, Cosmos, the community and the self.

Create your own visual image of healing.

When we wake up and follow a new route map, we start to glimpse ourselves within a living planet and we find our purpose in the Cosmos. Once we see ourselves as having a meaningful role in that sacred universe, as the reflecting and thinking part of that universe, our actions acquire a moral purpose to reduce greenhouse gas emissions, protect biodiversity and fight for social justice. We will find ourselves searching for the best in everyone, including ourselves. The point of our lives is not to consume more. It is to uphold this beautiful planet in our amazing universe for the brief span of our lives. We find tools to judge our actions and our beliefs, and to hold us when the going gets tough. We detect a sense of meaning and purpose across all of humanity.

We need a transformation towards sustainability in every aspect of society. Loving and spiritual qualities and practices for the Cosmos will help us get there. I invite you to find a comfortable place, perhaps a favourite spot in nature and undertake the following exercise.

 Invitation to Reflect

Consider the practices I have suggested for exploring our Cosmos; a Cosmos that has been expanding for 13.8 billion years and that has, amazingly, birthed Gaia in all her glorious complexity. Which of these practices resonate with you?

Create a large circle representing Planet Earth. Consider how ending violence towards human communities and ending systemic racial, gender, disability, LGBTQ+ and socio-economic injustices helps grow our planet. Map your ideas on your representation of planet Earth and make any connections you can see.

In what ways can you birth a deeper love for the more-than-human world, which is not simply about appreciation but also about protecting and saving?

Consider ways that you might share the practices and qualities in Figure 11.4 with others.

How might you bring the ideas of Meetings for Earth into your own community or organisation?

Notes

[138] For online versions of the Truth and Reconciliation Commission reports, see: https://www.sahistory.org.za/article/truth-and-reconciliation-commission-trc-0

[139] See *Slavery, Abolition and the University of Glasgow*, Report and Recommendations from the History of Slavery Steering Group September 2018, available at https://www.gla.ac.uk/media/Media_607547_smxx.pdf. The University won Times HE University of the Year 2020 for its work on addressing its historic links with slavery: https://www.timeshighereducation.com/news/times-higher-education-awards-2020-winners

[140] For this history, see https://www.themonastery.co.uk/our-story-2/

[141] See https://www.universetoday.com/39966/drake-equation-1/

[142] See X Kendi, I. 2019. pp: 232 – 233 and 237 – 238 for ideas.

[143] The growth of the carbon literacy programme at Manchester Metropolitan University demonstrates an organic way for the discussion on ethics and qualities to grow out from the academy: https://carbonliteracy.com/

[144] Some UK and US organisations, with links to others: https://www.resurgence.org/ https://www.greenspirit.org.uk/ https://www.findhorn.org/ https://fore.yale.edu

[145] See the UN on the need to use the UN SDGs as a guiding compass through the global crisis created by the COVID-19 pandemic: https://news.un.org/en/story/2020/05/1063742. For the effects of COVID-19 on the UN SDGs see https://unstats.un.org/sdgs/report/2020/

[146] See, for example, Ed Pilkington on the USA: https://www.theguardian.com/us-news/2020/may/28/us-coronavirus-death-toll-racial-disparity-inequality; the UN on gender inequality: https://news.un.org/en/story/2021/03/1087392; and the UN on human rights and inequality: https://news.un.org/en/story/2021/09/1101552.

Cycle 6: Germinating seeds of hope

"And whatever you can do, just do it and be happy by doing it. Whether you have achieved anything or not doesn't matter; just act. Living is with action. Not worrying, not thinking, not planning. A little bit of these things is fine, but the main thing is acting. That comes from the resilience in yourself."

(Satish Kumar, 2017: 8)

This sixth and final cycle brings together the practices and qualities from the five preceding cycles as a contribution to achieving solutions to our many planet-wide problems. Starting with interior changes to the self, we can learn to become more cosmologically influenced managers, activists and teachers. The four stories towards the end of Chapter 12, inspired by the Dream of the Earth, are examples of dynamic and intrinsically small exterior management practices that will provide you with inspiration for the journey ahead. As you reflect on the themes within those stories, take the time to create your own story of the Dream of the Earth.

Finally, I conclude this journey to hopeful futures by returning to the knowledge of ancient civilisations and our planet Gaia herself. We celebrate the knowledge of the cosmonauts, astronauts, and taikonauts who have seen the Earth from space, inspiring meditation on their reflections, as a backdrop to an Urgent Call for Wise Action. Through an extended Creative Learning Exercise – from the individual to the community, organisation, government and international levels and within each of the paradigms explored throughout the book - I will encourage us to set specific targets for the crucial decade ahead. With this Urgent Call to Wise Action, we can set off from Base Camp as artists rather than consumers, over the mountains, and onwards on our journey to a hopeful future.

CHAPTER 12: Becoming a cosmically influenced activist, manager and teacher

"We can more easily find one another and end our isolation as we form communities…and give expression to stories that demonstrate and celebrate the possibilities of Earth Community."
David Korten (2006: 355)

"Our house is on fire. I am here to say. Our house is on fire."
Greta Thunberg (2019:19)

"Experience in conservation projects has shown that positive change will only last for the long term if local communities are fully involved in developing the plans and directly feel the benefit of rising biodiversity."
David Attenborough (2020: 180)

"The forces of doomism and despair mongering remain active, and we must call them out whenever they appear."
Michael Mann *(2021: 257).*

We are walking on Dartmoor, a band of GreenSpiriters from across England, enjoying a day walk together. At the start of our walk, we encounter a group of soldiers training. Startled, we walk between them. They ignore us, watching each other, guns out, running down the hill and crouching low, shouting instructions. It is a sharp reminder that taking green and spirit out into the world is not easy.

Over the top of the hill, the beautiful moors are spread out before us. Some of us stride out for a longer walk up the hill, led by the fitter members of our company. Every so often, we pause to share a poem, something someone has appreciated, or a reflection. As we walk, we hear skylarks trilling overhead. I concentrate and am rewarded with the sight of a tiny flash of life soaring above me. I am reminded of how precious it is to hear these birds and how rare they are in my city life. I recall walking on the South Downs behind Brighton when I was a child and hearing skylarks, a constant part of our lives. My mother loved these birds, they were part of her native Iveragh, and the heroes of the beautiful song, "I have seen the lark soar high at noon, heard her song up in the blue." The skylarks on Dartmoor remind me of writer Michael McCarthy's love of butterflies and what they mean in his life. When we stop, the wind in our faces, the horizon away in the distance, we each offer our reflections. I talk about the skylarks and that I no longer hear them very often. Michael McCarthy says that when we love we must love fiercely because what we love may not be here next year. So, we must love the skylarks now in the knowledge that they are threatened and vulnerable. Love them fiercely and act on their behalf.

Introduction

António Guterres, General Secretary of the United Nations, wants every country to declare a climate emergency until the world reaches net zero carbon emissions. Many cities and regions have already declared a Climate Emergency. Throughout this book, I have argued that the dedicated long-term, decade-by-decade, generation-by-generation work needed to overcome this emergency requires each of us to live within our planet and our cosmos. The Climate Emergency is a Cosmological Emergency. We are changing the structure, environment and ecology of our planet on cosmological proportions and time scales. We need to stand up to what we are physically doing with cosmological wisdom and loving spiritual qualities. This chapter explores what happens when we become cosmologically-influenced managers, community activists, teachers and parents. It explores *internal* changes to our thinking and emerging *external* action in the world. I offer four stories (following page 376) to illustrate the development of my own ideas, and how cosmological thinking influenced my practice. As I emphasise the importance of sharing hopeful actions, I invite you to create your own stories.

Community, as a site in which to become a cosmologically-influenced practitioner, can be a location for creating music, gardening, knitting, reading and community orientated activism of all kinds. Community may refer to our interest or identity groups, or to where we live.[147] A second site of practice is learning and teaching. We are all learners throughout our lives and a journey of life-long and life-wide learning offers us many opportunities to learn individually and with each other. A third site is in the management of our own lives or organisations. In our individual lives, we manage where we live, how we eat, sleep and organise our lives, what we buy, what we consume and how we heat our homes. Managing an organisation encompasses many professional and voluntary categories, including educational and academic, community, NGOs and charities, local government, health and business.

◯ **Hopeful Companions**

Resources for Action
United Nations Secretary General Antonio Gutérres urges countries to declare a climate emergency. The Guardian, 12 December 2020: https://www.youtube.com/watch?v=lhlJGxm4rzl

Wunderling. N. et al, 2021. Interacting tipping effects increase risk of climate domino effects under global warming. Earth Systems Dynamics, 12 pp. 601-619. European GeoSciences Union: https://esd.copernicus.org/articles/12/601/2021/

Climate Emergency Declaration and Mobilization in Action 2022: https://www.cedamia.org/

Experiments in transforming into Cosmic practice

Dreams of managing that move between self, community, planet and Cosmos can seem far removed from our current paradigms. We can sometimes feel powerless in the face of so many challenges. My late tutor, Chris Seeley, urged me to delve deeper into a participative universe. I did this by using all my senses to enter into the present and expressing what I discovered through reflection and writing captured at the beginning and end of each day. During this process, Chris observed that she trusted that I could change local government work practices into cosmic practice, and back into daily practice, and illustrate that process from my own experience. Ever since, I have been experimenting with fostering hopeful futures through planting seeds of wider paradigms in all areas of my life, nurtured by song, music and poetry.

Assessments of management or community development practice typically centre on outputs and outcomes. The effective spending of public funding is often a priority. This can sometimes be easy to measure. In neighbourhood regeneration, for example, one can count the number of new jobs created or trees planted. In community development, it's easy to record the number of activities, the number of people involved, and their feelings about those activities. Official reports allow us to piece together how communities were impacted and the long-term changes made. In addition to delivering these types of outputs and outcomes, I became interested in widening human-based practice into cosmological practice. I created an additional set of outputs and outcomes that emerged over time and continue to develop. These include assessing changes to the **interior** thinking that underpins external action, such as ideas about nature, climate, the planet and the Cosmos, and changes to **exterior** action arising from this thinking that results in changes to management, community and teaching practice.

Over two decades, I have used story to shape my practice, seeking to make manifest the Dream of the Earth. My stories respond to Thomas Berry's suggestion that our way into the future is to return to the depths of the Cosmos to find the energy to take us forward. These stories point towards solutions within wider paradigms. The overall outcomes are still in the process of being dreamed, and the stories demonstrate steps along the way.

◯   **Hopeful Companion**

Book
Harrison, L. 2018. *Dream Big Little Leader.* A board book for toddlers about heroines of colour. London: Puffin.

Seeley. C. 2006. '*Wild margins playing at work and life.*' Centre for Action Research in Professional Practice, University of Bath. Available at: https://people.bath.ac.uk/mnspwr/doc_theses_links/c_seeley. html

---

<u>Creativity</u>
Sinead O'Connor: *My Singing Bird*: https://www.youtube.com/watch?v=FHJJCCMEo2w

Prince Ea: *Man Vs Earth* https://www.youtube.com/watch?v=VrzbRZn5Ed4&t=3s

Drew Dellinger: *Hieroglyphic Stairway*: https://www.youtube.com/watch?v=fjc4rmJdA3k

Newton Harrison: *Apologia Mediterranean*: https://ecoartscotland.net/2020/03/13/newton-harrison-3-recent-videos-including-apologia-mediterranean/#more-5532

 Creative Learning Exercises

Drawing on the examples in the Hopeful Companions resources, identify creative ways to become more cosmologically influenced in your daily life.

As you work through this chapter, use your favourite form of creativity to capture the ideas using this method.

Collect examples of songs, poetry, music or art to inspire you on this journey to become part of the planet and Cosmos.

Interior practices

My interior management practices include three areas of action – the call of Gaia, bringing the Cosmos into my thinking and understanding that everything is connected.

The Call of Gaia

The first set of practices as a manager, teacher and activist involve listening to Gaia and her creatures and embedding this listening in my thinking and practice while acknowledging the importance of human healing and development. These interior practices are within the control of each of us and are open to all.

Listening to the call of Gaia has become part of me. After several years of collecting newspaper and magazine cuttings, images of threatened species were with me all the time. Gaia was ever present in my thoughts, and I began to see this as a practice that might be important for my management work. I sensed the need to assess my practice through the eyes of Gaia's Graveyards while meeting more traditional targets, such as sticking to budgets, staff health and safety or teaching in an engaging manner. Through journaling and reflection on practice, another set of criteria to assess performance emerged – Gaia and the crisis facing our ecosystems. One weekend in 2008, for example, I cut the following stories from newspapers: a jellyfish invasion in the Mediterranean that threatened other marine life; the death of young puffins through choking because adult puffins are now feeding on sandpiper eels that have moved farther north because of global warming; the likely extinction of many shark species. I reflected on James Lovelock's observation that we continue to not think about Gaia in our actions despite the planet's desperate need for our careful attention. I reflect that I go to work, walk up the stairs, into my office, make a cup of tea and start work; and all the time the seas and the animals are dying.[148] These cuttings encouraged me to register for a PhD which ultimately led to this book. As I continue to collect the cuttings, my actions evolve. I take note of what is happening in one story and put it together with another, making connections, listening to our planet. I join the stories to the long Cosmic history that birthed such exquisite and complex forms of life. Through text and images, I bring the voices of the creatures into workshops, seminars and tutorials.

I use these stories not to elicit grief but to share the determination and need for urgent action and fierce love by individuals and organisations. All the time, I seek to find ways to bring Gaia into my work and my community. Over a decade later, the story of the puffins is amplified for other creatures. Animals are dying of starvation because they don't have enough food or because their stomachs are filled with the plastic they have inadvertently eaten. As I share stories of polar bears, Italian bears, jaguars, seals off the coast of Namibia, other stories from Gaia stand out; the failure of the English Cricket Board to tackle a culture of racism within the sport, the murder of a young woman through male violence in Ireland, the plight of the people of Afghanistan and Ukraine. It seems that we need to create **a daily practice** of Gaia's Graveyards in our paid and unpaid work. Such a practice of bearing witness will interweave the crisis of biodiversity with the need to address social injustice and all forms of inequality, so that they become a central strand in our thinking.

Principles of bearing witness to what is happening to Gaia

1. Embrace our living planet by developing your own practice of bearing witness to biodiversity loss, climate change and social injustice in all its forms.

2. Create a regular reminder to yourself to take action and maintain a balanced action research practice.

3. Teach others (students, children, friends, neighbours, colleagues) through a process of inquiry and action research.

4. Engage with the evidence of what is happening to the planet through your heart.

5. Encourage businesses, politicians and organisations to engage with the practice of bearing witness every day as an on-going orientation towards ecological and social justice based business, law-making and governance.

6. Become a participant in the living Earth by embracing a radical paradigm shift centred on social and racial justice and take urgent wise action to restore the planet.

7. Embed a reflective, spiritual, social justice and ecological dimension into your personal and professional practice.

⃝ Hopeful Companions

Resources for bearing witness to the science of what is happening to our planet Earth. Try to read at least some of the scientific reports behind the headlines.

Books
Thunberg, G. 2022. (ed) *The Climate Book.* London: Allen Lane. Over a hundred experts join Greta to explore the climate, what we've done to the planet and what we need to do.

State of the Cryosphere Report. 2022. *Global Losses, Global Impacts. We cannot negotiate with the melting point of ice.* International Cryosphere Climate Initiative. Offers sobering projections for what will happen to the cryosphere (mountain glaciers and snow, permafrost, Artic sea ice, polar oceans) under different degrees of global warming: https://iccinet.org/statecryo2022/

Websites
Consider following an environmental website. For example: https://www.theguardian.com/uk/environment

---

> https://www.bbc.co.uk/news/topics/cnx753jenyjt/environment
>
> International Union for the Conservation of Nature (IUCN). 2022. Red List of Threatened Species: https://www.iucnredlist.org/en

Developing a Gaian sense of 'True North'

Listening to Gaia and what she is going through led me to re-orientate my ideas of where I was going. Self-development writer Stephan Covey (1989) suggests finding one's own true north, one's own sense of direction, while futurist Hardin Tibbs (1999) expands this to include the environment and the planet. In Chapter 10, I traced the spiritual journey of searching within ever-expanding practices. I came to see this as tracking towards the best I could be, towards my own spiritual and professional 'true north', which includes the wellbeing of other beings. A distinctive characteristic of this emerging true north was that it was not merely a direction, but also how to forge the path north through action research and extended ways of knowing.

By asking myself what Gaia would see as the right approach to an issue, this sense of true north encouraged me to make management decisions that developed and protected a more holistic approach to service delivery. This included making the argument that community development should include community gardening and tree planting, the creation of hedgehog highways by residents' groups, and encouraging students to plant trees. My sense of true north is continuously challenged and fed by the practice of bearing witness. For example, working on revisions for this book, I evolved an understanding that bearing witness for Gaia is part of the struggle of bearing witness for Black Lives Matter. Allissa Richardson (2020: 187) records the long history of bearing witness to violence against black communities in the US through "slave narratives, black newspapers and magazines, urban radio, televised civil rights era news broadcasts, black blogs and websites and now, by witnesses with smartphones". This resonates with bearing witness to what is happening to our planet.

Personal healing and spiritual values are part of the practice for Gaia

Reflection on our treatment of Gaia led me back to James Lovelock (1988), who argues that we are abysmal at taking care of Gaia. How can we take care of planet Earth, he asks (p. 228), when we cannot care for our own personal health? Reflecting on my work practices in the 2000s, I recognised that I was heavily focused on work and did not have a holistic attitude towards life. In a 2007 journal extract, I wrote that the Dream of the Earth must also be a dream for oneself and one's home and family. I concluded that paid employment must be rooted in ideas of healing, self-development, life, health and wellbeing. Often, I was only reminded of the importance of health when a work colleague or neighbour died. As I scrutinised my work practice, I reflected on individual weaknesses and came to understand that dreaming must be part of the mess and imperfection of daily life. I acknowledged how far our dreams are from reality, how hard it is to maintain both, to let go of ego, and to balance ego, self-esteem and good work. Such reflections continued over the years as I struggled to learn to take care of myself and maintain a continuous holistic balance in my life. The spiritual healing described in Chapter 10 was a response to the pressures of work and my desire for a holistic life and included spiritual practices and understanding of the Cosmos as awe-inspiring and a source of strength and energy. These practices are essential if we are to respond to the challenges facing Gaia and society.

As I developed management and community practices, I was attentive to the spaces within organisations that allowed room for these qualities. For example, leadership development coaching encourages ongoing reflection while strength-based approaches to career development encourage dreaming and wellbeing. The events of 2020 brought health and wellbeing, inequality and racism to the fore. This has expanded to include organisational wellbeing and the importance of both resilience and tackling racism in organisations (Runneymeade Trust, 2021). There is increased attention paid to the damaging effects of experiencing racism, with a report outlining the mental health effects of racism on women of colour in the workforce (Gyimach et al., 2022). Without the qualities and skills of resilience, employees, and society in general, may not be able to cope with the shock of pandemics and other future threats (see OECD, 2021; Deakin, 2021). To promote resilience, many organisations are now offering spaces for reflection, spirituality and practices such as yoga and meditation. To tackle racism and the threat to wellbeing, organisations are introducing structural change, as for example the Race Equality Charter in Higher Education.

The importance of spirituality in the workplace and communities is now emerging in, for example, UNESCO Learning Cities.[149] Given that healing, loving and spiritual qualities are part of developing resilience, there is the opportunity for workplaces to become more receptive to our living planet and awe-inspiring Cosmos.

⭘ **Hopeful Companions**

Organisations
The Organization for Economic Co-operation and Development (OECD) report on resilience highlights the role of government: https://www.oecd.org/coronavirus/policy-responses/building-resilience-to-the-covid-19-pandemic-the-role-of-centres-of-government-883d2961/

Learning cities, see: https://unesco.org.uk/learning-cities/

Bringing the Cosmos into our daily thinking

Learning to add a cosmological dimension to my thinking was part of the development of my management, teaching and community practices. Over many years, I have learned to act within ever expanding frameworks of vision. I am driven by Thomas Berry's insight that we must return to the Cosmos to get the energy to go forward, given the scale of obstacles in our way and the tasks needed to overcome them.

Being part of the Cosmos

What started as journal entries reflecting challenges or difficulties at work, began to be juxtaposed by cosmological observations from books or the news. In 2009, for example, I meditated on the sheer size of the solar system, on the 19 trillion miles to the edge of the Oort Cloud, on the fact that the distance from the Earth to the Sun is one astronomical unit (AU) and from Earth to Pluto is about forty AU and from Earth to the centre of the Oort Cloud is 50,000 AU (Bryson, 2003: 24). Over the years, I have continued to meditate on the scale of the Cosmos, taking the six leaps described in Chapter 6. I continue to juxtapose reflections on my day with reflections on scientific exploration of the Cosmos and, where I can, I bring these stories of the Cosmos into conversations in paid and voluntary work and at home, in the belief that such an approach opens up spaces in our thinking. I open workshops by playing Carl Sagan's *Pale Blue Dot* video and his reflections on planet Earth "as a mote of dust suspended in a sunbeam" (1994).[150] These encourage participants to think critically and cosmologically about our values and society's relationship with violence to other humans.

Understanding neighbourhoods within expanding contexts/learning to become part of the Cosmos

Becoming part of the Cosmos gives us the understanding and energy to tackle the challenges we face. My cosmological thinking developed further as I meditated on the metaphor of moving up and down through the levels of the universe. In my work with Neighbourhood Renewal, I started to notice conversations about scale. At a regional seminar on the development of community empowerment in the North West of England, one officer observed that issues in neighbourhoods often relate to scale. He reflected that, as officers, we needed to differentiate between local issues and those that are sub-regional and regional. Each scale requires a different response. As I listened to this, I reflected on how such notions of scale might help develop wider ways of thinking. Similarly, unemployment research conducted in an area of high unemployment and poverty demonstrated the importance of creating links between employers at local authority and sub-regional levels (NWIEP, 2009; 2010).

My thinking was also influenced by expanding the concept of 'neighbourhood'. The National Geographic map of our cosmic neighbourhood that came unannounced through our front door at the Millennium transformed my use of the word *neighbourhood*, allowing me to use it to illustrate different scales, from the local all the way up to our neighbouring galaxies. Such an extension of the word 'neighbourhood' helps to extend our thinking. For example, I have used it in workshops with residents and councillors to encourage them to think of how neighbourhood streets connect to the scale of the planet and Cosmos.

Despite severe cutbacks due to austerity, the concept of neighbour-hoods and neighbourhood work survive in local government and policing in the UK, and have the potential to expand the sense of community. Dena Freeman (2020) suggests that we need to see the world as a whole and see ourselves as part of a global society in which we build spaces and institutions for local community participation. The goal of UN SDG 4, Quality Education, is to provide all learners with knowledge and skills for sustainable development through global citizenship. Such insights help to create links between what happens to us as individuals and what happens to the planet at ever-expanding scales. Perceiving the world as a whole helps us to understand the billions of years it has taken to get to where we are, and possibilities for the future on this sort of scale.

Developing thinking over cosmological time

We must also learn to understand the connections between everything through the dimension of time. Peter Drucker (1955: 14) suggests

> "There is one major factor in every management problem, not properly speaking, a fourth function of management, but an additional dimension, time. Management always has to consider the present and long-range future."

Long-range thinking is not a characteristic often developed at either national or local scales. The passage of time is most obvious in teaching as, each year, learners move on and new ones join. Communities also have an inbuilt sense of time as children are born and grow up at the same time as older people die. However, this long-term understanding of time is rarely reflected in government policies or neighbourhood initiatives. In 2010, Geoff Fordham undertook an assessment of the New Deal for Communities Programme, one of the national regeneration initiatives for disadvantaged areas. He lamented its short-term nature and how it ended when national policy changed. Into these short time scales, I started to develop interior practices to appreciate cosmological timescales through which the world in which I work, live and manage were created. This involved engaging with the New Universe story from the Big Bang to the present, and led me to reflect that what we need are managers whose thinking can move back and forward across these vast timescales. From an encounter with an ancient piece of sandstone (recounted in Chapter 2), I began to engage with a timescale for community work, which reached back 320 million years into the past and the same number of years into the future.

Curt Stager's (2011) *Deep Future* had a profound influence on my thinking. Stager asks us to think back to the Palaeocene-Eocene Thermal Maximum, 55 million years ago, writing (p. 68), "For something close to 170,000 years, the PETM forced the world into an exceptionally heated state that bears a striking resemblance to our extreme emissions scenario." As a result, the planet warmed by 5° to 6° degrees centigrade, the oceans suddenly acidified and, to survive, species had to move extensively. As global temperatures rise so quickly in the Anthropocene, time is not on our side. In a 2020 report in *The Guardian*, ReWilding Britain stated in stark terms the challenges facing wildlife: "Global heating is shifting Britain's climate zones by up to 5km (3.1 miles) each year, outpacing wildlife's ability to adapt and survive."

However, it is not only past cosmological time we should care about. Stager (2011) suggests that, in order to take seriously what we are doing to the planet, we must think forward 100,000 years into a future, at which time, under extreme climate change scenarios, our carbon footprint will begin to decline. Beyond that timescale, there are the millions of years yet to come during which the Earth will still be habitable. Such timescales are slow, immense and completely different to those within which we now operate. Within my practice, I have tried to influence long-term thinking, or cathedral thinking, as Greta Thunberg calls it (see Lalenti, 2020).[151] Meanwhile, regeneration or the great transition to a solar economy requires that we think on generational timescales. Psychologist Abram Maslow (1962) describes the need for a slow revolution to change society for the better. Although the practices suggested in this chapter and book can seem small, they offer a way to change paradigms and mindsets. Like water dripping on a rock, slow but faithful practices can bring about great change. As Verse 78 of the Tao Te Ching says, "Nothing in the world/is softer than water/but we know it can wear away the hardest of things".

Participation

Yet another characteristic of the Cosmos is participation. In Chapter 7, I explored the participatory methods of second-person action research, teaching, learning and community development. However, in many organisations and government services, participation is no more than tokenistic. A key element of cosmological thinking is that everyone is needed, not simply for the moment, but over time. This approach to participatory empowerment and democracy is essential for hopeful futures. Throughout this book, I have provided examples of decades-long community involvement that continues despite challenges and barriers. This includes participation in policy, strategy and practice on the ground. Participation can be seen in the work of the NGOs Involve and Climate Assembly UK to reach net zero carbon emissions by 2050.[152] Organisations in the fields of health and social care, social justice and global development make the argument for resources to be made available to support participation.

Understanding that everything is connected

Thomas Berry (1999) argues that the universe is a communion of subjects rather than a collection of objects. Over time, seeing the interconnectedness of all my actions has become part of how I see the world and my practice. Every action must bring every other action with it. In Chapter 8, I explored personal responses to glimpsing the Dream of the Earth, and I have embedded this growing understanding within my community and management work. The seven mountains of Gaia's Equation have become an extended view of practice, underpinning how I see the world: *love + cosmology + ecology + regeneration + action research + systems + participation = a new worldview.* In every piece of work, voluntary or paid, in management, teaching and community development settings, I have endeavoured to include as many of these concepts as possible. For example, in the mid-2000s, I actively embraced the Egan Wheel created for the Deputy Prime Minister from a review of skills for sustainable communities (ODPM, 2004a), and have since used this in meetings and training. The Egan Wheel depicts sustainable communities as consisting of eight interlocking elements (Figure 12.1), including governance, the environment, equity, housing, society and culture. The regional learning provider RENEW NW used the Egan wheel to explain the holistic and interconnected nature of regeneration. I adapted the language and examples, in order to use the Egan wheel for sustainable community development, so that it relates directly to the experiences of the staff or community members involved. I also use this practice with students to illustrate ideas from their experience or examples from the news. In 2020, love is referred to as kindness or wellbeing; ecology as insects, wildflowers, hedgehogs and bug lines;

participation as employee voice; and equity as BLM and racial justice, gender equality and reducing inequalities.

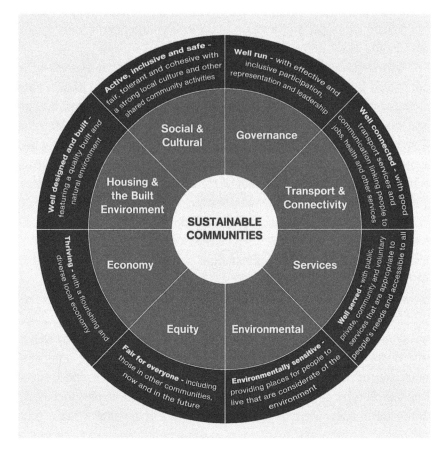

Figure 12.1: The Egan Wheel, integrated components of Sustainable Communities. (Source: RENEW NW Legacy Document 2009. Available under Creative Open Government Licence of the UK National Archives: https://tonybaldwinson.files. wordpress.com/2014/05/renew-northwest-collected-works-2005-to-2008- 9780957260610-v3.pdf)

The United Nations Sustainable Development Goals are yet another interconnected way to see the world. They are now central to the teaching of global concerns, responsible enterprise, business, ethics and sustainability at the Business School where I teach. Each SDG is clearly connected to each of the others, allowing for an interconnected sense of the planet. Such an interconnected approach has often resulted in me being asked to 'focus' on one specific area: empowerment, the environment, wellbeing. However, through developing a cosmological understanding, I have tried to share a vision of the world, which is whole, not divided into silos, and a vision of Earth from the International Space Station, the Moon and beyond.

Working to develop a long-term understanding that everything is connected brings with it a deep appreciation of the need for total system change that will re-create and connect government, legal systems, religion and the economy. Such developments are already taking place. While the European Union might not yet advocate a cosmological approach, it has a clear understanding of the need for a complete system change. In 2014, Hans Braining, Executive Director of the European Environment Agency, suggested that we must concentrate on the structural and systemic causes of the challenges we face, rather than on individual issues, as we have done since the 1970s. The UN SDG adds the human and social justice dimensions to the environmental issues affecting the world. The IPPC Working Group Report 2022 'Mitigations of Climate Change' offers clear examples of how climate change can be tackled through working with Indigenous Peoples and local communities, creating nature-focused solutions, protecting and restoring nature (IPPC, 2022b). Work by NGOs affiliated to the UN have highlighted the need to add more anti-racist perspectives to the UN SDGs. The European Parliament and Council together agreed the Eighth Environment Action Programme, running to 2030, which acknowledges the systemic nature of the challenges ahead, prioritising biodiversity loss, toxic environments and encouraging a circular economy. These must be added to the map of the journey ahead and they require a mind-set very different to the current 'take, make, use, trash' approach. Such systemic change is at the opposite end of the spectrum to each individual's span of control or influence, reinforcing the need for participatory methods that encourage individuals, communities, businesses and governments to work together (Sustainable Consumption Round Table, 2006, Raworth, 2017).

○ **Hopeful Companions**

Resources for Action
Integrating the Elimination of Systemic Racism, and Racial and Ethnic Discrimination, into the Implementation of the SDGs, Report by the Society for the Psychological Study of Social Issues (SPSSI), 21 September 2020: https://www.spssi.org/index.cfm?fuseaction=Page.ViewPage&PageID=2609

8th European Environmental Action Programme: https://ec.europa.eu/environment/strategy/environment-action-programme-2030_en

Forum for the Future School of System Change offers resources for working systemically for ecological futures, including a newsletter, educational courses and a regular blog: https://www.forumforthefuture.org/school-of-system-change

Answering the call of the Dream of the Earth – growing external practices

Extending the boundaries of current projects

I have found the concept of the 'well tempered radical' (Meyerson & Scully, 1995) to be a most useful way to think about how to survive and flourish within an organisation, when introducing and promoting radical ideas. A range of management practices can be developed to embrace more holistic or Gaian paradigms. For instance, NWTWC and NNW were commissioned to deliver regional empowerment workshops to share knowledge and experiences between neighbourhood practitioners across the North West of England. At these workshops we introduced practices such as individual reflection and storytelling to encourage and support participants to share ideas and improve their practice. Story telling allows participants to share ideas in their own words, encouraging a different narrative to emerge and a sense of individual ownership and empowerment. Regional seminars organised by RENEW NW played a similar role with professionals and community members engaged in regeneration. Participants learned together about innovation and good practice to support wellbeing, effective neighbourhood governance, diversity and inclusion, and regional sustainability. As facilitator and occasional contributor, I introduced elements of Dreaming of the Earth, such as using the *Earthrise* photograph as a motivational tool and the Egan Wheel to explore the importance of combining ecological sustainability with social justice. From the early 2000s, a neighbourhood warden scheme was created to tackle anti-social behaviour and domestic violence in neighbourhoods and encourage communities to work together on local projects. Gradually, more environmental issues were introduced, including waste management and encouraging pride in the neighbourhood. The concept developed further into District Centre Wardens, whose sole charge was improving local environments. With their portable litter collection bins and stopping to chat to local people, wardens became popular with traders and locals alike. Training for wardens expanded to include health and safety, carbon literacy, community cohesion and community development.[153]

A decade later, developments in higher education have begun to link local communities to initiatives offering carbon and sustainability literacy training. The Carbon Literacy Project for example, seeks to bring such training to all sections of the community, using the train-the- trainer model to extend wider into society.

◯ Hopeful Companion

Articles
Meyerson, D. and Scully, M. 1995. Tempered radicalism and the politics of ambivalence and change. *Organization Science*, 6(5): 585-560: https://ideas.wharton.upenn.edu/wp-content/uploads/2018/07/Meyerson-Scully-1995.pdf

---

Encouraging the birthing of ecological dreams

One external management practice involves growing opportunities in the workplace to birth ecological dreams and put them into action. This can be achieved through establishing a sustainability group for community development and working with local authorities and with other public bodies and non-governmental organisations on issues such as promoting energy efficiency, environmental issues, or how a village, town or organisation can become carbon neutral[154] and support biodiversity. A wide variety of stakeholders should be encouraged, bringing people together, adding green perspectives to community development approaches, and creating safe spaces where practice can be debated (Kemmis, 2001; Miller, 2019).

Adding an ecological dimension to an existing practice or project is another helpful way to encourage wider thinking. For example, through NWTWC, small quantities of seed money were distributed regionally over two years, as catalysts for neighbourhood-based community empowerment initiatives. Those of us involved in organising created an initial list of ideas for projects to be implemented. I proposed several green ideas, such as retrofitting houses and growing fruit and vegetables. I held out for these project ideas to be included, even though they felt left field at times, and were challenged by some senior managers, and one project on healthy eating and another that supported prisoners to grow food were funded. Yet another example was supporting and participating in an interdisciplinary partnership project to explore green transport. Through collaboration between the local university, the NWTWC and local voluntary projects, an imaginative week-long workshop was developed in which community members participated in a series of journeys by bike, train, canal and bus around Greater Manchester to explore and compare different forms of sustainable transport. The events turned out to be joyful, fun and emancipating in turn. The week ended with a daylong event hosted by Manchester Metropolitan University Youth and Community Department to share and celebrate green ideas.

Carpe Diem: creating holistic dreams for arising opportunities

In 1989, Lester Milbrath recommended the creation of ideas and plans that will be ready to put into action when society is ready for change. Naomi Klein (2015) has more recently reinforced this suggestion in *This Changes Everything*. A recurrent theme of this book is that we already have the solutions to hand. We simply need the drive, funding and organisation to put them into action. One aspect of interior management work explored earlier is to prioritise the gathering of information and ideas about how we can get to hopeful futures. The result of this interior work is to gather dreams for the work ahead which, with the right resources, people, and opportunities, will bring about the changes needed.

Having ideas to hand when opportunities present themselves is invaluable. In 2014, Creative Rusholme supported the idea of creating a Universe Walk in the local park but was unable to source the funding. Nearly a decade later, proposals to develop a long-term strategic plan and funding bid for the local community museum created opportunities to re-visit the idea. Such a project would require far more resources than those available from local funding sources. Sometimes, such ideas fail to get off the ground. Inspired by the Transition movement, for example, our street residents' committee twice applied for and failed to win funding for a carbon descent plan. But it was still worth the try, because it clarified our shared vision, and a much smaller proposal for carbon literacy training proved successful and one house was retrofitted through a regional pilot scheme.

In the mid-2010s, I researched how to implement ideas of Earth as community and a Cosmic society. I journaled about having a 'National Strategy on Earth as Community' with associated funding and implementation streams. But then Brexit and other societal upheavals occurred and these ideas seemed very far away. The global pandemic briefly helped create a space to consider these ideas again, but this was fleeting. Other projects come to light but have to end at a certain point, in luck (or faith) to be resurrected again. The NLights series of inspirational speakers on ecological and social justice described in Chapter 7, which ended in Manchester in 2016, provided inspiration for the opportunities at the Association of Sustainability Practitioners in 2021.

◯ Hopeful Companions

Creativity
Klein, N. 2015. [Film] *This Changes Everything*. Directed by Avi Lewis. A Klein Lewis Production and Louverture Films Production. The Book, Documentary and Impact Project: https://thischangeseverything.org/

Organisations

Climate Fresk, a French based organisation operating internationally, which aims to provide quality climate education for individuals and groups: https://climatefresk.org/

Hawkin. P. (ed). 2018. *Drawdown: The Most Comprehensive Plan Ever Proposed to Reverse Global Warming*. London: Penguin. Includes the world's leading resource for climate solutions: https://www.drawdown.org/ and free six video units to learn about climate solutions. For the trailer see: https://www.drawdown.org/climate-solutions-101

Centre for Alternative Technology: https://cat.org.uk offers practical solutions towards a zero carbon world.

Faithfulness

Studying Thomas Berry's life, it is clear that it took a lifetime to develop his understanding of the Dream of the Earth, and the Great Work facing humanity (Tucker et al., 2019). Faithfulness is a key characteristic of being a cosmologically influenced manager, activist or teacher. I started my journey with the Dream of the Earth and delved deeper into a participative universe. This developed into imagining what Gaian and cosmological practice might look like within the realities and practicalities of everyday working life. This was an ongoing reflective journey, continually pulling and pushing practice, captured through journaling. There was also the constant challenge and messiness in managing service delivery, staff and the difficulties of external circumstances, together with juggling home and family life.

A key part of this practice is having the determination when things go wrong to go back to listening to the planet and becoming part of the Cosmos and its ancient and beautiful history. I have achieved this through journaling, but we all have our own ways to reconnect, such as walking, stargazing, poetry, music and Earth prayer. We must have the determination to understand the cosmic dynamics of the universe and the faithfulness of the sun, to appreciate gravity as love and that the qualities of kindness, compassion and tolerance arise from the structures of the universe. My personal work with community development, teaching and management has human echoes of the eons of time taken to create the Cosmos, our galaxy, our solar system and life on our planet. Slowly building brick by brick to empower people to grow sustainable communities and to sense cosmological futures reflects the millions of years that it has taken life to grow and evolve on our planet. If funding stops or actions are not given the green light by those more powerful, then we must have the faithfulness to start all over again, energised by the billions of years that life has been growing on our planet.

 Invitation to Reflect

Such practices result in being consciously aware and undertaking actions in ever expanding spheres growing outwards to the Cosmos. Reflect on the following:

You are part of Gaia and the Cosmos. How does your work, both in paid employment and at home, in the community, and so on, currently reflect this? What practices can you alter or add to further reflect that you are part of Gaia and the Cosmos?

Identify the dominant paradigm in your place of work or in your home setting. Consider how you might introduce aspects of wider paradigms into these contexts.

Reflect on the concept of inner and outer journeys. How can you apply this in your own practice? If this seems too challenging, try to break it down and reflect on individual interventions over time.

Finding a sympathetic friend, peer or mentor with whom to share your experiences can be very empowering.

Stories: Dreaming the Dream of the Earth in practice

This section contains four stories, revised from journal entries, recounting my own lived experiences of practicing these paradigms in a variety of contexts spanning many years. I share them as practical examples of how these beliefs have shaped my work practice. They are offered in the hope that you will go on to create stories of Dreaming the Earth from your work, family and community experiences, which can be shared as examples of how we can change the world for the better.

Story 1: Steps towards community development for humans and the more-than-human

In the 2000s, community development work in Stockport Council, Greater Manchester, provided support to communities and individuals and tackled wide-ranging neighbourhood issues. I was heavily involved in a partnership of community development practitioners to develop a more strategic basis for the service. The strategy created by this partnership combined a vision for building individual and community group capacity and creating sustainable communities. The vision committed to 'a healthy and sustainable' borough, including diversity, health and flourishing communities, allowing for several dimensions of the *Dream of the Earth* to be introduced into a mainstream council strategy. The Local Strategic Partnership, the main public sector cross-organisational structure of the borough, adopted the strategy.

The Community Development Strategy (2006) envisioned the following:

- "Communities are flourishing, trust is widespread, and diversity is celebrated
- Geographical communities and communities of identity play an active and vibrant part in service delivery and governance
- Improved quality of life in communities is achieved
- Citizens and communities are engaged in creating a healthy and sustainable Stockport
- Community development support is developed to the highest standards"

Inspired by this, the North West Together We Can empowerment partnership aimed to create a regional vision for community development to be shared widely among local communities, local authorities, health and other public services. A consultative process involved a series of workshops across the region over two years. The regional vision combined ecology with social justice issues and capacity building. The vision stated,

> "In twenty years' time, communities across the region will be empowered, healthy, resilient and cohesive.... Poverty and disadvantage will have been substantially reduced through the enterprise and creativity of communities.... The regional economy will be at the forefront of ecological progress. This will be achieved through the support of a thriving community development profession...networked across the region." (NWTWC, 2011).

While the strategies can be critiqued – including addressing further the root causes of poverty and the involvement of the voluntary sector for example – such perspectives could be included in any future work.

These two examples reveal how strategic support and resources can be developed to help grow flourishing communities, diversity and trust, decarbonise society and tackle biodiversity loss. Neither survived the onset of austerity in the 2010s but remain pioneering work to provide green shoots for the future.

◯ **Hopeful Companions**

Book
Tam, H. (ed). 2021. *Tomorrow's Communities: Lessons from Community Transformation in the age of Global Crisis.* Bristol: Bristol University Press.A

Films
Nobel Peace Prize Laureate Wangari Maathai talks about her community work to empower women and local communities and plant trees: https://www.youtube.com/watch?v=1HXFdWD3HMs

Organisations
Black History Stockport, a Project which aims to discover Stockport's African and Caribbean Heritage: https://blackhistoryinstockport.com/

The International Association for Community Development Strategic Plan champions sustainable development and climate justice, equality and human rights: https://www.iacdglobal.org/iacd-strategic-plan-2020-2024/

Story 2: Neighbourhood working and excellence in management

Investors in Excellence (IiE) is an international quality award which assesses performance in leadership, delivery, resources and outcomes. It is awarded to public and private businesses and to business units within larger organisations. In 2005 and 2008, I headed the Social Inclusion Unit, working alongside a team of four managers and their staff to achieve this Award. The Unit gained recognition for its work delivering the best standards of service to local communities. As a Unit, we adapted our language to challenge the top-down culture prevalent throughout the Local Authority, for example, changing 'customers' to 'communities', and emphasised the participation of staff and communities in service delivery. The ethos of the Unit, for collaboration in ways of working, not competition, was also drawn out. In working for the Award, care was taken to address common critiques including being simply a tick box exercise and not involving front line staff.

To protect community and neighbourhood warden work, the IiE award was adopted by the regional training service Neighbourhoods NW and turned into a specific Neighbourhood Management Excellence Framework Award for neighbourhood practitioners. The Award highlighted excellent performance management when working with neighbourhoods and made space for community development principles such as diversity, inclusion and participation. Austerity brought an end to these services and to the Neighbourhood Management Excellence Framework. As an independent not for profit organisation, the National Association of Neighbourhood Management continued to champion the cause of neighbourhood management until 2021.

Past and current threads now weave together in my teaching of responsible management and sustainability. In 2020 the National Association of Neighbourhood Management sought to highlight the importance of neighbourhood work and to call for it to be an integral part of the post-pandemic world. The European Foundation for Quality Management (EFQM) Award now aligns itself with the UN Sustainable Development Goals (UNSDG), while the Local Government Association charts growing interest in local authorities to develop the UN SDGs within their services. Neighbourhood work has developed beyond service co-ordination to community wealth building. The Ellen MacArthur Foundation now teaches excellence in management, centring on sustainability and creating a closed loop economy. The dream of achieving the highest standards of management in the delivery of services for human communities and the planet continues.

⭕ Hopeful Companions

Books
Clare Goff with a Foreword by Liz Richardson and Ben Lee. 2020. *Neighbourhood working beyond the pandemic: How Covid-19 has shone a spotlight on the power of local approaches.* London: Shared Intelligence and the National Association of Neighbourhood Management: http://localneighbourhood.org/wp-content/uploads/2020/09/Neighbourhood-working-beyond-pandemic-070920b.pdf

Brown, M. and Jones, R. 2021. *Paint your Town Red: How Preston Took Back Control and Your Town Can Too.* London: Repeater.

RENEW North West: *The Collected Works 2005 – 2008.* Available under Creative Open Government Licence of the UK National Archives: https://tonybaldwinson.files.wordpress.com/2014/05/renew-northwest-collected-works-2005-to-2008-9780957260610-v3.pdf

Story 3: Growing green spirituality in the community

GreenSpirit is a national charity that I have been involved with for many years. Its mission statement is "An engaged spirituality for a Living Earth". Members of the charity take the journey to develop the practices and qualities of a Cosmos- and planet-based spirituality in environments that seek to be supportive and safe. With a thriving governance structure, including an active council reporting to annual general meetings, the charity operates a policy of remaining self-funded and operating within its financial resources and, therefore, cannot be halted by government polices of austerity while dancing lightly on the Earth. The work of GreenSpirit includes annual gatherings, spring walking breaks, summer weeks in Wales, a network of local groups, various one-off events and collaborative partnerships with likeminded organisations and individuals. Following the inspiration of Alan Shephard's book service, a major strand of work is reaching out through an open email newsletter, creating ideas and practice through the regular magazine, and book publications.

Local GreenSpirit groups across England and Wales are an integral part of the work. In the 2010s, we formed one such local group in Greater Manchester, with the members prepared to share the work. We agreed on a self-organising structure, with a volunteer co-ordinator who planned meetings and organised publicity. During our events we shared exercises such as the Council of All Beings and Walking the Universe Story and visiting a local allotment to understand principles of permaculture and organic farming. Other activities included a regular reading group and working closely with the community at St Agnes Church, which hosted many of our meetings. The focus of each local group is different. Some ritually celebrate the changing seasons at the Equinoxes and the Celtic festivals of Samhain, Imbolc, Beltane and Lughnasadh. Others grow relationships with faith communities, refugee communities and green activists. The local group in North Lancashire and Cumbria inspired author Noel Charlton to conceive of *Meetings for Earth* groups, described in Chapter 11, as a way to spread green spirituality. A series of discussions with local group members in 2016, found that for some, local groups provide an opportunity to reflect, meditate on what it means to follow green spirituality and an opportunity to be replenished and nourished. For others, these groups provide opportunities for green activism. The work of such groups combines 'being' with acting and embodying visions of sustainable and cosmological futures. Reflecting these multi-dimensional roles, the GreenSpirit website contains a green action tool kit that encourages practical action, together with resources to celebrate green spirituality. GreenSpirit continues to reflect and develop, as it takes its spiritual practices and voice out into the world, presently working on diversity and inclusion. As a charity, it is a testament to the power of volunteers working together faithfully over decades, of sharing ideas and learning, and of contributing to creating the Dream of the Earth.

◯ Hopeful Companions

Resources for Action
Free articles to download on green spirituality and a living planet, suitable for use in community and educational settings: https://www. greenspirit.org.uk/magazine-past-articles/

Resurgence and Ecologist: regular programme of events on themes related to our living planet: https://www.resurgence.org/take-part/resurgence-events.html

Findhorn Foundation: transformational learning experiences: workshops, events, retreats, daily inspiration. Offered online and face to face: https://www.findhorn.org/workshops/

Story 4: Transformational learning

While developing a new two-year Masters in Responsibility and Business Practice, the teaching staff at the School of Management in Bath, wanted to create an ongoing community of learners with a common grounding in action research. The solution? An email community, open to anyone who had completed the programme, which I duly joined. Over twenty years later, this community is still thriving and is a place where knowledge and experience, skills and ideas are shared for the creation of a better world.

Our learning methods are simple and have remained the same over two decades. We freely share knowledge, skills and experience, and respond to calls for help from group members. The key to the success of the email learning group is that it is grounded in the shared experience of a two-year developmental and action research learning project. In 2017, alumni of the Master's programme, myself included, successfully negotiated to become a self-organising community, through dedicated volunteer efforts to keep going and a firm determination to 'keep the flame alight'.

The long-term nature of this community is unique, allowing for the tracking of outputs and outcomes of transformational learning, including the outcomes of the curriculum. The practice-based vision at the core of action research is "to contribute to the flourishing of human and ecological communities of which they are part" profoundly influenced many of the students who participated. Graduates of the programme have taken these learning approaches and developed them in other settings and contexts. Three teachers on the course, Judi Marshall, Gill Coleman and Peter Reason (2011), gathered thirty alumni stories, including using action research to build reconciliation and restoration in post conflict communities, growing food in the inner city and bringing system change into company business strategies. Alumna Jane Riddiford (2021) has also gathered her experiences of working with action research, ecology, community and young people, to demonstrate outcomes of trust, shared purpose and transformational learning.

The alumni community is now part of the Association of Sustainability Practitioners (ASP), an open access practitioner group that shares knowledge, practice and ideas on action research, management and sustainability. Throughout 2021, I worked with fellow directors to develop Earth Conversations, offering both inspiring topic speakers alternating with speakers on action research, finding a format to mirror the basic structure of the Masters and echoes of the work of NLights. These two communities offer a living model for the long-term sharing of transformational learning for hopeful futures, at a minimal cost, which can be adapted to multiple settings.

⭕ Hopeful Companions

Examples of using action research for sustainability.

The Advertising Industry: video of the film about the Good Life 2030 Project by the Purpose Disruptors organisation, exploring the role of the advertising industry in creating a sustainable future and panel discussion at COP 26: https://www.youtube.com/watch?v=gM5CKnbzJyo

Community Development: Guanaratne, L. and De Zoysa, M. 2011. A journey of dialogue, peace and inner peace. in Marshall et al. (eds). *Leadership for Sustainability*. London: Routledge, pp. 215-219.

Engineering: Ainger, C. and Fenner, R. 2013. *Sustainable Infrastructure: Principles into Practice,* ICE Publishing: https://www.icevirtuallibrary.com/doi/book/10.1680/sipp.57548

Inquiry and Ethics: *Satish Kumar: Abundant Love,* Rattanani et al, 2023

Youth and Community: United Nations. 2021. Climate Adaptation: Interview with Dr. Jane RTEDxRotherhide. Talk by Jane Riddiford: https://www.youtube.com/watch?v=y6uJ1l9IDqg

Networks
Find and explore networks which can support you on your journey to hopeful futures. See for example the Association of Sustainability Practitioners: https://sustainabilitypractitioners.org/

Reflections

This cycle started with the call of the UN Secretary General at the 2020 Climate Ambition Summit that all counties declare a state of Climate Emergency until we have reached zero carbon emissions. I have drawn out ways to grow our thinking and actions to contribute to bringing about these changes, with a focus on setting out inner and outer practices in an emerging community, and teaching and management practice within a wider paradigm, all the while operating within the current dominant, mechanistic paradigm. I have touched on some of the challenges facing the 'well-tempered radical' and explored the type of practice that can be created as bridges between work in the current paradigm and work in a wider paradigm, using existing resources, staff and services. Through story, I have given examples of where the Dream of the Earth might inspire practice, creating tangible outputs and outcomes, and I have suggested that creating such hopeful stories from our practice is an important task for the present.

 Invitation to Reflect

Reflect on and create your own stories.

Think of a Dream for Planet Earth with which you have been involved, no matter what its size or shape. Is this dream in its infancy? Has this dream ended or is it ongoing? Try to create an image or drawing of that dream in your journal.

Recount a story of something positive you have done which helps the Dream of the Earth. Reflect on what you did and describe the good and the challenging parts. Find a way to tell your own and other positive stories for change at home, in the community or at work.

Find ways to amplify these positive stories and encourage others to do the same.

Notes

[147] See the International Association of Community Development Practice Insights magazines, for examples of work with a wide range of communities globally. Magazines are free to download at https://www.iacdglobal.org/practice-insights-magazine/

[148] For this effect but reflected at the larger level of society, see: https://www.theguardian.com/commentisfree/2022/may/29/observer-view-70-years-warnings-environment

[149] See for example, the PASCAL observatory Faith and Spirituality Learning Cities Network: http://lcn.pascalobservatory.org/blog/blogentry/news/busy-year-pascal-lcn-faith-based-learning-city-development-network

[150] Sagan, C. 2009. Pale Blue Dot video: https://www.youtube.com/watch?v=wupToqz1e2g

[151] For the full speech to the European Parliament following the fire at Notre Dame Cathedral, see: https://www.youtube.com/watch?v=cJAcuQEVxTY

[152] See examples of Involve's work: https://www.involve.org.uk/our-work and the full report on reaching net zero by 2050 in the UK: https://www.climateassembly.uk/

[153] At the time, these ideas were often too radical to surface within the senior levels of the local, regional or national state and later, when austerity hit, were jettisoned.

[154] See http://www.goingcarbonneutral.co.uk/

Chapter 13: Our destination in sight
Orbiting Gaia

"So, on one hand you look at your safe haven on Earth and then you turn around…and see that there is not a lot of habitable planets or moons around you. You sort of feel like you need to take care of the precious gift you've been given."
Anousheh Ansari, Iranian-American space traveller (in Gondarzi, 2006)

"Those seven days, 23 hours and five minutes [on the Mir Space Station] changed my life. When you have seen the whole world through your window there is no us and them, no politics."
Muhammed Faris, Syrian cosmonaut (in Garthwaite, 2016)

"We need a coalition of hopers, enablers and imaginers."
Anne Karpf (2021)

"The climate crisis crystallises these facts: We have to save the world. We have to change it, and ourselves. It's not too late."
Vanessa Nakate (2021: 200)

The academic year 2020/21 is a strange one. Due to COVID-19, we are teaching online, two or three colleagues together with the students. I am excited to be teaching a brand-new course on global concerns for sustainable development. Included is content on how businesses both large and small are responding to the United Nations Sustainable Development Goals (UN SDGs). At the start of the course, we invite each of the first-year students to choose the SDG which speaks most to them. We highlight the WWF report that all SDGs can be addressed through nature. Each online session begins with a catchup on what's happening to the planet through the lens of the three pillars of sustainable development. One of my colleagues recommends David Attenborough's A Life on Our Planet: Witness statement and Vision for the Future, in which the author argues we need to work with nature, with nature friendly technology, to solve the challenges of the world. Attenborough writes that we are not alone in our task to address the devastating losses of biodiversity we have caused. We have nature alongside us, created over billions of years. We need to work in partnership and collaboration with nature and Life. I glimpse suddenly in these lines the journey in this book — that the powers of the universe, over billions of years, are here for us, not by demand but by invocation. Earth and all her life forms are our community and can help us if we genuinely seek to work together and collaborate. Our task is simple, Attenborough argues — to rewild the world to save biodiversity if we are to save ourselves.[155]

When we teach about the UN SDGs, we teach about the importance of nature. We teach about social justice, gender equality, ending inequalities, discrimination and racial injustice. At the end of each written assignment, the students include a reflective appendix. Students write about how the course has opened their eyes to what is happening to the world, the steps they are taking to change their lifestyles and sometimes the actions they are considering for their future careers. In the spring term, in response to the isolation of the pandemic, a new Student-Staff-Community Sustainability Group emerges. We end the year with a pilot course teaching the UN SDGs and Climate Action in the community. The first session takes place on Zoom and the second in nature, with the rain drumming on our umbrellas, as we sit in a circle and learn and debate together.[156]

Introduction

In this final chapter, I reflect on the journey to locate our learning within ourselves, our communities, our planet and our Cosmos. I bring together many of the techniques and practices which I have used and explored throughout this book. I curate a set of practical tools to help you to undertake your own learning journey.

I return to the cosmonauts, astronauts and taikonauts who are the first living beings to leave planet Earth in her 4,500,000,000-year history and return to share their experiences. On each of their missions, despite following precise and hectic schedules, they had time to see the Earth from a wholly different vantage point, and to appreciate her beauty and fragility. I invite you to meditatively consider their reflections and take their experiences with you into your own first-person practice. Let their reflections be a source of inspiration for the journey and action ahead. For the journey into the Cosmos is not simply a journey of discovery, but also a Call to Urgent and Wise Action - action to celebrate, protect and champion our planet and especially the more-than-human world.

In Chapter 1, I introduced Base Camp. I traced how planet Earth is in desperate trouble, due to unprecedented threats to biodiversity, the effects of the climate emergency, and human induced disasters, such as the COVID-19 pandemic. I identified how the current decade is critical in the fight against climate change. I traced global social justice issues, the ongoing racism and discrimination faced by many communities, attacks on indigenous lands, cultures and livelihoods, and the hunger and poverty suffered by millions around the world. I explored shoots of positive action, with countries committing to the Paris Climate Agreement to limit global warming at well below 2° Celsius – and preferably 1.5° – compared to pre-industrial levels and with ongoing work to implement the UN SDGs and social movements for justice around the world. I concluded that despite these actions, major challenges remain.[157]

Figure 13.1: It's now or never if the world is to stave off climate disaster.
(Source: Fiona Harvey, The Guardian, 5 April 2022)

In Chapter 2, I opened 'windows' onto wider ways of seeing the world with a family of paradigms that allow us to grow within the community of our planet and our Cosmos. These paradigms enable us to see each other not as other, but as kin, going back 13.8 billion years. We can learn again to see our planet as living and as sacred and forge a new respect for the equality of all human beings and the unique nature of our planet in the Cosmos. Out of this wider understanding, we can begin to express our love for each other and for our planet home and find the motivation and energy needed for dedicated long-term action.

To make this family of paradigms meaningful, I examined a range of first- and second-person research practices that we can undertake in our daily lives through multiple learning cycles. These require few resources and are open to all. I inquired into a range of exploration and discovery practices, including those leading us into loving and spiritual qualities and into individual and communal participation in our Cosmos. I now want to bring many of these elements together to conclude this handbook, guiding you and others to access and explore your Call to Urgent and Wise Action.

This final guide to facilitate your Call falls into four sections:

The elements of an action research toolkit: A summary of many of the key techniques I have found powerful on my journey.

The Journey of the Cosmos: A Call to Urgent and Wise Action: bringing together the need for immediate action guided by wisdom and reflection.

Painting a picture of the Dream of the Earth: An extended practical Creative Learning Exercise guiding you to identify your own path to Urgent and Wise Action.

Concluding remarks: A final section, exploring launching your own journey and transition of ideas to action.

Given the fundamentally practical aims of this chapter, I have also included many Invitations to Reflect, Creative Learning Exercises and Hopeful Companions which can be used to further explore the ideas discussed.

The elements of an action research toolkit: Powerful first- and second-person research practices that we can undertake in our daily lives

Here I have brought together six inspirational tools explored at length throughout this book, which together provide crucial guidance to access new futures and the actions needed to call this future into being. While each practice has been discussed iteratively throughout these chapters, in each case I have highlighted particular examples of discussion and exploration to aid those who would like to develop the concepts and techniques further.

Opening windows into new futures – images of awe and wonder

Visual images – still and moving – are an immediate and accessible window into the power of the Cosmos. They can incite awe, wonder and understanding. Many have been moved and inspired by the stunning beauty of the Earth from the Apollo missions and of the far reaches of the Cosmos from the Hubble and James Watt telescopes.[158] Together with images of the natural world here on Earth, we have the inspiration we need to dream a flourishing future.

However, images of a participative world view have been with us for millennia. Primack and Abrams (2006) point to images from Ancient Egypt to illustrate how that civilisation imagined itself as a Cosmic participant, physically supporting the heavens, while the Hindu *Mahabharata* saw creation initiated in the churning of the milky ocean (what we today call the Milky Way) above and the ocean below (Mura, 1972).[159] These images remind us that such knowledge is ancient and deep but, in our rush towards technological futures, we have begun to forget it. Now we must reclaim it.

Throughout this book I have illustrated key concepts and ideas with visual images. For example see Chapter 11, showing the scale used to allow individuals and groups to 'walk' the universe story, from the big bang to the present (Figure 11.2 on page 329).

Metaphor: Sometimes, visual images alone cannot fully explain what we are trying to understand. The use of metaphor can be equally evocative in guiding our understanding of our place in the Cosmos – from the very big to the very small.

Both ancient and modern metaphors can help our understanding. Thich Nat Hanh (2009) describes Indra's Net from the *Avatamsaka Sutra* as made up of many jewels, each of which shines and glitters and reflects the others, demonstrating the interdependence of the entire universe.[160]

Figure 13.2: The ancient Egyptians view of upholding the Cosmos.
(Source: Joel Primack & Nancy Abrams, 2006: 43)

Abrams and Primack (2011) suggest that the use of metaphor is key to understanding how we live in the universe. They present their own metaphors, including the 'cosmic uroboros' discussed in Chapter 11, and recommend that we each create our own metaphors for living in a participative universe (Figure 11.3 on page 334).

Opening windows through a family of paradigms and emerging cosmologies

Protecting our Earth requires that we appreciate how precious and unique it is. Starting in Chapter 2 and then continuing throughout this book I have explored different ways to experience and perceive the planet and the Cosmos through a family of paradigms that open us up to deep perception:

- Being open to different perspectives beyond our own and understanding that we each view society differently.
- The constellation of beliefs and practices which we share within particular communities.
- The awareness that being part of a living planet and Cosmos affects everything we do

---

 Invitation to Reflect

How can we make these paradigms real in our lives? The astronauts, cosmonauts and taikonauts participated in encountering the universe directly. I invite you to reflect on their observations.

After returning from the very first orbit of the planet by a human, Yuri Gagarin reflected:

> "Orbiting Earth in the spaceship, I saw how beautiful our planet is. People, let us preserve and increase this beauty, not destroy it!"[161]

Apollo 11 command module pilot, Michael Collins, described his chance to have his own personal cosmic perspective:

> "I enjoyed the fact that I was on one side of this little satellite of our planet...and if I looked in the other direction, there was God knows what: only me and the rest of the universe. I liked that feeling, being a part of the rest of the universe instead of being a part of the solar system." *(*in Kelley, 1988: 54)

The experience of seeing the Earth on the return journey from the moon was life changing for Apollo 14 astronaut Edgar Mitchell:

> "...it was a beautiful, harmonious, peaceful looking planet, blue with white clouds, and one that gave you a deep sense... of home, of being, of identity. It is what I prefer to call instant global consciousness...and I got a sense of being alive." (Overview Institute of Australia, 2021)[162]

Reflecting on orbiting the Earth for eight days in September 1992, Mae Jeimison, engineer, doctor and astronaut, and first Black woman in space reflected:

> "Once I got into space, I was feeling very comfortable in the universe. I felt like I had a right to be anywhere in this universe, that I belonged here as much as any speck of stardust, any comet, any planet."[163]

◯ **Hopeful Companions**

<u>Films</u>
Leland Melvin. From NLF Player to NASA Astronaut. 27 February 2018, AARP videos: https://www.youtube.com/watch?v=P4Tommp9HXY

Astronaut Peggy Whitson First Female Commander of the Space Station. 23 August, 2017. Movers videos: https://www.youtube.com/watch?v=tCRVs42maAs

 Creative Learning Exercises

As we near the end of this journey, use any medium (e.g., text, collage, drawing, photography, etc.) to reflect on your participation in our living planet and Cosmos.

Reflect on what it means to live in the planet and Cosmos as well as in your home and street.

Reflect on the inspiration you feel from being part of this very ancient universe.

Think ahead to millions of years into the future. What do you see? What will our planet and the Cosmos be like then?

Use this reflection as inspiration and motivation for the journey ahead and for the actions you need to take, drawing your inspiration from the gift of living in this awesome universe.

Learning to operate within the Cosmos and planet, using the action research tool kit

In Cycle Two (chapters 3, 4 and 5), I first described the characteristics of transformative learning and action research. The journey ahead draws out the contours and possibilities of a new map, created through a range of first- and second-person action research practices.

As we seek to take the practical daily steps to live within a wider Cosmos and planet, the metaphor of 'living up and down the levels of the universe' can be helpfully applied to our daily lives. No matter our circumstances, it is always possible to practice seeing ourselves within an amazing planet and Cosmos. Just as we have become accustomed to seeing ourselves as global citizens, with families living around the world, so we can see ourselves as citizens of the Solar System and the Milky Way Galaxy, and as children of the Universe that has birthed us over a period of 13.8 billion years.

Equipped with the action research tool kit and with ideas for new maps, I hope you will explore these forms of inquiry to create your own journey into hopeful futures, sharing with others as you go. Through extended ways of knowing and creativity, these ideas can develop and grow for each one of us. The outcomes of action research aim for flourishing human and ecological communities, which can help guide action. Action research can provide every one of us with the tools to find and answer our own calls to action.

Practices for self: A focus on our own ethical, reflective and spiritual conduct. At the level of the self, first-person practices allow us to participate in a journey into loving and spiritual qualities. Along the way, we can explore and learn how to live metaphorically up and down between ourselves, our communities, our planet and our Cosmos and engage in a process of dreaming the Dream of the Earth. Such practices can help to grow a wider sense of self within our daily lives and can be undertaken individually or with others. They can be introduced into playful and reflective practices in learning and as part of growing resilience and well-being in neighbourhoods and organisations. Chapters 5, 6 and 10 explore practical examples.

Practices for Community: A focus on learning and acting together, engaging in first- and second-person participatory learning. By nurturing growth in our communities, we plant seeds of participatory learning and practices for broader hopeful futures. Together we need to create powerful stories to share about our future, to encourage each other into action. Together, we can participate in transformational learning approaches to issues of social and ecological justice, to the UN SDGs, and to being part of our planet and Cosmos. These practices for community can be practiced everywhere, in family discussions, in neighbourhood WhatsApp groups, in faith and community meetings, in work team events and in meetings for Earth. Chapters 4, 7 and 12 give examples of where these practices have been successfully developed.

Practices for our planet: Our practices for the planet call us to bear witness to threatened species and communities living with injustice, as we seek to understand how all the parts of the planet work as one to make the life which sustains us all. Together we can learn that each one of us – human and more-than-human, trees, animals and plants – can create new dreams for the whole Earth. Such practices and understandings can bear fruit in all aspects of life. We can use these practices in small and large businesses, in schools and universities, in hospitals and health care settings, in NGOs, trade unions and legal practices. Examples of using these practices are given in Chapters 6 and 8.

Practices for our Cosmos: Practices for our Cosmos require us to open new windows, to see the planet and Cosmos differently and to seek to live into them, thus delving deeper into a participative universe and explore the qualities and practices for a wonder filled and meaningful Cosmos. As cosmologically influenced practitioners, managers, parents, teachers, business people, and health workers, we seek to link the challenges that we and those around us face in an interconnected whole, understanding and acting on the connections between racism and discrimination, the global need for health care such as vaccines and clean water, violence against women, biodiversity loss and the climate emergency, local and global justice, poverty and inequality. That understanding comes from the practice of imagining back 13.8 billion years and forward 320 million years. In such a quest, we must search for cosmological values and ethics on which to base our society. Explorations of learning these practices for our Cosmos are given in Chapters 9 and 11.

 Creative Learning Exercises

Reflect on the practices of inquiry that you have encountered in the preceding chapters, and consider other inquiry practices that have not been included in this book.

> Identify those that will help you to get closer to participating in our Cosmos and encountering our living planet.

> Choose one inquiry practice that has meaning for you from each of the levels of self, community, planet and Cosmos.

Consider creative ways to represent your chosen inquiry practices. For example, you might consider creating a collage from natural materials in the garden or park, taking photographs, drawing, knitting or embroidery.

Find a place to display this representation near where you work or in your notebook.

Consider ways to put these inquiry practices into action in your home, workplace or community.

Healing, loving and spiritual qualities

As I bore witness through collecting cuttings over the years, I spent time with the terrible and growing plight of planet Earth. I have found that themes are repeated, becoming more urgent and threatening. What was once scientific prediction has now become reality. In January 2022, CO_2 levels stood at 418.19 pp million at the Mauna Loa monitoring station. In 2021, the highest methane emissions ever were recorded and NASA and NOAA recorded that the eight warmest years on the planet had been in the last decade.[164] Insects are losing the battle with climate change (Milman, 2022) and wildfires burning through increased heat and land clearance threaten poor communities and nature's ability to recover (Immerwahr, 2022). COVID-19 had a dramatic impact on social justice, setting back work to achieve the UN Sustainable Development Goals, including action to reduce poverty and hunger.[165] The UN Refugee Agency reports that increasing numbers of people around the world are displaced by the climate crisis and by war and violence. The global pandemic, for example, increased people's experience of grief and loss and stress and uncertainty all around the world (Nakate, 2021). The work to explain what is happening to nature and get meaningful action takes its toll on the health of activists (Monbiot, 2022).

A key element of the work ahead is healing ourselves and our communities, nature and the climate, the cosmological effects of our carbon emissions on the planet, and structural discrimination racism and social injustice. These journeys into healing, loving and spiritual qualities that encompass a sacred Cosmos highlight the interconnectedness of social and ecological justice are explored in Chapters 3, 10 and 11.

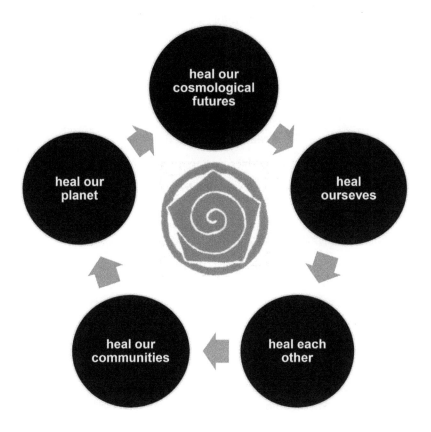

Figure 13.3: Cycles of healing for hopeful futures.
(Source: Kettleborough, 2023)

Exploring ethics and values for the Ecozoic

We cannot make decisions to care for the planet in our daily lives until we are governed by ethics and values for the planet and the Cosmos (Milbrath, 1989). As a cosmologically influenced manager, mother, community activist and student, ethics and values are an important part of my journey. The ethics and values explored throughout this book point to a fundamentally different basis for living in the Ecozoic as we move away from those that dominate the Anthropocene (see for example in Chapter 3 and Chapter 10).

We can engage with these ethics within the four quadrants of self, community, planet and Cosmos, developing values and ethics journeys across all traditions and cultures. These contribute to an ecumenical journey of sharing and debate within our communities, businesses and governments. In such a process, the values of respect and listening are crucial.

 Creative Learning Exercises

Reflect on the values and ethics explored throughout this book.

Identify your personal values and ethics for creating hopeful futures.

Identify other values and ethics required for the Dream of the Earth and living in a participative universe.

Consider ways that you can discuss and debate these values and ethics in your home, community and workplace.

Knowledge in a suitcase and on a mobile phone

As an essential part of the action research tool kit, literature helps facilitate this journey of healing. With information available to almost all of us with a few taps on a keyboard or swipes of a screen, scholarship is no longer the preserve of universities, although they remain important explorers and receptacles of knowledge. There are many forms of learning open to each one of us. Public libraries across the world provide access to knowledge and to the internet, essential doors for communities and worth defending always (Ovenden, 2020).

The *Hopeful Companion* boxes throughout this book contain many of the resources that have guided me. These are the voices of those devoted to studying Gaia and the Cosmos, those who speak compassionately and with courage for justice and equality, those who teach about action research, those who teach about building anti-racist and gender equal societies. They are the voices of global institutions seeking to build a world free of hunger and poverty, a world with compassion for refugees and the homeless, a world that fights against climate change and for biodiversity. These are also the voices of dreamers, whose inspirational words help each one of us to become dreamers too.

We need to get these resources onto every mobile device and into public and organisational libraries so that they are available to all, facilitating the planting of seeds for participative learning in our streets and organisations. Without knowledge, we cannot enact the solutions that already exist or dream of new ones. We cannot take wise action without the ability to learn about ideas, paradigms and different ways of acting. Without knowledge linked to participatory learning, we cannot meaningfully discuss and debate the different options, solutions and support needed.

Through the myriad examples of participatory learning in Chapters 3, 4 and 7, there emerge endless possibilities for communities to learn together.

The Journey of the Cosmos: A Call to Urgent and Wise Action

Experimenting and learning with these various tools and bearing witness to the state of our planet provide a call for each one of us to engage in Urgent and Wise Action.

Urgent action is needed this decade to hold off the cosmological effects of mass extinction of species and the overheating of the planet that will put human civilisation in crisis. Urgent action needs to become part of our daily thinking; we live in a Climate Emergency.

However, this is not merely a call for urgent action, but for Wise Action too. We need loving and spiritual qualities as the basis for living. The call for wise action must be built on qualities of faithfulness, love, grief and hope over many years. If you are unsure of your own call to wise action, then I hope that this journey has inspired you to feel your way forward. Talk to your friends, family, colleagues or faith communities. Gail Bradbook (in Taylor, 2020), co-founder of Extinction Rebellion in the UK, says that we have a choice between a dystopian future and a hopeful future. Which it will be depends on each one of us. Ugandan climate activist Vanessa Nakate urges members of society to mobilise to pressurise governments to act immediately to adopt the UN SDGs and ensure that the voice of the global south is heard and the intersectionality of the challenges facing humanity acknowledged.[166] In finding urgent and wise action to take, we need to bring all issues together, as Brazilian climate activist Kaime Silvestre explains: "The fight for climate justice is a fight of justice itself, and must include the fight for social justice and racial justice" (in Nakate, 2022:198).

Throughout, I have explored solutions arising from the work and initiatives of many people and organisations, ranging from overarching paradigms to specific actions, for example see Chapters 1, 2, 7, 8, 11 and 12.

From the perspective of the Dream of the Earth (Chapter 8) and a participative universe (Chapters 9 & 11), all the challenges we face are interlinked and must be tackled holistically at every level of society. Technological solutions to the current climate and environmental crisis must be explored and enacted within the ethics and values laid out in this book. However, no solutions, technological or otherwise, should be enacted without ensuring gender, racial and all other forms of social equality. Nature-based solutions must be integral to the goals of all the 17 UN SDGs. The technology already exists to deliver a fossil free future, and proposals, such as the Green New Deal, combine international fairness, meaningful employment and environmental protection (see Karpf, 2021; Brown, 2021). To prevent insects succumbing to climate change requires the creation of networks of resilient habitats (Buglife, 2022);[167] similarly, saving fish requires marine reserves for 30% of the oceans by 2030 (Fair Seas, 2022).[168]

To avoid doom and cynicism, we can take specific actions as individuals, alongside campaigning for actions for governments to cut CO_2 (Vidal, 2022). Likewise, as individuals, we can create effective and real action on the UN SDGs, such as Marcus Rashford's campaigning to end food poverty in the UK or Greta Thunburg's rise from obscurity starting with an individual school strike in August 2018. We can explore aspects of society, such as sport, to learn the roots of racism, and through learning with each other and through education, take action to create more equal societies (Holding, 2021; Rafiq, 2021). National organisations can participate, such as a newspaper championing an end to femicide (Guardian, 2021)[169] and, on an international level, the UN Refugee Agency helping communities in Afghanistan (2022). The central role of communities is reflected around the world – planting trees in Bhutan (Adepitan, 2021), sea grass in Plymouth Sound (O'Neill, 2021) and protecting nature in the Amazon (Abelvik-Lawson, 2020). We can learn how everything is interconnected and, to preserve species, we need to reduce consumption and change production methods, working together to change the laws (Greenfield, 2022).

○ **Hopeful Companions**

Articles
IPCC, 2022: Climate Change 2022: *Mitigation of Climate Change. Contribution of Working Group III to the Sixth Assessment Report of the Intergovernmental Panel on Climate Change* [Shukla, J., Skea, R. Slade, A. Al Khourdajie, R. van Diemen, D. et al. (eds.)]. Cambridge University Press, Cambridge, UK and New York, NY, USA. doi: 10.1017/978100915792

Meyer, C. et al: Transforming the Stories we tell about change from 'issue' to 'action': https://iopscience.iop.org/article/10.1088/1748-9326/abcd5a/pdf

Films
Rockström, J. 2021. *On 'Breaking Boundaries' and the Climate Crisis*: Rockström answers questions from climate activists: https://www.youtube.com/watch?v=SQxfKypJ2JA

Resources for Action
Carrington, D. 2022. World is coming close to irreversible change say climate experts. 28 October, The Guardian. Outlines four key global reports on greenhouse gas emissions and action needed: https://www.theguardian.com/environment/2022/oct/27/world-close-to-irreversible-climate-breakdown-warn-major-studies

Anti-racist Wales Action Plan. What we are going to do to make Wales anti-racist: https://gov.wales/anti-racist-wales-action-plan

Living Earth Community Mickey et al, 2020. Open source book: https://fore.yale.edu/publication/books/Living-Earth-Community

Creative Learning Exercises

Consider your own call to urgent and wise action and be inspired by the cosmonauts, astronauts and taikonauts whose words will energise you for the tasks ahead.

What is your own Call to Urgent and Wise Action?

In what ways can you integrate this Call to Action into your own daily life?

If you have already established your Call to Action, how are you nourished in your work?

What does or will inspire and sustain you to faithfully follow your Call to Action over years and when the outlook is bleak?

Consider ways to bring your sources of inspiration and your Call to Action together.

Paint me a picture of the Dream of the Earth and Zero Carbon by 2030...[170]

In this section, I set out potential paths to the Dream of the Earth. I explore an extended practical Creative Learning Exercise which can act as a guide to help you identify your own path. From this Creative Learning Exercise you can extract those elements which most inspire and speak to you as your own personal Call to Urgent and Wise Action.

Throughout the book, I have described ways through the mountains that will help us to navigate safely to the valley at the other side, and a land of ecological and social justice, where we will live in harmony with the Earth. Satish Kumar urges us to become artists of sustainable futures rather than passive consumers. The route ahead might be through music, spirituality or tree planting. From the seeds of ideas scattered throughout these pages, you can grow a forest of hopeful futures which will mature long after you are no longer here.

How can we handle the complexity of taking action across multiple levels of society, within the planet, Cosmos, community and ourselves, and across so many different issues? Throughout the book, I have offered inspirational ideas for actions that can be achieved by individuals and communities with minimal additional resources, and by sympathetic staff or

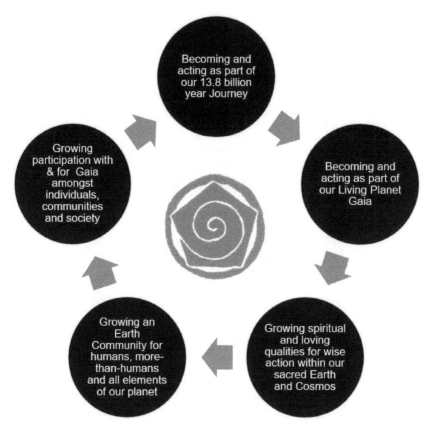

Figure 13.4: Our Journey to Wise and Urgent Action through five Dreams of the Earth for citizens of planet Earth and the Cosmos. (Source: Kettleborough, 2023)

tempered radicals working in public and private organisations.

Now we return to the inspiration of Thomas Berry's Dream of the Earth. What follows in an extended Creative Learning Exercise describing five interconnected paradigms for society to live by as we make the journey towards hopeful futures. Each suggests a dream for how we might live our lives true to each paradigm, as citizens of planet Earth and the Cosmos.

Five Creative Learning Exercises :

Read the following five interconnected cosmic paradigms and explore the potential actions described:

> As you go through each of the five paradigms/ Dreams of the Earth, Identify **one** action that you feel is achievable and worthwhile.

> Identify **one further action** from each paradigm that calls you and that you can visualise yourself putting time and energy into.

Once you have completed this exercise, you will have ten actions to match the decade ahead, from the early 2020s to early 2030s, the time within which, the IPCC tells us, we need to make a difference.

Creative Learning Exercise: *Dream of the Earth*:

1. Becoming part of our 13.8-billion-year journey

We are part of the universe, from its origins 13,800,000,000 years ago. As children of this profound history, we can learn to care deeply about the future of our planet and all of Life.

As citizens of planet Earth and the Cosmos:

<u>Individuals, families and communities</u>
We make time to participate in the great age of the universe, appreciating our origins in the stars and the gifts of the sun.

> We listen to what the cosmonauts, astronauts and taikonauts tell us of planet Earth from space.

We listen to the wisdom and stories of Indigenous Peoples and Elders and learn different ways to tell the Journey of the Universe story.

> We find creative ways to tell the story to our children and to our neighbours.

<u>Educators, artists and scientists</u>
We ask all educators to teach the Journey of the Universe to students of all ages.

> We create Journey of the Universe Walks in neighbourhoods and parks and encourage children and adults to walk them regularly so that the 13.8 billion years of our history becomes a shared sacred walk.

We ask artists to create stories, images, artworks and pieces of music that reflect and celebrate the age of the Universe and its long transformational history.

> We ask scientists and students in higher education to teach the story of the universe to local communities, schools and widely at all levels of society, helping participants understand the awe-inspiring nature of Life on Earth.

<u>Local, regional, national and international government</u>
We encourage governments of whatever size to frame their work and their journey within the history of the Universe.

> We encourage governments at all levels to enshrine in their laws and actions the unique nature of life on Earth and that extinction is forever, within a 13.8-billion-year history.

<u>Businesses large and small</u>
We encourage businesses to see their enterprise within the long history of the Universe, to appreciate their part in keeping this history going and to re-frame their operations and business models in the light of this.

We encourage businesses to give employees time to participate in learning about the history of the Universe.

We encourage the sharing of visual images of the Universe and the planet as part of work and organisational settings.

Wider society
We encourage the idea of Meetings for Earth to be shared and developed widely in all sections of society.

We work to weave an understanding of the unique nature of life and Earth, within the Journey of the Universe, in all institutions, faith communities, organisations and the media. From this understanding of the cosmological history of our planet, we work to immediately reduce and end greenhouse gases, plastic and all other waste, recognising the Climate Emergency.

We develop cosmological perspectives, seeing our planet from the perspective of deep time.

We seek to act our true age of 13.8 billion years in all our actions for nature and justice, in achieving the UN SDGs and seeing planet Earth as our one and only home.

We work, out of our cosmic history, to create peace, justice and strong institutions across our communities on planet Earth; grow mediators and conflict resolution specialists; end the arms trade; create racial justice organisers and community development workers; and end violence to women.

We learn to see our planet from the viewpoint of the planet Saturn and work towards peace and justice between nations.

For Everyone
We take seriously our moral and ethical responsibilities to the Cosmos and to our planet. We work together to help all of Life and our human communities through the extreme weather, drought, fires and melting of ice caused by our greenhouse gas emissions, to create a cosmological future for our fellow humans and Life on planet Earth.

Creative Learning Exercise: *The Dream of the Earth*

2. Becoming part of Our Living Planet, Gaia

Our planet is alive and we must respect and work with every part of her.

As citizens of planet Earth and the Cosmos:

<u>Individuals, families and communities</u>
We find our own special place in nature and get to know it through our senses.

We grow plants and trees in our homes, gardens and parks.

We develop a daily practice of bearing witness as a way to understand ecological and social injustice.

We encourage everyone to participate in learning to care for nature.

We seek to restore biodiversity, from the local to the global.

We care for neglected land to restore nature and grow local food.

We work together to create thousands of miles of nature corridors, starting from our own homes, to facilitate the movements of animals, insects and birds.

We advocate for local and national economies that ensure that everyone has enough within the planet's boundaries.

<u>Educators, artists and scientists</u>
We encourage scientists to work with government, business and local communities, on solutions to preserve and restore biodiversity and end greenhouse gas emissions by 2038.[171]

We draw on the skills of artists, musicians and other creatives to teach about our living Earth and to encourage the restoration of Gaia.

We encourage schools to explore and adopt eco- and forest school-type initiatives and learn about protecting endangered species.

We develop adult education in its widest form, so that all can learn about their living planet and how to take care of her.

We encourage universities to develop eco campuses and to preserve and restore local biodiversity, creating links, networks and projects with their local communities.

We ask scientists to work with artists and educators to share knowledge and understanding of climate tipping points facing our living Earth and the need for urgent action.[172]

We ask all educational establishments and faith communities, working with scientists and artists to teach carbon literacy to all ages and sections of society, including regular refresher courses, as a major educational project.[173]

Local, regional, national and international government
We ask governments to enshrine the rights of indigenous peoples and nature in law and international treaties.-

We ask governments to advocate for rewilding the land and sea, working with and protecting the rights of local and indigenous communities, to create marine and terrestrial reserves, with a target of 30% by 2030 and 50% by 2050.

We ask governments to support biodiversity around the world, with nations paying their contribution to the great rain forests in proportion to their carbon emissions.

We work, through all levels of government, to address the needs of refugees and asylum seekers, creating strategies to address the effects of climate change and the devastation of natural systems.

Businesses large and small
We work towards all businesses adopting a business model centred on Life and Gaia, adopting such models as the Natural Step, Doughnut Economics, Cradle to Cradle and the Circular Economy, seeking to restore ecological systems.

We ask all businesses to switch from seeing nature as a dead resource to a living planet within an awe inspiring and wonder filled Cosmos which sustains us and all life on Earth.

Wider society
We work together to understand how Life in all her forms is threatened by climate change and use our collective power to halt greenhouse emissions and biodiversity loss.

We link our understanding of how our living planet has been plundered with the effects of racism and colonialism, bringing together organisations that advocate for an end to racism and the decolonialisation of society with those that advocate for Gaia.

We develop the leadership of Indigenous women to lead the restoration of nature.

We link respect for human health and mental wellbeing with the health of the planet and act for both.

We debate together, using participatory approaches, the features of an international global economic order that ensures all people have enough within the boundaries of nature and of the planet.

We work for the UN SDGs 2030, adopting nature-based solutions where possible.

For everyone
We pledge our allegiance to urgently preserving and restoring our Living Planet, working for social justice, drawing motivation from our sense of awe and wonder at the Cosmos and our ancient, shared history.

Creative Learning Exercise: *The Dream of the Earth*

3. Growing loving and spiritual qualities within our sacred Earth and Cosmos

Loving and spiritual qualities need to be the basis for all our actions as we are filled with awe and wonder at being alive and being inhabitants of our planet and Cosmos.

As citizens of planet Earth and the Cosmos:

For individuals, families and communities
We grieve together, from love and humility, for what we are doing to the climate, to Life and to social justice.

> **We** develop healing for ourselves, our communities, our planet and our cosmological futures.

We share a Cosmic Road Map for Loving and Spiritual Qualities and encourage individuals, communities, institutions, faith groups, and organisations to create their own for flourishing futures for the human and the more-than-human.

Educators, artists and scientists
> **We** learn to use the the sciences and creative arts to develop loving and spiritual qualities for our planet, and to inspire awe and wonder for the Cosmos.

We work with people of all ages to share these ideas and values in formal and informal educational settings, and in life-wide and life-long learning.

> **We** ask scientists to share and teach their discoveries of how our planet and Cosmos works, so that we all gain understanding, compassion and motivation. [174]

We share and teach the United Nations Universal Declaration of Human Rights, as part of loving and spiritual qualities, to communities from the young to the old.

Local, regional, national and international government
> **We** encourage governments at every level to work with people of all and no faiths to create societies based on qualities of love, forgiveness, tolerance, kindness and respect towards humans and more-than-humans.

We ask governments to fund peace and kindness projects in all parts of society.

> **We** ask governments to implement the international agreements and fund the resources needed for poorer countries with lower carbon emissions to adapt to climate change, and mitigate against loss and damages.[175]

Businesses large and small
We ask businesses and investors to invest, operate, advertise and sell their products and services on ethical lines, respecting communities, Gaia and the Cosmos.

We encourage businesses to adopt wellbeing strategies and to include mindfulness, reflection and resilience in their business models, for their human communities and to address restoring Life.

We ask businesses to encourage their staff to volunteer and to seed fund local projects on meditation and creating kindness and loving and spiritual qualities in communities.

Wider society
We encourage faith communities to offer their wisdom and spiritual insights to all, irrespective of faith, as humanity's shared wisdom traditions.

We enter a period of repentance and remorse for slavery, the destruction of indigenous cultures, ecology and the climate. We ask forgiveness of each other and resolve to start again from such repentance. We set up Truth and Reconciliation Commissions at different levels of society to help us do this work and address the need for reparations.

We employ skilled mediation workers to work through local, regional and national conflict and create and support diverse and inclusive communities, analysing and working on trigger points for conflict.

We share ideas of the Earth as living and our Cosmos as sacred. Out of such a spiritual sense of worth and love for our planet, we work for societies to be based on anti-racism, and for the rights of all, including the well-being of women, disabled communities, LGBTQ+ communities and economically disadvantaged communities.

We seek to create a peaceful world, ending the era of nuclear weapons and ending armaments in the world, prioritising work to peacefully address conflict.

We learn and debate together issues of peace with regard to failing states and countries with repressive regimes, linked to the United Nations organisations and mediators, and to find actions to support communities.

We seek, out of love and kindness for each other and for nature, to support individuals, businesses and governments to drastically lower carbon emissions and our impact on the Earth, setting and monitoring annual global targets to 2038 and beyond. Such targets to be collected by street, ward, town, city, rural area and region, nation and continent and shared widely through various forms of media.

We tackle achieving the UN SDGs, universal human rights and social justice out of the spiritual qualities of love and respect and awe and wonder for Life and the Cosmos, encouraging the participation of all in democratic political parties.

Everyone
We encourage the recognition of each individual's potential and value as part of the wider interconnected whole.

We work together to develop loving and spiritual qualities in sociey and create ethics and values for a living Earth and an awe-inspiring Cosmos.

Creative Learning Exercise: *The Dream of the Earth*

4. Growing Earth as Community for humans and more-than-humans

Everything is part of one community – soil, rocks, animals, climate, seas, water, insects, birds, people from every background.

As citizens of planet Earth and the Cosmos:

Individuals, families and communities
We explore together our understanding of Earth as Community, discovering how every part of planet Earth is interconnected and interdependent.

> **We** experiment, learn, debate and create dreams in our streets and neighbourhoods for the entire Earth Community.

Educators, artists and scientists
We ask educators, scientists and artists to share how we can achieve the UN SDGs by 2030, seeking to get individuals and communities to understand root causes of problems.[176]

> **We** ask artists and scientists to set up Citizens Assemblies in towns and cities, to teach ideas and work out how to achieve net zero greenhouse gas emissions and socially just local communities by 2038.

We ask artists to teach creatively the principles of the Earth Charter and Earth Democracy for Justice, Peace and Sustainability.

> **We** ask educators, artists and scientists to work with different forms of media to share ideas about Earth as Community.

Local, regional, national and international government
We encourage governments to commission and act on National Cross-Party Reports on hunger, poverty and social justice challenges to addressing biodiversity loss and achieving a net zero emissions society, fast tracking the report to be produced in months.[177]

> **We** propose Policy Action teams[178] composed of individuals from all walks of life to investigate different aspects of these challenges.

We ask governments to establish and act on National Strategies for Earth Renewal.[179] To include, for example, a Green New Deal Strategy, a Racial Justice Strategy, a Gender Equality Strategy, an Equalities Strategy, a Preservation of Biodiversity and Restoration of Climate Strategy and an Integrated Mental Health and Health and Social Care Strategy.

We ask governments to promote Race Equality Charters based on the principles of Black Lives Matter to create communities, organisations and societies free of systemic racism and discrimination.

We ask local government to fund Neighbourhood Wardens for Earth Renewal to work with communities and other organisations on recycling, reducing waste, growing food, supporting refugees and asylum seekers and helping resolve community tensions.[180]

We establish a Policy Unit in each Local Authority to help all sections of society to reduce greenhouse gas emissions year on year to reach 50% reductions by 2030 and net zero by 2038, increase renewable energy, and work for biodiversity and social equity. [181]

We set up, through government, Universal Income for all, encouraging citizens to use their time to become carers, artists and makers for Earth as Community.

We ask government to raise taxes for United Nations institutions, and tax and restrain the multinationals, abolishing international tax havens, using the proceeds to fund urgent and wise actions.

We mandate governments to set targets and fund the adaptations needed by communities and nations globally to adapt infrastructure and society to the effects of climate change.

Businesses large and small
We dream to turn our businesses upside down, to start from the principles of Earth as Community and then profit for humans.

We ask businesses large and small to offer free participative learning on Earth as Community to their Boards, investors, staff, fellow businesses and local communities.

We ask businesses to include nature as the major stakeholder in their business.

Wider society
Where we can, we ask national and local government to help. We approach NGOs, celebrities, faith communities, businesses, charities, trusts, foundations and use crowd sourcing to create funds for these approaches.

We seek to mobilise women in relation to their needs, their caring responsibilities, and the challenges they face, such as violence, and how these issues relate to Earth as Community.

We bring together members of society in local areas, to establish how we can build anti-racist societies and how we can educate all on the achievements of Black, indigenous and people of colour and the history of slavery and colonialism.

We consider how to create a nature-rooted National Health and Wellness Service, linked to social and community care.

We work together to hold all media accountable by users and with oversight from democratic institutions to ensure that the media do not endanger democracy.

For everyone

We encourage everyone to mobilise and to work faithfully over years together to achieve Earth as Community for all the human and more-than-human children, grandchildren and to the seventh generation.

Creative Learning Exercise: *The Dream of the Earth*

5. Growing participation across society and planet Earth

Participation is the foundation on which we can create our hopeful futures. Working with, involving and listening to everyone builds respect. Working in participation with nature and our planet means we honour our fellow species and wider planet.

As citizens of planet Earth and the Cosmos:

<u>Individuals, families and communities</u>
We participate in learning, setting goals to learn and imagine new hopeful futures from the bottom up, joining with other individuals and communities.

We ask civil society organisations and institutions to learn, teach and share ideas about participatory learning and participatory democracy.

We respectfully participate, debate and learn together , including on social media, to develop and implement policies and practices to build anti-racist, gender equal and anti-discrimination societies where everyone can flourish and play a full part in society. We link this work with the UN SDGs, to *'Leave no-one behind'.*

<u>Educators, artists and scientists</u>
We encourage educators to teach members of society, through creative and participatory methods, about sustainability and ways to take action.

We ask educators at all levels to learn and teach about action research, reflection, participative democracy, creativity and resilience, paradigms and experimenting with how we learn.

We encourage educators in higher education to explore methods of participatory democracy and seek to embed these in workplaces, communities, trade unions, companies and political parties.

We ask local art galleries and museums, art and music colleges to become creative hubs to encourage participation in the dreams of the Earth.

We encourage educational establishments to explore different paradigms and teach students to see themselves as part of our planet and Cosmos, from the very young to the very old.

We ask universities and colleges to see themselves as resources for their communities and businesses, through research, ideas, global links and action, helping create hopeful futures.

We encourage each university student to participate in their local community and help create solutions.

> We encourage scientists to participate with local communities and share their knowledge widely and encourage citizen science through all ages.

Local regional, national and international government
We encourage all levels of government to facilitate participation in lifelong and life-wide learning around sustainable futures.

> We support voluntary organisations, charities, NGOs, business, local and national government and health services to provide resources for people to participate in society.

We encourage grants for individuals and community groups to create local projects to solve local challenges.

> We encourage government to resource community development workers in every locality to work to involve communities in neighbourhood activities, tackling injustice and going green.

We encourage local public services to fund a wide range of places for communities to meet, starting with the very local.

> We support local libraries to share resources for hopeful futures and lending schemes using all media resources.

We ask all levels of government to encourage their citizens to participate in learning about protecting human rights for citizens of the planet.

Businesses large and small
> We encourage businesses to participate with their local communities, creating volunteering links and bringing resources into communities

We ask businesses to participate with Life around them – in their geographical area and in their supply chains, to preserve and restore.

> We encourage businesses to build diversity, inclusion and equality into their strategies through participation with employees and the community.

Wider society
We seek resources to create local and regional partnerships to draw representatives of all parts of society to work together from all walks of life. [182]

We learn from faith and social movements and encourage participation in social justice, peace and nonviolence, climate justice and restoring nature, joining democratic political parties at all levels.

We support communities and create global links, seeking participation in global decision-making bodies to create global citizens.

We encourage participation in the development of technology for a better world, controlled through democratic systems and based on morals, ethics and values for Earth as Community.

For Everyone
We seek to create vast social movements to address the climate emergency and biodiversity loss and achieve social justice, sharing information widely and actively seeking involvement from all parts of society and all citizens of Planet Earth.

Invitation to Reflect

You have now read each of the interconnected Cosmic paradigms Reflect on each of these five paradigms in turn, exploring the following ideas and questions:

• Reflect on the ideas in these paradigms in relation to your own life and experiences.

• Are there any ideas you think are missing and need to be included? Can you add to your own Dreams of the Earth?

Following these reflections, do you need to change any of the ten actions you have chosen?

Using colours, keep a record of these reflections.

The interconnected nature of these paradigms is important. To make them manageable, the following Creative Learning Exercise seeks to bring ideas together over a ten-year cycle.

 Creative Learning Exercises

Record each of the ten actions you have chosen from the Creative Learning Exercise on page 404.

Draw a visual representation of each of your ten actions or search online for an image.

Create a timeline of the next ten years on a large piece of paper. For each year, add your target actions, drawings and pictures to each year of your timeline.

Don't forget: the paradigms are all interconnected (Figure 13.4). Can you capture this in your Timeline?

Set yourself tasks to follow the timeline.

Share your timeline as widely as you possible with family, friends and work colleagues.

Once you have completed this exercise, you will have ten actions to match the decade ahead, from the early 2020s to early 2030s, the time within which, the IPCC tells us, we need to make a difference. You will have created your own Dream of the Earth.

Concluding thoughts: Being the change and driving the change we need to see in the world

Creating stories for emerging cosmologies

As we create and take these actions, we must consider how we will build the groundswell of support needed to transform our societies. Throughout this book, I have traced the deep-seated challenges facing our planet and her inhabitants. Our dominant worldview is orientated towards a consumerist, racially unjust and growth addicted society. This paradigm is promoted and sustained by advertisers, the media, corporate stakeholders and vast wealth inequalities. Now is our time to reclaim our voices and the role of the dreamer and cosmologist and tell Earth enhancing stories to ourselves and to each other.

This Handbook seeks to tell other stories and to encourage you to create your own stories or retell stories you hear in your own words and voice. We have wonderful voices to share. The stories told by the astronauts, cosmonauts and taikonauts teach us of the fragility of our planet. Physicists teach us of the great age of the universe and that we have been part of it from the beginning. Biologists and Earth scientists teach us the challenges facing the planet and work to develop practical solutions. Social scientists have developed ways of learning that are reflective, participative, lifelong and life wide. Philosophers and spiritual teachers help us to perceive the world differently through exploring qualities and practices. Community members show how by taking dedicated action and involving everyone we can improve our streets and neighbourhoods. Across the world, activists are working to create better, more hopeful futures, traced by many authors and writers. Many of the thinkers introduced in these pages propose the need to create stories that can hold our dreams and help us step into the future.

Not only must we create stories of hope for ourselves, we must share them, to fill our families, communities, and places of work and learning with positivity and energy.

Stories must be about both the journey and the destination. Throughout this book I have provided Hopeful Companions to explore how we can replace stories of doom and gloom with stories of inquiry, curiosity and discovery. The Creative Learning exercises and Invitations to Reflect, offer ways to share stories that explore why we fail and celebrate when we pick ourselves up and start again. The Action Research Toolkit introduced throughout the book and brought together in this concluding chapter encourages us to continue to ask questions, continue to inquire, continue to create stories together and never give up.

Just as humanity's journey to the moon in the 1960s helped stimulate the first environmental movement, perhaps our dreams of Mars will enable us to become part of our wider Cosmos.[183] Can we learn to see ourselves as part of the Cosmos reflecting on herself? Such a vision can bring moral purpose and meaning to our lives, as we meet social and ecological challenges justly and ethically.

Each of us must tell stories from our own place, time and perspective. There is no universal place from which these stories emerge. The power of such an approach allows many voices and perspectives to be heard. It highlights the potential of encouraging children, young people and students to tell their own stories and to encourage members of communities to be part of the project to share our new cosmologies through whatever media are available.

 Invitation to Reflect

An abiding message from the cosmonauts, astronauts and taikonauts is one of peace and co-operation. I invite you to meditate on the following.

First cosmonaut Yuri Gagarin wrote,

> "Looking at the earth from afar you realise it is too small for conflict and just big enough for co-operation."

From the Mir Space Station, Syrian cosmonaut Mohammed Faris' observation that no human politics can be seen from the vantage point of space, was reflected in his life. Faris had to flee Syria along with millions of his country people, finding safety in Turkey, where he teaches astronomy and space, acknowledging the generosity of his adopted homeland to refugees (in Garthwaite, 2016).

When the International Space Station celebrated its twentieth birthday in 2020, astronaut Leland Melvin reflected,

> "When you think about those 20 years of the people, gay, straight, Muslim, Christian and Catholic, atheist, these different colours, these different lifestyles – all these people were able to come together and build something from one module to this international outpost the size of a football field without fighting, without warring. That is worthy of a peace prize."
>
> (Davenport, 2020)

Creative Learning Exercises

Create your own story or stories of hopeful futures. By creating, amplifying and putting such stories out into the world, you start to create different futures.

Create a story of a journey to hopeful futures that brings together self, community, Earth and Cosmos.

Create a story in a different medium, e.g., painting, photograph, woodwork, etc. Think of ways to share this with others.

As we create stories of hope, we grow communities for the future and strengthen all those who take wise action.

Figure 13.5: A stellar cradle in the Rosette Nebula, 5,000 light years away. Seeing our human journey as a part of the Cosmos. (Source: NASA, 2010. https://www.nasa.gov/ image-feature/rosette-nebula-gives-birth-to-stars)

Creating communities and constructing hopeful futures

The construction of hopeful ways into the future, from the methods and practices set out in this book, symbolises our journey to new paradigms – the dreams of the Earth. Such new journeys will be made by individuals and communities, working together with businesses, governments, NGOs, faith communities and all parts of society.

Creating community has been a theme throughout this journey. I have explored the richness of human communities to take these ideas forward. The stories have demonstrated how human communities can follow the example of more-than-human communities. We can create visions through transformative learning, creating forests and learning communities together, planting seeds as we go, nourished by the planet of which we are a part.

Planet Earth from Saturn – A Cosmic journey

On Christmas Eve 1968, William Anders took the photograph that was to become known as Earthrise and humans saw the Earth rise from behind the moon for the first time. Four years later, the crew of Apollo 17 took a photograph of Earth, titled Blue Marble, from 18,000 miles away.

The account of this journey, from self to community to Gaia, now reaches the Cosmos. Voyagers 1 and 2 blasted off from Cape Canaveral in 1977. Thirteen years later, Voyager 1 turned its face to home and took one last photograph of its home planet before she became too far away to be visible. That Pale Blue Dot, that pixel of reflected light, seen through the rings of Saturn, is our home.

In 2013, NASA repeated this iconic shot from nine hundred million miles away to capture another hauntingly beautiful portrait of our home planet. This time, NASA encouraged humanity to wave for the camera! Today, both Voyagers have travelled beyond the heliosphere and are now in interstellar space and, against all the odds, still communicating with us. There is hope that they will continue to transmit data back to Earth until the end of the 2020s. By then, humanity needs to have made big strides towards our hopeful future. The journeys of Voyagers 1 and 2 into the unknown is a metaphor for our own journey. As Carl Sagan (1981) wrote, as a species "we are on the shores of the cosmic ocean, we have put our toes in and waded out a little...."

◯ **Hopeful Companions**

Films
Animation of the journeys of Voyagers 1 and 2 through the solar system: https://www.youtube.com/watch?v=xZIB8vauWSI

For accounts of the Voyager 1 and 2 missions over the past 40 years, including videos: https://voyager.jpl.nasa.gov/frequently-asked-questions/

For a minute-by-minute Mission Status update in real time, see the Nasa website: https://voyager.jpl.nasa.gov/mission/status/

Our journey ends...

Finally…to the children who started this story. They are grown up now and I play 'save the animals' with my grandchildren, hugging trees together. The birds in our garden are still hanging in there, filling the garden with their song, perching and pecking at the branches in the holly bush in front of my window.

My hope has been to convey a sense of cosmic awe and what that might mean for everyday practice. I set out to guide you in finding your own maps, to use and adapt tools and practices and to act as a guide as you create your own journey into hopeful futures.-

Above all, I hope that you now see the journey ahead differently – as necessary, challenging, but exciting. As I continue my way on my journey which will last a lifetime, I wish you well on yours and send my love and support with you on your travels.

...with a new start

I end where I began, with our planet and Cosmos, and the reflections of three space explorers.

In 1963, Russian engineer Valentina Tereshkova was the first woman in space. Her first message back to Earth was:

"Ya chaika, Ya chaika, [I am Seagull] I see the horizon. A light blue, a beautiful band. This is the Earth. How beautiful it is. All goes well" (in Gibson, 2014: 53)

The Cosmos teaches us humility and spirituality. It also inspires us. Indian astronaut Kalpana Chawla, who died in the Columbia Shuttle accident in 2003 wrote (in Jackson, 2017),

> "The path from dreams to success does exist. May you have the vision to find it, the courage to get on to it and the perseverance to follow it."

Finally, astronomer Dr. Tayyaba Zafar (2020) is also clear about the journey ahead:

> "Don't give up on your mission. I didn't. We have one life and must live it to the fullest. Each one of us has a shining star inside us and we need to follow it; seek guidance from it."[184]

Bon voyage.

I leave you with a very special ◯ Hopeful Companion

Kelley, K. 1988. *The Home Planet and Reflections of Earth*. Reading, Mass: Addison Wesley Publishing.

Informative, challenging and optimistic large format book of Earth photography and space traveler's testimony to the fragility and beauty of the Earth. Produced by the Association of Space Explorers and in co-operation with the Soviet Agency Mir, to share the wonders of Planet Earth.

Notes

[155] Attenborough, 2019. p. 121.

[156] See Randles et al (2023) and Wadham et al (2923) for accounts by staff and students of how the work of the Student-Staff-Community Sustainability Group has developed.

[157] See the UN General Secretary's October 27 response to the UNEP Global Emissions Report 2022, on the day my youngest granddaughter was born, calling for climate action on all fronts immediately: https://www.youtube.com/watch?v=mCkUcJUuCPE

[158] https://www.nasa.gov/mission_pages/webb/main/index.html

[159] Mura M. 1972. Tabing Temple Painting depicting 'Adiparwa – Churning of the Milky Oceans' Anthony Forge Collection, E74177, https://australian.museum/learn/cultures/international-collection/balinese/the-churning-of-the-milky-ocean-balinese-paintings-e74163-and-e74177/

[160] To illustrate interdependence, Thich Nat Hanh describes how humans may feel they only need their lungs to breathe yet breathing also needs the mountains and the forests (page 19).

[161] Quoted in Lebedev, L., Romanov, A. and Luk'ianov, B. 1973. Sons of the Blue Planet, https://quotes.yourdictionary.com/author/yuri-gagarin/581629

[162] https://www.overviewinstituteaustralia.org/the-overview-effect

[163] See: https://www.azquotes.com/author/19683-Mae_Jemison and https://prologue.blogs.archives.gov/2020/03/30/mae-jemison-first-black-woman-in-space/

[164] Davis, J. 2022. The last eight years have been the hottest on record. National History Musuem. 14th January: https://www.nhm.ac.uk/discover/news/2022/january/last-eight-years-have-been-the-hottest-on-record.html

[165] See reports from the UN on the need to use the UN SDGs as a compass in the times of global crisis created by the COVID-19 pandemic: https://news.un.org/en/story/2020/05/1063742

[166] In 2020, Vanessa Nakate was invited to became one of seventeen Young Leaders for the Sustainable Development Goals. In her book, The Bigger Picture, Nakate explores the importance of the UN SDGs both within Africa and the whole world, while also linking to the importance of working for racial and social justice.

[167] Buglife B-Lines. 2022 https://www.buglife.org.uk/our-work/b-lines/

[168] Fair Seas. 2022. Building a movement of Ocean Stewardship, https://fairseas.ie/

[169] Guardian. 2021. End femicide: The aims of our campaign. 13 November, https://www.theguardian.com/society/2021/nov/13/end-femicide-the-observers-campaign

[170] See the song 'Paint Me a Picture of Ireland', written by John Broderick and sung by Séan Keane, from the Album Never Alone, 2013, Dublin: Circin Rua Tao.

[171] Although many nations have a target of 2050 for net zero greenhouse gas emissions, the IPPC 2018 report and the UNEP 2022 report call for drastic cuts within the next ten years.

[172] https://www.theguardian.com/environment/2022/sep/08/world-on-brink-five-climate-tipping-points-study-finds

[173] https://carbonliteracy.com/what-on-earth-is-carbon-literacy/

[174] See NASA Scientist Peter Kalmus on what is happening to the Earth: https://www.theguardian.com/commentisfree/2022/apr/06/climate-scientists-are-desperate-were-crying-begging-and-getting-arrested and the report from Sky News on progress between COP 26 and COP 27, and a response with Peter Kalmus': https://news.sky.com/story/what-a-difference-a-year-makes-how-the-world-has-changed-since-cop26-as-cop27-approaches-12737401?dcmp=snt-sf-twitter

[175] https://www.france24.com/en/asia-pacific/20220910-un-chief-says-never-seen-climate-carnage-like-pakistan-floods

[176] For example: https://www.irishtimes.com/opinion/2022/08/13/world-hunger-is-not-an-inevitability-its-politics/

[177] See for example, the work of the Social Exclusion Unit: https://api.parliament.uk/historic-hansard/written-answers/1999/nov/29/social-exclusion-unit

[178] See the 18 Policy Action teams for the National Strategy for Neighbourhood Renewal: https://dera.ioe.ac.uk/9947/1/National_strategy_for_neighbourhood_renewal_-_Policy_Action_Team_audit.pdf

[179] https://www.bristol.ac.uk/poverty/downloads/keyofficialdocuments/Neighbourhood%20Renewal%20National%20Strategy%20Report.pdf

[180] https://eprints.lse.ac.uk/4591/

[181] For resources and an innovation hub for local government, communities and businesses, see: https://cat.org.uk/info-resources/zero-carbon-britain/

[182] See accounts of collaborative working in partnerships, with examples from regeneration organisation Groundwork and the Mersey Basin Campaign in Barton et al. (2020)

[183] https://www.nasa.gov/topics/moon-to-mars See also the UN Outer Space Treaty (1966): https://www.unoosa.org/oosa/en/ourwork/spacelaw/treaties/introouterspacetreaty.html

[184] https://pakistan.timesofnews.com/breaking-news/dr-tayyaba-zafar-a-stargazer-lands-up-in-antarctica.html

Acknowledgements

Many people have contributed to my thinking and to the development and production of this book. I am grateful to them all.

I offer particular thanks and appreciation:

To those members of my family who have gone before, for their inspiration and support. To my mother, Catherine Josephine Kettleborough, for her love of poetry, the women's movement and the wisdom and spirit of the universe; to my father, Allan John Kettleborough, for his love of literature, education and learning, for his love of golden moments, his belief in family, and in his siblings, Neville, Patrick and Eunice. To my grandmothers, Helena Murphy and Kathleen Mary Kettleborough, for demonstrating love and care in action. To my aunts and uncles, Helena Murphy, Brid and Eamonn Langford, Moira Murphy and Ita and Tómas Murphy-Mitchell, for bringing me up every summer of my childhood with love, between the mountains and the sea.

To the organisations which have enabled me to spend my career working towards values that I believe in, including the two organisations who have book-ended my career. To the students at Manchester University Student Community Action demonstrating their power to help local communities in the 1970s. To staff and students at Manchester Metropolitan University who use collaborative working to create new educational partnerships for change; and to those working on Decolonising the Curriculum who freely share ideas, resources and actions.

To members of the women's movement in Manchester, my colleagues in local authorities, NGOs and local communities, and local councillors and MPs across the North West of England, who have shown that it is possible to work together to grow a better world.

To members of the community development movement locally, nationally and internationally, for their continued demonstration of what communities can achieve.

To members of GreenSpirit who share a belief in being part of the wider Cosmos. To the Thomas Berry Manchester Friends and the global ecumenical community that keeps his work alive. To members of the Faith Learning City Development Network for holding spirituality central to learning.

To the originators of the Masters in Responsibility and Business Practice (RPB) at Bath University – Judi Marshall, Gill Coleman and Peter Reason. To Judi who has given me ongoing academic and personal support ever since – through my PhD programme at Lancaster University and beyond. To my late Tutor, Chris Seeley. To alumni of the Masters Programme and the Association of Sustainability Practitioners for sharing knowledge and experience.

To members of my local community in Rusholme who work to make it a better place to live for humans and for nature. To my neighbour, Elaine Bishop, for working together on community projects and for continued encouragement.

With appreciation and thanks to the individuals who have given ideas, feedback and support as I wrote this book – Ahmed Ali, Stephen Allen, Nick Beddows, Elizabeth Boylan, Terry Biddington, Jean Boulton, Rob Browning, Gabriel Chanan, Eve Davidson, Jo Frankham, Simon Hicks, Chris Holmes, Jill Holmes, Liz Jayne, Donna Jones, Gwyn Jones, Clive Larsen, Rosalyn Marron, Jane Morris, Ian Mowll, Cliodhna Mulhern, Kelvin Ravenscroft, Peter Reason, Ita Ryan, Konstantina Skritsovali, Phoebe Spence, Sally Randles, Jagdish Rattanani, Anne Tucker, Helen Wadham, Marcin Wozniak and Xin Qi. Your comments were gratefully received and helped to develop this book. Any remaining challenges belong to me alone.

To my wonderful editor, Martina Tyrrell, for her understanding of and sympathy with my ideas and her meticulous work to redraft and encourage right through to the final chapters!

To Helen Hart, Anna Brownbridge and the design team at SilverWood Books for their work and support in design, production and promotion of this book – above and beyond the call of duty!

With grateful thanks to my family for their support. To Nóra Barton Kettleborough for kind and long term editorial assistance. To Ita Barton

Kettleborough for exploring and debating ideas and to Merewyn Owtram Algie for sharing play and nature based learning. To my aunt, Nóra Ryan Murphy, and her husband, Phil, for their continued attentiveness and encouragement. To my brother, Allan óg Kettleborough, for ongoing interest and for encouraging my work. To my grandchildren Eddi, Livvy, Jarvis and Lola for the love and hope they give me.

To my civil partner, Phil, who has created our lovely garden, my working environment, edited the first version of this book and worked on the design. You encouraged me to enrol on the RBP over three decades ago and have supported Gaia's Graveyards, even as the house filled up, and my master's and PhD research. Above all, thank you for constantly believing in me and my ideas and for being my companion in life and joy.

To the nature outside my study window – blue tits, sparrows, blackbirds and robins who delight me with their song; frogspawn in the spring; and the great Ash Tree who has been my unfailing companion for four decades; may you stay strong in dangerous times.

To our Living Planet Gaia and our Sacred Cosmos who have become my companions and inspiration for seeking to do the best that I can in their service.

With thanks to the following for generously giving me permission to use:

Figures:

Erna Colebrook (11.2), Ita Kettleborough (8.1), Joel Primack and Nancy Abrams (11.3 & 13.2), Kate Sibthorpe (7.3), Mike Pumford (1.1) and Phil Barton (1.1 & 1.2).

The International Platform on Biodiversity and Ecosystem Services (3.1), The Living Doughnut Lab (3.2), NASA (1.3, 1.4 & 13.5), RENEW NW (12.1), The United Nations (5.1) and Wikipedia (2.1).

Thanks to Geoff Mead for permission to use the late Chris Seeley's illustration (4.3).

Figures 0.1, 9.1 & 13.1 copyright Guardian News and Media Ltd 2022.

Quotations:

Thanks to Mary Evelyn Tucker and John Grim who, on behalf of the estate of the late Thomas Berry, gave permission to use his quotes throughout the book and offered support.

Thanks to Peter Reason and Melanie Newman for permission to use material from *The Stories of the Great Turning*.

The author has made every effort to ensure accuracy. Should you find any errors please contact her via The Centre for Connected Practice website (https://c4cp.net). There you will also find all weblinks referenced in this book, accurate at the time of publication.

About The Author

Helena Kettleborough is a writer, speaker and advocate for social and environmental change. Holding a Master's in responsible enterprise and a PhD in management, learning and leadership, she has worked extensively for equalities, community development and neighbourhood regeneration.

Currently teaching Responsible Business Practice and Sustainable Development at Manchester Metropolitan University, Helena is active in her local neighbourhood and with faith groups, addressing grief for biodiversity loss and climate change and the need to take action. She is a director of the Association of Sustainability Practitioners and established the Centre for Connected Practice in 2015. She is a founding committee member of her local residents' association in inner city Manchester. She has published extensively in practice, academic and education journals and books.

Helena draws on her career as a senior manager in Local Authorities delivering community development, learning and neighbourhood regeneration services across North West England as examples of what communities can achieve together as well as her experience as a mother, neighbour and campaigner.

Helena is currently leading a university/community joint project to plant 470 trees in her neighbourhood, having successfully planted 47. Next stop 4,700!

You can find out more about Helena and her research and learning work at https://c4cp.net and her work in the community on the same website and clicking 'Creative Rusholme'.

References

Abelvik-Lawson, H. 2020. Meet the Indigenous community that's fighting deforestation – and winning. *Greenpeace*, 30 November, https://www. greenpeace.org.uk/news/meet-the-indigenous-community-thats-fighting-deforestation-and-winning/

Abraham, J. 2019. Our oceans broke heat records in 2018 and the consequences are catastrophic. *The Guardian*, 15 January, https://www. theguardian.com/environment/climate-consensus-97-per-cent/2019/ jan/16/our-oceans-broke-heat-records-in-2018-and-the-consequences-are-catastrophic

Abram, D. 1996. *The Spell of the Sensuous*. New York: Random House, Vintage.

Abram, D. 2010. *Becoming Animal, an Earthly Cosmology*. New York: Pantheon Books.

Abrams, N. 2015. *A God that Could be Real: Spirituality, Science and the Future of Our Planet*. Boston: Beacon Press.

Abrams, N. and Primack, J. 2011. *The New Universe and the Human Future: How a Shared Cosmology Could Transform the World*. London: Yale University Press.

Adam, T. 2008. A review of narrative ethics. *Qualitative Inquiry*, 14 (2): 175–94.

Adepitan, A. 2021. Planting trees in Bhutan. In *Climate Change: Ade on the Frontline*, BBC 2, https://www.bbc.co.uk/teach/class-clips-video/ geography-ks3-gcse-planting-trees-bhutan/zmsqdp3

Al-Anon. 1973. *One Day at a Time in Al-Anon*. New York: Al-Anon Family Group HQ.

Albrecht, G., Sartore, G., Connor, L., Higginbotham, N., Freeman, S., Kelly, B., Stain, H., Tonna, A. and Pollard, G. 2007. Solastalgia: the distress caused by environmental change. *Australasian Psychiatry*, 15: sup1, S95–S98, DOI: 10.1080/10398560701701288

Allen, S. 2017. Learning from friends: Developing appreciations for unknowing in reflexive practice. *Management Learning*, 48(2), 125–139.

Alliot, M. 1970. *The Poems of John Keats*. London: Longman.

Almond, R.E.A., Grooten M. and Petersen, T. (eds). 2020. *Living Planet Report 2020: Bending the curve of biodiversity loss*. WWF, https://www.wwf.org.uk/sites/default/files/2020-09/LPR20_Full_report.pdf

Amigo, I. 2020. When will the Amazon reach a tipping point? *Nature*, 578: 505–507, https://www.nature.com/articles/d41586-020-00508-4

Anderson, P. 2001. Marine mammals in the next one hundred years: Twilight for a Pleistocene megafauna? *Journal of Mammalogy*, 82(3): 623–629, https://doi.org/10.1644/1545-1542(2001)082<0623:MMITNO>2.0.CO;2

Andrews, K. 2021. *The New Age of Empire: How Racism and Colonialism Still Rule the World*. London: Allen Books.

Arday, J., and Mirza H. (eds.) 2018. *Dismantling Race in Higher Education Racism, Whiteness and Decolonising the Academy*. London: Palgrave.

Argyris, C. and Schon, D. 1974. *Theories in Practice: Increasing Professional Effectiveness*. San Francisco CA: Jossey-Bass.

Armstrong, K. 2006. *The Great Transformation: The World in the Time of Buddha, Socrates, Confucius and Jeremiah*. London: Atlantic Books.

Arshad, A. 2021. Decolonising the curriculum. How do I get started? *Times Higher Education,* September, 2021, https://www.timeshighereducation.com/campus/decolonising-curriculum-how-do-i-get-started

Asahi Glass Foundation. 2012. *Blue Planet Prize Laureates Environment and Development Challenges: The Imperative to Act,* https://www.iucn.org/sites/dev/files/import/downloads/blue_planet_prize_laureates_paper_feb_2012.pdf

Aslin, H. and Blackstock, K. 2010. 'Now I am not an expert in anything': Challenges in undertaking transdisciplinary inquiries across the social and biophysical sciences, in Brown, V., Harris, J and Russell, J. (eds.). *Tackling Wicked Problems Through the Transdisciplinary Imagination*. Abingdon, Oxon: Earthscan, pp 117 -129.

Assadourian, E. 2017. EarthEd: Rethinking Education on a Changing Planet, in The Worldwatch Institute, *State of the World, Earthwatch Series, EarthEd Rethinking Education on a Changing Planet*, Washington: Island Press, pp. 5–20.

Attenborough, D. 2020. *A Life on Our Planet: My Witness Statement and a Vision for the Future.* London: Ebury.

Azhar, A. 2021. *Exponential: How Accelerating Technology is Leaving us Behind and What to do About it.* London: Penguin Random House.

Baldwin, M. 2001. The co-operative inquiry as a tool for professional development. *Systemic Practice and Action Research*, 15(3): 223–235.

Banerji, A. 2018. India's 'worst water crisis in history' leaves millions thirsty. *Everything News, Reuters*, 5 July, https://www.reuters.com/article/us-india-water-crisis-idUSKBN1JV01G

Barber. B. 1995. *Jihad vs McWorld.* New York: Ballantine Books.

Barborough Kettleton (2015). *Gaia's Graveyards: Timeline.* Exhibited Terre Verte Art Gallery, Launceston. Retrieved from http://c4cp.net/creativity/ (viewed May 2015)

Barnes, S. 2018. *Rewild Yourself: 23 Spell binding Ways to Make Nature More Visible.* London: Simon and Schuster.

Bartocci, G., Grossi, G., Meuro, S. and Ebdon, C. 2022. The journey of participatory budgeting: Systematic literature review and future research directions. *International Review of Administrative Services*, 1–18, https://journals.sagepub.com/doi/pdf/10.1177/00208523221078938

Barton, P. (2015). *Gaia's Graveyards: Washing line* Exhibited at St Agnes Church Stockport. Retrieved from http://c4cp.net/creativity/ (Viewed November 2015)

Barton, P. and Bishop, E. 2019. *Stories of a Manchester Street.* Manchester: History Press.

Barton, P., Handley, J., Wilmers, P., Sharland, R. and Menzies W. 2021. Place based leadership revisited: Partnerships in environmental regeneration in North West England, 1980–2010, A Practitioners Perspective. *Voluntary Sector Review*, 12(1): 91–121, https://doi.org/10.1332/204080521X16106634435216

Bateson, G. 1972. *Steps to an Ecology of Mind.* London: University of Chicago Press.

Bateson, G. and Bateson, M. 2005. *Angels Fear, Towards an Epistemology of the Sacred.* New Jersey: Hampton Press.

BBC News. 2016. Who was Caroline Herschel?, 16 March, https://www. bbc.co.uk/news/science-environment-35823012

Beaumont, M. 2008. Paradigm change? in Bogenreiter-Feigl, E. (ed.). *Paradigmenwechsel?* Vienna: Verbandes österreichischer Volkshochschnlen., pp.61-63.

Belenky, M., Clinchy, B., Goldberger, N. and Tarule, J. 1986. *Women's Ways of Knowing: The Development of Self, Voice and Mind.* New York: Basic Books.

Benöhr. J and Lynch, P. 2018. Should rivers have rights? *Yale 360,* 18 August, https://e360.yale.edu/features/should-rivers-have-rights-a-growing-movement-says-its-about-time

Benson, M. 2014. *Cosmigraphics: Picturing Space Through Time.* New York: Abrams.

Berners-Lee, M. and Clark, D. 2013. *The Burning Question.* London: Profile Books.

Berry, T. 1988. *The Dream of the Earth* Republished (2015) Berkeley CA: Counterpoint Press.

Berry, T. 1999. *The Great Work: Our Way into the Future.* New York: Bell Tower.

Berry, T. 2006. *Evening Thoughts: Reflecting on Earth as Sacred Community.* Tucker ME (ed) Berkely CA, Counterpoint Press

Berry, T. 2009. *The Sacred Universe. Earth, Spirituality and Religion in the Twenty First Century.* Tucker ME (ed). New York: Columbia.

Bekhout B., Galasso N., Lawson M., Morales P., Taneja A., Pimentel D. 2021. *The Inequality Virus.* Oxfam International Report, https://www. oxfam.org/en/research/inequality-virus

Biddington, T. 2021. *Multifaith Spaces, History, Development, Design and Practice.* London: Jessica Kingsley.

Black. A., Crimmins. G. and Jones. J. 2017. *Reducing The Drag: Creating V Formations Through Slow Scholarship and Story,* https://core.ac.uk/download/pdf/211500868.pdf

Blinkcoe, K. 2009. Re-educating the person, in Stibbe, A. (ed.). *The*

Handbook of Sustainability Literacy, Skills for a Changing World, Totnes: Green Books.

Bloom, W. 2011. *The Power of Modern Spirituality.* London: Piatkus.

Bird, K and Pitman L. 2020. How diverse is your reading list? Exploring issues of representation and decolonisation in the UK. *Higher Education,* 79: 903–920, https://link.springer.com/content/pdf/10.1007/s10734-019-00446-9.pdf

Bridle, S. 2003. Comprehensive compassion: An interview with Brian Swimme. *What is Enlightenment?* 19, 2 July, http://thegreatstory.org/SwimmeWIE.pdf

Boden, R., Greenwood, D., Hall, B., Levin, M., Marshall., M., and Wright, S. 2015. Action research in universities and higher education worldwide, in Bradbury, H. (ed.). *Sage Handbook of Action Research,* 3rd edition. London: Sage. pp 281–290.

Boff, L. 1995. *Ecology and Liberation: A New Paradigm.* Maryknoll, NY: Orbis.

Boff, L. 1997. *Cry of the Earth, Cry of the Poor.* Maryknoll, NY: Orbis.

Bohle, S. 2012. *Cause and Effect, Visualising Sustainability.* Berlin: Gestalten.

Botkin, J., Elmandjra, M. and Malitza, M. 1979. *No Limits to Learning, Bridging the Human Gap: A Report to the Club of Rome.* Oxford: Pergamon.

Boyce-Tilman, J. 2016. *Experiencing Music, Restoring the Spiritual.* Oxford: Peter Lang.

Boyce-Tillman, J. and Roberts, S. 2019. *Enlivening Faith: Music, Spirituality and Christian Theology.* Oxford: Peter Lang Books.

Bradbury, H. 2003. Sustaining the heart of action researchers: An interview with Joanna Macey. *Action Research Journal,* 1(2): 208–223.

Bradbury, H. 2015. (eds) The Sage Handbook of Action Research. London: Sage.

Bradbury Huang, H., Brydon-Miller, M., Gaya Wicks, P., Embury, D., and Lifvergen S. (eds.). 2013. ARJ since 2003: Celebrating 10 for 10. *Action Research,* 11(3): 215–217.

Bradbury, H., Glenzer, K., Columbia, D., Kjellström, S., Aragon, A., Warwick, R., Traeger, J., Apgar, M., Friedman, F., Hsia, H., Lifvergren, S., and Gray, P. 2019. What is good action research?: Quality choice points with a refreshed urgency. *Action Research Journal*, 17(1): 14–18, https://doi.org/10.1177%2F1476750319835607

Bradbury, H., Glenzer, K., Apgar, M., Embury, D., Friedman, V., Kjellström, S., Childers-McKee, C., Hsia, H., Ortiz, A., Gray, P., Bun Ku H., Parenti M., Traeger, J., Warwick, R., Devicha, S. 2020. *Action Research Journal's* seven quality choice points for action-oriented research for transformations. *Action Research Journal,* 18(1) 3–6, DOI: 10.1177/1476750320904562

Brooks, M. 2020. Here. There. Everywhere? Is the universe conscious? *New Scientist*, 2 May, 3280: 39–44.

Brooksbank, A. 2020. *Mummy Goes to Market. A Counting Book.* London: Walker Books.

Brother Lawrence. 1923.*The Practice of the Presence of God.* London: Mowbray and Co.

Brown, G. 2021. *Seven Ways to Change the World.* London: Simon and Schuster.

Brown, V., Harris, J. and Russell, J. 2010. *Tackling Wicked Problems Through the Transdisciplinary Imagination.* Abingdon, Oxon: Earthscan.

Browne, B. 2004. Imagine Chicago: A methodology for cultivating community. *Journal of Community and Applied Social Psychology*, 14: 394–405.

Bruner, J. 1968. Two modes of thought, in Mercer, N. (ed.). *Language and Literacy from an Educational Perspective. Volume 1, Language Studies.* Milton Keynes: OUP, pp. 99-112

Bryn K. and Bryan J. 2020. *My Mummy is a Firefighter.* London: Butterfly.

Bryon-Miller, M. 2008. Ethics and action research: Deepening our commitment to principles of social justice and redefining systems of democratic practice, in Reason, P. and Bradbury, H. (eds.). *The Sage Handbook of Action Research, Participative Inquiry and Practice*, 2nd edition. London: Sage, pp. 199–210.

Bryon-Miller, M., Aranda, A., and Stevens, D. 2015. Widening the circle: Ethical reflections in action research and the practice of structured ethical reflection, in Bradbury, H. (ed.). *Handbook of Action Research,* 3rd edition. London: Sage, pp. 596–607.

Bryson, B. 2003. *A Short History of Nearly Everything.* London: Transworld.

Bull, A. 2022. Yorkshire cricket's great divide: 'We've got to stop looking over the fence at each other.' *The Guardian,* 18 June.

Burns, D. 2007. *Systemic Action Research: A Strategy for Whole System Change.* Bristol: Policy.

Byron N. and Adeola, D. 2019. *Look Up!* London: Penguin.

Bryon, N. and Adeolo, D. 2022. *Rocket Rules: Ten Little Ways to Think BIG.* London: Puffin.

Burnell, C. 2020. *I am not a label. 34 People with Disabilities.* London: Wild Eyed Editions.

Burnton, S. 2022. Rafiz at Auschwitz: If this doesn't move you there is something wrong. *The Guardian,* 1 May, https://www.theguardian.com/sport/2022/may/01/azeem-rafiq-at-auschwitz-if-this-doesnt-move-you-theres-something-wrong

Cameron, J. 1995. *The Artists Way.* London: Pan Books.

Capra, F. 1996. *The Web of Life.* London: HarperCollins.

Carrington, D. 2011. Mass tree deaths prompt fears of Amazon 'climate tipping point'. *The Guardian,* 3 February, https://www.theguardian.com/environment/2011/feb/03/tree-deaths-amazon-climate

Carrington, D. 2013. CO_2 at its highest level for more than 3m years, Greenhouse gas passes 400 parts per million. The Guardian, 11 May.

Carrington, D. 2019. Record heat in world's oceans is 'dire warning' on climate crisis. *The Guardian,* 14 January, https://www.theguardian.com/environment/2019/dec/03/decade-of-exceptional-heat-likely-to-be-hottest-on-record-experts-say

Carrington, D. 2020. Coronavirus: Nature is sending us a message says UN Environment Chief. The Guardian, 25 March, https://www.theguardian.com/world/2020/mar/25/coronavirus-nature-is-sending-us-a-message-says-un-environment-chief

Carrington, D. 2021. Amazon rainforest now emitting more CO_2 than it absorbs. *The Guardian,* 14 July.

Carrington, D. 2022. World is coming close to irreversible change, say climate experts. The Guardian, 20 October.

Carson, R. 1962. *Silent Spring.* London: Penguin Classics.

Carter R. 2019. *The City is my Monastery: A Contemporary Rule of Life.* Norwich: Canterbury Press.

Ceballos, G., Ehrlich, P., and Dirzo, R. 2017. Biological annihilation via the ongoing sixth mass extinction signalled by vertebrate population losses and declines. *Proceedings of the National Academy of Sciences* (PNAS), doi:10.1073/pnas.1704949114

Centre for Alternative Technology. 2019. *Zero Carbon Britain: Rising to the Climate Emergency.* Wales: CAT, https://cat.org.uk/info-resources/zero-carbon-britain/research-reports/zero-carbon-britain-rising-to-the-climate-emergency /

Chanan, G. and Miller, C. 2013. *Rethinking Community Practice, Developing Transformative Neighbourhoods.* Bristol: Policy Press.

Chankseliani, M. and McCowan, T. Higher Education and the Sustainable Development Goals. High Educ 81, 1–8 (2021). https://doi.org/10.1007/s10734-020-00652-w

Charlton, N. 2008. *Understanding Gregory Bateson: Mind, Beauty, and the Sacred Earth.* Albany: State University of New York Press.

Christie, D. 2013. *The Blue Sapphire of the Mind, Notes for a Contemplative Ecology.* Oxford: Oxford University Press.

Clarke, C. 2002. *Living in Connection: Theory and Practice of a New World-View.* Warminster, UK: Creation Spirituality Books.

Cobb, J. 2001. Protestant theology and deep ecology: the failure of anthropocentrism, in Barnhill D. and Gottlieb R. (eds.) *Deep Ecology and World Religions*, New York: State University of New York Press, pp. 213 - 228

Cobb, S., Kettleborough, H., Leathlean, D. and Wozniak, M. 2016. I Love Learning: Innovating for Creativity. *Creative Academic Magazine*, 4a, pp. 86–88. http://www.creativeacademic.uk/uploads/1/3/5/4/13542890/cam_4a.pdf

Connor, S. 2014. We'll miss the invertebrates when they are gone. *The Independent,* 25 July.

Cooke, B., and Cox. J. 2005. *Fundamentals of Action Research, Volume 1, The Early Years.* Sage Benchmarks in Social Research series. London: Sage.

Bradshaw, C.J., Ehrlich, P., Beattie, B., Ceballos, G., Crist, E., Diamond, J., Dirzo, R., Ehrlich, A., Harte, J., Harte, M., Pyke, G., Raven, P., Ripple, W., Saltré, F., Turnbull, C., Wackernagel, M., Blumstein, D. 2021. Underestimating the challenges of avoiding a ghastly future. *Frontiers of Conservation Science*, https://doi.org/10.3389/fcosc.2020.615419

Calaprice, A. 2011. *The Ultimate Quotable Einstein*. Princetown and Jerusalem: Princetown University Press and Hebrew University of Jerusalem.

Covey, S. 1989. *The Seven Habits of Highly Effective People* London: Free Press.

Cox, B. and Cohen, A. 2011. *The Wonders of the Universe*. London: Collins.

Cox, B. and Cohen A. 2015. *The Human Universe*. London: William Collins.

Craig, G. 2017. *Community Organising against Racism*. Bristol: Policy Press.

Cranton, P. 2006. *Understanding and Promoting Transformational Learning: A Guide for Educators of Adults*. 2nd edition. San Francisco, CA: Jossey-Bass.

Crenshaw, K. 1991. Mapping the margins: Intersectionality, identity politics and violence against women of colour. *Stanford Law Review*, 43(6): 1241–1299.

Cunliffe, A. 2010. Crafting qualitative research: Morgan and Smircich 30 years on. *Organizational Research Methods,* 14(4): 1–27.

Cullinan, C. 2002. *Wild Law Governing People for Earth*. Claremont, South Africa: Silver Ink.

Cunningham, I. 2003. Reg Revans – an appreciation: The life of a learning guru. *Development and Learning in Organizations*, 17(3): 4–6.

Davenport, C. 2020. Humans have been living aboard the International Space Station for 20 years. What comes next? *The Washington Post,* 1 November, https://www.washingtonpost.com/technology/2020/11/01/space-station-20-years-anniversary/

Davies, P. 2006. *The Goldilocks Enigma: Why the Universe is Just Right for Life*. London: Penguin.

Department of Communities and Local Government (DCLG). 2006. *The Community Development Challenge Report.* London: CLG.

De Chardin, T. 1936/1975. *Toward the Future.* New York: Harcourt.

Deakin, R. 2021. Wellbeing, in Wilkinson, A. and Dundon, T. (eds) *Contemporary Human Resource Management,* 6th edition. London: Sage.

Dean, B. and Prablant, S. 2020. *Me, my Dad and the End of the Rainbow.* London: Simon and Schuster.

Deane-Drummond, C. 2017. *A Primer in Eco Theology: Theology for a Fragile Earth.* Eugene, OR: Cascade Books.

De Botton, A. 2012. *Religion for Atheists.* London: Penguin Books.

De Mello, A. 1984. *The Song of the Bird.* New York: Image, Doubleday.

De Mello, A. (ed. Stroud, J.F.). 1990. *Awareness.* London: Fount.

Denzin, N. and Lincoln, Y. (eds.) 2015. *Handbook of Qualitative Research,* 5th edition. Thousand Oaks: Sage.

De Vaal, E. 1997. *Living with Contradiction: An Introduction to Benedictine Spirituality.* Norwich: Canterbury Press.

Devlin, H. 2018. Cosmic dawn: Astronomers detect signals from first stars in the universe. *The Guardian,* 28 February, https://www.theguardian.com/science/2018/feb/28/cosmic-dawn-astronomers-detect-signals-from-first-stars-in-the-universe

Dey, M., White, W., and Kaur, S. 2021. *The Pay and Progression of Women of Colour. A Literature Review.* London: Fawcett Society and the Runneymede Trust: https://www.fawcettsociety.org.uk/the-pay-and-progression-of-women-of-colour-literature-review

Dick, B. 2010. Action research literature 2008–10: Themes and Trends. *Action Research,* 9(2): 122–143.

Dick, B., Stringer, E., Huxham, C. 2009. Conclusion: Final reflections, unanswered questions. *Action Research,* 7(1): 117–120.

Donald, P., Collar, N., Marsden S., and Pain D., 2013. *Facing Extinction. The World's Rarest Birds and the Race to Save Them.* London: Christopher Helm.

Dorling Kindersley 2016. *Great City Maps, A Historical Journey Through Maps, Plans and Paintings.* London: Dorling Kindersley.

Drucker, P. 1955. *The Practice of Management.* London: Heinemann.

Ducrocq, A. 2011. *Petite Anthologies Spirituelle pour Reenchanter le Quotidien.* Paris: Albin Michel.

Duggan, J. and Sebastian, J. 2016 to present. *Post Colonialism and Religions Series*: London: Palgrave Macmillan.

Duncan, G. 2015. Innovations in appreciative inquiry: Critical appreciative inquiry with excluded Pakistani women, in Bradbury, H. (ed.). *The Sage Handbook of Action Research,* 3rd edition. London: Sage. pp 55–63.

Easwaran, E. (translator). 2007. *The Chandogya Upanishads,* 2nd edition. Tomales, California: Nilgiri Press.

Elder, Z. and Gilbert, I. (ed) 2011. *Full on learning: Involve me and I'll understand,* Bancyfelin , Wales: Crown House.

Elgin, D. 2009. *Our Living Universe.* San Francisco: Berrett-Koehler.

Elhacham, E., Ben-Uri, L., Grozovski, J., Bar-On, Y. and Milo R. 2020. Global human-made mass exceeds all living biomas. *Nature* 588, 442–444, https://doi.org/10.1038/s41586-020-3010-5

Eliot, T.S. 1963. *Collected Poems 1909–1962.* London: Faber and Faber.

Ellis, C. and Bochner, A. 2000.Autoethnography, personal narrative, reflexivity: Researcher as subject, in Denzin, N. and Lincoln, Y. (eds.). *Handbook of Qualitative Research,* 2nd edition. Thousand Island CA: Sage Publications, pp. 733–769.

Embery, D. 2015. Action research in an online world, in Bradbury, H. (ed.). *Sage Handbook of Action Research,* 3rd edition. London: Sage, pp. 529–535.

Emmott, S. 2013. *10 Billion.* London: Penguin.

England, E. 1988. *Keeping a Spiritual Journal.* East Sussex: Highland Books

Equal Rights Trust. 2016. Interview with Kimberlé Crenshaw and Patricia Shulz: Intersectionality in promoting equality. *Equal Rights Review*, 16: 209–219.

Eriksson, P. and Kovalainen, A. 2008. *Qualitative Methods in Business Research.* London: Sage.

Essex University. 2022. *Decolonising the Curriculum: Decolonising Your Reading Lists*: https://library.essex.ac.uk/edi/readinglists

European Commission. 2022. Environment Action Programme to 2030, https://ec.europa.eu/environment/strategy/environment-action-programme-2030_en

Fair Seas. 2022. Building a movement of Ocean Stewardship, https://fairseas.ie/

Fals-Borda, O. 2001. Participatory (action) research in social theory: Origins and challenges, in Reason, P. and Bradbury, H. (eds.). *Handbook of Action Research, Concise Paperback Edition*, London: Sage, pp. 27 -37.

Fals-Borda, O. 2006. The North-South convergence: A 30-year first person assessment of PAR. *Action Research,* 4(3): 351–358.

Filho, W., Raath, S., Lazzarini, B., Vargas V., de Souza L., Anholon R., Quelhas, O., Haddad R., Klavins M., Orlovic V. 2018. The role of transformation in learning and education for sustainability. *Journal of Cleaner Production*, 199: 286–295.

Fisher, D., Rooke D. and Torbert, B. 2002. *Personal and Organisational Transformations Through Action Inquiry,* 2nd edition. Boston: Edge Works.

Flanagan, B. and Weatherall, D. 2013. *Sustainable Consumption in the UK: A Selection of Case Studies.* London: IPPR.

Fordham, G. 2010. *New Deal for Communities Programme: Achieving a Neighbourhood Focus for Regeneration. The New Deal for Communities National Evaluation Final Report Vol 1.* Sheffield: Sheffield Hallam University and Communities and Local Government, https://www.shu.ac.uk/-/media/home/research/cresr/reports/n/ndc-achieving-neighbourhood-focus-regeneragion-vol1.pdf

Forman, M. (ed.). 1935. *The Letters of John Keats.* Humphrey Milford: OUP.

Foucault, M. 1979. *Discipline and Punish: The Birth of the Prison.* London: Vintage.

Fox M. 1983. *Original Blessing.* New Mexico: Bear and Company.

Fox, M. 1991. *Creation Spirituality: Liberating Gifts for the Peoples of the Earth.* San Francisco: Harper.

Fox, M. 2020. *Julian of Norwich: Wisdom in a Time of Pandemic and Beyond.* USA: iUniverse.

Freeman, D. 2020. *Can Globalisation Succeed? A Primer for the 21st Century.* London: Thames and Hudson.

Freire, P. 1970/1996. *Pedagogy of the Oppressed.* London: Penguin Books.

Freire, P. 2004. *Pedagogy of Hope: Reliving Pedagogy of the Oppressed.* London: Continuum.

Garthwaite, R. 2016. From astronaut to refugee: How the Syrian spaceman fell to Earth. *The Guardian*, 1 March, https://www.theguardian.com/world/2016/mar/01/from-astronaut-to-refugee-how-the-syrian-spaceman-fell-to-earth?CMP=Share_iOSApp

Gawain, S. 1978/2016. *Creative Visualisation.* California: New World Library.

Gearty, M. and Marshall, J. 2021. Living life as inquiry: A systemic practice for change agents, systemic practice and action research. *Systemic Practice and Action Research.* 4: 441–462, https://doi.org/10.1007/s11213-020-09539-4

Geertz, G. 1973. *The Interpretation of Cultures.* London: Harper.

Gerhardt, S. 2004. *Why Love Matters: How Affection Shapes a Baby's Brain.* London: Routledge.

Gibbons, J. 2016. Choosing to fail: An interview with Professor Kevin Anderson. *ThinkorSwim*, 21 March, https://www.thinkorswim.ie/choosing-to-fail-prof-kevin-anderson-interviewed/

Gibson. K. 2014. *Women in Space.* Chicago: Chicago Review Press.

Gifford, R. 2015. 33 reasons why we can't think clearly about climate change. *New Scientist.* 8 July.

Gilchrist, A. 2004. *The Well-Connected Community: A Networking Approach to Community Development.* Bristol: Policy Press.

Gilchrist, A. and Taylor, M. 2011. *The Short Guide to Community Development*, 1st edition. Bristol: Policy Press.

Goff, P. 2019. *Galileo's Error: Foundations for a New Science of Consciousness.* London: Routledge.

Goldberg, N. 1986. *Writing Down the Bones.* Boston, MA: Shambhala.

Goldenberg, S. 2014. Western Antarctic icesheet collapse already begun scientists warn. *The Guardian,* 12 May, https://www.theguardian.com/environment/2014/may/12/western-antarctic-ice-sheet-collapse-has-already-begun-scientists-warn

Gondarzi, S. 2006. Interview with Anoushah Ansari, the first female space tourist. *Space.com*, 13 September, https://web.archive.org/web/20060920022453/http://space.com/missionlaunches/060915_ansari_qna.html

Goodell, J. 2018. *The Water Will come: Rising Seas, Sinking Cities, and the Remaking of the Civilised World*. Carlton VIC, Australia: Black Inc.

Goodwin, B. 1999. Reclaiming a life of quality. *Journal of Consciousness Studies*, 6(11): 293–55.

Goodwin, B., Mills, S. and Spretnak, C. 2001. Participation in the living world. *Revision*, 23(3): 26.

Gordon, G. 2001. Transforming lives: Towards bicultural competence, in Reason, P. and Bradbury, H. (eds.). *The Sage Handbook of Action Research Concise Paperback Edition*. London: Sage, pp. 243–252.

Gordon, G. 2007. *Towards Bicultural Competence Beyond Black and White*. Stoke-on-Trent: Trentham Books.

Ghosh, A. 2021. *The Nutmeg's Curse: Parables for a Planet in Crisis*. London: John Murray.

Grant, S. and Humphries, M. 2006. Critical evaluation of appreciative inquiry: Bridging an apparent paradox. *Action Research*, 4(4): 401–418.

Greenfield, P., Harvey, F., and Lakhani, N. 2022. Poor nations 'paying twice' for climate breakdown. The Guardian. 8 November 2022.

Gray, L. 2010. Man's greed wiping out life in the oceans. *The Daily Telegraph,* 5 October.

Gribben, G. 2011. *The Reason Why: The Miracle of Life on Earth*. London: Penguin.

Gribben, J and Gribben M. 2009. *He Knew He Was Right: The Irrepressible Life of James Lovelock and Gaia*. London: Allen Lane.

Grieten, S., Lambrechts, F., Bouwen, R., Huybrechts, J., Ronald R., and Cooperrider, D. 2018. Inquiry into appreciative inquiry: A conversation with David Cooperrider and Ronald Fry. *Journal of Management Inquiry,* 27(1): 101–114.

Grooten, M. and Almond, R.E.A. (eds.) 2018. *Living Planet Report 2018: Aiming Higher.* WWF, Gland, Switzerland, https://www.wwf.org.uk/sites/default/files/2018-10/wwfintl_livingplanet_full.pdf

Guardian. 2021. End femicide: The aims of our campaign. 13 November, https://www.theguardian.com/society/2021/nov/13/end-femicide-the-observers-campaign

Guardian Editorial. 2022. The world's poor need help to deal with a crisis that they did not cause. 13 June, https://www.theguardian.com/commentisfree/2022/jun/12/the-guardian-view-on-an-indian-summer-human-made-heatwaves-are-getting-hotter

Gustaven, B. 2003. Action research and the problem of the single case. *Concepts and Transformations*, 8(1): 87–93.

Guterres, A. 2020. Making peace with nature is the defining task of the 21st Century. *United Nations Climate Change,* 2 December, https://unfccc.int/news/un-secretary-general-making-peace-with-nature-is-the-defining-task-of-the-21st-century

Gvaenta, J. and Cornwall, A. 2015. Power and knowledge, in Bradbury, H. (ed.). *Sage Handbook of Action Research*, 3rd edition. London: Sage, pp. 465–471.

Gyimah, M., Azad, Z., Begum, S., Kapoor, A. Ville L., Henderson A., Dey, M. 2022. *Broken Ladders: The Myth of Meritocracy for Women of Colour in the Workplace.* London: Fawcett Society and the Runnymede Trust: https://www.runnymedetrust.org/partnership-projects/broken-ladders

Hall, S. 2015. Exxon knew about climate change almost forty years ago. *Scientific American,* 26 October, https://www.scientificamerican.com/article/exxon-knew-about-climate-change-almost-40-years-ago/

Hamera, J. 2011. Performance ethnography, in Denzin, N. and Lincoln, Y. (eds.). *Handbook of Qualitative Research*, 4th edition. Thousand Oaks: Sage, pp. 317–330.

Hanh, T.N. 1995. *Living Buddha, Living Christ.* London: Rider.

Hanh, T.N. 2010. *You Are Here: Discovering the Magic of the Present Moment.* Colorado: Shambala.

Hanh, T.N. 2009. Indra's net. *Resurgence and Ecologist*, 256, Sept/Oct: 18–19.

Hanish, C. 1970: The personal is political in *Notes of the Second Wave*, http://www.carolhanisch.org/CHwritings/PIP.html

Harding, S. 2006. *Animate Earth: Science, Intuition and Gaia.* Cornwall: MPG Books.

Harding, S. 2022. *Gaia Alchemy: The Reuniting of Science, Psyche and Soul.* Vermont: Bear and Company.

Harley, A. and Scandrett, E. 2019. *Environmental Justice, Popular Struggle and Community Development.* Bristol: Policy Press.

Harrop, E., Hyde, S. and Ronan, O. 2022. 'How integrated conceptions of earth rights and human rights in indigenous traditions can teach the Global North about true sustainability'. In Pathak, Y.V. and Adityanjee, A. (eds) *Human Rights, Spirituality and Religious Freedom: Perspectives from the Dharmic and Indigenous Cultures.* Kovidnam Vani, Delaware, USA.

Harvey, F. 2019. Decade of exceptional heat likely to be the hottest on record, experts warn, *The Guardian,* 3 December, https://www.theguardian.com/environment/2019/dec/03/decade-of-exceptional-heat-likely-to-be-hottest-on-record-experts-say

Harvey, F. and Carrington, D. 2019. UN warns unprecedented cuts in emissions needed. *The Guardian,* 26 November, https://www.theguardian.com/environment/2019/nov/26/united-nations-global-effort-cut-emissions-stop-climate-chaos-2030

Harvey, F. 2021. Ice melting at record rate, 23-year global study reveals. *The Guardian,* 26 January, https://www.theguardian.com/environment/2021/jan/25/global-ice-loss-accelerating-at-record-rate-study-finds

Harvey, F., Kassam, A., Lakhani, N., and Dhillon, A. 2022. Burning planet: Why are the world's heatwaves getting more intense? *The Observer,* 19 June, https://www.theguardian.com/world/2022/jun/18/burning-planet-why-are-the-worlds-heatwaves-getting-more-intense

Haugaard, M. 2012. Power and truth. *European Journal of Social Theory,* 15(1): 73–92.

Hawken, H. 2007. *Blessed Unrest.* New York: Viking/Penguin.

Hay, L. 1984. *You Can Heal Your Life.* California: Hay Publishers.

Henderson, H. 1996. *Building a Win-Win World.* San Francisco, CA: Berrett-Koehler.

Heron, J. 1996. *Co-operative Inquiry, Research into the Human Condition.* London: Sage.

Heron, J. 2006. *The Complete Facilitator's Handbook.* London: Kogan Page.

Heron, J. and Reason, P. 1997. A participatory inquiry paradigm. *Qualitative Inquiry,* 3(3): 274–294.

Heron, J. and Reason, P. 2001. The Practice of Co-operative Inquiry: Research with rather than on people in Reason, P. and Bradbury, H. (Eds.), *Handbook of Action Research: Participative Inquiry and Practice.* London: Sage. pp. 179-188.

Higgins, P. 2012. *Earth is our Business: Changing the Rules of the Game.* London: Shepheard-Walwyn.

Holding, M. 2021. *Why We Kneel, How We Rise.* London: Simon and Schuster.

Homer-Dixon, H. 2006. *The Upside of Down: Catastrophe, Creativity and the Renewal of Civilisation.* London: Souvenir Press Ltd.

Honore, C. 2004. *In Praise of Slow.* London: Orion.

Hulme, M. 2009. *Why We Disagree About Climate Change: Understanding Controversy, Inaction and Opportunity.* Cambridge: Cambridge University Press.

Human Development Reports. 1989-2021, http://hdr.undp.org/en/global-reports

Hutchins, R. 1968. *A Learning Society: A Britannica Perspective.* London: Penguin.

ICCA Consortium. 2021. *Territories of Life: 2021 Report.* ICCA Consortium Worldwide, https://report.territoriesoflife.org

Illeris, K. 2009. *Contemporary Theories of Learning: Learning Theorists in Their own Words.* Abingdon: Routledge.

Illeris, K. 2017. *How we Learn: Learning and Non-Learning in School and Beyond.* London: Routledge.

Illich, I. 1971. *Deschooling Society.* New York: Harper and Row.

Immerzeel, W.W., Lutz, A.F., Andrade, M. et al. 2020. Importance and vulnerability of the world's water towers. *Nature,* 577: 364–369, https://doi.org/10.1038/s41586-019-1822-y

Independent Newspaper. 2010. The dead sea. Microscopic life crucial to the marine food chain is dying out. The consequences could be catastrophic. *The Independent Newspaper,* 29 July.

IACD: International Association for Community Development. 2018. People, place and power, Dundee edition. *Practice Insights Magazine*, 16, https://www.iacdglobal.org/wp-content/uploads/2020/06/IACD-Practice-Insights-WCDC2019-website-version.pdf

IPBES. 2019. *Summary for policymakers of the global assessment report on biodiversity and ecosystem services of the Intergovernmental Science-Policy Platform on Biodiversity and Ecosystem Services.* IPBES Secretariat, Bonn, Germany, https://doi.org/10.5281/zenodo.3553579

IPCC. 2018: *Global Warming of 1.5°C. Summary for Policymakers,* https://www.ipcc.ch/site/assets/uploads/2018/10/SR15_SPM_version_stand_alone_LR.pdf

IPPC. 2019a: *Climate Change and Land,* https://www.ipcc.ch/site/assets/uploads/sites/4/2020/02/SPM_Updated-Jan20.pdf

IPCC. 2019b. *Special Report on the Ocean and Cryosphere in a Changing Climate. Summary for Policy Makers*, https://www.ipcc.ch/site/assets/uploads/sites/3/2019/11/03_SROCC_SPM_FINAL.pdf

IPPC. 2021. *The Physical Science Basis. Contribution of Working Group I to the Sixth Assessment Report of the Intergovernmental Panel on Climate Change. Summary for Policy Makers.* Cambridge University Press, https://www.ipcc.ch/report/ar6/wg1/downloads/report/IPCC_AR6_WGI_SPM.pdf

IPPC. 2022a. *Climate Change 2022: Impacts, Adaption and Vulnerability, Summary for Policy Makers, Working Group 11 Contribution to the Sixth Assessment Report of the IPPC.* February, https://www.ipcc.ch/report/ar6/wg2/

IPCC. 2022b. Summary for Policymakers, in *Climate Change 2022: Mitigation of Climate Change. Contribution of Working Group III to the Sixth Assessment Report of the Intergovernmental Panel on Climate Change*, doi: 10.1017/9781009157926.001

International Programme on the State of the Oceans (IPSO). 2013. State of the oceans report. *Marine Pollution Bulletin,* 74(2): 491–552, http://www.stateoftheocean.org/wp-content/uploads/2015/10/State-of-the-Ocean-2013-report.pdf

Jackson, L. 2017. *A Galaxy of Her Own: Amazing Stories of Women in Space.* London: Century.

Jarvis, P., Holford, J. and Griffin, C. 2003. *The Theory and Practice of*

Learning, 2nd edition. New York: Routledge.

Jarvis, P. 2006. *Towards a Comprehensive Theory of Human Learning. Vol 1: Lifelong Learning and the Learning Society.* London: Routledge.

Jasper, K. 1953/2021. *The Origin and Goal of History. London: Routledge Classics.*

Jeffers, S. 1987/2019. *Feel the Fear and Do it Anyway.* London: Vermillion.

Jha, A. 2010. Plight of the bumblebee: £10m search begins for cause of a perilous decline. *The Guardian,* 22 June.

Johnson, K. (2019) *Reaching for the Moon: The Autobiography of NASA Mathematician Katherine Johnson.* London: Atheneum Books

Joseph-Salisbury, R. and Connelly, L. 2021. *Anti-Racist Scholar-Activism.* Manchester: Manchester University Press.

Jowit, J. 2010. Case for saving species more powerful than climate change. *The Guardian,* 22 May.

Kaplan, A. 2002. *Development Practitioners and Social Process: Artists of the Invisible.* London: Pluto Press.

Karpf, A. 2021. *How Women Can Save the Planet.* London: Hurst and Co.

Keats, J. and Gittins, R. 1970. Axioms in philosophy: Letter to John Hamilton Reynolds (May 3, 1818), in Gittings, R. *Letters of John Keats: A New Selection, 1795–1821.* Oxford: OUP.

Kemmis, S. 2001. Exploring the relevance of critical theory for action research: Emancipatory action research in the footsteps of Jurgen Habermas, in Reason, P. and Bradbury, H. (eds.). *The Sage Handbook of Action Research.* London: Sage, pp. 94–105.

Kendall, G. 2019. Apollo 11 anniversary: Could an iPhone fly me to the moon? *Independent,* 9 July, https://www.independent.co.uk/news/science/apollo-11-moon-landing-mobile-phones-smartphone-iphone-a8988351.html

Kendi, I. X. 2019. *How to be an Antiracist.* London: Bodley Head.

Kendi I. X. and Lukashevshy, A. 2020. *Antiracist Baby.* New York. Random House.

Keremane, G. and McKay, J. 2011. Using photostory to capture irrigators' emotions about water policy and sustainable development objectives: A case study in rural Australia. *Action Research*, 9(4): 405–425.

Kettleborough, H. 2011. Thinking out of the box: Introducing action research into neighbourhood practice in the Northwest of England, in Marshall, J., Coleman, G. and Reason, P. (eds.). *Leadership for Sustainability: An Action Research Approach*. Sheffield: Greenleaf. pp. 89–94.

Kettleborough, H. 2014. *Joining self to community, planet and cosmos, a first-person inquiry of discovery and understanding*. PhD, Lancaster University School of Management.

Kettleborough, H. 2019. Gaia's Graveyards: Bearing witness as first-person inquiry. *Action Research Journal,* 17(3): 292–322 DOI: 10.1177/147675031881888

Kettleborough, H. and Kettleborough N. 2013 Discovering that we live in an ancient and beautiful universe, in Reason, P. and Newman, M. (eds.). *Stories of the Great Turning*. Bristol: Vala. pp 149–158.

King, D., Browne, J., Layard, R., O'Donnell, G., Rees, M., Stern, N., Turner, A. 2015. *A Global Apollo Programme to Combat Climate Change*. London: LSE, https://cep.lse.ac.uk/pubs/download/special/Global_Apollo_ Programme_Report.pdf

King, M.L. Jr. 28 August, 1963. I Have A Dream, March on Washington for Jobs and Freedom. Text of the speech: http://freedomsring.stanford. edu/?view=Speech

Klein, N. 2015. *This Changes Everything*. London: Penguin.

Kolb, D. 1984. *Experiential Learning*. Englewood Cliffs, NJ: Prentice-Hall.

Kolbert, E. 2006. *Field Notes from a Catastrophe*. London: Bloomsbury.

Kolbert, E. 2014. *The Sixth Extinction. An Unnatural History.* London: Bloomsbury.

Kolbert, E. 2021. *Under a White Sky: The Nature of the Future*. London: Bodley Head.

Kollwewe J. 2019. Half of the world's pay goes to 10% of workers despite fall in inequality. *The Guardian*. 5 July.

Korner, S. and Bellin-Hader, F. 2009. The 7000 Eichen of Joseph Beuys: Experiences after twenty-five years. *Journal of Landscape Architecture,* 4(2): 6–19.

Korten, D. 2006. *The Great Turning: From Empire to Earth as Community.* Bloomfield CT: Kumarian Press.

Kristiansen, M. and Bloch-Poulsen, J. 2008. Working with 'not knowing' amid power dynamics among managers: From fault finding and exclusion towards co-learning and inclusion, in Reason, P. and Bradbury H. (eds.). *Sage Handbook of Action Research, Participative Inquiry and Practice,* 2nd edition. London: Sage. pp. 463–471.

Kuhn, T.S. 1962 (1996). *The Structure of Scientific Revolutions.* London and Chicago: The University of the Chicago Press.

Kumar, S. 2007. *The Spiritual Compass: The Three Qualities of Life.* Totnes, Devon: Green Books.

Kumar, S. 2009. *Earth Pilgrim. In Conversation with Echan Deravy and Maya Kumar Mitchell.* Cambridge: Green Books.

Kumar, S. 2017. Soil, soul and society: Towards sustainable cities, in Kettleborough, H. and Barton, P. (Guest eds.), *GreenSpirit Magazine,* 'Green Spirituality in the Community' Edition. London: GreenSpirit. pp. 6-7.

Kumar, S. 2019. *Elegant Simplicity: The Art of Living Well.* Canada: New Society Publishers.

Kurio, J. and Reason, P. 2021. Voicing rivers through ontopoetics: A co-operative inquiry. *River Research and Applications,* 38: 376–384.

Kwok, M., Palmer, M., and Ramsey, J. (translators) and Chan, K. (calligraphy). 1993. *Tao Te Ching: A New translation.* Shaftesbury, Dorset: Element.

LaChance, S. 2001. *Cultural Addiction: The GreenSpirit Guide to Recovery.* California: North Atlantic Books.

Lakoff, G. 2010. Why it matters how we frame the environment. *Environmental Communication,* 4(1): 70–81, DOI: 10.1080/17524030903529749

Lakoff, G. 2009/2011. Why environmental understanding or 'framing' matters: An evaluation of the EcoAmerica Summary Report. *The Huffington Post,* https://www.huffpost.com/entry/why-environmental-underst_b_205477

Lalenti, V. 2020. *How Deep Time Thinking Can Help Earth Now.* Boston: MIT.

Lamb, R. 1980. *World Without Trees: Man's Devastation of his Environment.* London: Magnum Books.

Laszlo, E. 2001. Planetary vision: What it is and why we need it. *ReVision,* 23(4): 2–3.

Lather, P. 1991. *Getting Smart Feminist Research and Pedagogy With/in the Postmodern.* New York: Routledge.

Lau, W., Sharan. J., Bailey, R., Cook. E et al. 2020. Evaluating scenarios towards zero plastic pollution. *Science,* 369(6510): 1455–1461.

Lave, J. and Wenger, E. 1991. *Situated Learning: Legitimate Peripheral Participation.* Cambridge: Cambridge University Press.

Le Page, M. 2021. Dry soils mean Europe's trees are dying at a faster rate. *New Scientist.* 20 November: 14.

Ledwith, M. 2005. *Community Development: A Critical Approach.* Bristol: Policy Press.

Ledwith, M. 2020. *Community Development: A Critical and Radical Approach,* 3rd edition. Birmingham: Venture Press.

Legett, T. 2018. How Volkswagen tried to cover up the emissions scandal. BBC News, 5 May, https://www.bbc.co.uk/news/business-44005844

Lenton, T. and Watson, A. 2011. *Revolutions that Made the Earth.* Oxford: Oxford University Press.

Lenton T., Dutreuil S., and Latour B. 2020. Life on Earth is hard to spot. *The Anthropocene Review,* 7(3): 248– 270. DOI: 10.1177/2053019620918939

Leopold, A. 1946 (1968). *A Sand County Almanac.* Oxford: OUP.

Lewis, N. and Shore, C. 2019. From unbundling to market making: Reimagining, reassembling and reinventing the public university. *Globalisation, Societies and Education.* 17(1): 11–27. ISSN 1476-7724.

Lincoln, Y., Lynham, S. and Guba, E. 2011. Paradigmatic controversies, contradictions, and emerging confluences revisited, in Denzin, N. and Lincoln, Y. (eds.). *Handbook of Qualitative Research,* 4th edition. Thousand Oaks: Sage. pp. 97–128.

Local Government Association. 2021. *Health Inequalities: Ethnicity and COVID-19,* https://www.local.gov.uk/our-support/safer-and-more-sustainable-communities/health-inequalities-hub/health-inequalities-3

Louv, R. 2011. *The Nature Principle, Human Restoration and the End of the Nature Deficit Disorder.* North Carolina: Algonquin Books.

Lovelock, J. 1988/1995. *The Ages of Gaia: A Biography of Our Living Earth.* Oxford: Oxford University Press.

Lovelock, J. 2006. *The Revenge of Gaia: Why the Earth is Fighting Back and How We Can Still Save Humanity.* London: Allen Lane.

Lovelock, J. 2007. Forward, in Midgley, M. (ed.) *Earthly Realism: The Meaning of Gaia.* Exeter: Societas, pp. 1–2.

Lovelock, J. 2009. *The Vanishing Face of Gaia: A Final Warning.* London: Allen Lane.

Lovelock, J., Rees, M., Randall, L, Kump, L., Radford, T., Pope, V. et al. 2015.*The Earth and I.* Kohn, Germany: Taschen.

Lovelock, J. and Margulis, L. 1974. Atmospheric homeostasis by and for the biosphere: The Gaia hypothesis. *Tellus*, XXV1: 1–2 http://www.jameslovelock.org/atmospheric-homeostasis-by-and-for-the-biosphere-the-gaia-hypothesis/

Ludema, J., Cooperrider, D., Barrett, F. 2001. Appreciative inquiry: The power of the unconditional positive question, in Reason, P. and Bradbury, H. (eds.). *Handbook of Action Research.* London: Sage, pp. 155–165.

Ludema, J. and Fry, R. 2008. The practice of appreciative inquiry, in Reason, P. and Bradbury, H. (eds.). *The Sage Handbook of Action Research, Participative Inquiry and Practice.* London: Sage, pp. 280–296.

Lukes, S. 1974 (2005). *Power: A Radical View,* 2nd edition. London: Palgrave Macmillan.

Lydall, R. 2012. William: 'We must end killing or our children will not see these animals'. *The Evening Standard,* 19 June.

Lyons, O. 2004. The Ice is Melting. Address to the 24th Annual E. F. Schumacher Lectures, https://centerforneweconomics.org/publications/the-ice-is-melting/

Maathai, W. 2008. *Unbowed: One Woman's Story.* London: Arrow Books.

MacDonald, G. 1984/2017. *Ordering your Private World.* Nashville: Thomas Nelson.

MacRae, D. 2022. Azeem Rafiq: The ECB needs a reset of its morals and values. *The Guardian,* 21 January, https://www.theguardian.com/

sport/2022/jan/21/azeem-rafiq-cricket-ecb-needs-a-reset-of-its-morals-and-values-simple-as-that

Macy, J. and Brown, M. 1998. *Coming Back to Life: Practices to Reconnect Our Lives, Our World*. Gabriola Island, BC: New Society Publishers.

Macy, J. and Johnstone, C. 2012. *Active Hope: How to Face the Mess We're in Without Going Crazy*. Navato, California: New World Library.

Macy, J. 2013. Preface, in Reason, P. and Newman, M. (eds.). *Stories of the Great Turning*. Bristol: Vala, pp. 5–8.

Maguire, P. 2001. Uneven ground: Feminisms and action research, in Reason, P. and Bradbury, H. (eds.). *Handbook of Action Research*. London: Sage. pp. 60–70.

Mann, M. 2021. *The New Climate War*. London: Scribe.

Margulis, L. and Sagan, D. 1997. *Microcosmos: Four Billion Years of Microbial Evolution*. California: University of California Press.

Marshall, J. 2001. Self-reflective inquiry practices, in Reason, P. and Bradbury, H. (eds.). *Handbook of Action Research*. London: Sage, pp. 335–342.

Marshall, J. 2004. Living systemic thinking: Exploring quality in first-person action research. *Action Research*, 2(3): 305–325.

Marshall J. 2008. Finding form in writing for action research, in Reason, P. and Bradbury, H. (eds.). *The Sage Handbook of Action Research: Participative Inquiry and Practice*, 2nd edition. London: Sage, pp. 682–694.

Marshall, J. 2011. Images of changing practice through reflective action research. *Journal of Organizational Change Management*, 24(2): 244–256.

Marshall, J. 2016. *First Person Action Research: Living life as Inquiry*. London: Sage.

Marshall, J. and Reason, P. 2003. *Approaches to Action Research* (DVD). Centre for Action Research in Professional Practice: University of Bath, School of Management.

Marshall, J., Coleman, G. and Reason, P. (eds.) 2011. *Leadership for Sustainability: An Action Research Approach*. Sheffield: Greenleaf Publishing.

Marten, A. 2008. Action research on a large scale: Issues and practices, in Reason, P. and Bradbury, H. (eds.). *The Sage Handbook of Action Research: Participative Inquiry and Practice*, 2nd edition. London: Sage. pp 394–406.

Maslow, A. 1962/1998. *Maslow on Management*. New York: John Riley.

Maughan, E. and Reason, P. 2001. A co-operative inquiry into deep ecology. *ReVision*, 23(4): 18–24.

Mathews, F. 2016. Do the deepest roots of a future ecological civilisation lie in Chinese soil? *Australian Academy of the Humanities*. 2016. *Learning from the Other: Australian and Chinese Perspectives on Philosophy.* 2014 and 2015 Symposia, Australian Academy of the Humanities and the Chinese Academy of Social Sciences (Canberra Australian Academy of the Humanities).

Matthiessen, P. 1978. *The Snow Leopard*. London: Penguin.

Mayo M. 1997. *Imagining Tomorrow: Adult Education for Transformation*. Leicester: National Institute of Continuing Education.

McCarthy, M. 2015. *The Moth Snowstorm: Nature and Joy*. London: John Murray.

McIntosh, A. 2001. *Soil and Soul, People versus Corporate Power.* London: Aurum Press.

McIntosh, A. and Carmichael, M. 2016. *Spiritual Activism: Leadership as Service*. Cambridge: Green Books.

McKenzie, D and Swails, B. 2019. 'If the climate stays like this, we won't make it,' say those on the frontline of Africa's drought. CNN, 15 December, https://edition.cnn.com/2019/12/14/africa/climate-change-southern-africa-intl/index.html

McNiff, J. and Whitehead, J. 2011. *All you Need to Know About Action Research,* 2nd edition. London: Sage.

McQuiston II, J. 1996. *Always We Begin Again: The Benedictine Way of Living*. Ridgefield, CT: Morehouse.

Mead, G. 2011. *Coming Home to Story: Storytelling Beyond Happily Ever After.* Bristol: Vala Publishing Co-operative.

Meadows, D., Meadows, D. and Randers, J. 1972. *The Limits to Growth: A Report for the Club of Rome's Project on the Predicament of Mankind.* New York: Universe Books.

Meadows, D., Meadows, D., and Randers, J. 1992. *Beyond the Limits: Confronting Global Collapse, Envisioning a Sustainable Future.* Vermont: Chelsea Green Publishing Company.

Meadows, D., Rangers, J. and Meadows, D. 2004. *Limits to Growth: The 30-Year Update.* London: Earthscan.

Melvin, L. 2018. *Chasing Space: An Astronaut's Story of Grit, Grace and Second Chances.* London: Harper Collins.

Merskin, D. 2010. Hearing voices: The promise of participatory action research with animals. *Action Research,* 9(2): 144–161.

Milbrath, L. 1989. *Envisioning a Sustainable Society: Learning Our Way Out.* Albany: State University of New York.

Milbrath, L. 1995. Psychological, cultural, and informational barriers to sustainability. *Journal of Social Issues,* 51(4): 101–120.

Millennium Ecosystem Assessment. 2005. Guide to Millennium Ecosystem Reports, http://www.millenniumassessment.org/en/index.aspx

Miller, C. 2019. *Participation at 45° Techniques for Citizen Led Change.* London: Compass.

Miller, J. and Quartey, A. 2022. *Leland Melvin, Leaders like Us.* USA: Rourke Educational Materials.

Milman, O. 2021. 2020 was hottest year on record by a narrow margin Nasa says. *The Guardian,* 14 January, https://www.theguardian.com/environment/2021/jan/14/2020-hottest-year-on-record-nasa

Milman, O. 2022. Nowhere to hide: How insects are losing the race against the climate crisis. *The Guardian.* 11 January.

Mitchell, J. 1971. *Women's Estate.* London: Penguin.

Monbiot, G. 2020. Extinction Rebellion is showing Britain what real democracy could look like. *The Guardian,* 16 September, https://www.theguardian.com/commentisfree/2020/sep/16/extinction-rebellion-britain-democracy-protest-westminster

Monbiot, G. 2022. Watching *Don't Look Up* made me see my whole life of campaigning flash before me. *The Guardian,* 4 January, https://www.theguardian.com/commentisfree/2022/jan/04/dont-look-up-life-of-campaigning?s=09

Mulhern, C. and Emmanuel, J. 2011. *Working with Possibility, Appreciative*

Inquiry in the NW, Stockport: NWTWC, http://www.assetbasedconsulting.co.uk/uploads/publications/NWTWC-appreciative-Inquiry.pdf

Muncey, T. 2010. *Creating Autoethnographies.* London: Sage.

Murray, R. 2013. *Writing for Academic Journals,* 3rd edition. Berkshire: Open University Press.

Myers, N. 1985. *The Gaia Atlas of Planet Management.* London: Gaia Books.

Myers, N. and Kent, J. 2005. *The New Gaia Atlas of Planet Management.* London: Gaia Books.

Nakate, V. 2021. *A Bigger Picture: My Fight to Bring a New African Voice to the Climate Crisis.* London: Macmillan.

National Education Union. 2022. *Anti-Racism Charter: The NEU's framework for developing an anti-racist approach:* https://neu.org.uk/anti-racism-charter

Neal, L. 2015. *Playing for Time: Making Art as if the World Mattered.* London: Oberon.

Neihardt, J. and Black Elk, N. 1932/2000. *Black Elk Speaks: as told through John G. Neihardt (Flaming Rainbow) by Nicolas Black Elk. Being the Life Story of a Holy Man of the Oglala Sioux.* Lincoln: University of Nebraska Press.

Nerantzi, C. and Gossman, P. 2018. Cross-boundary communities: An alternative vision for academic development. *Compass,* 11(2), http://dx.doi.org/10.21100/compass.v11i2.800

Nerantzi, C. 2019. Living in the uncomfort zone or towards a creativity manifesto. In Jackon, N., and Willis, J. (eds). 2019. *Encouraging Imagination and Creativity in Higher Education. Personal Manifestos, Creative Academic,*13(b): 22. http://www.creativeacademic.uk/manifesto.html

Nerantzi, C., Moravej, H., Iosifidou, I. and Nina Silva, L. 2020. Creativity interwoven into the fabric of learning, an example from a postgraduate nutritional science module, in Hunter, A. Gillaspy, E. Withnell, N. and Nerantzi, C. (eds.). *Our Creative Self: Understanding Perceptions of Creativity in Learning and Teaching.* Prism, 3(1): 34–39, https://doi.org/10.24377/prism.ljmu.03012011

New Scientist Leader. 2015. Critical thinking is needed throughout life, not just in science. *New Scientist,* 3051, 12 December.

Nicolson, T., Jones, D., Greenwood, A. 2022. *Decolonising the Curriculum Toolkit Guidance.* Manchester Metropolitan University Faculty of Science and Engineering and Faulty Narrowing the Awarding Gap Task Group, https://www.mmu.ac.uk/about-us/professional-services/uta/reducing-awarding-gaps/decolonising-the-curriculum-toolkit

Norwood, R. 1986/2009. *Women Who Love Too Much.* London: Arrow Books.

Nurse, A. (2022) *Reparations and Anti-Black Racism. A Criminological Exploration of the Harms of Slavery and Racialized Injustice.* Bristol: Bristol University Press.

NWIEP. 2009. *Employment in the North West.* Wigan: NWIEP.

NWIEP. 2010. *Tackling Unemployment in an Area of High Unemployment and Poverty.* Wigan: NWIEP.

NWTWC. 2011. *North West Together We Can Community Empowerment Awards.* Stockport: NWTWC.

Oates, M. 2015. *In Pursuit of Butterflies: A Fifty-Year Affair.* London: Bloomsbury.

ODPM. 2004a. The Egan Review of Sustainable Communities, https://www.ihbc.org.uk/recent_papers/docs/Egan%20Review%20Skills%20for%20sustainable%20Communities.pdf

ODPM. 2004b. *New Deal for Communities: The National Evaluation Annual Report, 2003/2004.* London: ODPM, Neighbourhood Renewal Unit.

OECD. 2021. *OECD Health at a Glance 2021,* https://www.oecd.org/health/health-at-a-glance/

Orr, D. 2002. Four challenges of sustainability. *Conservation Biology,* 16(6): 1457–1460.

Osborne, M. 2014. Why lifelong learning and why learning cities? *Pedagogy,* 87(7): 1067–1077, http://eprints.gla.ac.uk/97745/1/97745.pdf

O'Donogue, J. 2007. *Benedictus: A Book of Blessings.* Dublin: Transworld.

O'Donoghue, N. 1993. *The Mountain Behind the Mountain.* Edinburgh: T & T Clark.

O'Murchu, D. 2000. *Religion in Exile: A Spiritual Vison for the Homeward Bound.* Dublin: Gateway.

O'Neill, E. 2021. Seagrass planting programme gets underway. *Marine Conservation Society*, 21 April, https://www.mcsuk.org/news/seagrass-planting-programme-underway/

O'Shaughnessy, A. 1873 Ode, in *Music and Moonlight Poetry Collection*, 1874, https://www.poetryfoundation.org/poems/54933/ode-

Osieyo. M. 2017. Bearing witness: The Grenfell Tower fire and how to help when we feel helpless. *Digging Deeper*, 25 June, https://marionosieyo.com/2017/06/25/grenfell-tower-fire-how-to-help-when-feeling-helpless/

Otto, R. (translated by Harvey, J.). 1923/1958. *The Idea of the Holy*. Oxford: Oxford University Press.

Otto, R. (translated Bracey, R. and Payne, R.). 1933/2016. *Mysticism East and West: A Comparative Analysis of the Nature of Mysticism*. Eugene Oregon: WIPF & Stock.

Ovenden, R. 2020. *Burning the Books: A History of the Deliberate Destruction of Knowledge*. Harvard: Harvard University Press.

Packhard, V. 1957/2007. *The Hidden Persuaders*. Brooklyn, NY: IG Publishers.

Packham. C. 2008. *Active Citizenship and Community Learning*. Exeter: Community Matters.

Payden, L. 2021. *Save Our Soils Report*. Bristol: The Soil Association, https://www.soilassociation.org/media/22963/saving-our-soils-report.pdf

Peck, S. 1978. *The Road Less Travelled: A New Psychology of Love, Traditional Tales and Spiritual Growth*. London: Rider.

Pedler, K. 1979/1991. *The Quest for Gaia: A Book of Changes*. London: Paladin.

Pedler, M. 1997. *Action Learning in Practice*. Aldershot: Gower.

Pedler, M. and Burgoyne, J. 2008. Action learning, in Reason, P. and Bradbury, H. (eds.). *Sage Handbook of Action Research, Participative Inquiry and Practice*, 2nd edition. London: Sage. pp. 319–332.

Pedler, M. and Trehan, K. 2009. Editorial: Management learning in a post-capitalist society. *Action Learning: Research and Practice*, 6(1): 1–3.

Penny, L. 2022. *Sexual Revolution: Modern Fascism and the Feminist Fightback*. London: Bloomsbury.

Perriton, L. 2001. Sleeping with the enemy? Exploiting the textual turn in management research. *International Journal of Social Research Methodology*, 4(1): 35–50.

Pidd, H., Barr, C., and Mohduin, A. 2020. Calls for health funding to be prioritised as poor bear brunt of COVID-19. *The Guardian*, 1 May, https://www.theguardian.com/world/2020/may/01/covid-19-deaths-twice-as-high-in-poorest-areas-in-england-and-wales

Pihkala, P. 2017. *Early Ecotheology and Joseph Sittler,* Zurich: Lit Verlag.

Piketty, T. 2014. *Capital in the 21st Century.* Cambridge: Harvard University Press.

Podger, D., Velasco, I., Luna, C., Burford, G. and Harder, M. 2013. Can values be measured? Significant contributions from a small civic society organisation through action research. *Action Research*, 11(1): 8–30.

Pope Francis. 2015. *Laudato Si': On Care for Our Common Home, Encyclical Letter.* London: Catholic Truth Society, http://www.vatican.va/content/francesco/en/encyclicals/documents/papa-francesco_20150524_enciclica-laudato-si.html

Porritt, P. 2007. *Capitalism as if the World Matters.* London: Earthscan.

Porritt, J. 2013. *The World We Made.* London: Plaidon Press.

Porritt, J. 2022. *Hope or Hell.* London: Simon and Schuster.

Power, C. 2013. The Truth Mandala, in Reason, P. and Newman, N. (eds.). *Stories of the Great Turning.* Bristol: Vala, pp. 85–93.

Primack, J. and Abrams, N. 2006. *The View from the Centre of the Universe: Discovering our Extraordinary Place in the Cosmos.* New York: Penguin.

Primavesi, A. 2003. *Gaia's Gift: Earth, Ourselves and God after Copernicus.* London/New York: Routledge.

Primavesi, A. 2009. *Gaia and Climate Change: A Theology of Gift Events.* London/New York: Routledge.

Primavesi, A. 2013. *Exploring Earthiness, the Reality and Perception of Being Human Today.* Eugene, Oregon: Cascade.

Pyrch, T. 2015. Teaching the heart of action research skills: Breaking free in the classroom, in Bradbury, H. (ed.). *Sage Handbook of Action Research*, 3rd edition. London: Sage, pp. 553–563.

Quincey, C., Mills, S., Robertson, J., Ladkin, D., Spretnak, C. and Ho, M. 2001. Participating in one another's lives and disciplines. *Revision,* 23(4): 6–11.

Rafiq, A. 2021. *Azeem Rafiq Witness Statement.* Digital, Culture, Media and Sports Committee, House of Commons, 21 November, https://committees.parliament.uk/publications/7832/documents/81586/default/

Rappaport, J. 2020. *Cowards Don't Make History: Orlando Fals Borda and the Origins of Participatory Action Research.* Durham, North Carolina: Duke University Press.

Raelin, J. 2009. Seeking conceptual clarity in the action modalities. *Action Learning, Research and Practice,* 6(1): 17–24.

Raine, K. 1988. S*elected Poems.* Ipswich: Golgonooza Press.

Randles, S., Wadham, H., Skritsovali, K., Hart, C., Hoque, S., Kettleborough, H., Klapper, R, Marron, R., Taylor, D. and Walley, L. With Clovis, A., Derbyshire, M., Devaney, M., Doig, G., Jones, D., Leigh, S., Louis, R., Margetson, M., Protopsaltis, T., Tucker, M., Twitchett, L., and Whiteley, C. (2023). Leveraging hope and experience: Towards an integrated model of transformative learning, community and leadership for sustainability action and change, in Purcell, W. and Haddock-Fraser J. (eds.). *The Bloomsbury Handbook of Sustainability in Higher Education.* London: Bloomsbury.

Ramamurthy, A. (2013) *Black Star, Britain's Asian Youth Movements.* London: Pluto Press.

Rattanani, J. with Iyengar, S., and Pearson, L. (2023) *Satish Kumar: Abundant Love* Axminster England: Triarchy Press

Ravenscroft, K. 2021. Seeing the World Anew. Responding to Thomas Berry's the Great Work. In Greene, H., Cone, L., Futch, G., Loyd, A., and Powell, M. 2021. *The Living Legacy of Thomas Berry.* EcoZoic Journal (6), pp 118–121: https://greenspirit.org.uk/pdf/EcozoicJournal-6.pdf

Raworth, K. 2017. *Doughnut Economics: Seven Ways to Think Like a 21st Century Economist.* London: Penguin Random House.

Reason, P. 2001a. Earth community: Interview with Thomas Berry. *Resurgence,* 204: 10–14.

Reason, R. 2001b. A participatory conversation about how the universe, our lives and science are participatory. *Revision,* 3(4): 12–17

Reason, P. 2005. Living as part of the whole: The implications of participation. *Journal of Curriculum and Pedagogy*, 2(2): 35–41.

Reason, P. 2007. *Earth as community: A Celebration of the Vision and Path of Thomas Berry.* London: GreenSpirit.

Reason, P. and Bradbury, H. 2001. Introduction: Inquiry and participation in search of a world worthy of human aspiration, in Reason, P. and Bradbury, H. (eds.). *Sage Handbook of Action Research.* London: Sage, pp. 1–14.

Reason, P. and Bradbury, H. (eds.) 2008. *The Sage Handbook of Action Research, Participative Inquiry and Practice*, 2nd edition. London: Sage.

Reason, P. and Caney, S. 2015. Action research and ecological practice, in Bradbury, H. (ed.). *Sage Handbook of Action Research*, 3rd edition. London: Sage, pp. 553–563.

Reason, P. and Goodwin, B. 1999. Towards a science of qualities in organisations: Lessons from complexity theory and postmodern biology. *Concepts and Transformations,* 4(3): 281–217.

Reason P. and Torbert, W. 2001a. Towards a transformational science: A further look at the scientific merits of action research. *Concepts and Transformations*, 6(9): 1–37.

Reason, R. and Torbert, W. 2001b. *Taking the metaphor of participation into our lives and practices. Revision,* 3(4): 2–3.

Reed, C. and Frisby, W. 2008. Continuing the journey: Articulating dimensions of feminist participatory research, in Reason, P. and Bradbury, H. (eds.). *The Sage Handbook of Action Research, Participative Inquiry and Practice*, 2nd edition. London: Sage, pp. 93–105.

Reinharz, S. 2010. *Observing the Observer.* Oxford: Oxford University Press.

RENEW NW. 2007. *Egan Wheel: Integrated components of sustainable communities.* Liverpool: RENEW NW.

Reynolds, M. 1998. Reflection and critical learning. *Management Learning,* 29(2): 183–200.

Re-Wilding Britain. 2020. Global heating threatens UK wildlife's ability to adapt and survive. *The Guardian,* 29 October, https://www.theguardian.com/environment/2020/oct/29/global-heating-threatens-uk-wildlife-ability-adapt-survive-rewilding-britain

Richardson, L. 2000. Writing: A method of inquiry, in Denzin, N. and Lincoln, Y. (eds.). *Handbook of Qualitative Research,* 2nd edition. Thousand Oaks, CA: Sage. pp 923–948.

Richardson, H. 2014. Pupils begin 'tough' new national curriculum, BBC News, 1 September, https://www.bbc.co.uk/news/education-28987787

Richardson, A. 2020. *Bearing Witness While Black: African Americans, Smartphones and The New Protest.* Oxford: Oxford University Press.

Riddiford, J. 2021. *Learning to Lead Together: An Ecological and Community Approach.* London: Routledge.

Riegal, R. 2014. World's second largest supertrawler enters Irish water. *Irish Independent,* 3 March, https://www.independent.ie/irish-news/worlds-second-largest-super-trawler-enters-irish-waters-30058458.html

Riley, S. and Reason, P. 2015. Cooperative inquiry: An action research practice, in Smith, J. (ed.). *Qualitative Psychology: A Practical Guide to Research Methods,* 3rd edition. London: Sage. pp. 168–198.

Rittel, H. and Weber, M. 1973. Dilemmas in a general theory of planning. *Policy Sciences,* 4: 155–169. US Environmental Protection Agency Archive, https://archive.epa.gov/reg3esd1/data/web/pdf/rittel%2bwebber%2bdilemmas%2bgeneral_theory_of_planning.pdf

Roberts, E. and Amidon, E. 1991. *Earth Prayers from Around the World: 365 Prayers, Poems, and Innovations for Honouring the Earth.* California: Harper San Francisco.

Rockström, J., Steffen, W., Noone, K., Persson, Å. et al. 2009. Planetary boundaries: Exploring the safe operating space for humanity. *Ecology and Society,* 14(2): 32, http://www.ecologyandsociety.org/vol14/iss2/art32/

Runneymeade Trust. 2021. *England's Civil Society Submission to the United Nations Commission on the Elimination of Racial Discrimination.* Runneymeade Perspectives, https://assets-global.website-files.com/61488f992b58e687f1108c7c/61bca661b8abd33d2f6f579c_Runnymede%20CERD%20report%20v3.pdf

Ryan, E. (ed.) 1994. *A Grateful Heart.* Berkeley: Conari Press.

Saad, L. 2020a. Do the work: An anti-racist reading list. *The Guardian,* 3 June, https://www.theguardian.com/books/booksblog/2020/jun/03/do-the-work-an-anti-racist-reading-list-layla-f-saad

Saad, L. 2020b. *Me and White Supremacy: How to Recognise Your*

Privilege, Combat Racism and Change the World. London: Quercus Books.

Sachs, J. 2015. The clean energy moonshot. *Hindustan Times,* 7 October, https://www.hindustantimes.com/analysis/the-clean-energy-moonshot/story-Eyr0Bsr2b9Zyk8lmq7MapJ.html

Sachs, J., Schmidt-Traub, G., Kroll, C., Lafortune, G., Fuller, G. 2019. *Sustainable Development Report.* New York: Bertelsmann Stiftung and Sustainable Development Solutions Network (SDSN).

Sagan, C. 1980 (1995). *Cosmos.* London: Abacus.

Sagan, C. 1985. *Contact.* London: Orbit.

Sagan, C. 1995. *Pale Blue Dot: A Vision of the Human Future in Space.* London: Random House.

Sample, I. 2014. The Milky Way is on outskirts of 'Immeasurable Heaven' supercluster. *The Guardian,* 3 September, https://www.theguardian.com/science/2014/sep/03/milky-way-laniakea-galaxy-supercluster-immeasurable-heaven

Sandel, M. 2012. *What Money Can't Buy: The Moral Limits of Markets.* Cambridge: Harvard University Press.

Sanghera, S. 2021. *Empireland: How Imperialism Has Shaped Modern Britain.* London: Viking.

Scharmer, O. 2007. *Theory U: Leading from the Future as it Emerges: The Social Technology of Presencing.* Cambridge, MA: The Society for Organizational Learning, Inc.

Schnor, J. 2008. Species matter. *Environmental Science and Technology,* 1 April, https://pubs.acs.org/doi/pdf/10.1021/es087061y

Schön, D. 1983. *The Reflective Practitioner: How Professionals Think in Action. London:* Basic Books.

Schumacher, E. 1973/2011. *Small is Beautiful: Economics as if People Mattered,* London, Harper Collins.

Seeley, C. 2011. Uncharted territory: Imagining a stronger relationship between the arts and action research. *Action Research,* 9(1): 83–99.

Seeley, C. and Reason, R. 2008. Expressions of energy: An epistemology of presentational knowing in action research, in Liamputtong P. and Rumbold, J. (eds.). *Knowing Differently: Arts Based and Collaborative*

Research. New York: Nova Science Publishers. Pp. 25–46.

Senge, P. 1990. *The Fifth Disciple: The Art and Practice of the Learning Organisation.* London: Random House Business Books.

Senge, P. and Scharmer, O. 2001. Community action research: Learning as a community of practitioners, consultants and researchers, in Reason, P. and Bradbury, H. (eds.). *Handbook of Action Research.* London: Sage, pp. 195–206.

Shah-Kazemi, R. 2007. *My Mercy Encompasses All: The Koran's Teachings on Compassion, Peace and Love.* Berlin: Dussman.

Shah- Kazemi, R. 2011. *Spiritual Quest: Reflections on Quranic Prayer According to the teachings of Iman Ali.* Institute of Islamic Studies. Occasional Papers 3.

Shiva, V. 2005. *Earth Democracy, Justice, Sustainability and Peace.* London: Zed Books.

Shiva, V. 2020. *Reclaiming the Commons. Biodiversity, Indigenous Knowledge and the Rights of Mother Earth.* London: Synergeticpress.

Singer, P. 1975/2015. *Animal Liberation.* London: Bodley Head.

Skolimowski, H. 1994. *The Participatory Mind: A New Theory of Knowledge and of the Universe.* London: Penguin Arkana.

Skolimowski H. 2015. *Dialogues with the Stars.* Michigan: Creative Fire Press.

Skrbina, D. 2007. *Panpsychism in the West.* Boston MA: MIT.

Slade, S. and Miller, V. 2019. *A Computer Called Katherine.* London: Hachette.

Smith, M. K. 2007 (2020). Basil Yeaxlee, lifelong learning and informal education. *The encyclopaedia of pedagogy and informal education*, https://infed.org/mobi/basil-yeaxlee-lifelong-learning-and-informal-education/

Smith, J. 2022. *Why Has Nobody Told Me This Before?* London: Penguin.

Soper, K. 2020. *Post Growth Living: For an Alternative Hedonism.* London: Verso.

Sparkes, A. 2002. Autoethnography: Self-indulgence or something more?, in Bochner, A. and Ellis, C. (eds.). *Ethnographically Speaking: Autoethnography, Literature and Aesthetics.* New York: Altima Press, pp. 209–233.

Sparkes, A. 2020. Autoethnography: Accept, revise, reject? An evaluative self reflects. *Qualitative Research in Sport, Exercise and Health*, 12(2): 289–302.

Spretnek, C. 2004. *Missing Mary: The Queen of Heaven and Her Re-emergence in the Modern Church.* New York: Palgrave MacMillan.

Stager, C. 2011. *Deep Future the Next 100,000 Years of Life on Earth.* New York: St Martin's Press.

Steffen, W., Richardson, K., Rockström, J., Cornell, S., Fetzer, I., Bennett, E., Biggs, R., Carpenter, S., de Vries W., Folke, C., Gerten, C., Heinke, D., Mace, M., Persson, G., Ramanathan, L., Reyers, V. and Sörlin, S. 2015. *Planetary boundaries: Guiding human development on a changing planet. Science,* 347(6223), https://science.sciencemag.org/content/347/6223/1259855.full

Steier, F., Brown, J., Mesquita da Silva, F. 2015. The world café in action research settings, in Bradbury, H. (ed.). *Sage Handbook of Action Research,* 3rd edition. London: Sage, pp. 211–219.

Stengers, I. 2018. *Another Science is Possible: A Manifesto for Slow Science.* Cambridge: Polity Press.

Sterling, S. 2001. *Sustainable Education: Re-visioning Learning and Change.* Schumacher Briefing No 6. Dartington: Schumacher Society/ Green Books.

Stirling, S. 2010. Learning for resilience or the resilient learner? Towards a necessary reconciliation in a paradigm of sustainable education. *Environmental Education Research*, 16(5–6): 511–528.

Stavos, J. Tores, C. and Cooperrider D. 2018. *Conversations worth having: Using Appreciative Inquiry to Fuel Productive and Meaningful Engagement.* London: Berrett-Kohler.

Stubley, P. 2019. Enough rainforests to fill 30 football pitches destroyed every minute last year. *The Independent.* 25 April.

Sufi, M. 2019. The battle for water: Growing violence around world's most precious resource. *The Guardian,* 31 December.

Sustainable Consumption Round Table. 2006. *I Will if You Will: Towards Sustainable Consumption.* London: Sustainable Development Commission and National Consumer Council.

Svoboda, E. 2013. The selfish benefits of compassion. *New Scientist,* 220(2939): 28–29.

Swan E. 2008. Let's not get too personal, critical reflection, reflexivity and the confessional turn. *Journal of European Industrial Training,* 32(5): 385–399.

Swimme, B. 1984. *The Universe is a Green Dragon.* Sante Fe: New Mexico: Bear & Company.

Swimme, B. 1996. *The Hidden Heart of the Cosmos.* New York: Orbis.

Swimme B. and Berry, T. 1992. *The Universe Story, From the Primordial Flaring Forth to the Ecozoic Era. A celebration of the Unfolding of the Cosmos.* San Francisco: Harper.

Swimme, B. and Tucker M. 2011. *Journey of the Universe,* New Haven: Yale University Press.

Tam, H. 2021. (ed) *Tomorrow's Communities: Lessons from community transformation in the age of Global Crisis.* Bristol: Bristol University Press.

Tarnas, R. 2000. A new synthesis: We seem to be moving toward a more integral world-view that is a dialectical synthesis of world and self. *Resurgence,* March/April: 8–11.

Tarnas, R. 2006. *Cosmos and Psyche: Intimations of a New World View.* New York: Plume.

Taylor, S., Rudolph, J. and Foldy, E. 2015. Teaching and learning reflective practice in the action science/action inquiry tradition, in Bradbury, H. (ed.). *The Sage Handbook of Action Research,* 3rd edition. London: Sage, pp 732–741.

Thoreau. H. 1854 (2017). *Walden: A Life in the Woods.* London: Vintage.

Thunberg, G. 2019. *No One is Too Small to Make a Difference.* London: Penguin.

Tibbs, H. 1999. Sustainability. *Deeper News,* 10(1): 1–76.

Tomren, T. 2021. The articles in this book and the discipline of Eco-theology in Andrianos L. and Tomren, T, (eds) 2021.*Contemporary ecotheology climate justice and environmental stewardship in world religions.* World Council of Churches: Embla Akademisk.

Torbert, W. 2001. The practice of action inquiry, in Reason, P. and Bradbury, H. (eds.). *Handbook of Action Research.* London: Sage, pp. 207–208.

Torbert, W. and Reason, P. 2001. A four-day feast of conversation at the Fetzer Institute. *Revision*, 23(3): 2.

Tosey, P. 2008. Once upon a time...tales of organisational learning. *The Learning Organisation*, 15(6): 454–462.

Toynbee, P and Walker, D. 2020. *The Lost Decade: The Hidden Story of How Austerity Broke Britain.* London: Faber.

Tremlett, G. 2013. Spanish sperm whale death linked to UK supplier's plastic. *The Guardian.* 9 March.

Tucker, M., Grim J. and Angyal A. 2019. *Thomas Berry: A Biography.* New York: Columbia University Press.

Turner-Vesslago, B. 2013. *Freefall: Writing Without a Parachute.* Bristol: Vala Publishing Company.

Tutu, D. 2000. *No Future Without Forgiveness.* London: Rider.

Tutu, D. and Tutu, M. and Abrams, D. (eds.) 2015. *The Book of Forgiving: The Fourfold Path for Healing Ourselves and Our World.* London: William Collins.

Tyukavina, A., Potapov P., Hansen M., Pickens A., Stehman S., Turubanova S., Parker D., Zalles V', Lima A., Kommareddy I., Song X., Wang L., Harris N. 2022. Global trends of forest loss due to fire from 2001 to 2019. *Frontiers in Remote Sensing*, https://www.frontiersin.org/article/10.3389/frsen.2022.825190

UN/Department of Economic and Social Affairs Economic Analysis Policy Brief #81: Impact of COVID-19 on SDG Progress, a Statistical Perspective, https://www.un.org/development/desa/dpad/publication/un-desa-policy-brief-81-impact-of-covid-19-on-sdg-progress-a-statistical-perspective/

United Nations Development Programme. 2011. *Sustainability and Equity: A Better Future for All.* Human Development Report, http://hdr.undp.org/sites/default/files/reports/271/hdr_2011_en_complete.pdf

United Nations Development Programme. 2019. *Beyond Income, Beyond Averages, Beyond Today: Inequalities in Human Development in the 21st Century.* Human Development Report, http://hdr.undp.org/sites/default/files/hdr2019.pdf

United Nations Development Programme. 2020. *The Next Frontier: Human Development and the Anthropocene.* Human Development Report, http://hdr.undp.org/sites/default/files/hdr2020.pdf

United Nations Development Programme. 2022. *New Threats to Human Security in the Anthropocene.* New York: United Nations, https://hdr.undp.org/content/2022-special-report-human-security

UNESCO. 1997. *Learning: The Treasure Within.* Paris: UNESCO.

UNESCO. 2015. *Rethinking Education: Towards a Common Good?* http://www.unesco.org/new/fileadmin/MULTIMEDIA/FIELD/Cairo/images/RethinkingEducation.pdf

UNESCO. 2021. Thinking Higher and Beyond: Perspectives on the Futures of Higher Education to 2050, 5 May, https://www.iesalc.unesco.org/eng/wp-content/uploads/2021/05/Thinking-Higher-and-Beyond_EN-_Format_FINAL.pdf

UNESCO. 2022. Knowledge driven actions: Transforming Higher Education for global sustainability: https://unesdoc.unesco.org/ark:/48223/pf0000380519

United Nations Environment Programme. 2021. *Faith for Change Initiative,* https://www.unep.org/about-un-environment/faith-earth-initiative

United Nations Environment Programme. 2022. Global Emissions Gap Report: https://www.unep.org/resources/emissions-gap-report-2022

United Nations Millennium Development Goals. https://www.un.org/millenniumgoals/bkgd.shtml

United Nations News Agency. 2020. Planet-warming trend continues: 2020 closes hottest decade on record. *UN Weather Agency,* 24 December, https://news.un.org/en/story/2020/12/1080882

United Nations Department of Economic and Social Affairs. 2021. SDG Knowledge: UNSDG 16, https://sdgs.un.org/goals/goal16

United Nations Environment Programme News. 2017. Indigenous people and nature: A tradition of conservation. 26 March, https://www.unep.org/news-and-stories/story/indigenous-people-and-nature-tradition-conservation

United Nations Sustainable Development. 2015. *Helping stakeholders shape new global goals for humanity's future, civil society and other stakeholders, leaving no one behind when implementing Agenda 2030,* http://www.stakeholderforum.org/fileadmin/files/SD2015%20Brochure%20%28online%29.pdf

United Nations Sustainable Development Goals Report. 2019. https://unstats.un.org/sdgs/report/2019/The-Sustainable-Development-Goals-Report-2019.pdf

United Nations Sustainable Development Goals Report. 2020. https://www.un.org/development/desa/publications/publication/sustainable-development-goals-report-2020

University College Union and Students Organising for Sustainability. 2021. COP 26 Campaign: Decarbonise and Decolonise 2030, https://www.ucu.org.uk/media/11630/COP26-campaign-decarbonise-and-decolonise-2030---quick-guide/pdf/Decarbonise_Decolonise_quick_guide_Jun21.pdf

University of Essex. 2022. *Decolonising the Curriculum,* https://library.essex.ac.uk/edi/readinglists

Valk, A. 2010. *Radical Sisters: Second Wave Feminism and Black Literation in Washington, D.C.* Urbana Chicago: University of Illinois Press.

Van der Kooij, J., Doret J. and Miedema, S. 2013. 'Worldview': The meaning of the concept and the impact on religious education. *Religious Education*, 108(2): 210–228, DOI: 10.1080/00344087.2013.767685

Vidal, J. 2011a. Arctic sea ice melts at fastest pace for 40 years. *The Guardian,* 12 September, https://www.theguardian.com/environment/2011/sep/11/arctic-ice-melting-at-fastest-pace

Vidal, J. 2011b. Imported plants bring diseases that threaten to kill millions of British trees. *The Guardian*, 23 October, https://www.theguardian.com/environment/2011/oct/23/trees-exotic-diseases-gardening

Vidal, J. 2022. It's the great green reset: 10 things Britain can do now to save the planet. *The Guardian*, 3 January, https://www.theguardian.com/commentisfree/2022/jan/03/great-green-reset-10-things-britain-save-planet-cop26

Vimela, P., Chan, Q., and Khan, A. 2011. Climate change impacts on water salinity and health. *Journal of Epidemiology and Global Health*, 1(7): 5–10, https://www.sciencedirect.com/science/article/pii/S2210600611000086

Vu, M. and Burton, V. 2019. Mindful reflexivity: Unpacking the process of transformative learning in mindfulness and discernment. *Management Learning,* 51(2): 207–226, DOI: 10.1177/1350507619888751

Waddell, H. 1927/1989. *Wandering Scholars*. University of Michigan Press.

Wadham, H. 2021. Agency as interspecies, collective and embedded endeavour: Ponies and people in Northern England, 1916–1950. *Journal of Historical Sociology*, 34(4): 550–572.

Wadham, H., Hart, C., Hashmi, A., Kettleborough, H., Marron, R., Randles, S., Skritsovali, K. and Tucker, M. (2023) Sustainability education beyond the classroom: how the "exploding university" nurtures collective intelligence across local and global communities. In: Handbook of Research on Implications of Sustainable Development in Higher Education. IGI Global, Hershey, PA, pp. 202-229.

Wakefield, T., Singh J., Murtuja, B., Bryant, P., and Pimbert, M. 2008. The jury is out: How far can participatory projects go towards reclaiming democracy?' in Reason, P. and Bradbury, H. (eds.). *The Sage Handbook of Action Research, Participative Inquiry and Practice*, 2nd edition. London: Sage, pp. 333–349.

Wals, A. and Corcoran, C. (eds.) 2012. *Learning for Sustainability in Times of Accelerating Change.* Netherlands: Wageningen Academic.

Ward, P. 2007. *Under a Green Sky: Global Warming, the Mass Extinctions of the Past and What They Can Tell us About the Future.* New York: Collins.

Waterman, H., Boaden, B., Burey, L. et al. 2015. *Facilitating large-scale implementation of evidence-based health care: Insider accounts from a co-operative inquiry.* BMC Health Services Research, DOI 10.1186/ s12913-015-0722-6

Watts. J. 2020. Arctic methane deposits starting to release, scientists say. *The Guardian*, 27 October, https://www.theguardian.com/science/2020/ oct/27/sleeping-giant-arctic-methane-deposits-starting-to-release- scientists-find

Watts, J. 2019. Human society under urgent threat from loss of Earth's natural life. *The Guardian*, 6 May, https://www.theguardian.com/ environment/2019/may/06/human-society-under-urgent-threat-loss-earth- natural-life-un-report

Weber, A. 2014. *Matter and Desire: An Erotic Ecology.* Vermont: Chelsea Green Publishing.

Weber, A. 2016. *The Biology of Wonder, Aliveness, Feeling and the Metamorphosis of Science.* BC, Canada: New Society Publishers.

Welsh Government. 2021. *An Anti-Racist Wales. The Race Equality*

Action Plan for Wales: Emerging Vision, Purpose, Values and Envisaged Future by 2030. Cardiff: Welsh Government, https://gov.wales/sites/default/files/consultations/2021-03/race-equality-action-plan-an-anti-racist-wales_2.pdf

Wenger, E. 2009. A social theory of learning, in Illeris, K. (ed.). *Contemporary Theories of Learning: Learning Theorists in their Own Words.* Abingdon: Routledge , pp 219–228.

Wetherbee, G., Baldwin, A. and Ranville, J. 2019. It is raining plastic: Open file report for the United States Geological Society, https://doi.org/10.3133/ofr20191048https://pubs.usgs.gov/of/2019/1048/ofr20191048.pdf

Whitney, D. and Trosten-Bloom, A. 2010. *The Power of Appreciative Inquiry: A Practical Guide to Positive Change,* 2nd edition. San Francisco: Barrett-Koshler Publishers.

Willoughby, G. and Tosey, P. 2007. Imagine Meadfield: Appreciative inquiry as a process for leading school improvement. *Educational Research, Administration and Leadership,* 35(4): 499–520.

Wilson, E.O. 2002. *The Future of Life.* London: Little Brown.

Wilson, E.O. 2016. *Half Earth and Our Planet's Fight for Life, New York:* Liveright.

Worldwatch Institute. 2017. *EarthEd: Rethinking Education on a Changing Planet.* Washington: Island Press.

World Sustainability Series. 2018–2022, https://www.springer.com/series/13384

Wozniak, M., Cobb, S. Kettleborough, H. and Leathlean, D. 2019. Working together collaboratively and in partnership to explore 'I learning' creative approaches to motivate and inspire students. *MMU Learning and Teaching in Action,* 13(1): https://ltiammu.files.wordpress.com/2021/05/12_wozniak_etal_working_together_i_love_learning.pdf

WWF. 2019. *Nature in all the Goals: How Nature-Based Solutions can Help us all Achieve all the Sustainable Development Goals.* WWF, https://wwfint.awsassets.panda.org/downloads/nature_in_all_goals_publication__2019__1.pdf

WWF. 2021. *Powering Nature: Creating Conditions to Enable Nature-Based Solutions,* https://wwfint.awsassets.panda.org/downloads/wwf_powering_nature_report.pdf

Xavantina, N. and Santarén. 2019. The Amazon is approaching an irreversible tipping point. *The Economist*. 3 August.

Yearly Meeting of the Religious Society of Friends (Quakers). 1995. *Quaker Faith and Practice: The Book of Christian Disciple of the Yearly Meeting of the Religious Society of Friends (Quakers) in Britain.*

Yorks, L. 2015. The practice of teaching co-operative inquiry, in Bradbury, H. (ed.). *Sage Handbook of Action Research*, 3rd edition. London: Sage, pp. 553–563.

Yorks, L., Arnold, A., James, L., Rees, A., Hoffman-Pinilla, H., and Ospina, S. 2015. The tapestry of leadership: Lessons from six co-operative inquiry groups of social justice leaders, in Bradbury, H. (ed.). *Sage Handbook of Action Research*, 3rd edition. London: Sage, pp. 487–496.

Yousafzai, M. 2013. *Speech to the United Nations Youth Assembly.* United Nations, 12 July, https://www.youtube.com/watch?v=3rNhZu3ttlU

Zafar. T. 2019. Dr. Tayyaba Zafar: A stargazer lands up in Antarctica. *Times of News*, 25 February, https://pakistantimesofnews.com/breaking-news/dr-tayyaba-zafar-a-stargazer-lands-up-in-antarctica.html

Zandee D. and Cooperrider D. 2008. Appreciable worlds, inspired inquiry, in Reason, P. and Bradbury, H. (eds.). *The Sage Handbook of Action Research, Participative Inquiry and Practice*, 2nd edition. London: Sage. pp. 190–198.

Zhao, J., Wright, A. and Dick, B. 2012. A practitioner in the academy: An interview with Bob Dick. *Action Research*, 10(4): 432–448.

Zimmerman, B. 2002. Becoming a self-regulated learner. *Theory into Practice*, 41(2): 64–70.

Index

Ingram Content Group UK Ltd.
Milton Keynes UK
UKHW010433100523
421505UK00001B/1